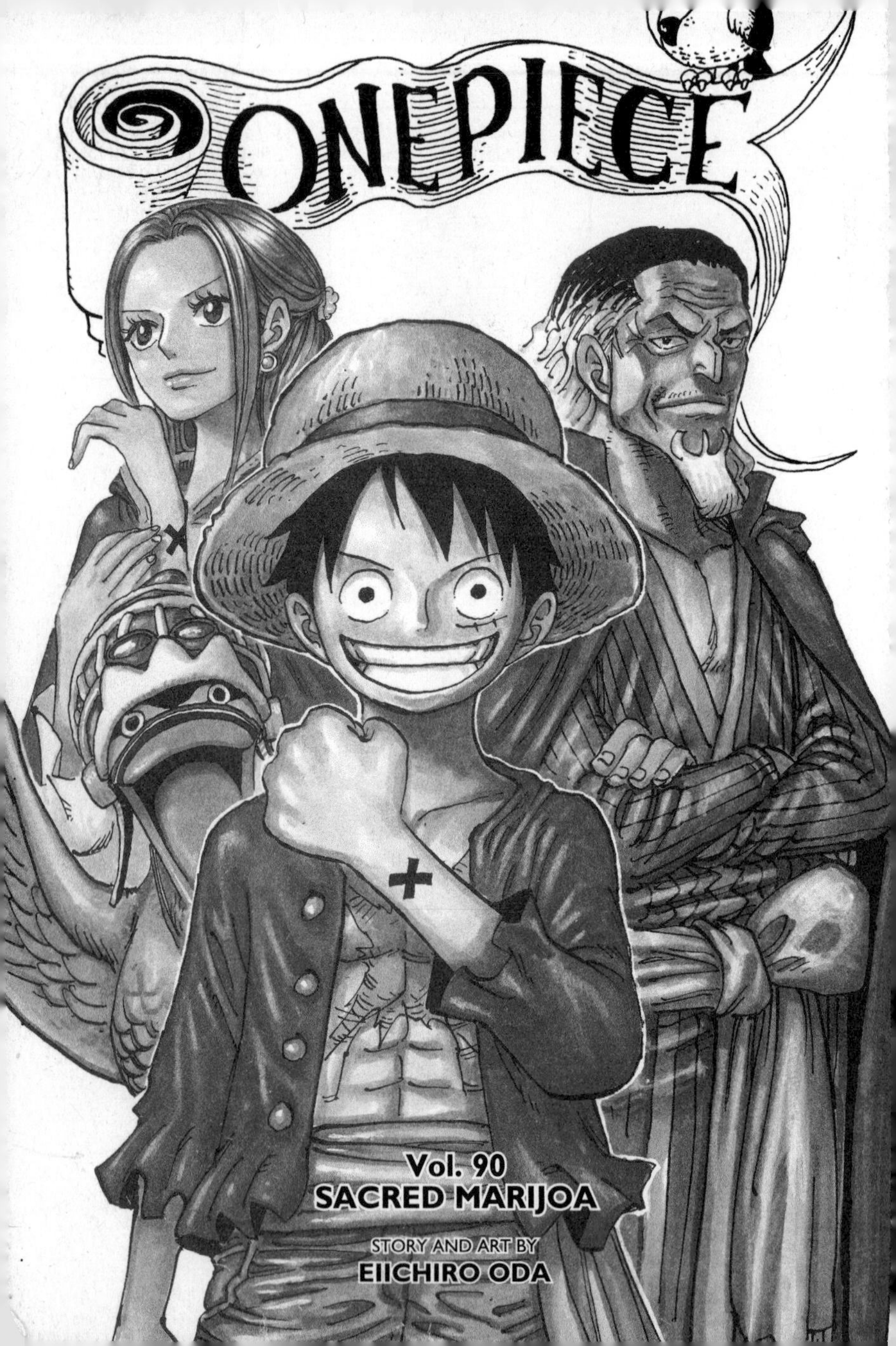
ONE PIECE
Vol. 90
SACRED MARIJOA
STORY AND ART BY
EIICHIRO ODA

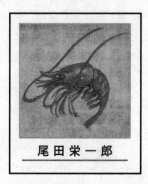

尾田栄一郎

What do you suppose is the plumpest thing in the world? You know how sometimes you can't help but think about this topic...for three hours? Maybe it's the cheeks of an indignant child. Or is it a butt? But I think in the end...it's got to be shrimp. Can we agree that it's shrimp?

Let volume 90 begin!!!

-Eiichiro Oda, 2018

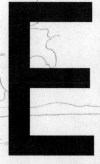

iichiro Oda began his manga career at the age of 17, when his one-shot cowboy manga **Wanted!** won second place in the coveted Tezuka manga awards. Oda went on to work as an assistant to some of the biggest manga artists in the industry, including Nobuhiro Watsuki, before winning the Hop Step Award for new artists. His pirate adventure **One Piece**, which debuted in **Weekly Shonen Jump** in 1997, quickly became one of the most popular manga in Japan.

Characters

The Straw Hat Crew

Tony Tony Chopper

After researching powerful medicine in Birdie Kingdom, he reunited with the rest of the crew.

Ship's Doctor, Bounty: 100 berries

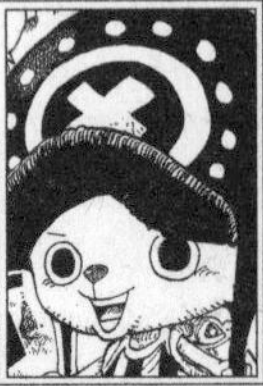

Monkey D. Luffy

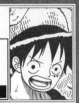

A young man who dreams of becoming the Pirate King. After training with Rayleigh, he and his crew head for the New World!

Captain, Bounty: 500 million berries

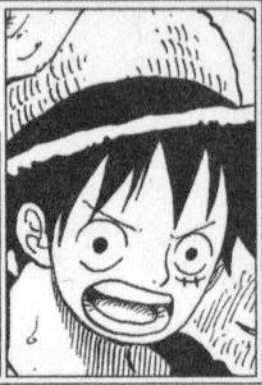

Nico Robin

She spent her time in Baltigo with the leader of the Revolutionary Army: Luffy's father, Dragon.

Archeologist, Bounty: ~~130 million berries~~

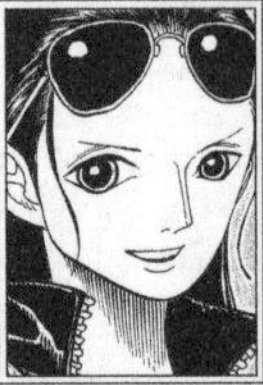

Roronoa Zolo

He swallowed his pride and asked to be trained by Mihawk on Gloom Island before reuniting with the rest of the crew.

Fighter, Bounty: 320 million berries

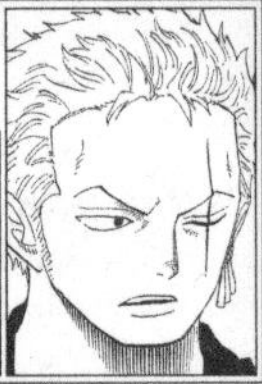

Franky

He modified himself in Future Land Baldimore and turned himself into Armored Franky before reuniting with the rest of the crew.

Shipwright, Bounty: 94 million berries

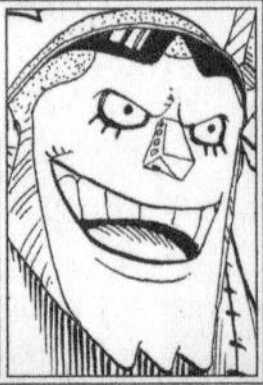

Nami

She studied the weather of the New World on the small Sky Island Weatheria, a place where weather is studied as a science.

Navigator, Bounty: 66 million berries

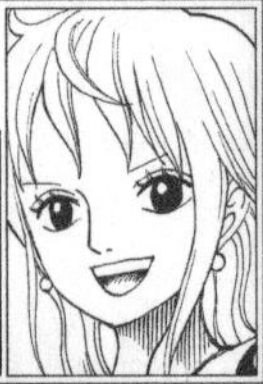

Brook

After being captured and used as a freak show by the Longarm Tribe, he became a famous rock star called "Soul King" Brook.

Musician, Bounty: 83 million berries

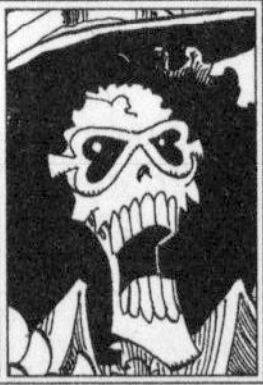

Usopp

He trained under Heracles at the Bowin Islands to become the King of Snipers.

Sniper, Bounty: 200 million berries

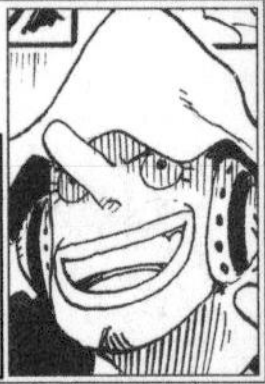

Shanks

One of the Four Emperors. Waits for Luffy in the "New World," the second half of the Grand Line.

Captain of the Red-Haired Pirates

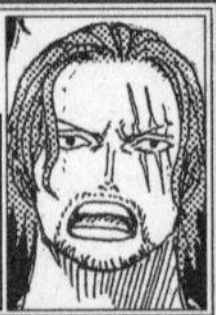

Sanji

After fighting the New Kama Karate masters in the Kamabakka Kingdom, he returned to the crew.

Cook, Bounty: 177 million berries

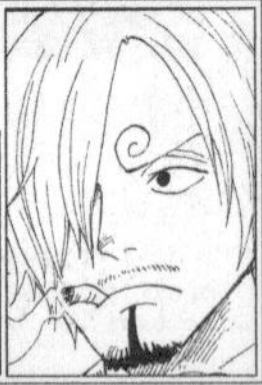

Big Mom Pirates

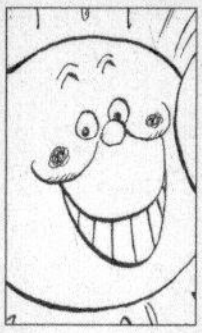

Prometheus the Sun

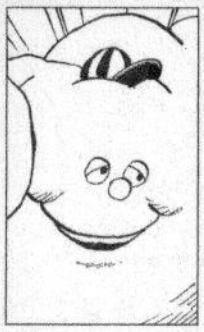

Zeus the Storm Cloud

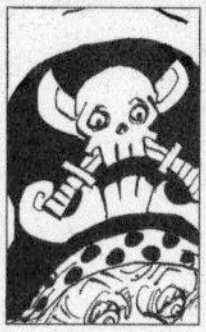

Napoleon the Bicorn Hat

Charlotte Linlin

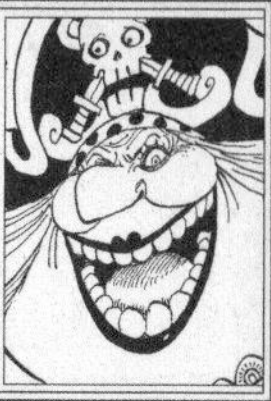

One of the Four Emperors. Known as Big Mom. Uses the Soul-Soul Fruit powers to pull life span from people.

Captain, Big Mom Pirates

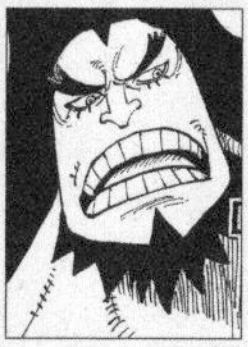

C. Oven

4th Son of Charlotte

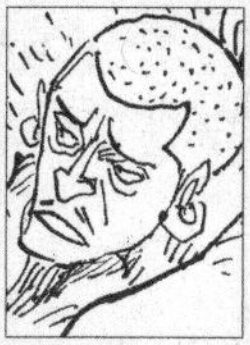

C. Daifuku

3rd Son of Charlotte

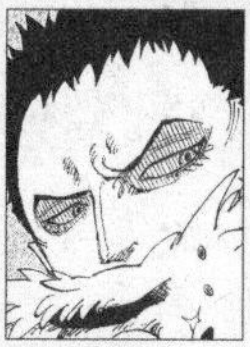

C. Katakuri (Sweet 3)

2nd Son of Charlotte

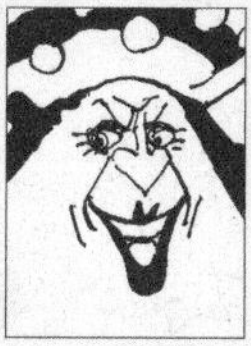

C. Compote

1st Daughter of Charlotte

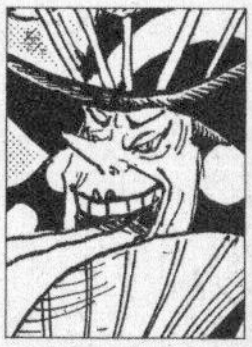

C. Perospero

1st Son of Charlotte

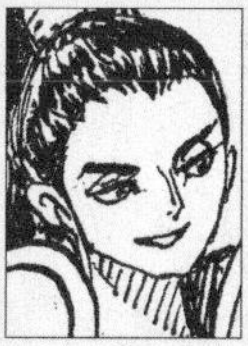

C. Cinnamon

16th Daughter of Charlotte

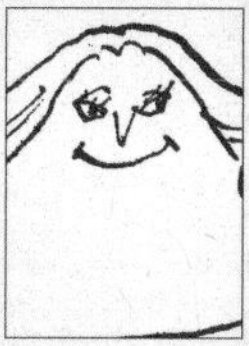

C. Citron

15th Daughter of Charlotte

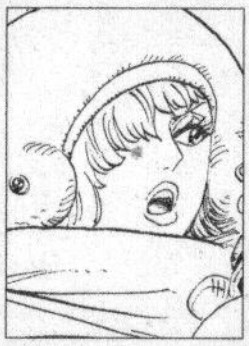

C. Smoothie (Sweet 3)

14th Daughter of Charlotte

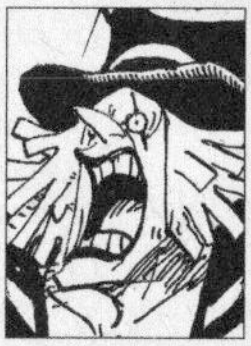

C. Montd'or

19th Son of Charlotte

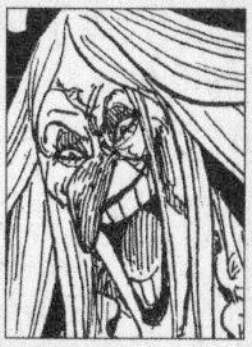

C. Brulee

8th Daughter of Charlotte

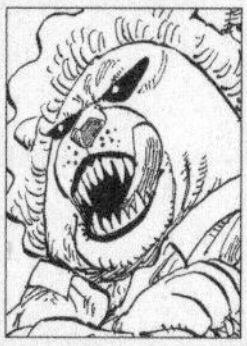

Pekoms

Fighter, Big Mom Pirates

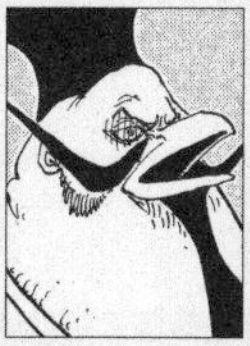

Count Niwatori

Fighter, Big Mom Pirates

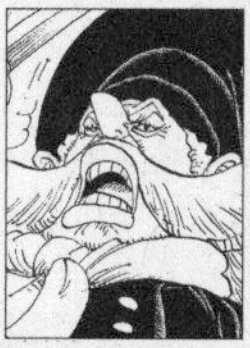

"Gourmet Knight" Streusen

Head Chef, Big Mom Pirates

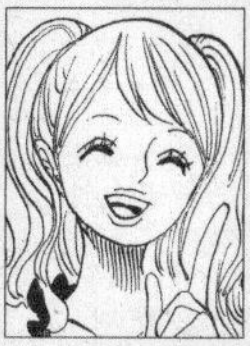

Charlotte Pudding

35th Daughter of Charlotte

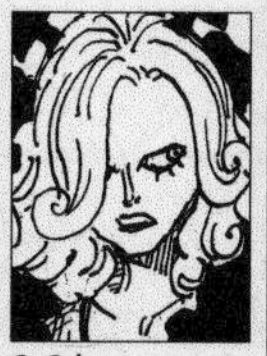

C. Galette

18th Daughter of Charlotte

Luffy enters a one-on-one battle with Katakuri to help the rest of the crew escape. Big Mom reaches the ship just as Sanji finishes the cake, luring her away... Meanwhile, Luffy triumphs in an extreme battle against Katakuri, and then throws off his pursuers to reach the crew. But the Big Mom Pirates' siege is fierce, and the ship sinks under a hail of cannon fire!

Germa 66

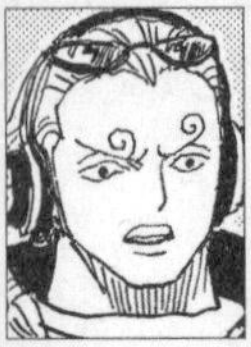

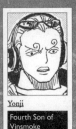

Yonji

Fourth Son of Vinsmoke

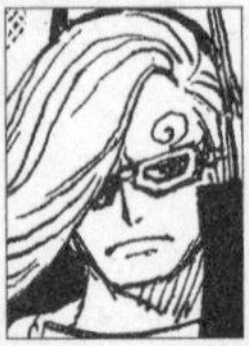

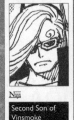

Niji

Second Son of Vinsmoke

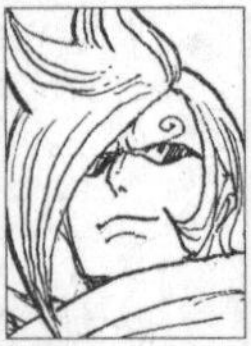

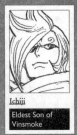

Ichiji

Eldest Son of Vinsmoke

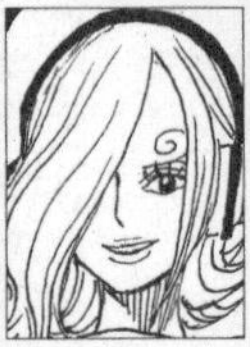

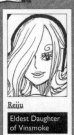

Reiju

Eldest Daughter of Vinsmoke

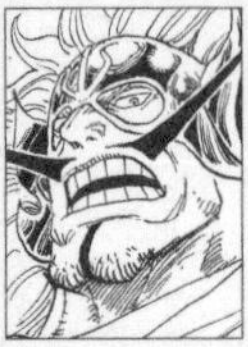

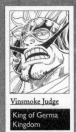

Vinsmoke Judge

King of Germa Kingdom

Sun Pirates

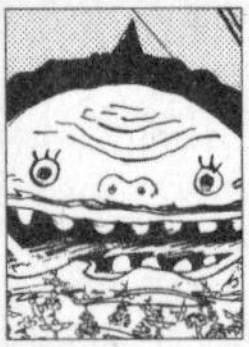

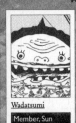

Wadatsumi

Member, Sun Pirates

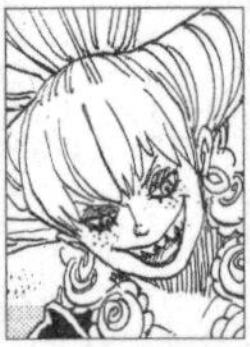

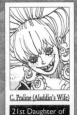

C. Praline (Aladdin's Wife)

21st Daughter of Charlotte

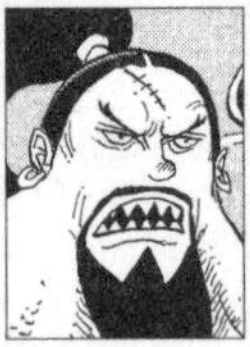

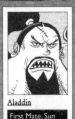

Aladdin

First Mate, Sun Pirates

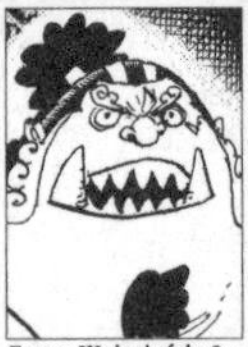

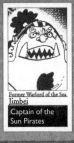

Former Warlord of the Sea
Jimbei

Captain of the Sun Pirates

Minks

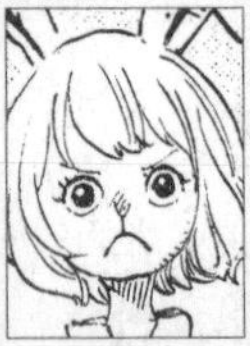

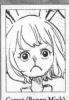

Carrot (Bunny Mink)

Battlebeast Tribe, Kingsbird

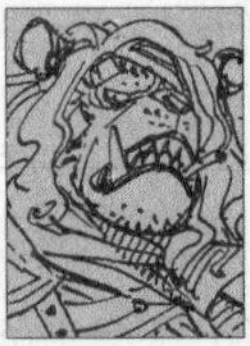

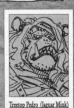

Treetop Pedro (Jaguar Mink)

Leader of the Guardians

Firetank Pirates

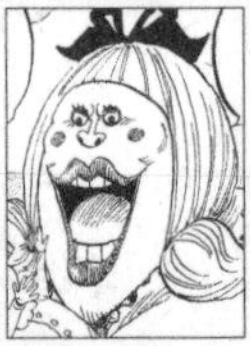

C. Chiffon (Bege's Wife)

22nd Daughter of Charlotte

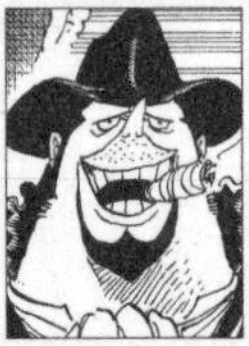

Capone "Gang" Bege

Captain of the Firetank Pirates

Story

After two years of hard training, the Straw Hat pirates are back together, first at the Sabaody Archipelago and then through Fish-Man Island to their next stage: the New World!!

Luffy and crew head into Big Mom's stronghold and successfully take back Sanji, who was stuck in a political marriage with Big Mom's daughter. They then join forces with Bege in a plot to assassinate Big Mom that ultimately fails. Big Mom then chases after the fleeing crew. Sanji decides to bake a new cake to placate Mama's rampage, and

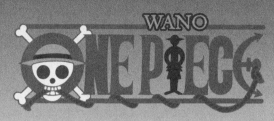

Vol. 90
SACRED MARIJOA

CONTENTS

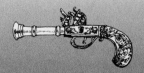

Chapter 901:

DON'T LET EVEN DEATH STOP YOU!!!

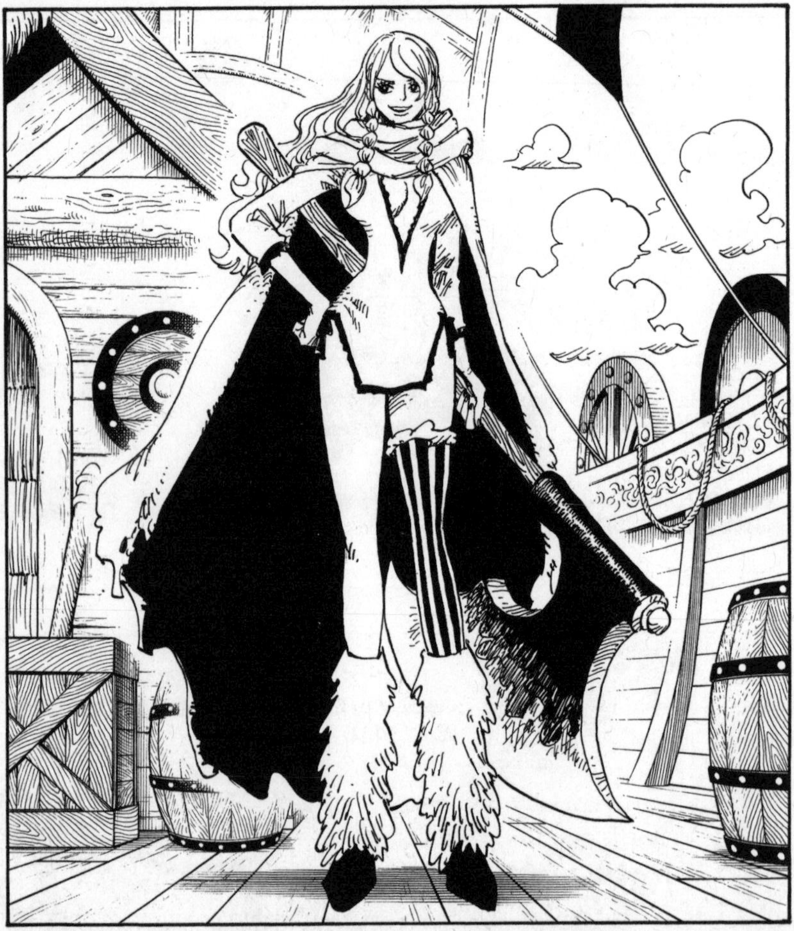

THE SAGA OF THE SELF-PROCLAIMED STRAW HAT FLEET, VOL. 32, HAJRUDIN: "BUGGY'S DELIVERY ESCAPEE LIST: DOCTOR GERD OF THE NEW GIANT PIRATES"

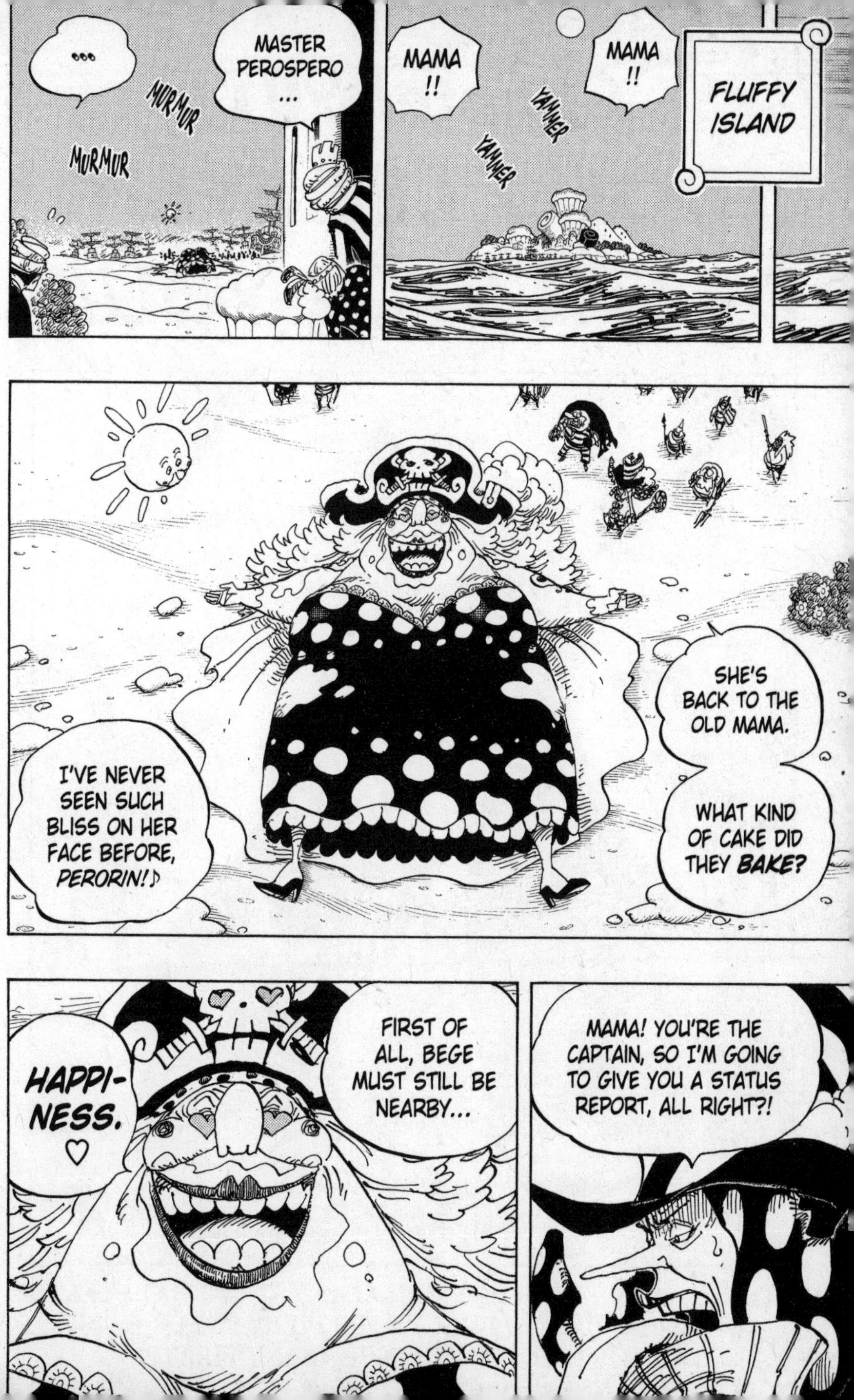
FLUFFY ISLAND
MAMA !!
YAMMER
MAMA !!
YAMMER
MASTER PEROSPERO ...
MURMUR
...
MURMUR
SHE'S BACK TO THE OLD MAMA.
WHAT KIND OF CAKE DID THEY BAKE?
I'VE NEVER SEEN SUCH BLISS ON HER FACE BEFORE, PERORIN!♪
MAMA! YOU'RE THE CAPTAIN, SO I'M GOING TO GIVE YOU A STATUS REPORT, ALL RIGHT?!
FIRST OF ALL, BEGE MUST STILL BE NEARBY...
HAPPI-NESS. ♡

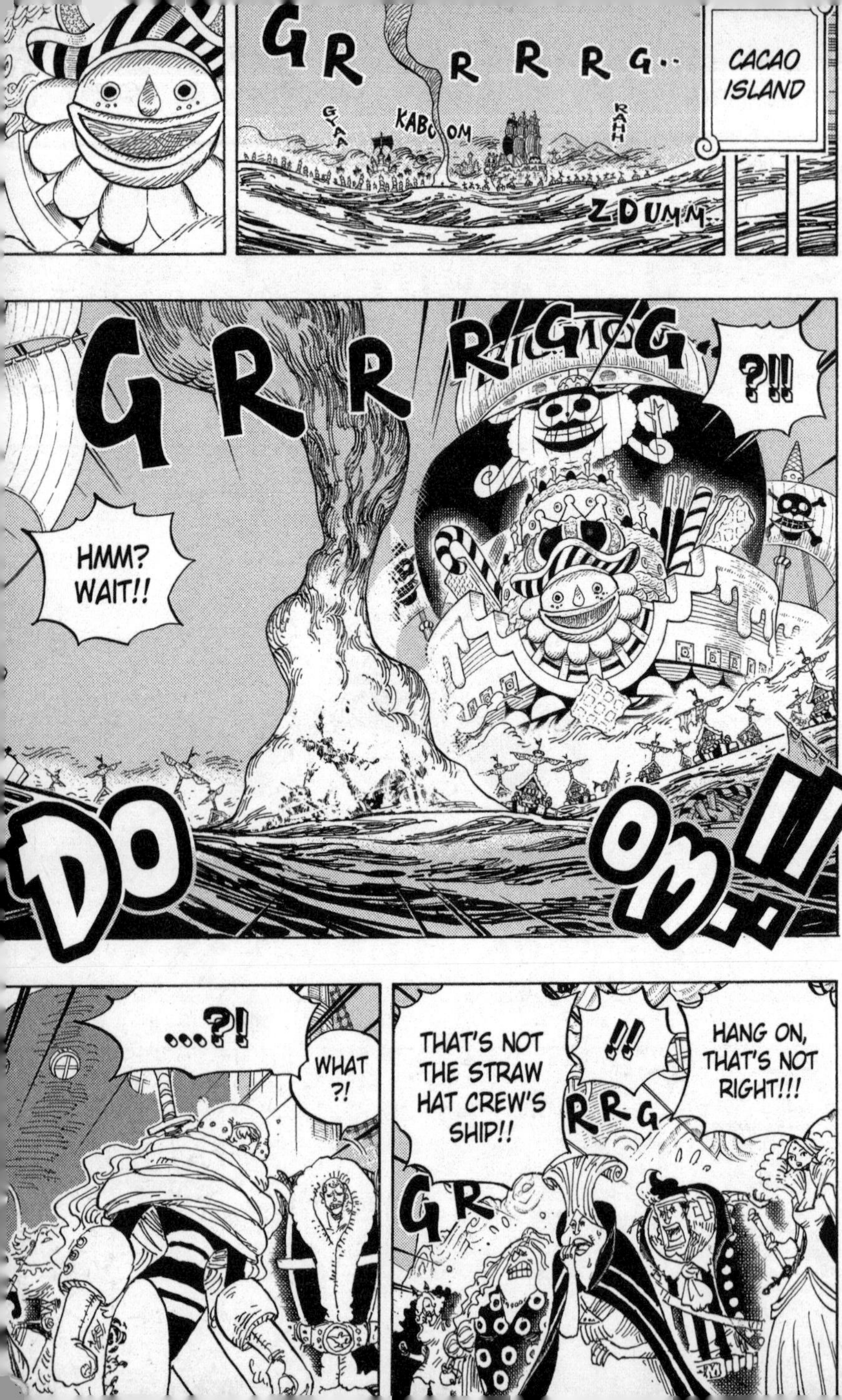
CACAO ISLAND
GRRRRG...
RAHH
KABOOM
GYAA
ZDUMM...
?!!
GRRRGGG
HMM? WAIT!!
DOOM..!!
HANG ON, THAT'S NOT RIGHT!!!
!!
THAT'S NOT THE STRAW HAT CREW'S SHIP!!
GRRRG
WHAT ?!
...?!

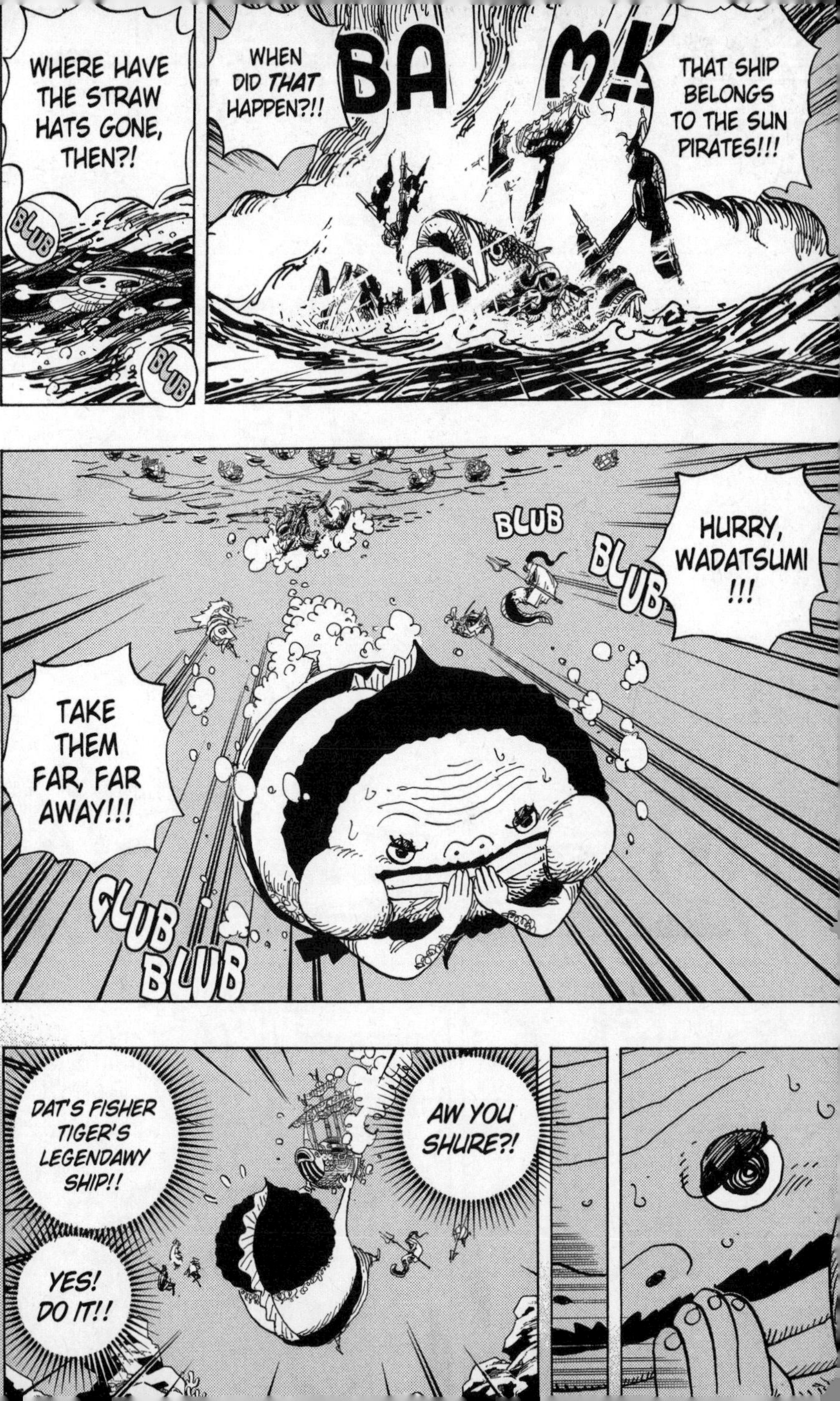
THAT SHIP BELONGS TO THE SUN PIRATES!!!
BAM!
WHEN DID THAT HAPPEN?!!
WHERE HAVE THE STRAW HATS GONE, THEN?!
BLUB
BLUB
HURRY, WADATSUMI!!!
BLUB
BLUB
TAKE THEM FAR, FAR AWAY!!!
GLUB BLUB
AW YOU SHURE?!
DAT'S FISHER TIGER'S LEGENDAWY SHIP!!
YES! DO IT!!

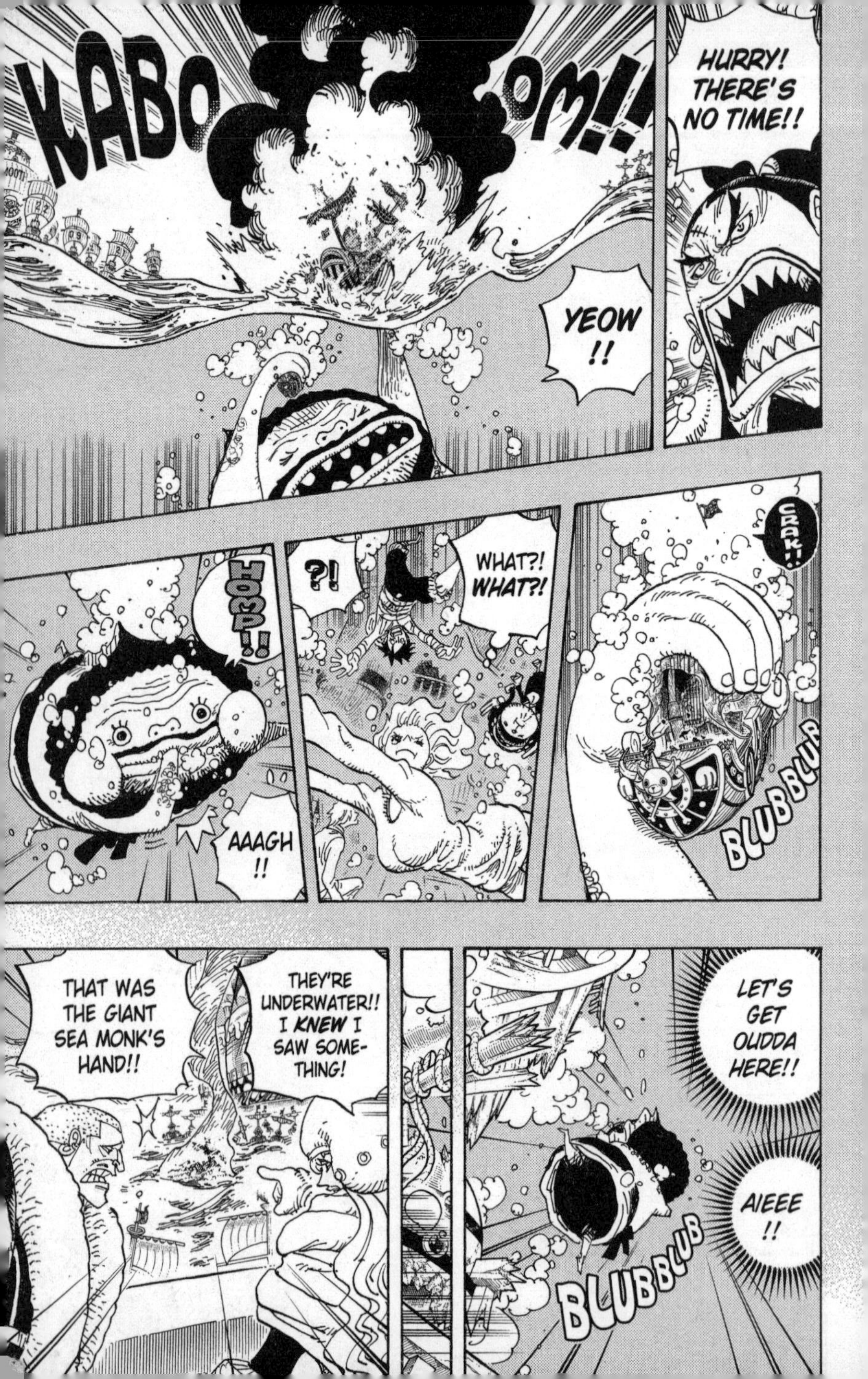
HURRY! THERE'S NO TIME!!
KABO OM!!
YEOW !!
CRAK!!
BLUB BLUB
WHAT?! WHAT?!
?!
HOMP!!
AAAGH !!
LET'S GET OUDDA HERE!!
AIEEE !!
BLUB BLUB
THEY'RE UNDERWATER!! I KNEW I SAW SOMETHING!
THAT WAS THE GIANT SEA MONK'S HAND!!

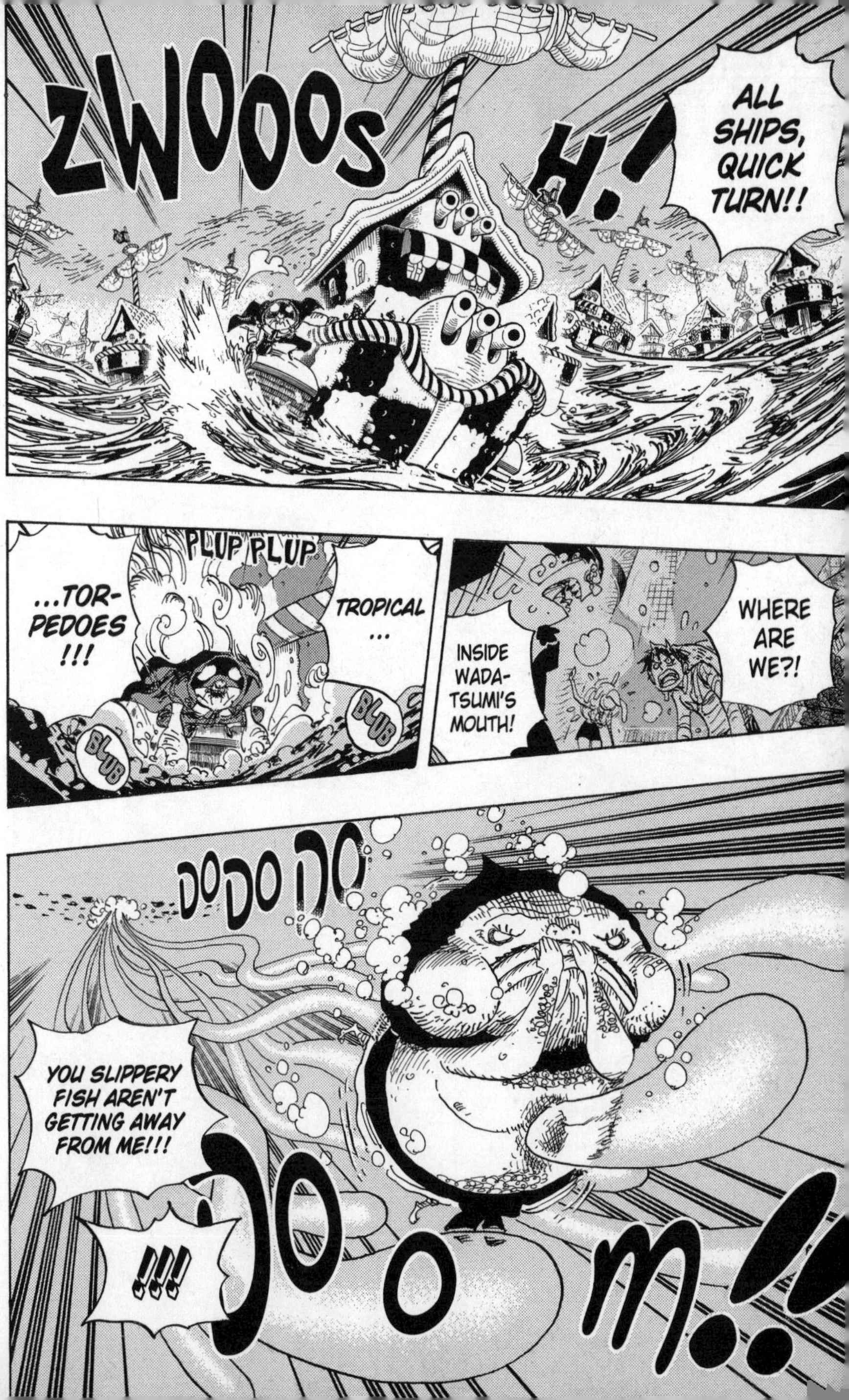
ALL SHIPS, QUICK TURN!!
ZWOOOSH!
WHERE ARE WE?!
INSIDE WADA-TSUMI'S MOUTH!
PLUP PLUP
TROPICAL ...
...TOR-PEDOES !!!
BLUB
BLUB
YOU SLIPPERY FISH AREN'T GETTING AWAY FROM ME!!!
!!!

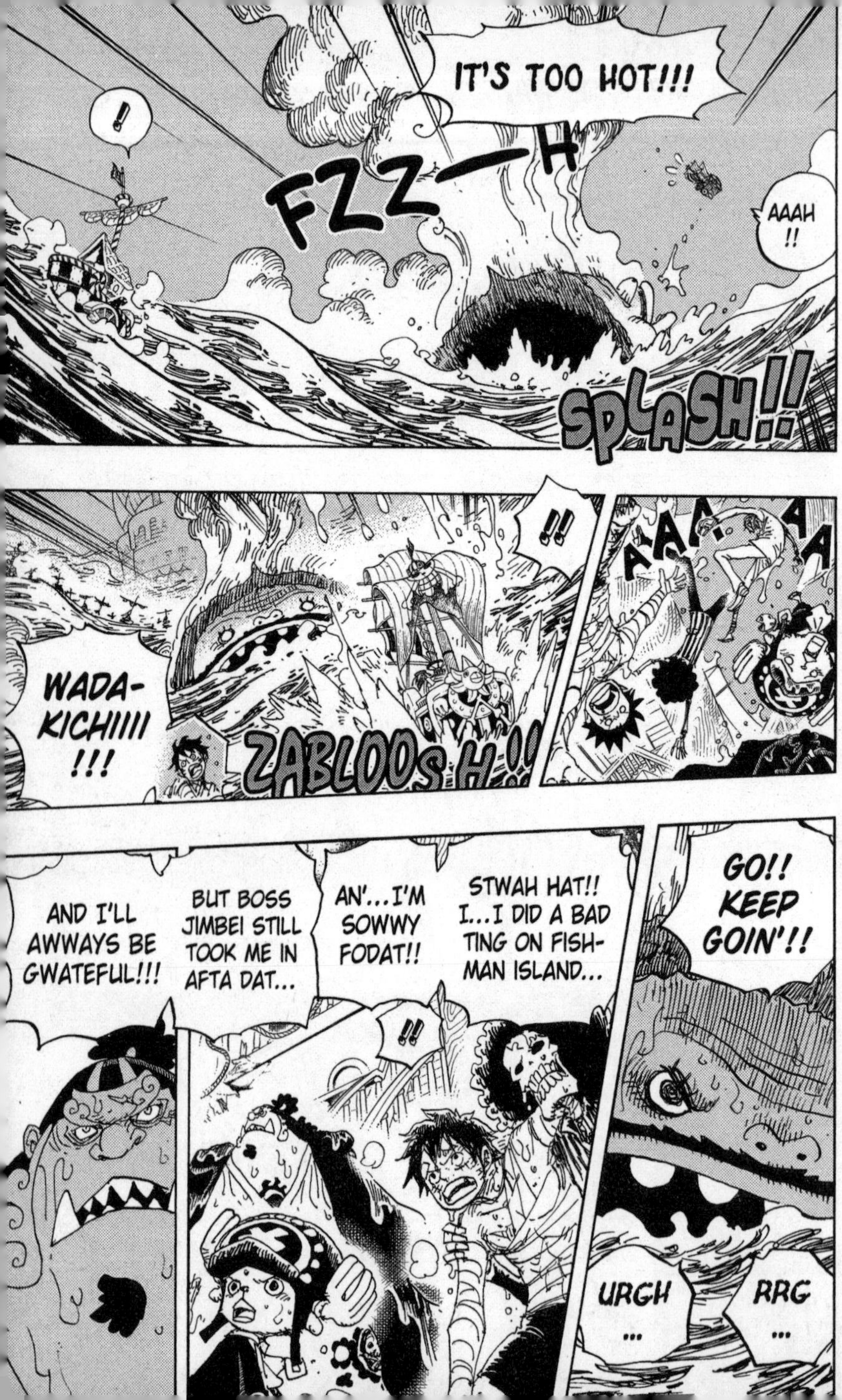
IT'S TOO HOT!!!
AAAH !!
!
FZZ—H
SPLASH!!
AAAAA
!!
WADA-KICHI!!!!!!!!
ZABLOOSH!!
GO!! KEEP GOIN'!!
RRG ...
URGH ...
STWAH HAT!! I...I DID A BAD TING ON FISH-MAN ISLAND...
AN'...I'M SOWWY FODAT!!
!!
BUT BOSS JIMBEI STILL TOOK ME IN AFTA DAT...
AND I'LL AWWAYS BE GWATEFUL!!!

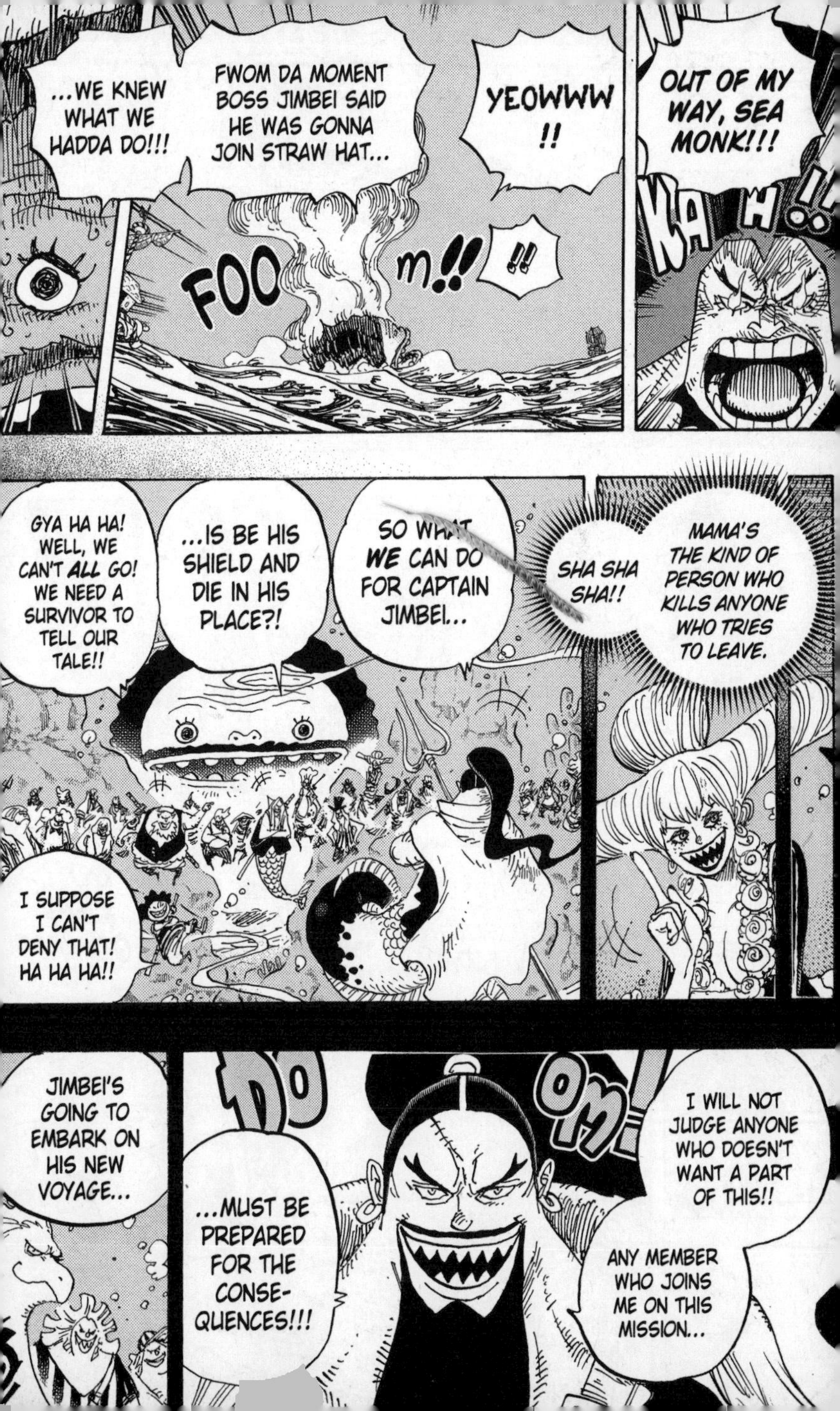
OUT OF MY WAY, SEA MONK!!!
YEOWWW!!
FWOM DA MOMENT BOSS JIMBEI SAID HE WAS GONNA JOIN STRAW HAT...
!!
FOOm!!
...WE KNEW WHAT WE HADDA DO!!!
MAMA'S THE KIND OF PERSON WHO KILLS ANYONE WHO TRIES TO LEAVE.
SHA SHA SHA!!
SO WHAT **WE** CAN DO FOR CAPTAIN JIMBEI...
...IS BE HIS SHIELD AND DIE IN HIS PLACE?!
GYA HA HA! WELL, WE CAN'T **ALL** GO! WE NEED A SURVIVOR TO TELL OUR TALE!!
I SUPPOSE I CAN'T DENY THAT! HA HA HA!!
I WILL NOT JUDGE ANYONE WHO DOESN'T WANT A PART OF THIS!!
DOOM!
ANY MEMBER WHO JOINS ME ON THIS MISSION...
...MUST BE PREPARED FOR THE CONSE- QUENCES!!!
JIMBEI'S GOING TO EMBARK ON HIS NEW VOYAGE...

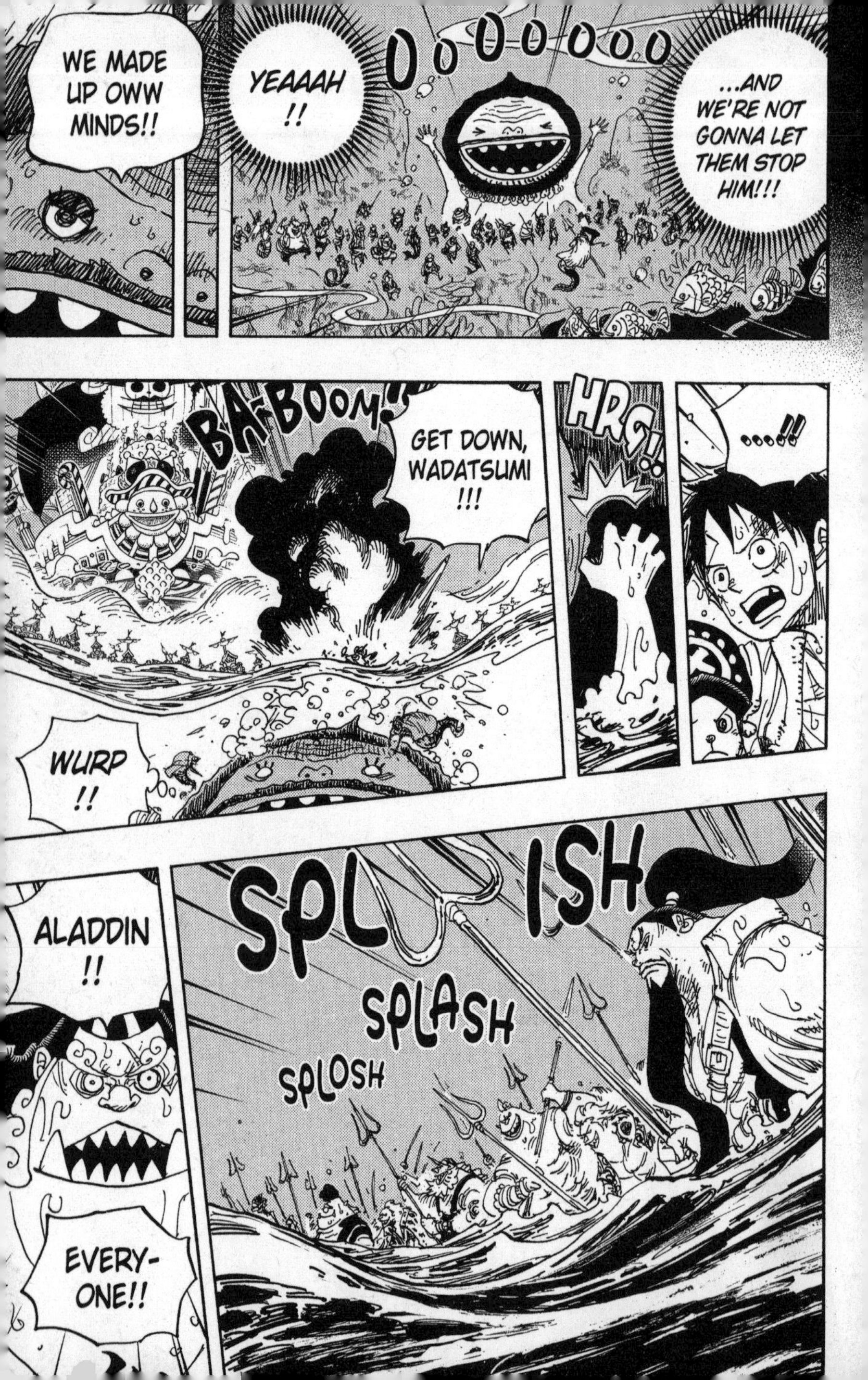
...AND WE'RE NOT GONNA LET THEM STOP HIM!!!
OOOOOOO
YEAAAH !!
WE MADE UP OWW MINDS!!
...!!
HRG!!
BA-BOOM!!
GET DOWN, WADATSUMI !!!
WURP !!
SPLISH
SPLASH
SPLOSH
ALADDIN !!
EVERY-ONE!!

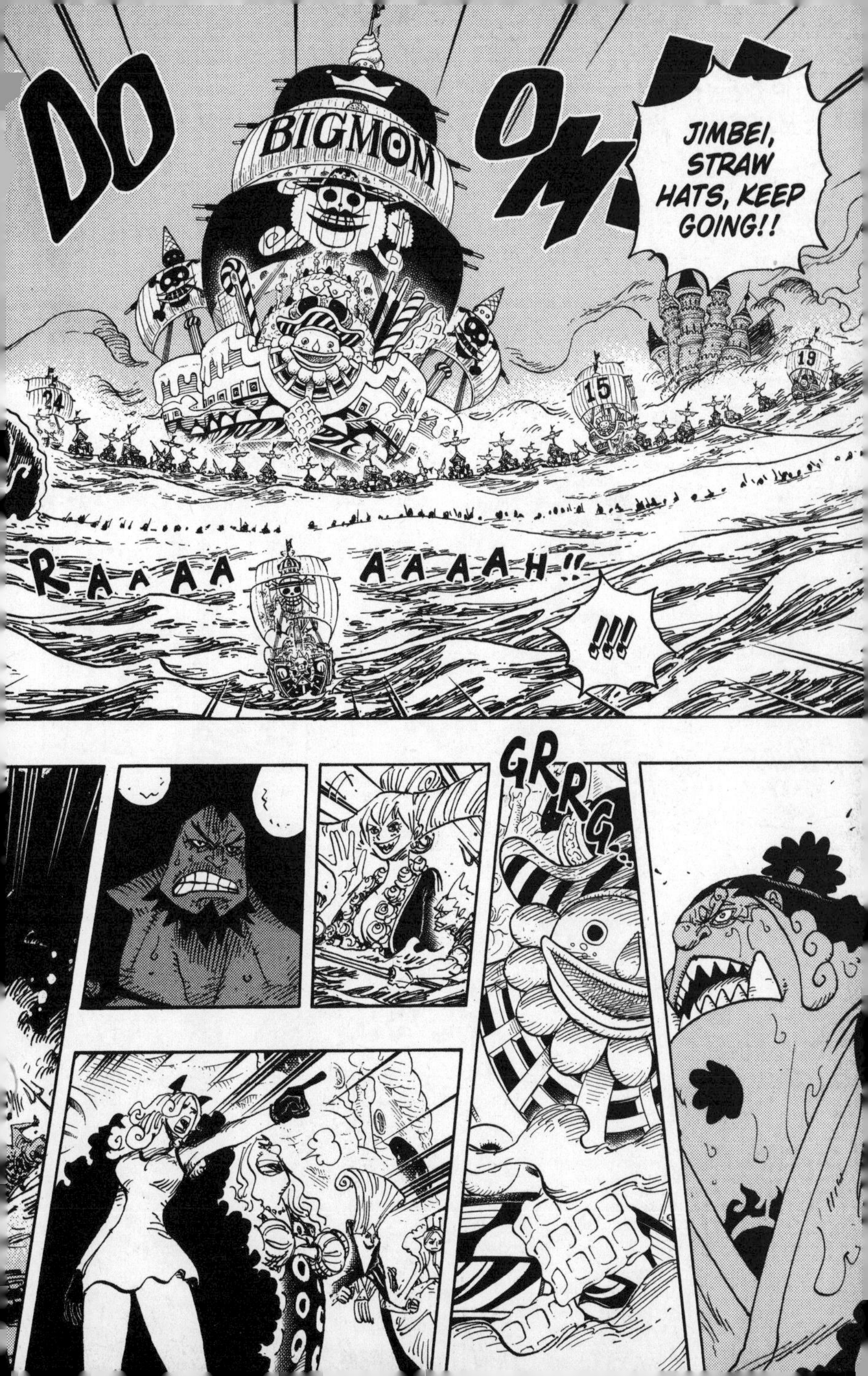
JIMBEI, STRAW HATS, KEEP GOING!!
DO
OM
RAAAA AAAAH!!
!!!
GRRRG

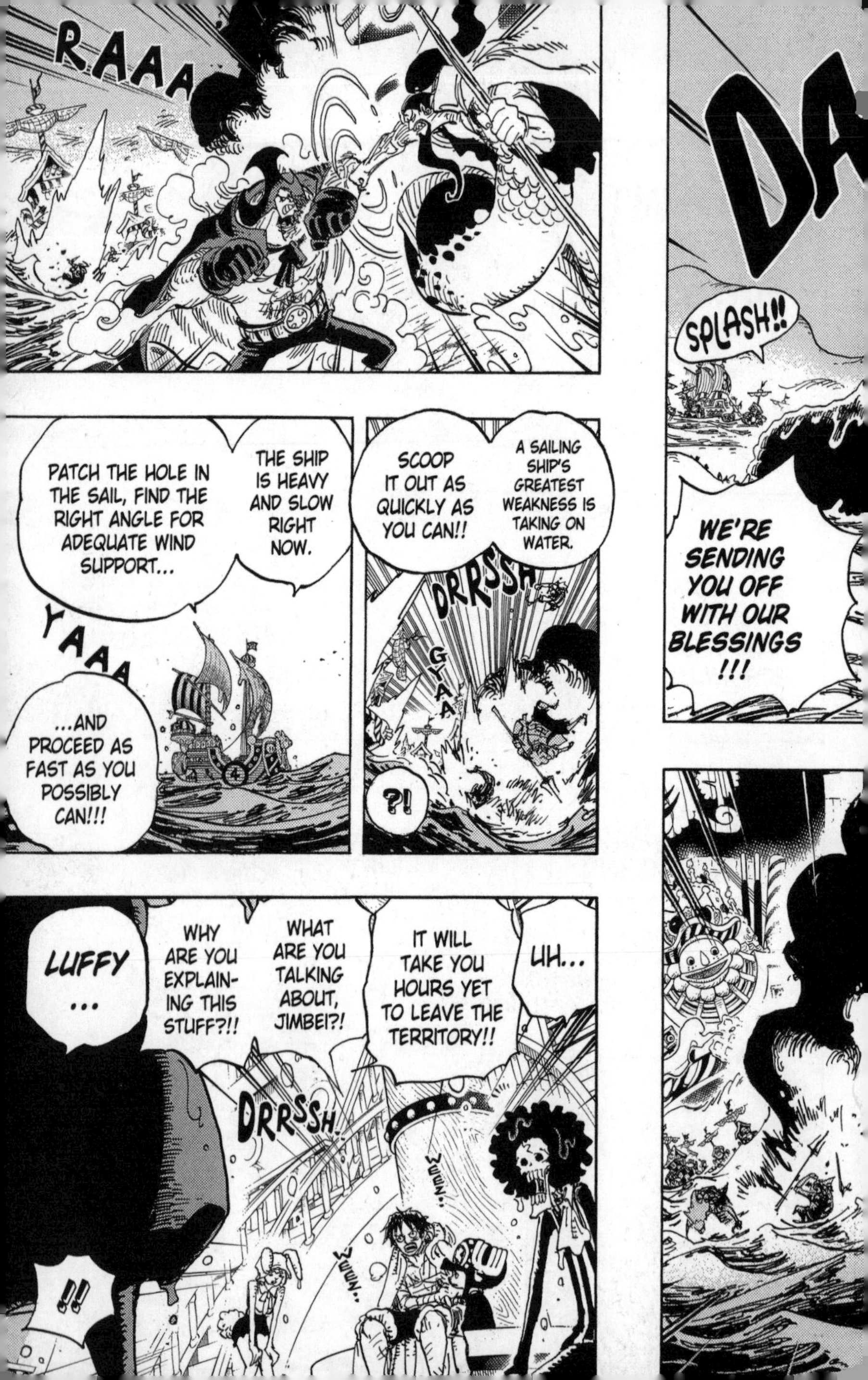
DA
SPLASH!!
WE'RE SENDING YOU OFF WITH OUR BLESSINGS!!!
RAAA
A SAILING SHIP'S GREATEST WEAKNESS IS TAKING ON WATER.
SCOOP IT OUT AS QUICKLY AS YOU CAN!!
DRRSSH
GYAA
?!
THE SHIP IS HEAVY AND SLOW RIGHT NOW.
PATCH THE HOLE IN THE SAIL, FIND THE RIGHT ANGLE FOR ADEQUATE WIND SUPPORT...
YAAA
...AND PROCEED AS FAST AS YOU POSSIBLY CAN!!!
UH...
IT WILL TAKE YOU HOURS YET TO LEAVE THE TERRITORY!!
WHAT ARE YOU TALKING ABOUT, JIMBEI?!
WHY ARE YOU EXPLAINING THIS STUFF?!!
LUFFY ...
DRRSSH
!!

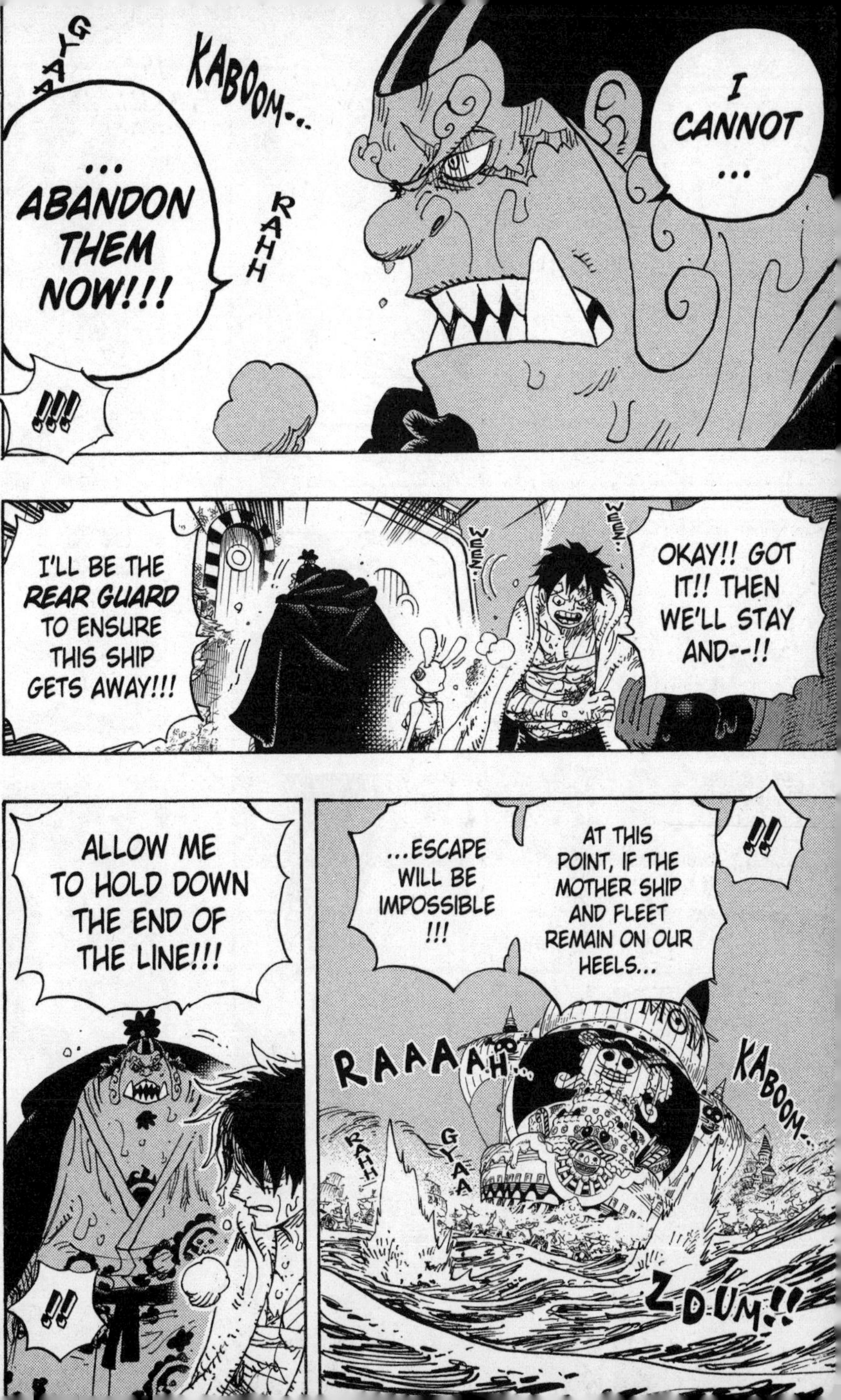
I CANNOT ...
KABOOM...
GYAAA
... ABANDON THEM NOW!!!
RAHH
!!!
OKAY!! GOT IT!! THEN WE'LL STAY AND--!!
WEEZ...
WEEZ...
I'LL BE THE REAR GUARD TO ENSURE THIS SHIP GETS AWAY!!!
!!
AT THIS POINT, IF THE MOTHER SHIP AND FLEET REMAIN ON OUR HEELS...
...ESCAPE WILL BE IMPOSSIBLE !!!
KABOOM...
RAAAAH...
GYAA
RAHH
ZDUM!!
ALLOW ME TO HOLD DOWN THE END OF THE LINE!!!
!!

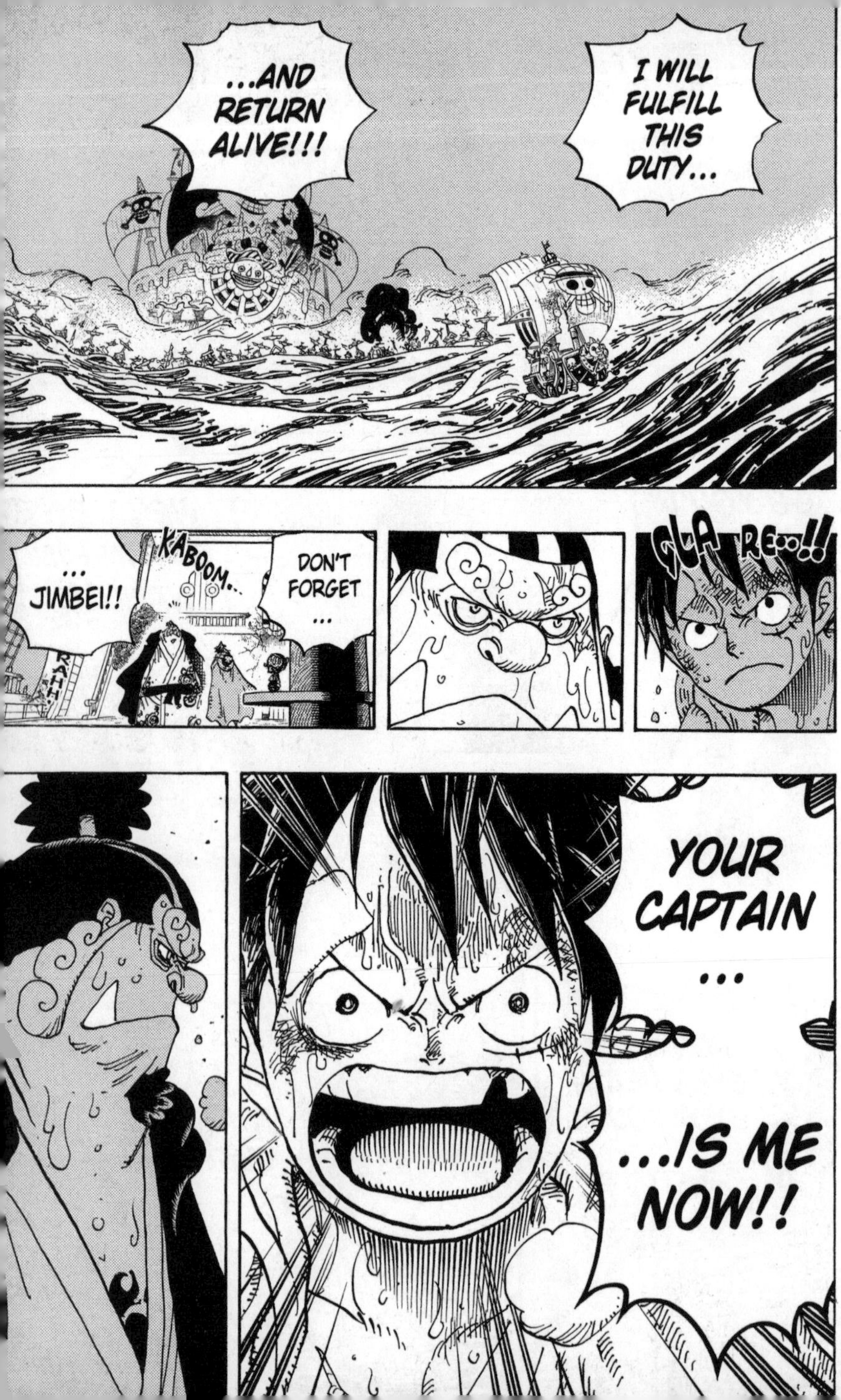
I WILL FULFILL THIS DUTY...
...AND RETURN ALIVE!!!
GLARE..!!
DON'T FORGET ...
KABOOM...
... JIMBEI!!
RAHH
YOUR CAPTAIN ...
...IS ME NOW!!

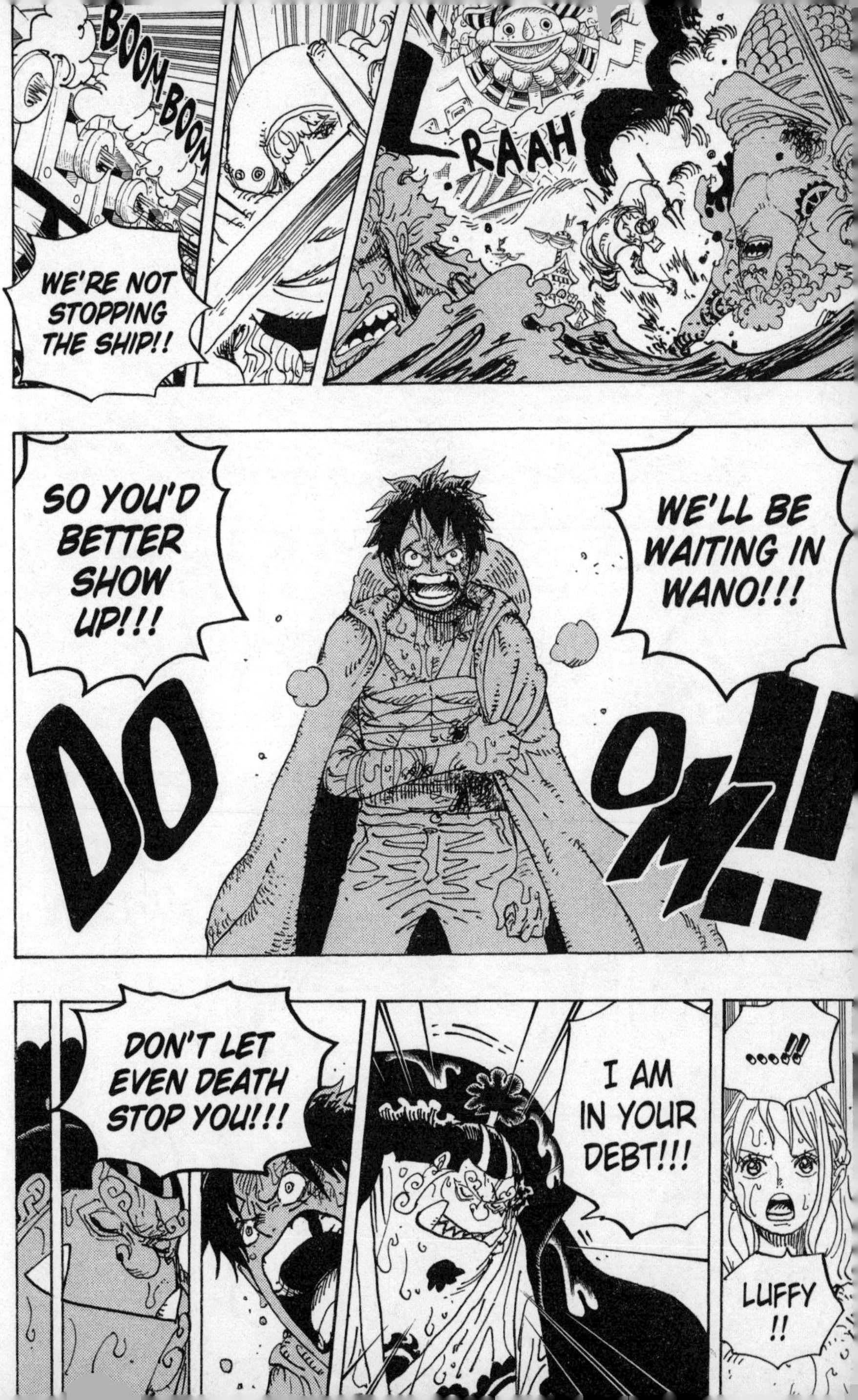
RAAH
BOOMBOOM
WE'RE NOT STOPPING THE SHIP!!
WE'LL BE WAITING IN WANO!!!
SO YOU'D BETTER SHOW UP!!!
DO
OM!!
...!!
LUFFY !!
I AM IN YOUR DEBT!!!
DON'T LET EVEN DEATH STOP YOU!!!

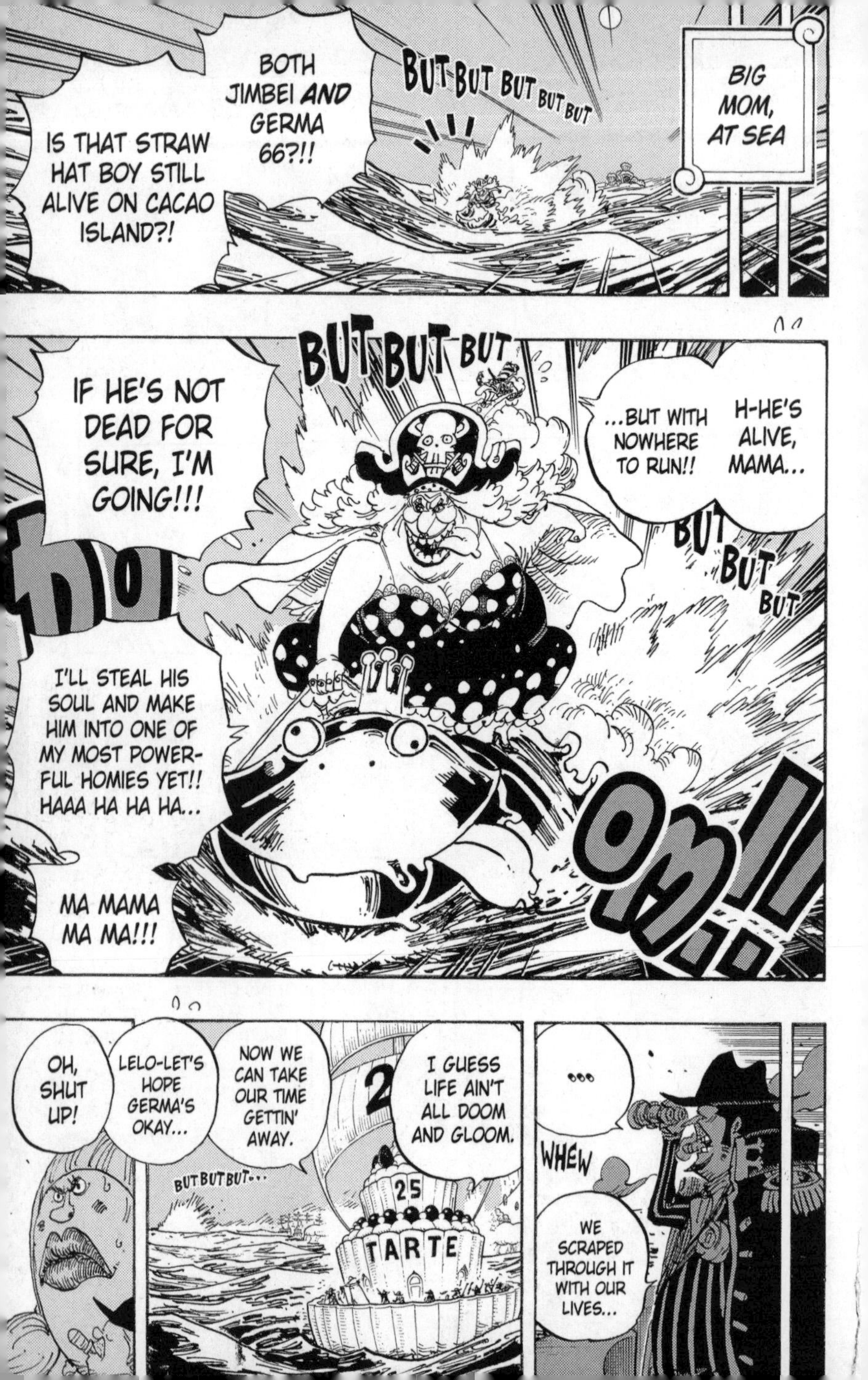
BIG MOM, AT SEA
BUT BUT BUT BUT BUT
BOTH JIMBEI AND GERMA 66?!!
IS THAT STRAW HAT BOY STILL ALIVE ON CACAO ISLAND?!
H-HE'S ALIVE, MAMA...
...BUT WITH NOWHERE TO RUN!!
BUT BUT BUT
BUT BUT BUT
IF HE'S NOT DEAD FOR SURE, I'M GOING!!!
I'LL STEAL HIS SOUL AND MAKE HIM INTO ONE OF MY MOST POWER-FUL HOMIES YET!! HAAA HA HA HA...
MA MAMA MA MA!!!
THOOM!!
...
WHEW
WE SCRAPED THROUGH IT WITH OUR LIVES...
I GUESS LIFE AIN'T ALL DOOM AND GLOOM.
NOW WE CAN TAKE OUR TIME GETTIN' AWAY.
2
25
TARTE
BUT BUT BUT...
LELO-LET'S HOPE GERMA'S OKAY...
OH, SHUT UP!

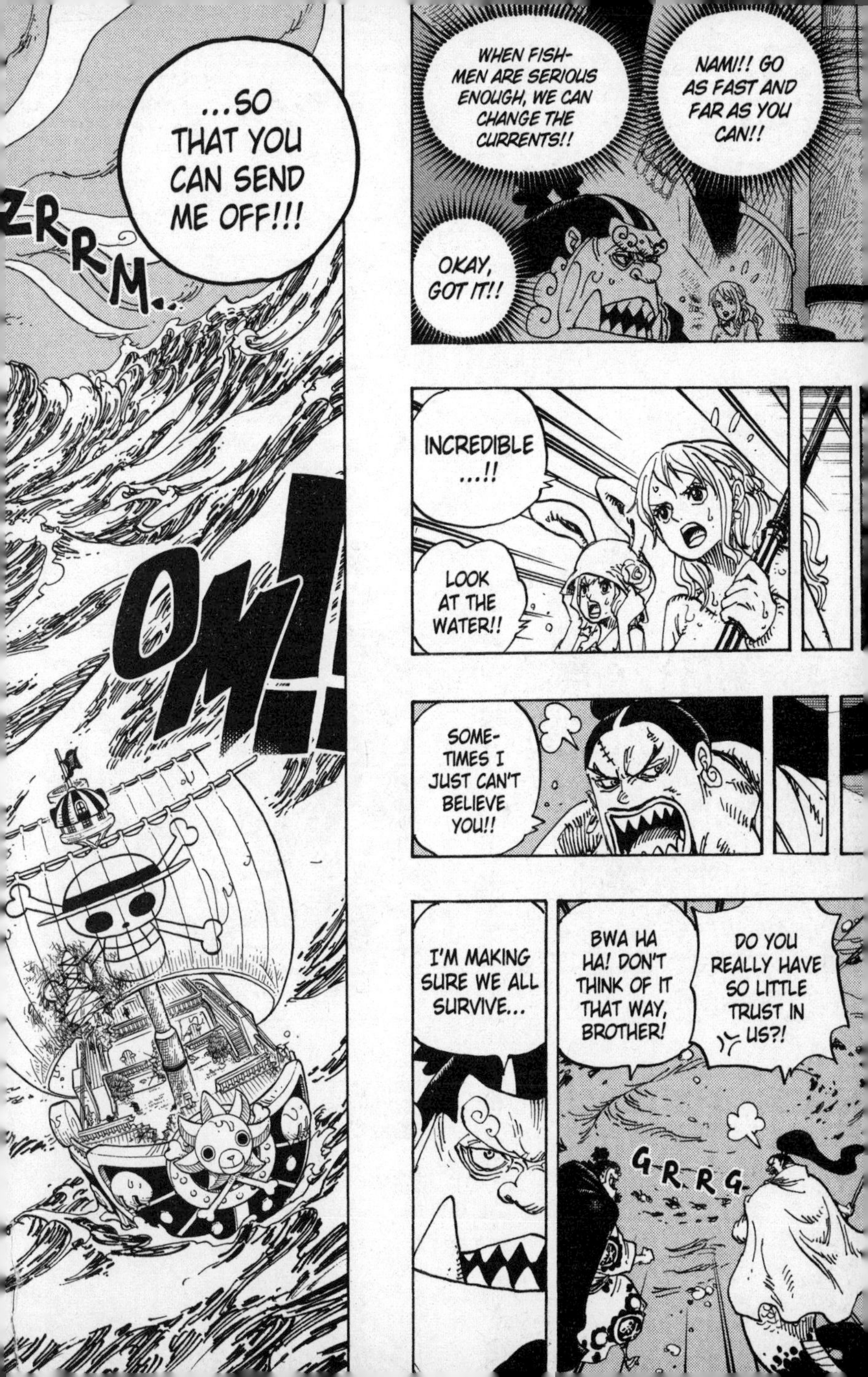
NAMI!! GO AS FAST AND FAR AS YOU CAN!!
WHEN FISH-MEN ARE SERIOUS ENOUGH, WE CAN CHANGE THE CURRENTS!!
OKAY, GOT IT!!
INCREDIBLE ...!!
LOOK AT THE WATER!!
SOME-TIMES I JUST CAN'T BELIEVE YOU!!
DO YOU REALLY HAVE SO LITTLE TRUST IN US?!
BWA HA HA! DON'T THINK OF IT THAT WAY, BROTHER!
I'M MAKING SURE WE ALL SURVIVE...
GRRG
...SO THAT YOU CAN SEND ME OFF!!!
ZRRRM..
OH!!

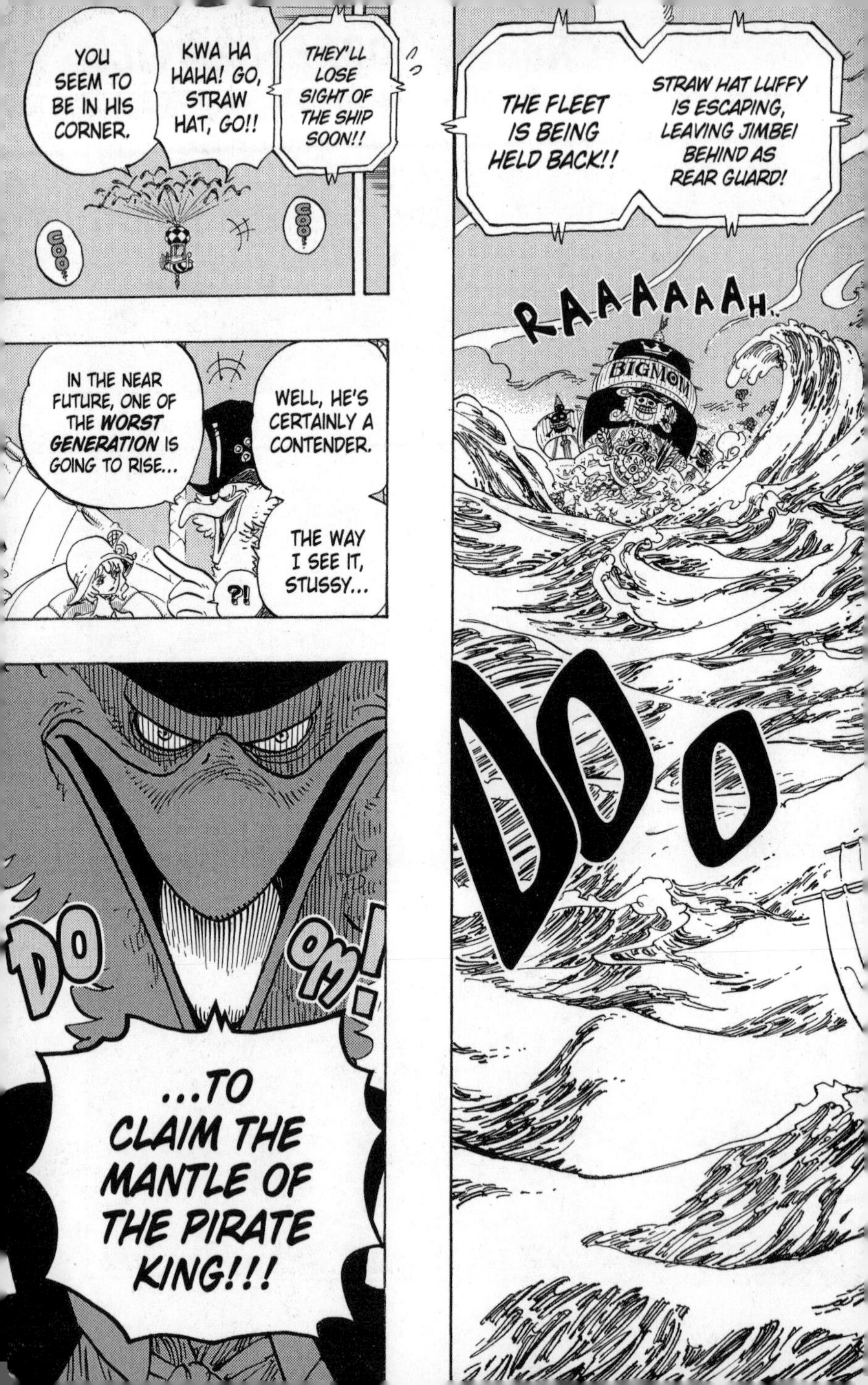
STRAW HAT LUFFY IS ESCAPING, LEAVING JIMBEI BEHIND AS REAR GUARD!
THE FLEET IS BEING HELD BACK!!
RAAAAAAH
BIGMOM
DOOO
THEY'LL LOSE SIGHT OF THE SHIP SOON!!
KWA HA HAHA! GO, STRAW HAT, GO!!
YOU SEEM TO BE IN HIS CORNER.
GOO
GOO
WELL, HE'S CERTAINLY A CONTENDER.
THE WAY I SEE IT, STUSSY...
?!
IN THE NEAR FUTURE, ONE OF THE WORST GENERATION IS GOING TO RISE...
DOOM!
...TO CLAIM THE MANTLE OF THE PIRATE KING!!!

Chapter 902: END ROLL

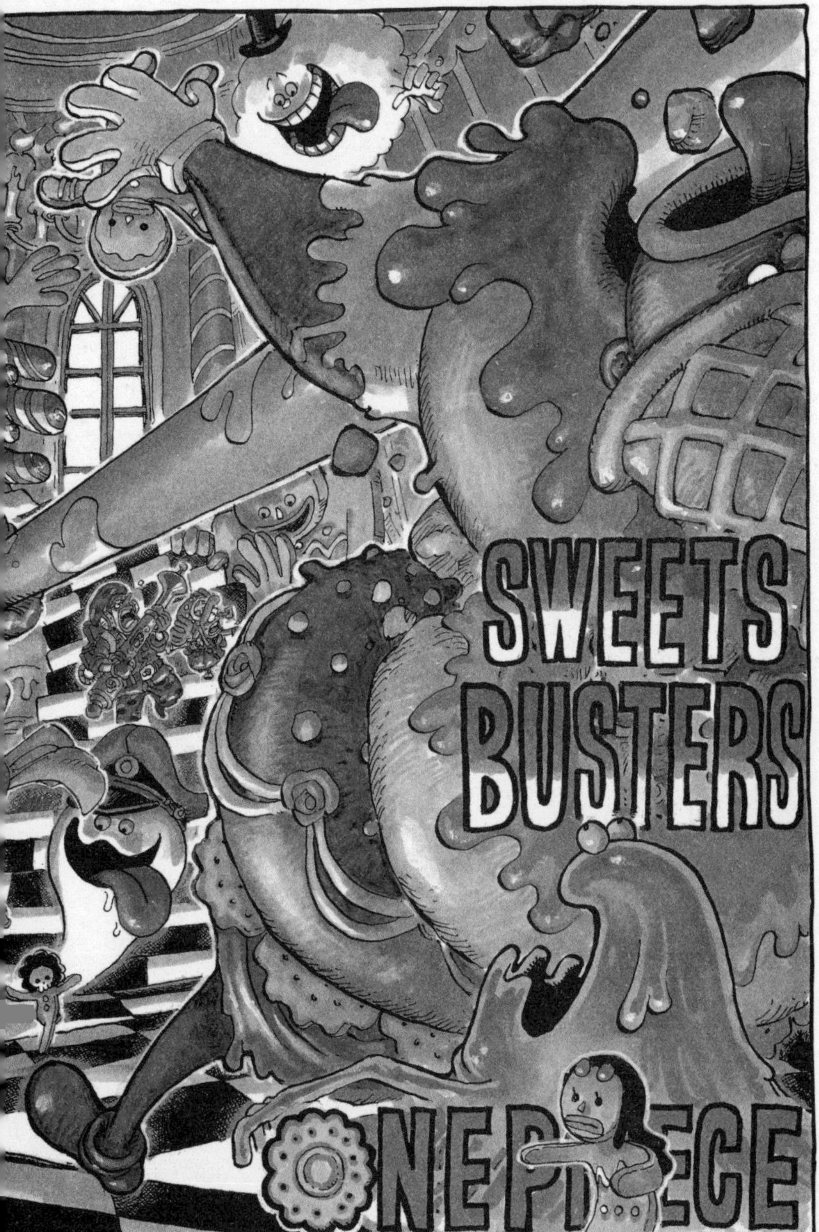
SWEETS BUSTERS
ONE PIECE

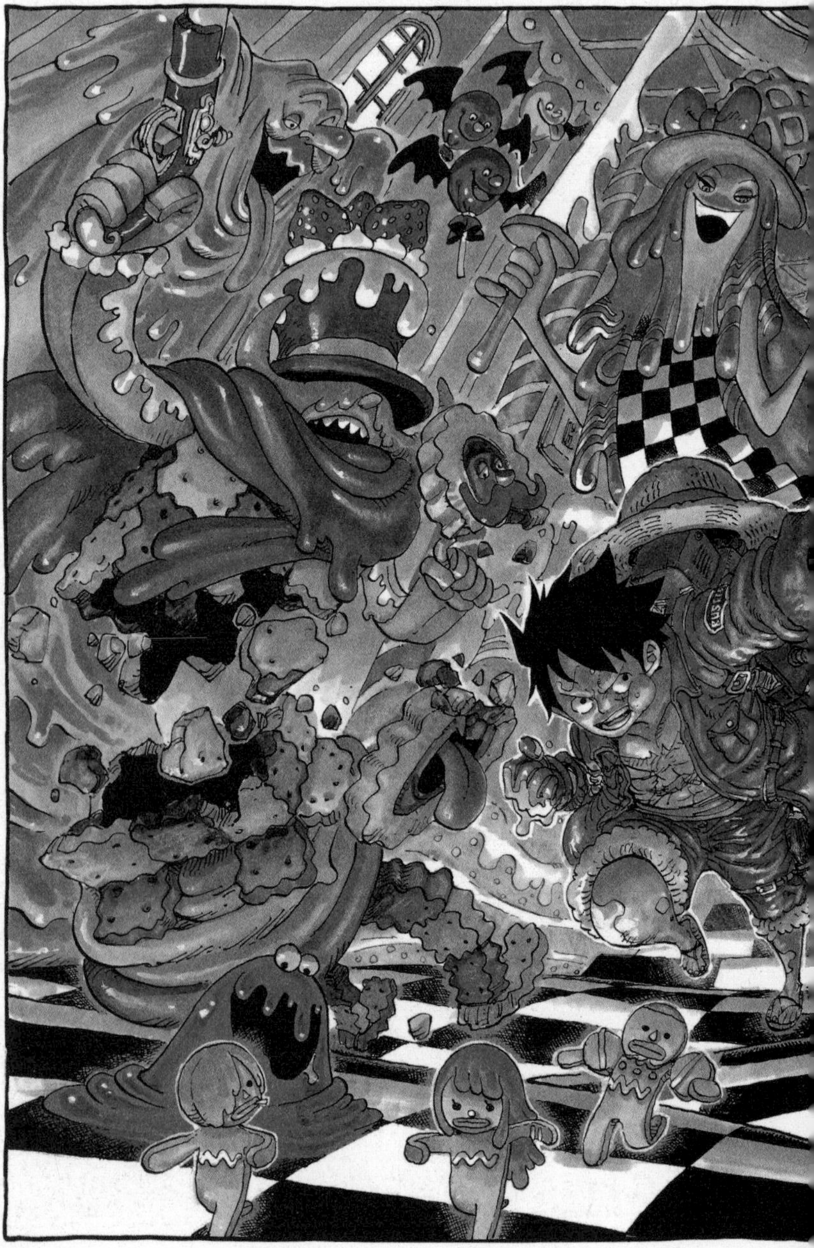

vol.90
ONE PIECE

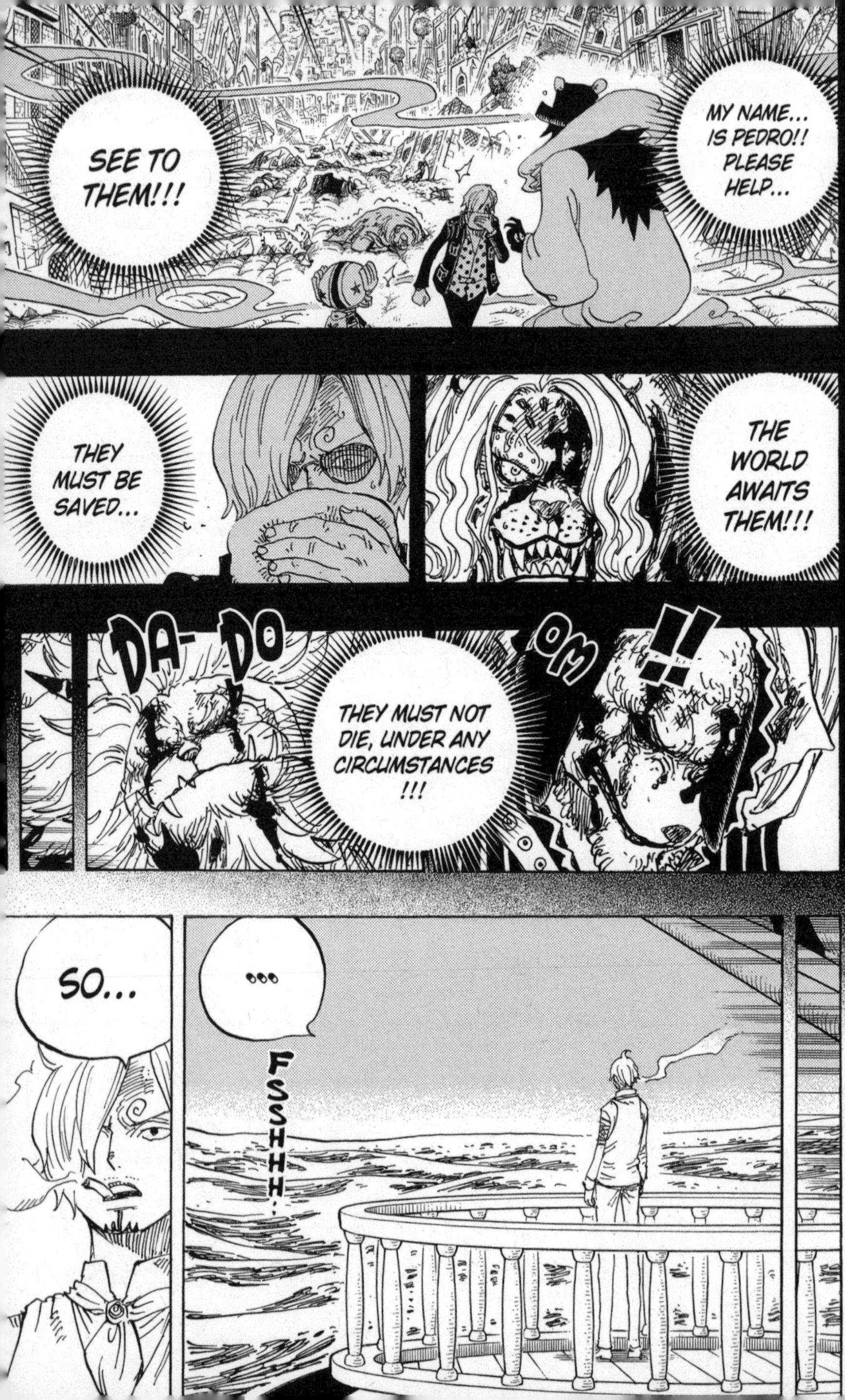
MY NAME... IS PEDRO!! PLEASE HELP...
SEE TO THEM!!!
THE WORLD AWAITS THEM!!!
THEY MUST BE SAVED...
DA-DOOM!!
THEY MUST NOT DIE, UNDER ANY CIRCUMSTANCES !!!
...
FSSHHH
SO...

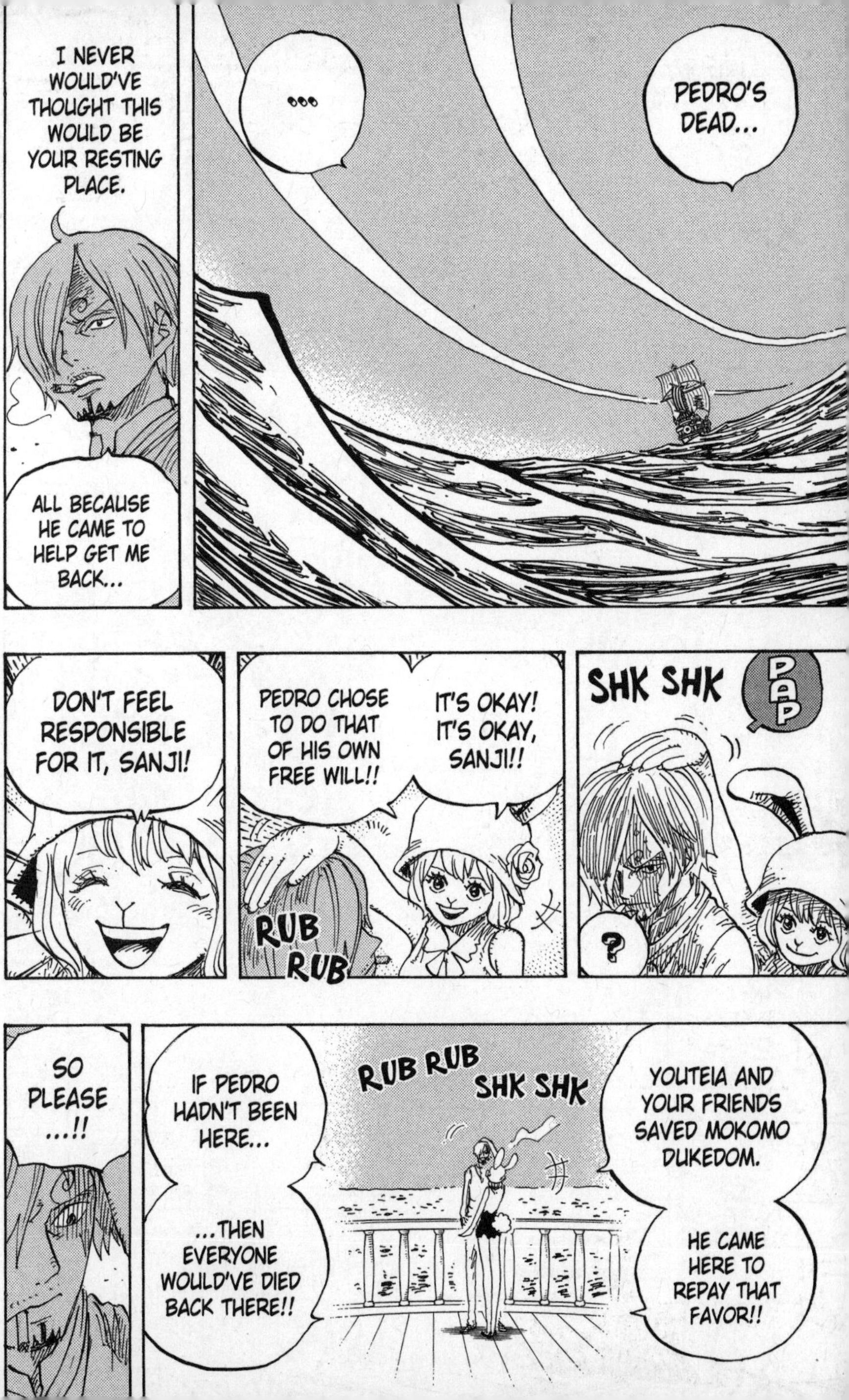

PEDRO'S DEAD...
...
I NEVER WOULD'VE THOUGHT THIS WOULD BE YOUR RESTING PLACE.
ALL BECAUSE HE CAME TO HELP GET ME BACK...
SHK SHK
PAP
?
IT'S OKAY! IT'S OKAY, SANJI!!
PEDRO CHOSE TO DO THAT OF HIS OWN FREE WILL!!
RUB RUB
DON'T FEEL RESPONSIBLE FOR IT, SANJI!
YOUTEIA AND YOUR FRIENDS SAVED MOKOMO DUKEDOM.
HE CAME HERE TO REPAY THAT FAVOR!!
RUB RUB
SHK SHK
IF PEDRO HADN'T BEEN HERE...
...THEN EVERYONE WOULD'VE DIED BACK THERE!!
SO PLEASE ...!!

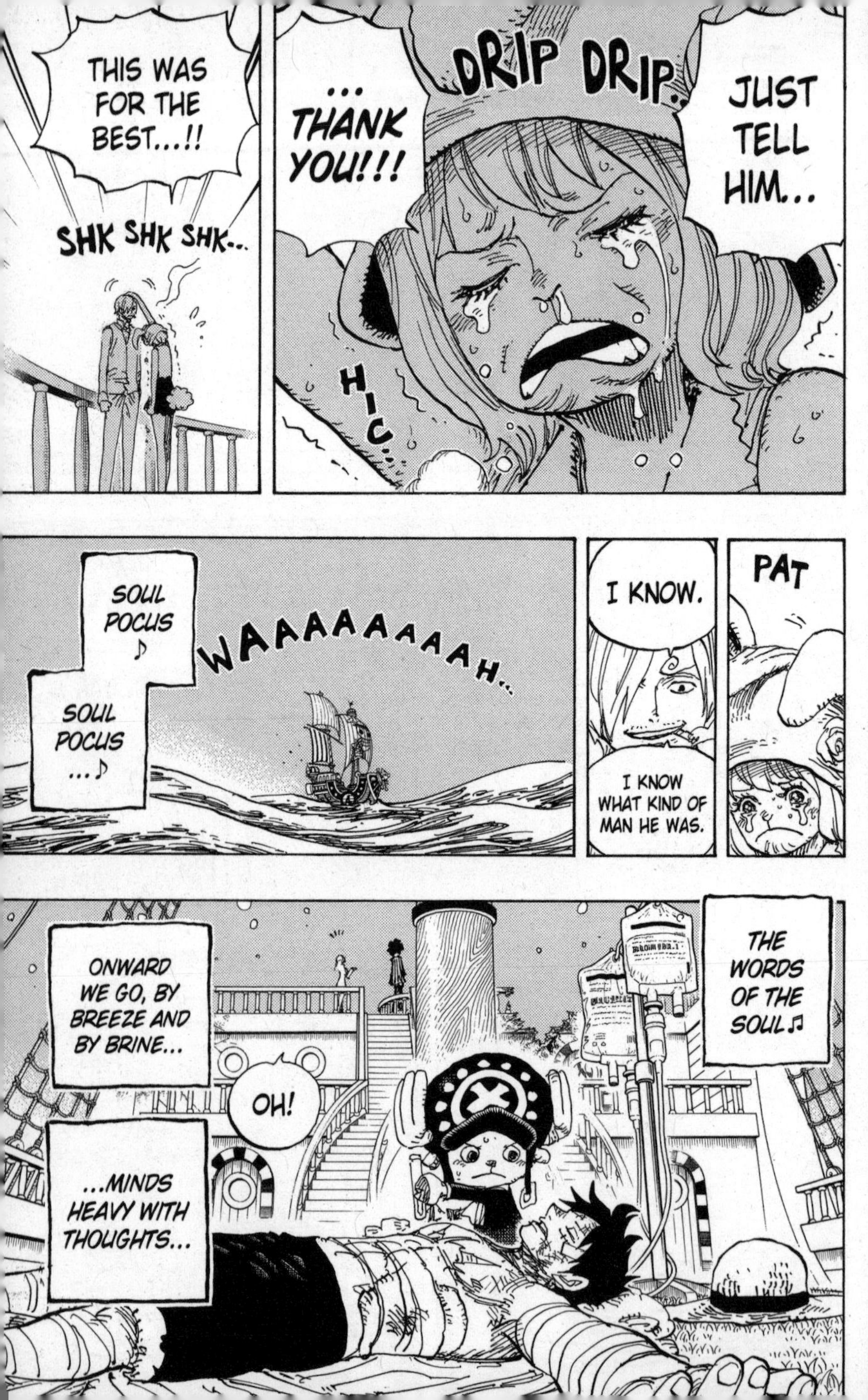
DRIP DRIP..
JUST TELL HIM...
...THANK YOU!!!
HIC..
THIS WAS FOR THE BEST...!!
SHK SHK SHK..
PAT
I KNOW.
I KNOW WHAT KIND OF MAN HE WAS.
SOUL POCUS ♪
WAAAAAAAAAH..
SOUL POCUS ...♪
THE WORDS OF THE SOUL♫
ONWARD WE GO, BY BREEZE AND BY BRINE...
OH!
...MINDS HEAVY WITH THOUGHTS...

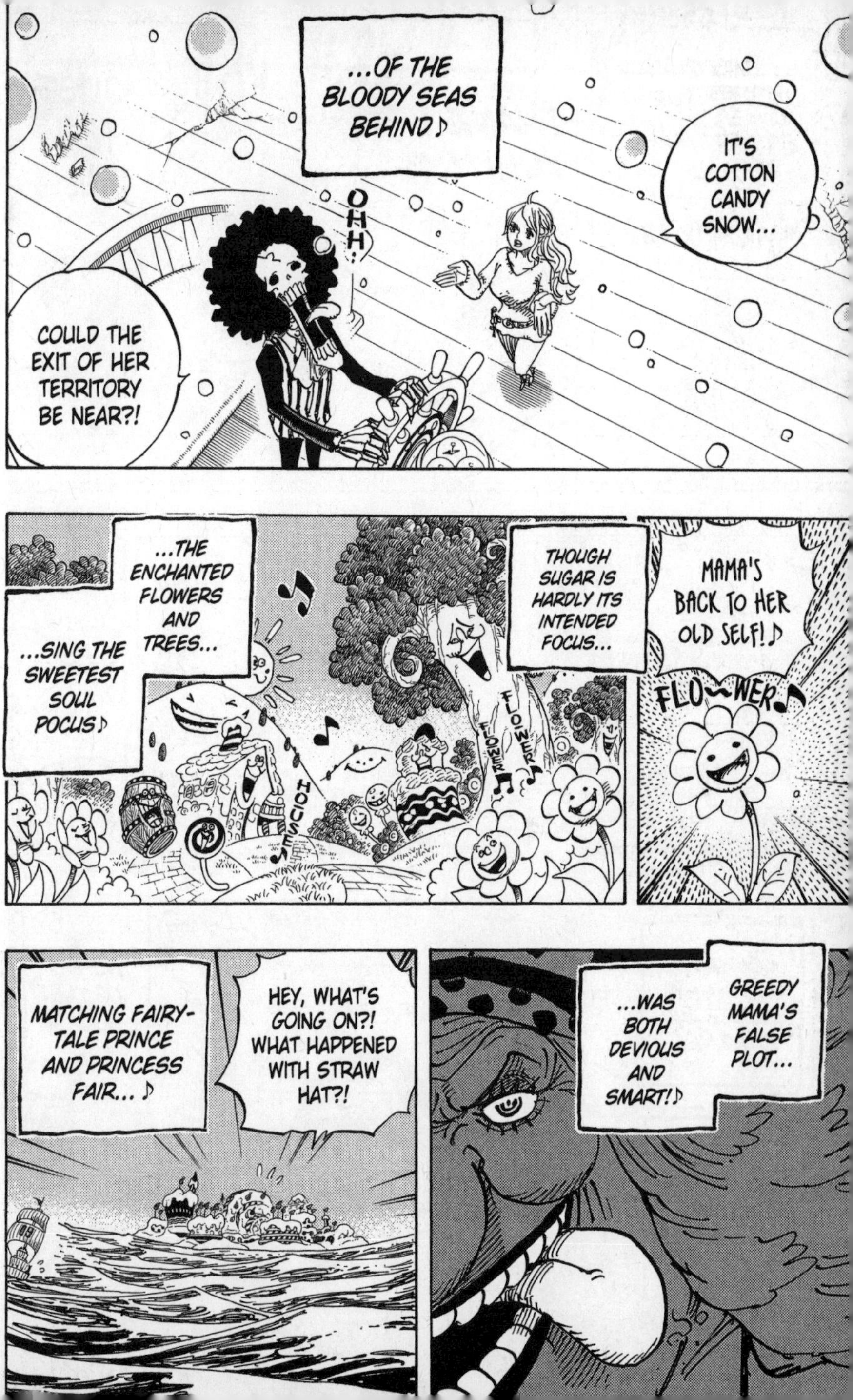
...OF THE BLOODY SEAS BEHIND♪
IT'S COTTON CANDY SNOW...
OHH!
COULD THE EXIT OF HER TERRITORY BE NEAR?!
MAMA'S BACK TO HER OLD SELF!♪
FLO~WER♪
THOUGH SUGAR IS HARDLY ITS INTENDED FOCUS...
...THE ENCHANTED FLOWERS AND TREES...
...SING THE SWEETEST SOUL POCUS♪
FLOWER♪
FLOWER♪
HOUSE♪
GREEDY MAMA'S FALSE PLOT...
...WAS BOTH DEVIOUS AND SMART!♪
HEY, WHAT'S GOING ON?! WHAT HAPPENED WITH STRAW HAT?!
MATCHING FAIRY-TALE PRINCE AND PRINCESS FAIR...♪

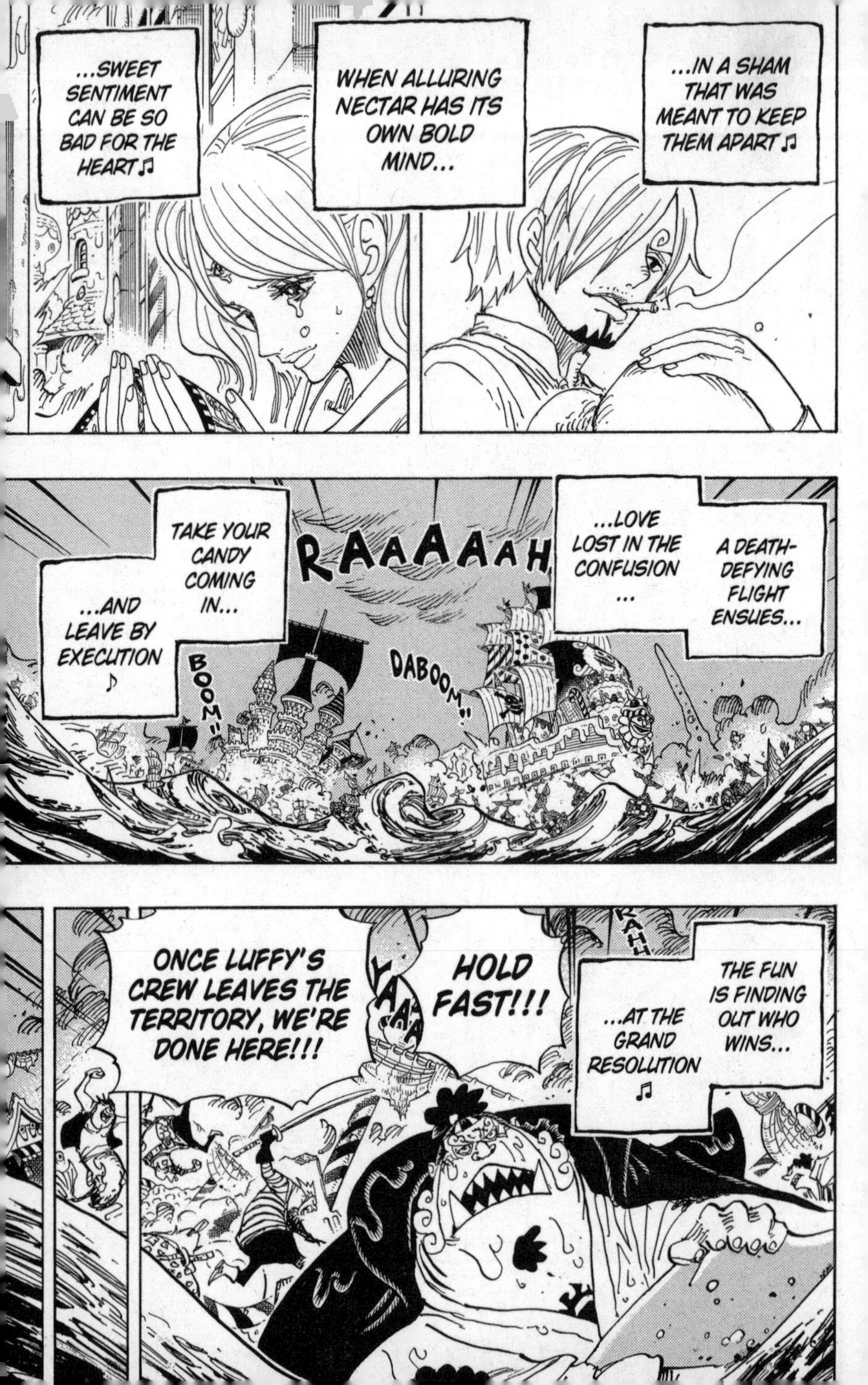
...IN A SHAM THAT WAS MEANT TO KEEP THEM APART ♫
WHEN ALLURING NECTAR HAS ITS OWN BOLD MIND...
...SWEET SENTIMENT CAN BE SO BAD FOR THE HEART ♫
A DEATH-DEFYING FLIGHT ENSUES...
...LOVE LOST IN THE CONFUSION ...
RAAAAAH
DABOOM!!
TAKE YOUR CANDY COMING IN...
...AND LEAVE BY EXECUTION ♪
BOOM!!
THE FUN IS FINDING OUT WHO WINS...
...AT THE GRAND RESOLUTION ♫
RAHH
HOLD FAST!!!
YAAAA
ONCE LUFFY'S CREW LEAVES THE TERRITORY, WE'RE DONE HERE!!!

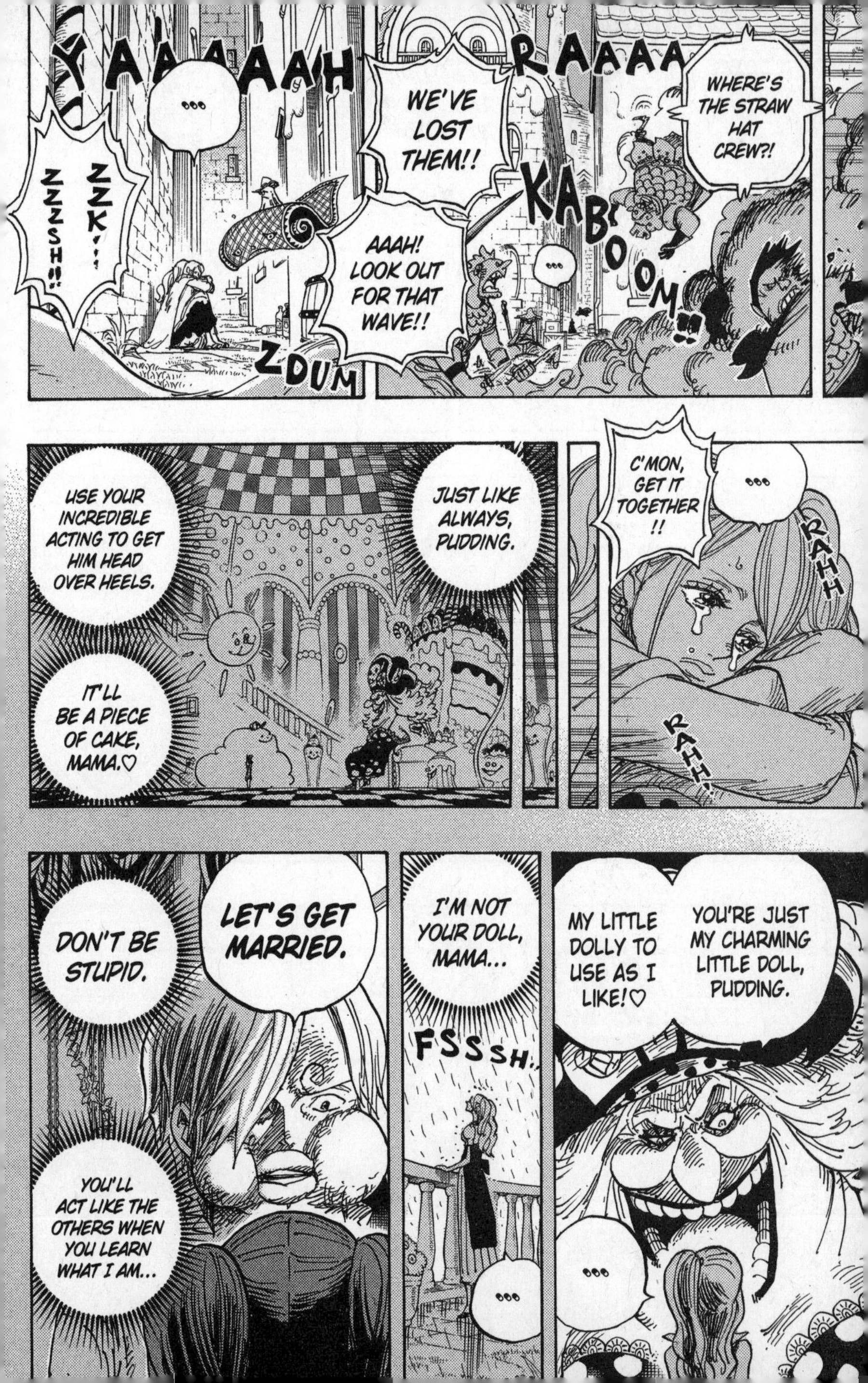
WHERE'S THE STRAW HAT CREW?!
RAAAA
KABOOM!!
WE'VE LOST THEM!!
AAAH! LOOK OUT FOR THAT WAVE!!
...
YAAAAAH
...
ZZK
ZZZSH!!
ZDUM
C'MON, GET IT TOGETHER!!
...
RAHH
RAHH!!
JUST LIKE ALWAYS, PUDDING.
USE YOUR INCREDIBLE ACTING TO GET HIM HEAD OVER HEELS.
IT'LL BE A PIECE OF CAKE, MAMA.♡
YOU'RE JUST MY CHARMING LITTLE DOLL, PUDDING.
MY LITTLE DOLLY TO USE AS I LIKE!♡
...
I'M NOT YOUR DOLL, MAMA...
FSSSH..
...
LET'S GET MARRIED.
DON'T BE STUPID.
YOU'LL ACT LIKE THE OTHERS WHEN YOU LEARN WHAT I AM...

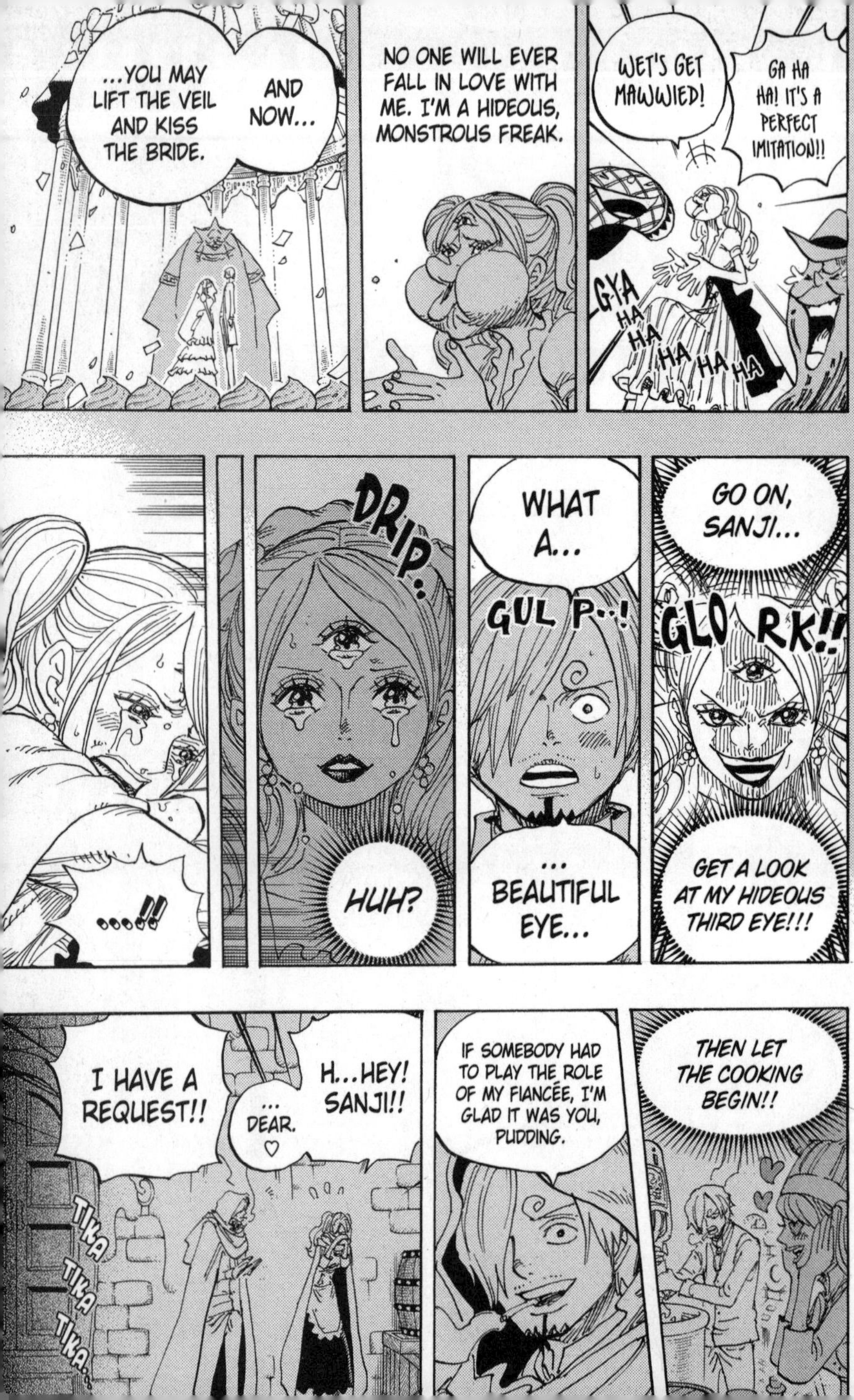
WET'S GET MAWWIED!
GA HA HA! IT'S A PERFECT IMITATION!!
GYA HA HA HA HA HA HA
NO ONE WILL EVER FALL IN LOVE WITH ME. I'M A HIDEOUS, MONSTROUS FREAK.
AND NOW...
...YOU MAY LIFT THE VEIL AND KISS THE BRIDE.
GO ON, SANJI...
GLORK!!
GET A LOOK AT MY HIDEOUS THIRD EYE!!!
WHAT A...
GULP..!
...BEAUTIFUL EYE...
DRIP..
HUH?
....!!
THEN LET THE COOKING BEGIN!!
IF SOMEBODY HAD TO PLAY THE ROLE OF MY FIANCÉE, I'M GLAD IT WAS YOU, PUDDING.
H...HEY! SANJI!!
...DEAR. ♡
I HAVE A REQUEST!!
TIKA TIKA TIKA TIKA..

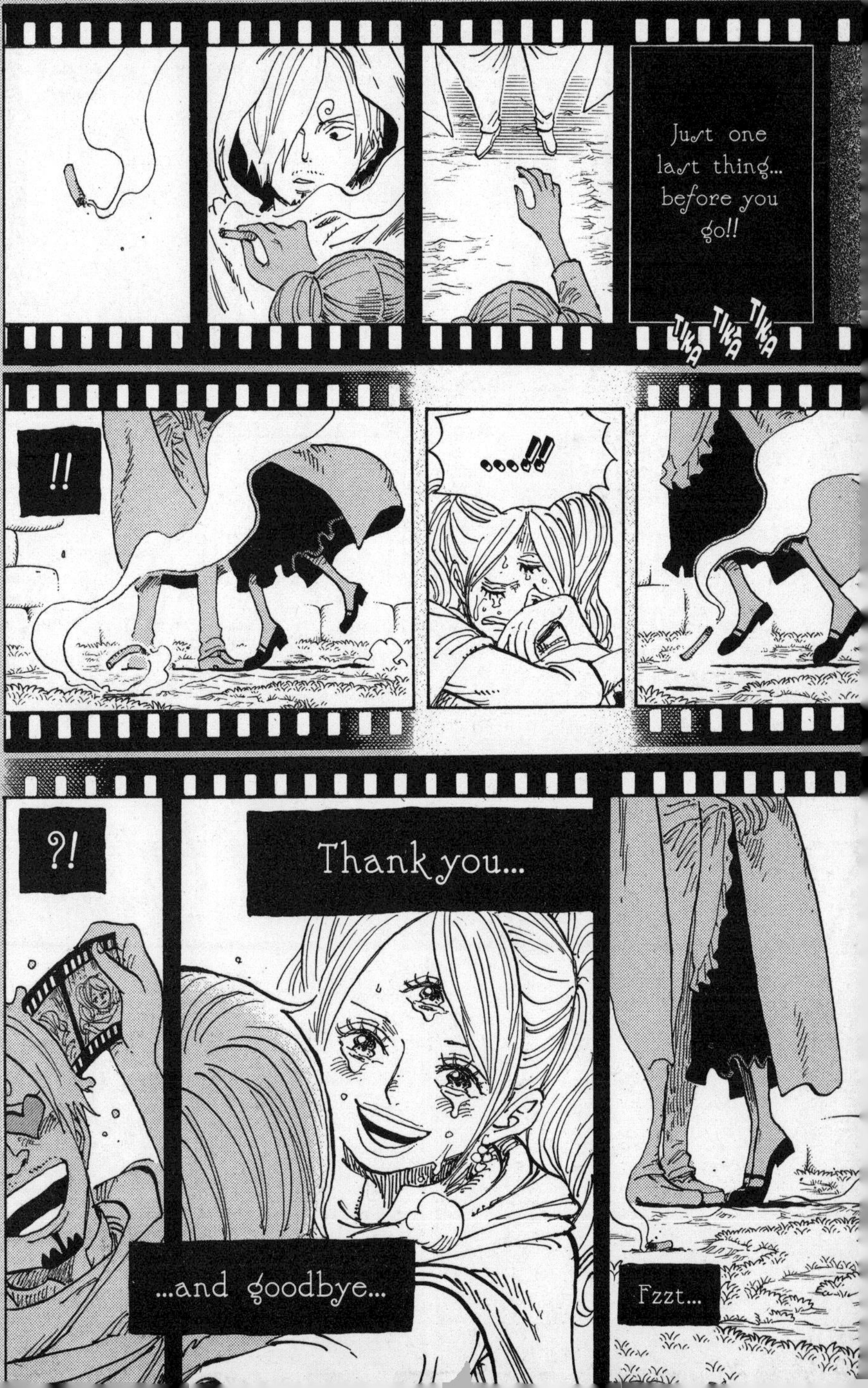
Just one last thing... before you go!!
TIKA TIKA TIKA
....!!
!!
Fzzt...
Thank you...
...and goodbye...
?!

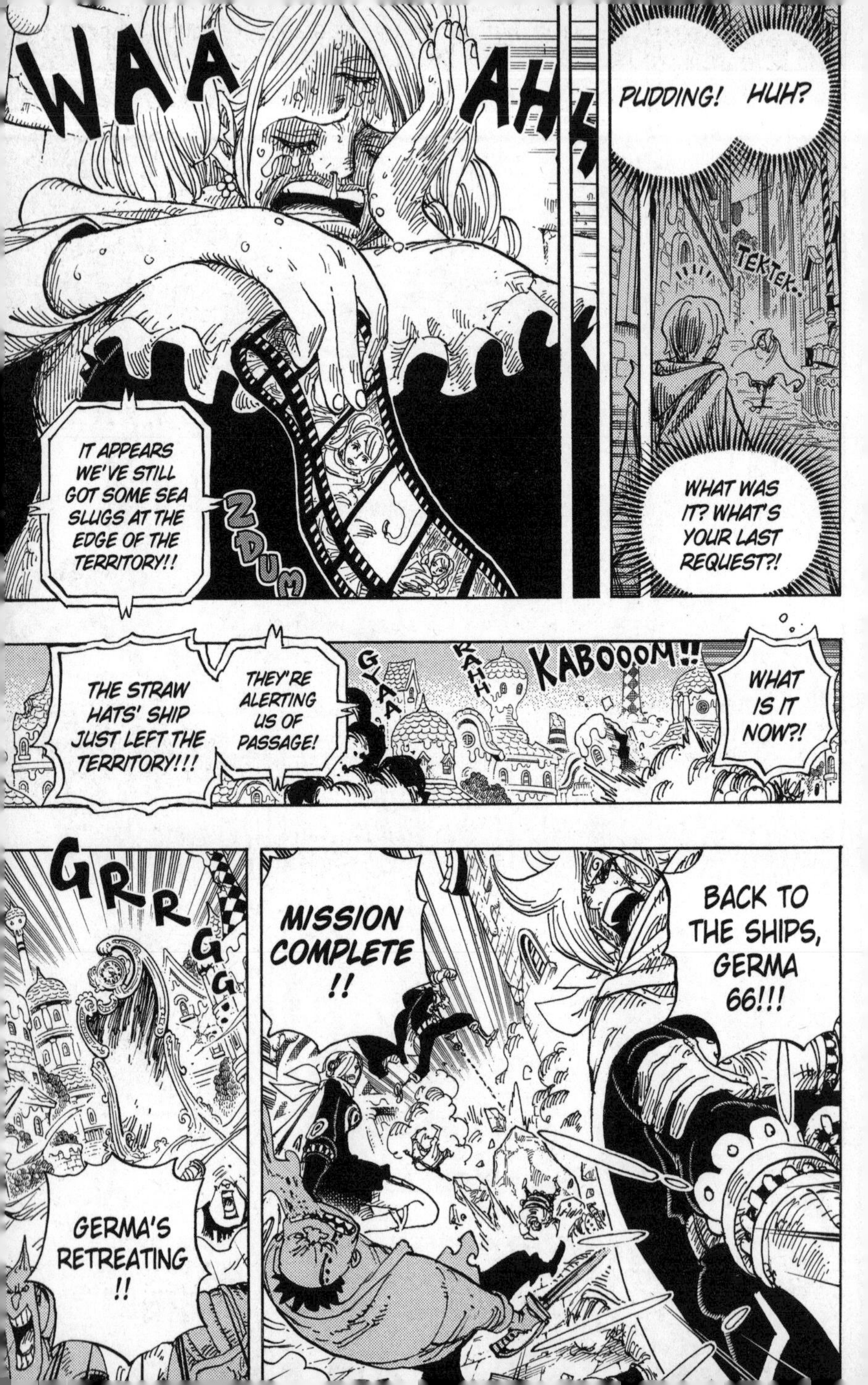
PUDDING! HUH?
TEKTEK..
WHAT WAS IT? WHAT'S YOUR LAST REQUEST?!
WAAAHH
IT APPEARS WE'VE STILL GOT SOME SEA SLUGS AT THE EDGE OF THE TERRITORY!!
ZDUM
WHAT IS IT NOW?!
KABOOOM!!
RAHH
GYAA
THEY'RE ALERTING US OF PASSAGE!
THE STRAW HATS' SHIP JUST LEFT THE TERRITORY!!!
BACK TO THE SHIPS, GERMA 66!!!
MISSION COMPLETE!!
GRRRGG
GERMA'S RETREATING!!

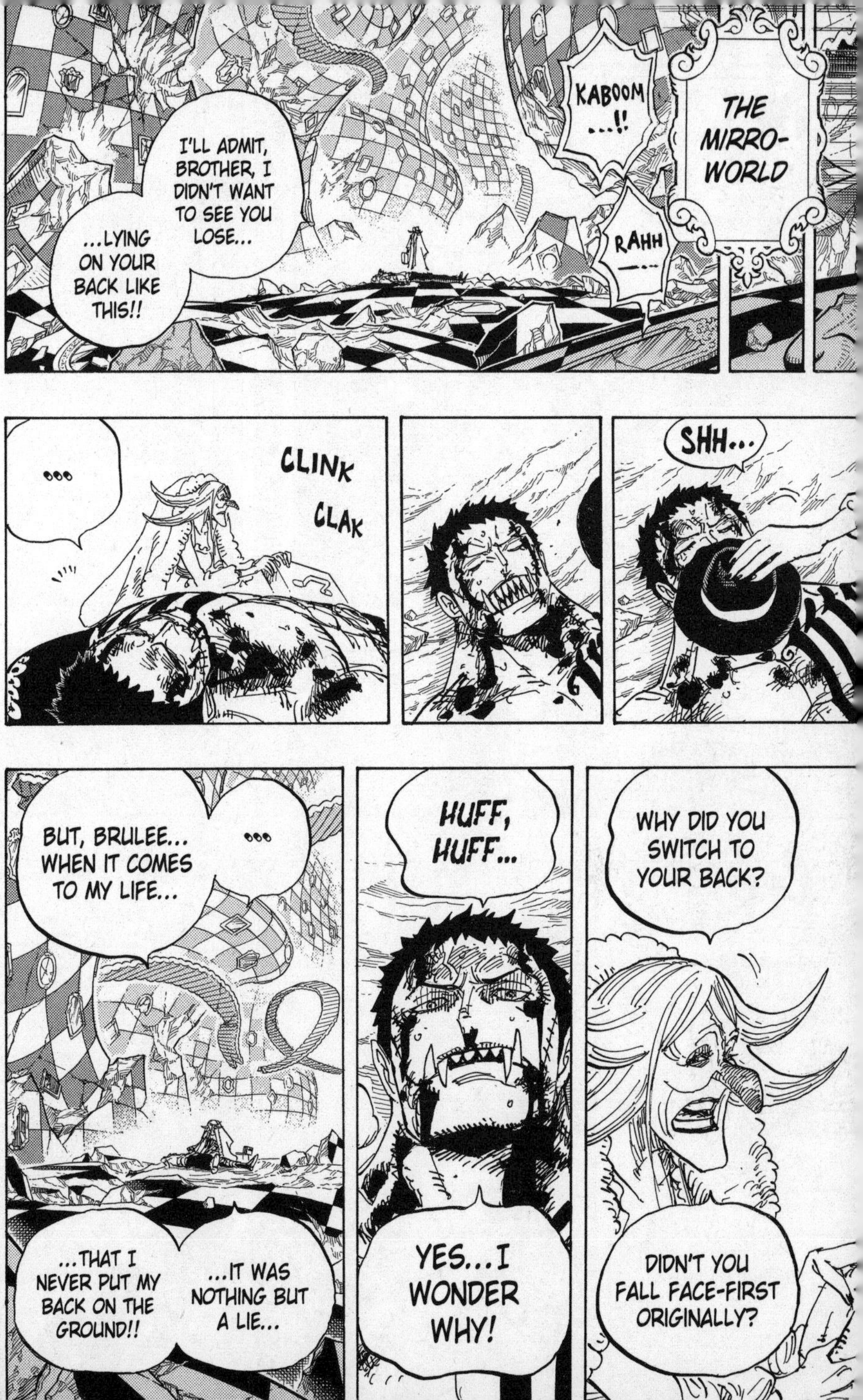
THE MIRRO-WORLD
KABOOM...!!
RAHH—...
I'LL ADMIT, BROTHER, I DIDN'T WANT TO SEE YOU LOSE...
...LYING ON YOUR BACK LIKE THIS!!
SHH...
...
CLINK
CLAK
WHY DID YOU SWITCH TO YOUR BACK?
DIDN'T YOU FALL FACE-FIRST ORIGINALLY?
HUFF, HUFF...
YES...I WONDER WHY!
...
BUT, BRULEE... WHEN IT COMES TO MY LIFE...
...THAT I NEVER PUT MY BACK ON THE GROUND!!
...IT WAS NOTHING BUT A LIE...

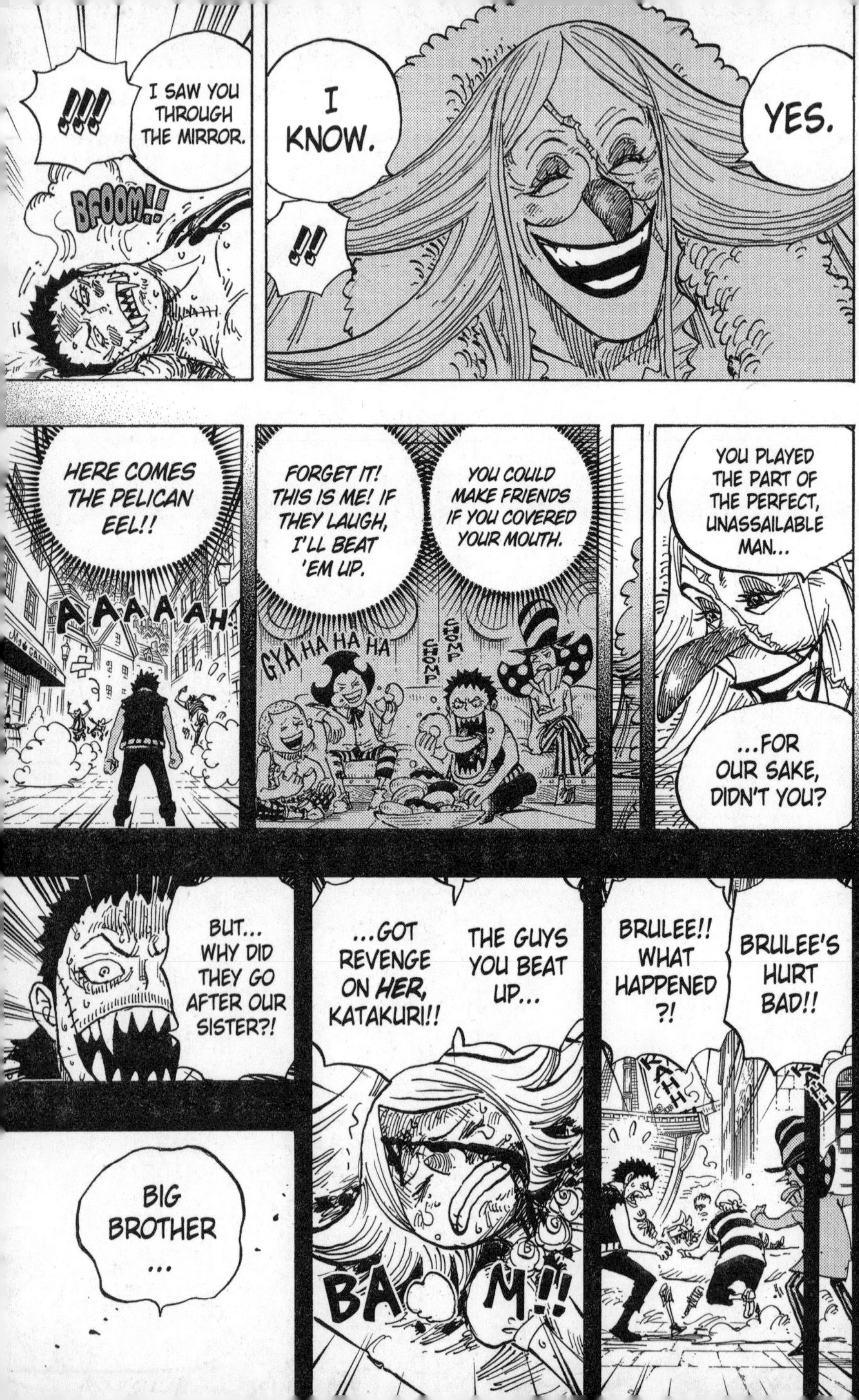
YES.
I KNOW.
!!
I SAW YOU THROUGH THE MIRROR.
!!!
BROOM!!
YOU PLAYED THE PART OF THE PERFECT, UNASSAILABLE MAN...
...FOR OUR SAKE, DIDN'T YOU?
YOU COULD MAKE FRIENDS IF YOU COVERED YOUR MOUTH.
FORGET IT! THIS IS ME! IF THEY LAUGH, I'LL BEAT 'EM UP.
CHOMP
CHOMP
GYA HA HA HA
HERE COMES THE PELICAN EEL!!
AAAAAH!!
BRULEE'S HURT BAD!!
BRULEE!! WHAT HAPPENED?!
KAHH
KAHH
THE GUYS YOU BEAT UP...
...GOT REVENGE ON HER, KATAKURI!!
BAM!!
BUT... WHY DID THEY GO AFTER OUR SISTER?!
BIG BROTHER...

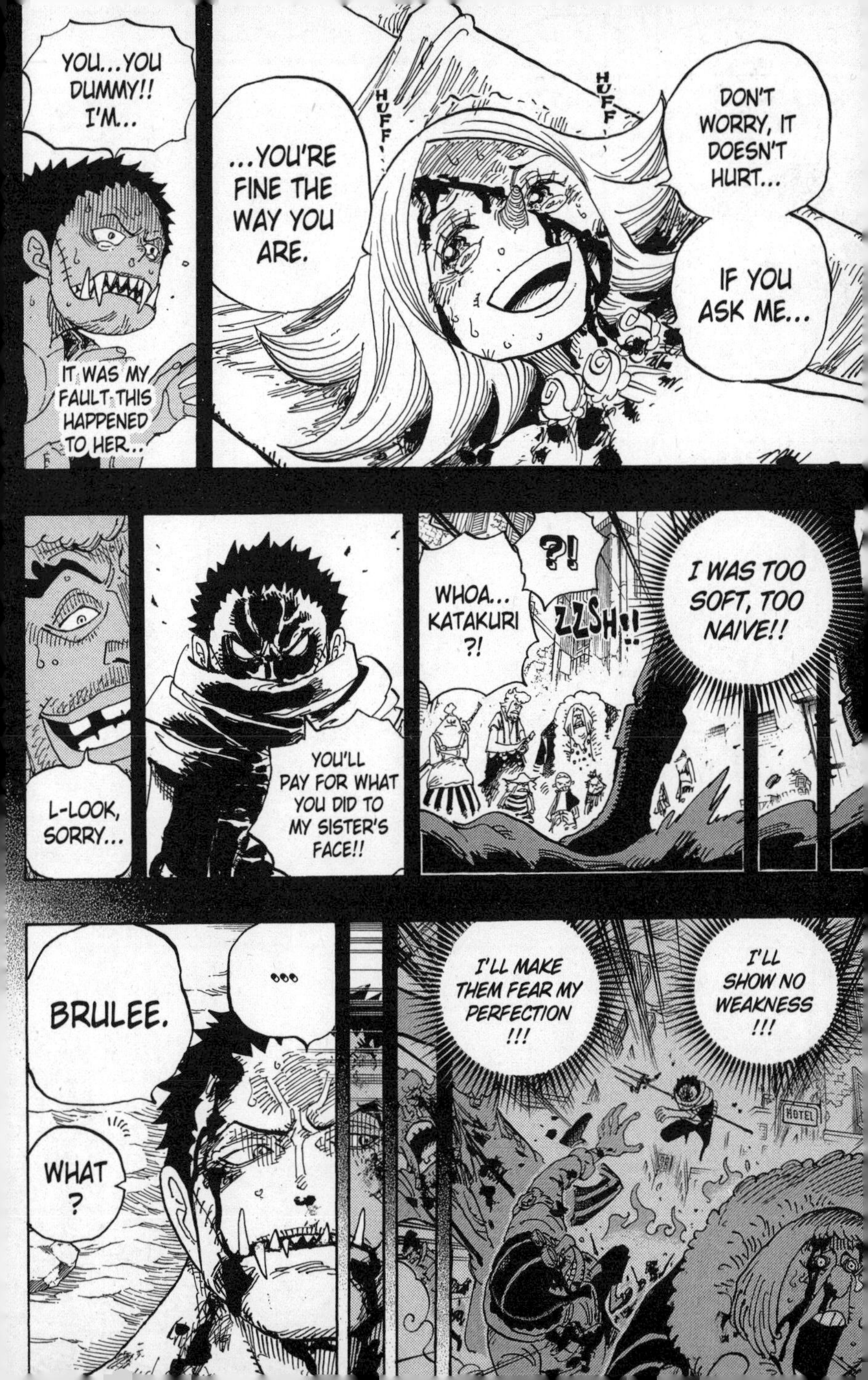
DON'T WORRY, IT DOESN'T HURT...
IF YOU ASK ME...
HUFF
HUFF
...YOU'RE FINE THE WAY YOU ARE.
YOU...YOU DUMMY!! I'M...
IT WAS MY FAULT THIS HAPPENED TO HER...
I WAS TOO SOFT, TOO NAIVE!!
?!
WHOA... KATAKURI ?!
ZZSH!!
YOU'LL PAY FOR WHAT YOU DID TO MY SISTER'S FACE!!
L-LOOK, SORRY...
I'LL SHOW NO WEAKNESS !!!
I'LL MAKE THEM FEAR MY PERFECTION !!!
HOTEL
...
BRULEE.
WHAT ?

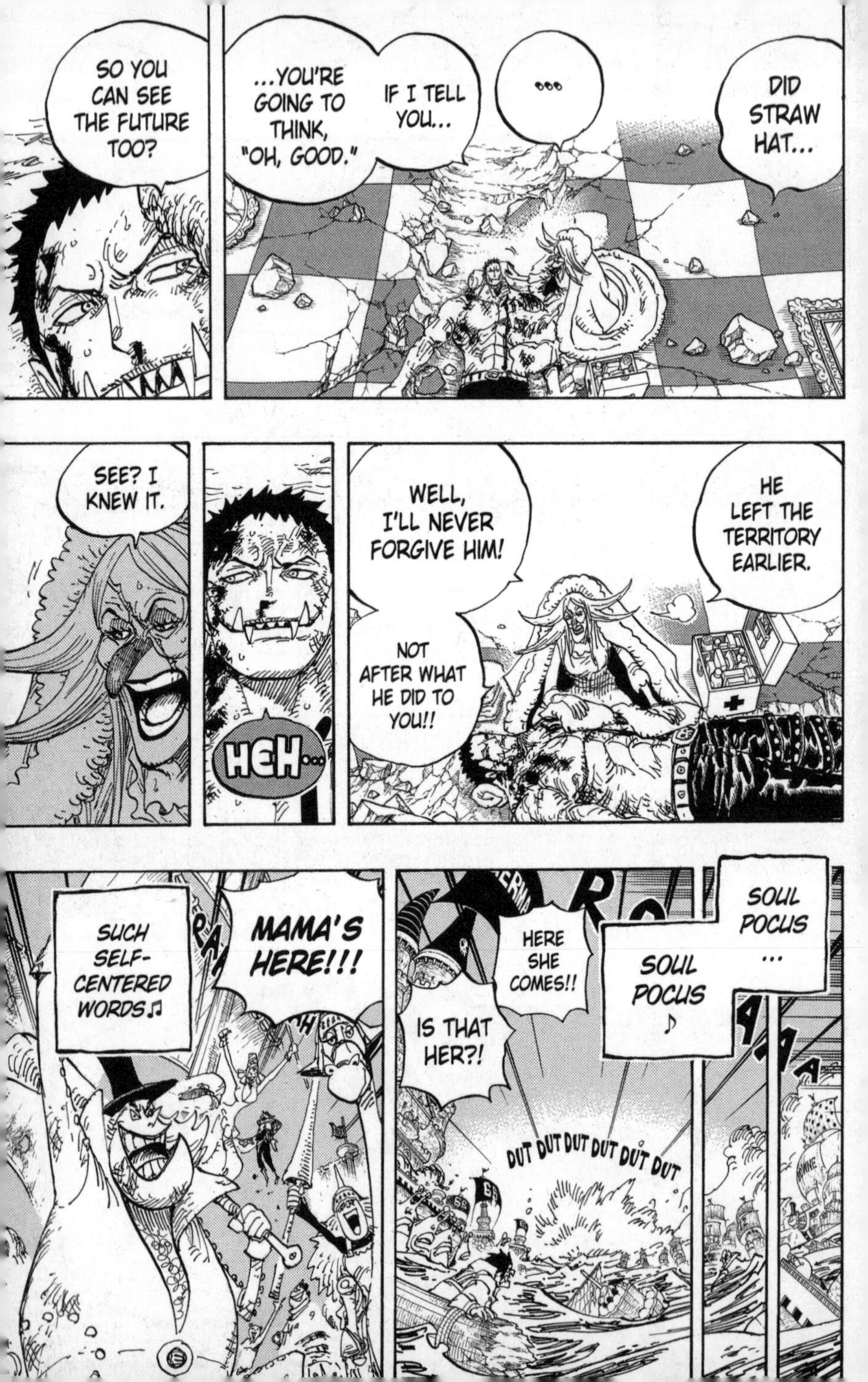
DID STRAW HAT...
...
IF I TELL YOU...
...YOU'RE GOING TO THINK, "OH, GOOD."
SO YOU CAN SEE THE FUTURE TOO?
HE LEFT THE TERRITORY EARLIER.
WELL, I'LL NEVER FORGIVE HIM!
NOT AFTER WHAT HE DID TO YOU!!
HEH...
SEE? I KNEW IT.
SOUL POCUS ...
SOUL POCUS ♪
HERE SHE COMES!!
IS THAT HER?!
DUT DUT DUT DUT DUT DUT
MAMA'S HERE!!!
SUCH SELF-CENTERED WORDS♫

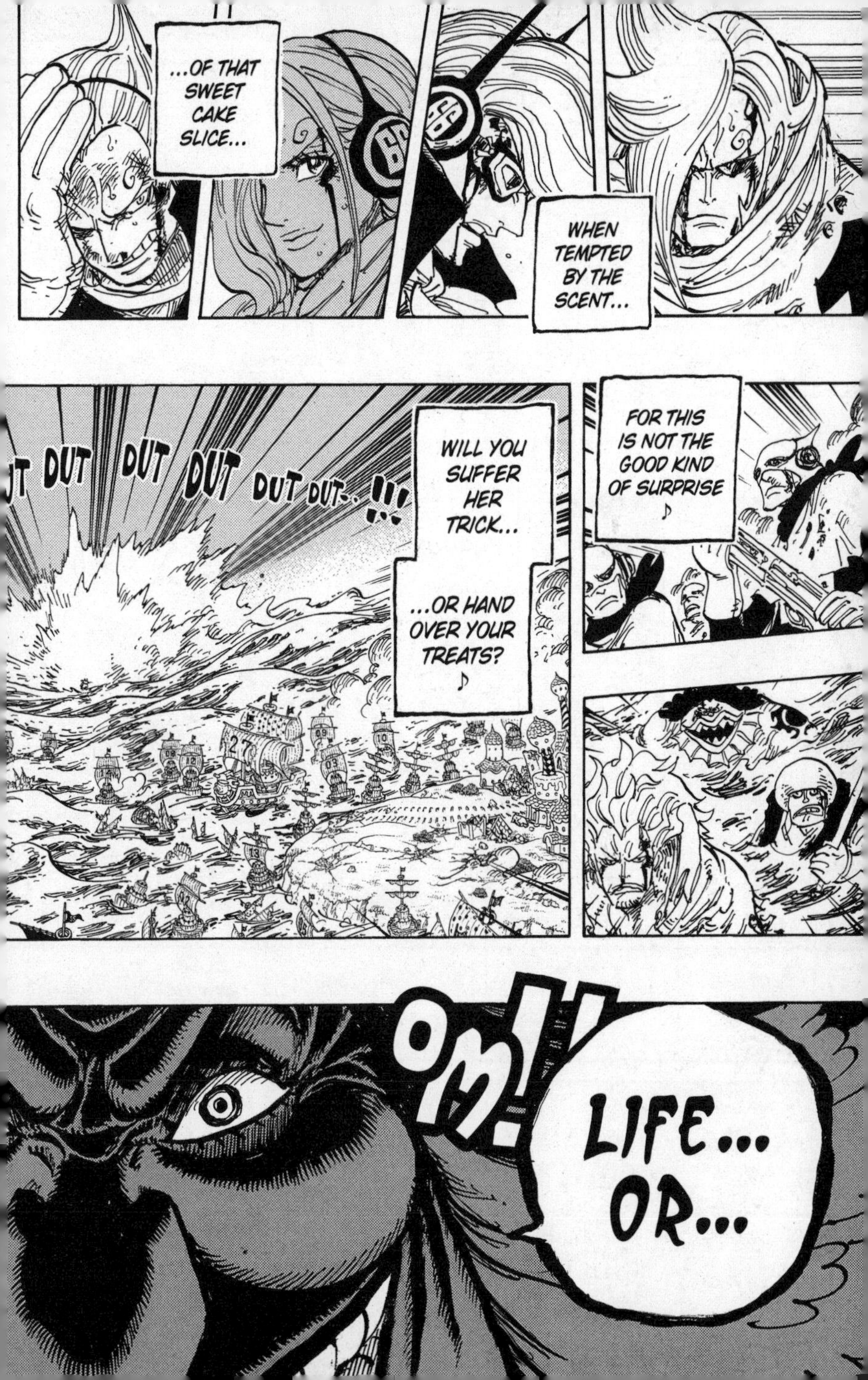
WHEN TEMPTED BY THE SCENT...
...OF THAT SWEET CAKE SLICE...
FOR THIS IS NOT THE GOOD KIND OF SURPRISE ♪
WILL YOU SUFFER HER TRICK...
...OR HAND OVER YOUR TREATS? ♪
DUT DUT DUT DUT DUT..!!!
OM!!
LIFE... OR...

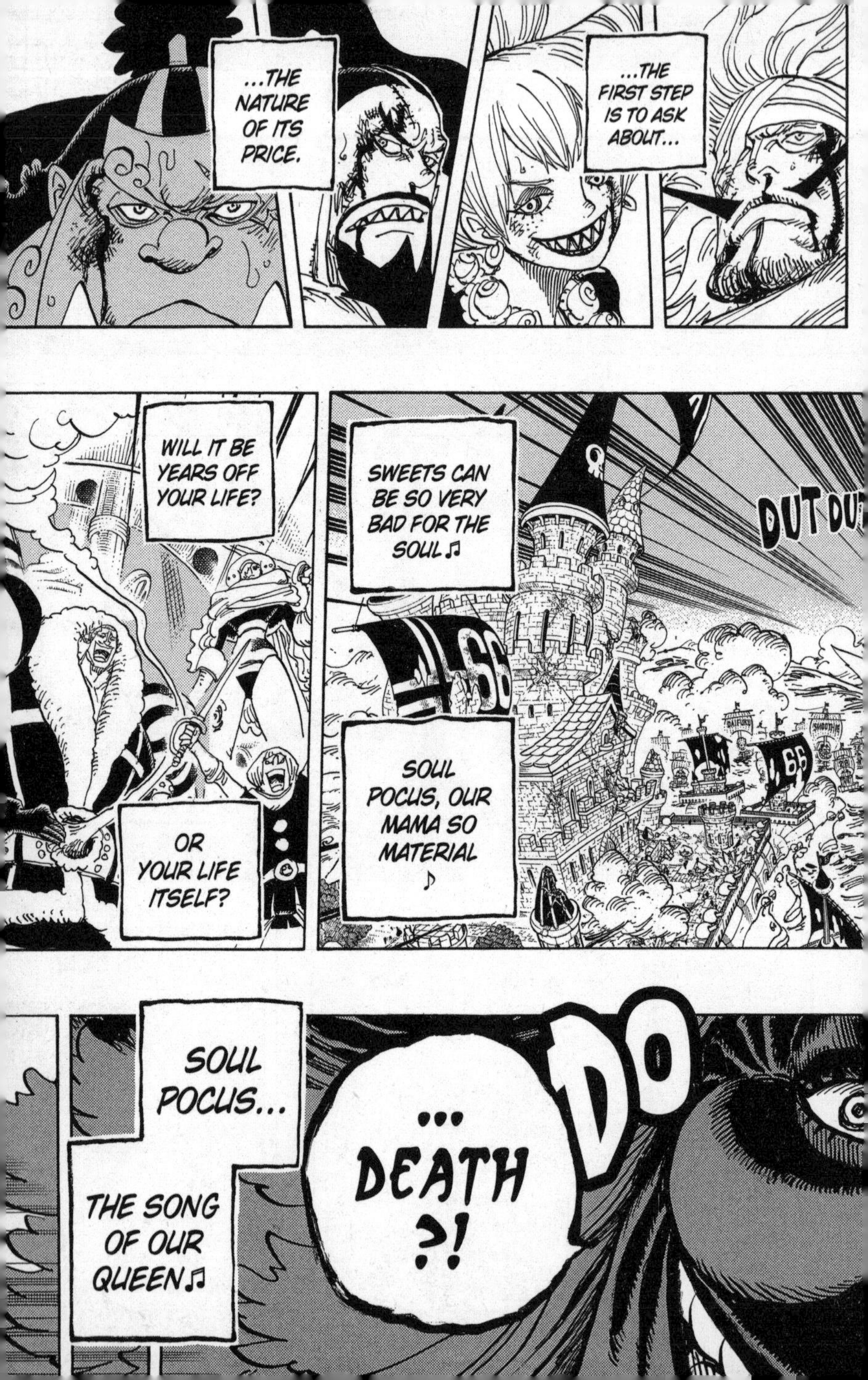
...THE FIRST STEP IS TO ASK ABOUT...
...THE NATURE OF ITS PRICE.
DUT DU
SWEETS CAN BE SO VERY BAD FOR THE SOUL♫
SOUL POCUS, OUR MAMA SO MATERIAL ♪
WILL IT BE YEARS OFF YOUR LIFE?
OR YOUR LIFE ITSELF?
DO
...DEATH ?!
SOUL POCUS...
THE SONG OF OUR QUEEN♫

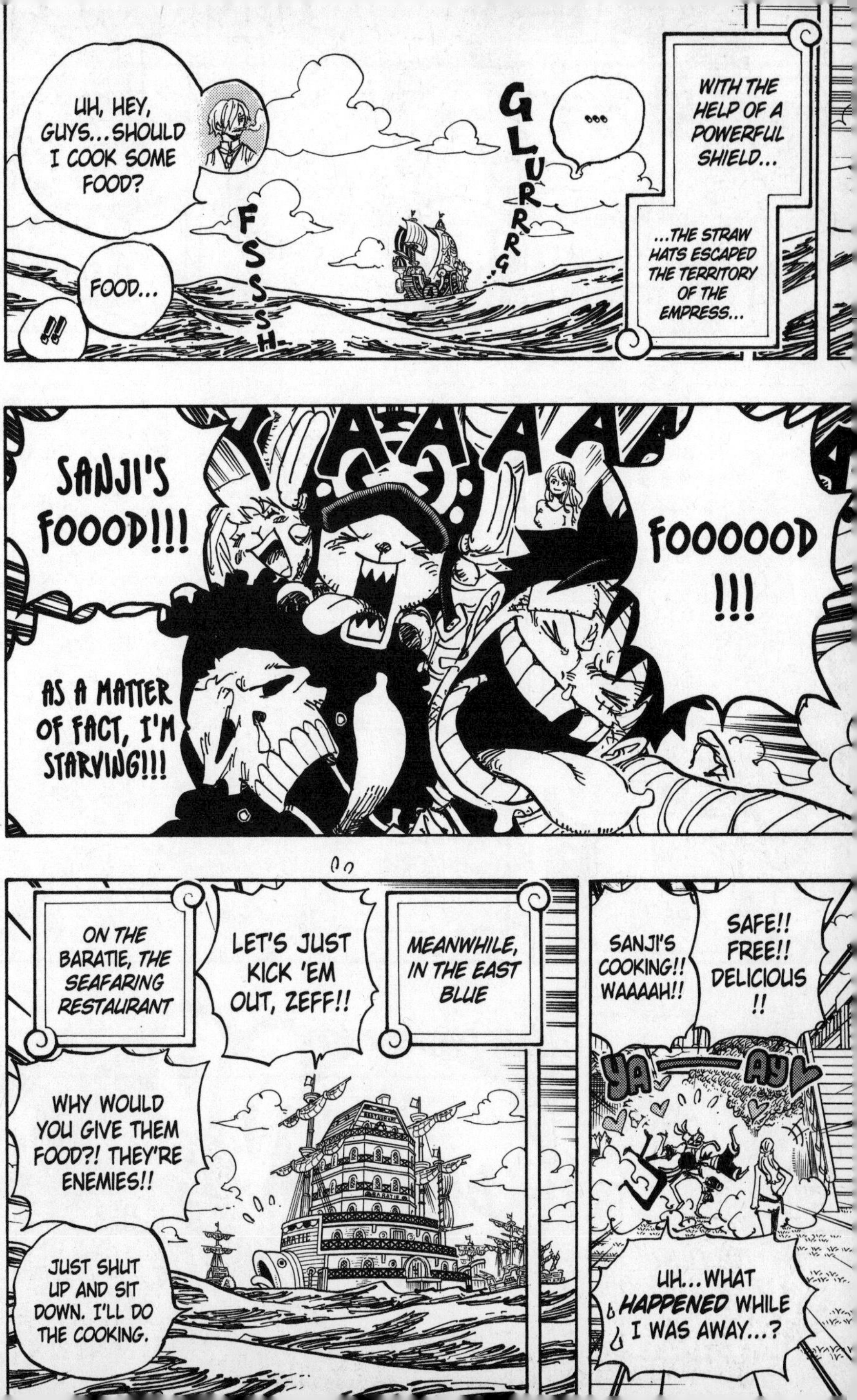
WITH THE HELP OF A POWERFUL SHIELD...
...THE STRAW HATS ESCAPED THE TERRITORY OF THE EMPRESS...
...
GLURRRRG
UH, HEY, GUYS...SHOULD I COOK SOME FOOD?
FSSSH
FOOD...
!!
FOOOOOD !!!
SANJI'S FOOOD!!!
AS A MATTER OF FACT, I'M STARVING!!!
SAFE!! FREE!! DELICIOUS !!
SANJI'S COOKING!! WAAAAH!!
YA—AY
UH...WHAT HAPPENED WHILE I WAS AWAY...?
MEANWHILE, IN THE EAST BLUE
LET'S JUST KICK 'EM OUT, ZEFF!!
ON THE BARATIE, THE SEAFARING RESTAURANT
WHY WOULD YOU GIVE THEM FOOD?! THEY'RE ENEMIES!!
JUST SHUT UP AND SIT DOWN. I'LL DO THE COOKING.

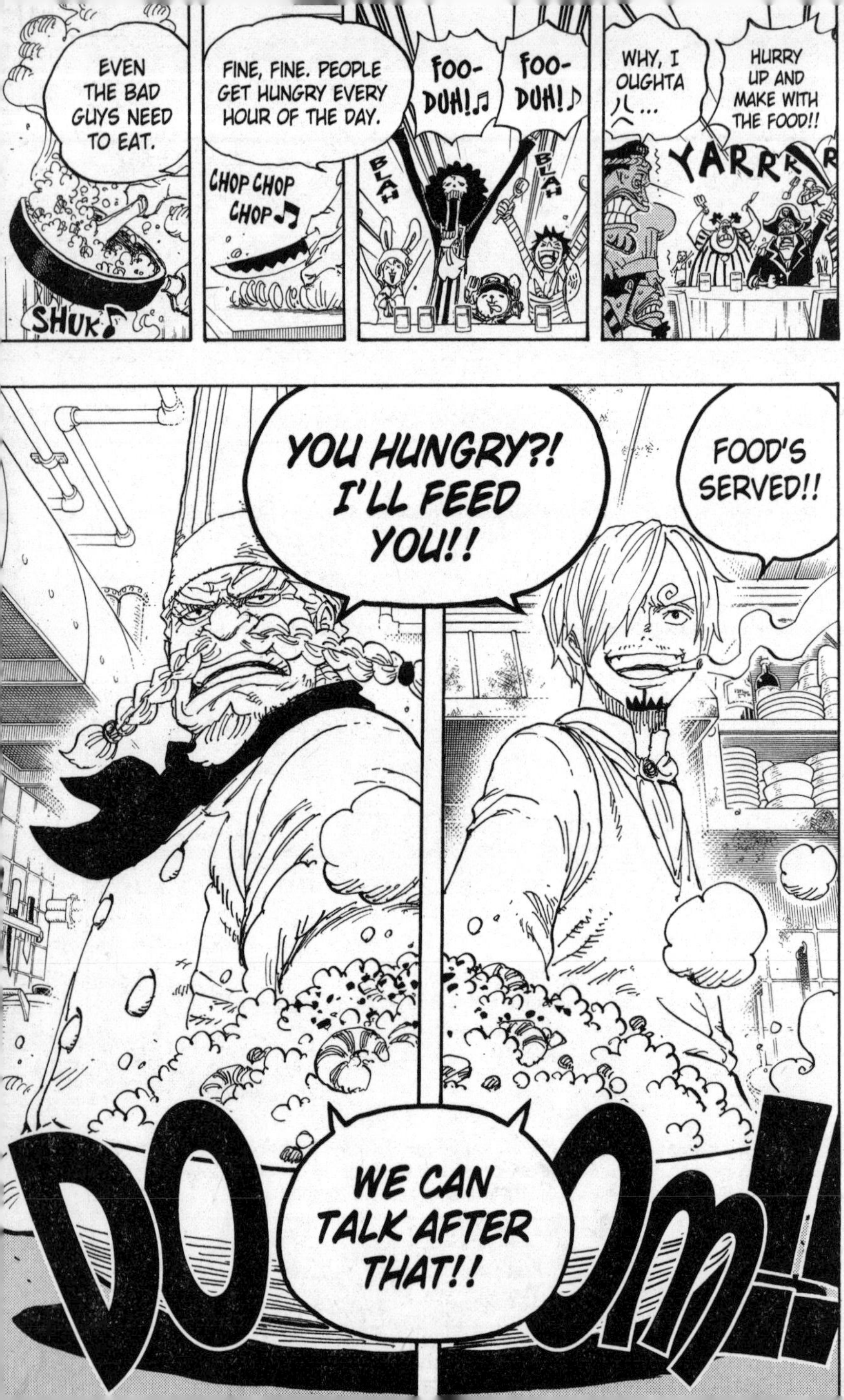
HURRY UP AND MAKE WITH THE FOOD!!
WHY, I OUGHTA...
YARRRR
FOO-DUH!♪
FOO-DUH!♫
BLAH
BLAH
FINE, FINE. PEOPLE GET HUNGRY EVERY HOUR OF THE DAY.
CHOP CHOP CHOP♫
EVEN THE BAD GUYS NEED TO EAT.
SHUK♪
FOOD'S SERVED!!
YOU HUNGRY?! I'LL FEED YOU!!
DOOOM!!
WE CAN TALK AFTER THAT!!

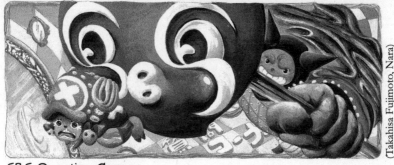

(Takahisa Fujimoto, Nara)

SBS Question Corner

Q: Hey, hey, hey! Step right up, folks! We're servin' some delicious chilled SBS for the summer months!

--Saya

A: Gosh, is it already that season? It sure has been hot lately. Hey, pal, I'll take a plate! Gotta love the sound of wind chimes as you eat. Ooh, already here? All right, let's give it a little taste.
Slurp slurp slurp, gulp. Mmm, that's the stuff. Nothing in the summer like nice chilled SB...
Hey, you started it without me!!! (Also, it's not summer.)

Q: Nami's dream is to draw a sea map of the entire world based on what she sees with her own eyes. Is she actually drawing that map?

--Kutsu Koko

SOMEDAY I'M GONNA NAVIGATE MY WAY ALL AROUND THE SEAS.
HA HA!!
AND WHEN I'VE SEEN EVERYTHING WITH MY OWN EYES, I'M GONNA MAKE A MAP OF THE WHOLE WORLD!!

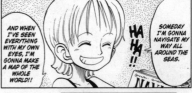

A: Of course she is. It's practically a daily ritual that she charts more after dinner. During the day when the story is moving, she has to give navigation directions, so she's usually on the deck instead.

Q: Heso, Odacchi!! I see where Chopper's looking on the cover page illustration of chapter 900… But please, don't let Chopper have a romantic interest. I want him to continue being **everyone's** Chopper! *(laughs)*

--Daiya

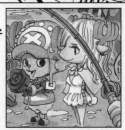

A: Milky the mink is the rare character whom Chopper can relate to as a person or as a reindeer. If Chopper really, truly falls in love, I cannot stop him. Because "Love is always a hurricane!!"

SO?! LOVE IS ALWAYS A HURRICANE !!
LOVE IS ALWAYS A HURRI-CANE!!
DOOM!!
THERE'S A SAYING IN THE EASTERN SEAS!
"LOVE IS ALWAYS A HURRICANE !!"

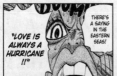

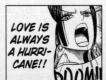

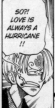

Chapter 903:
FIFTH EMPEROR

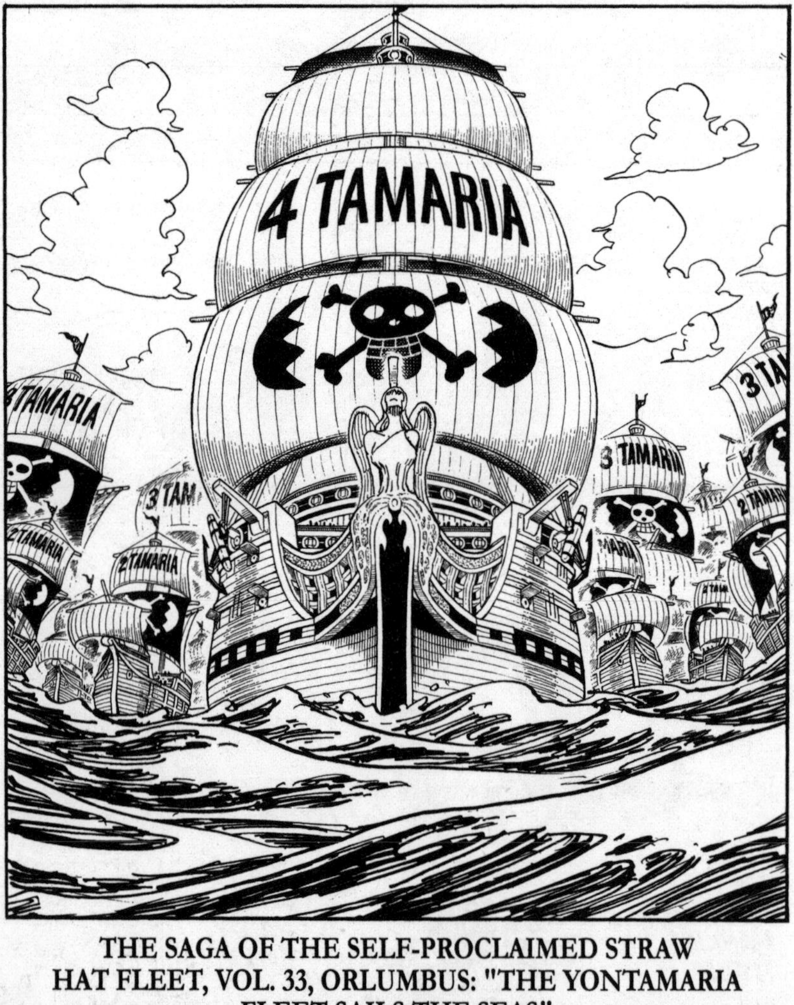

4 TAMARIA
3 TAMARIA
3 TAM
2 TAMARIA
2 TAMARIA
3 TAMARIA
3 TA

THE SAGA OF THE SELF-PROCLAIMED STRAW HAT FLEET, VOL. 33, ORLUMBUS: "THE YONTAMARIA FLEET SAILS THE SEAS"

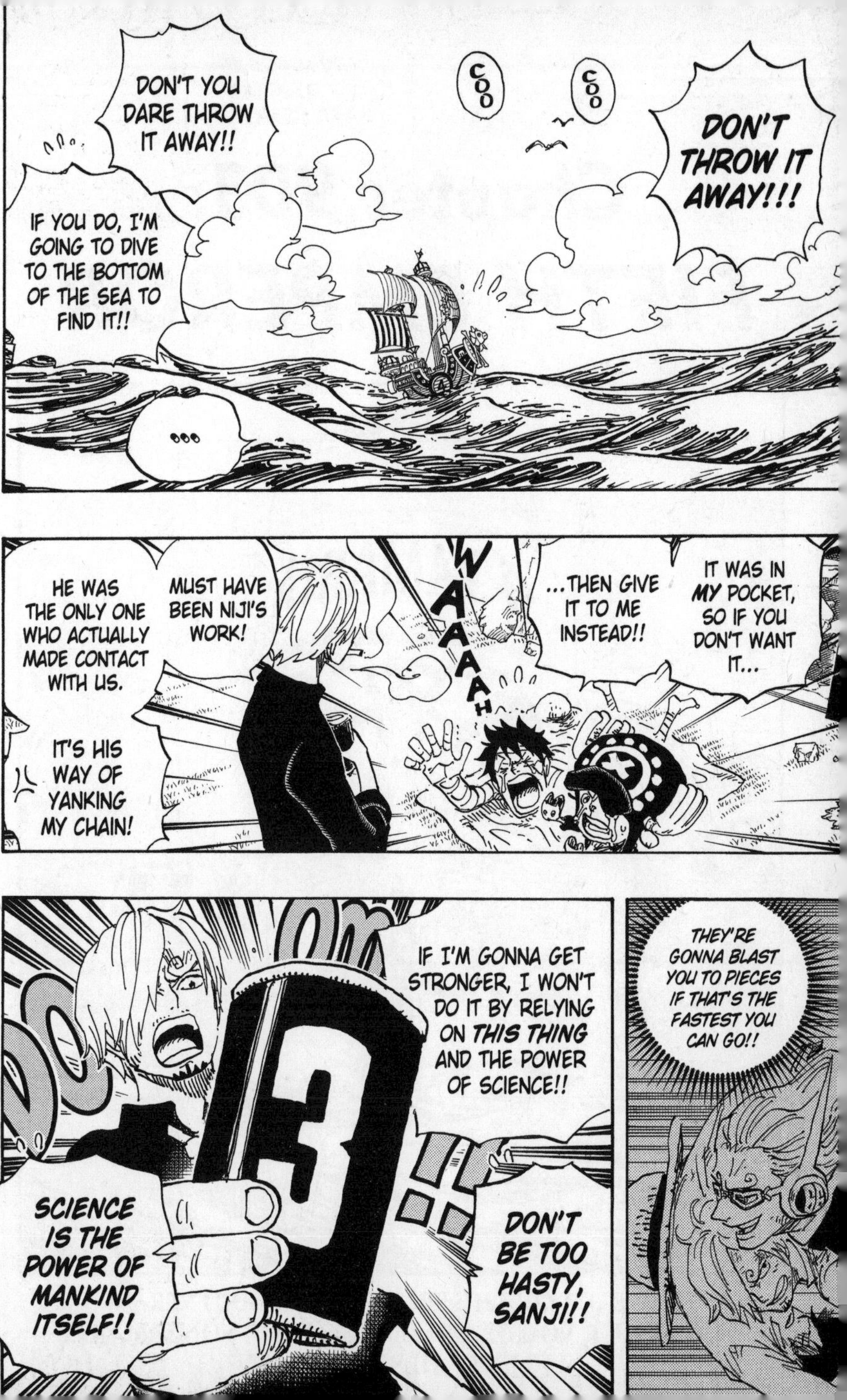
DON'T THROW IT AWAY!!!
COO
COO
DON'T YOU DARE THROW IT AWAY!!
IF YOU DO, I'M GOING TO DIVE TO THE BOTTOM OF THE SEA TO FIND IT!!
...
IT WAS IN MY POCKET, SO IF YOU DON'T WANT IT...
...THEN GIVE IT TO ME INSTEAD!!
WAAAAAH
MUST HAVE BEEN NIJI'S WORK!
HE WAS THE ONLY ONE WHO ACTUALLY MADE CONTACT WITH US.
IT'S HIS WAY OF YANKING MY CHAIN!
THEY'RE GONNA BLAST YOU TO PIECES IF THAT'S THE FASTEST YOU CAN GO!!
IF I'M GONNA GET STRONGER, I WON'T DO IT BY RELYING ON THIS THING AND THE POWER OF SCIENCE!!
DON'T BE TOO HASTY, SANJI!!
SCIENCE IS THE POWER OF MANKIND ITSELF!!
3

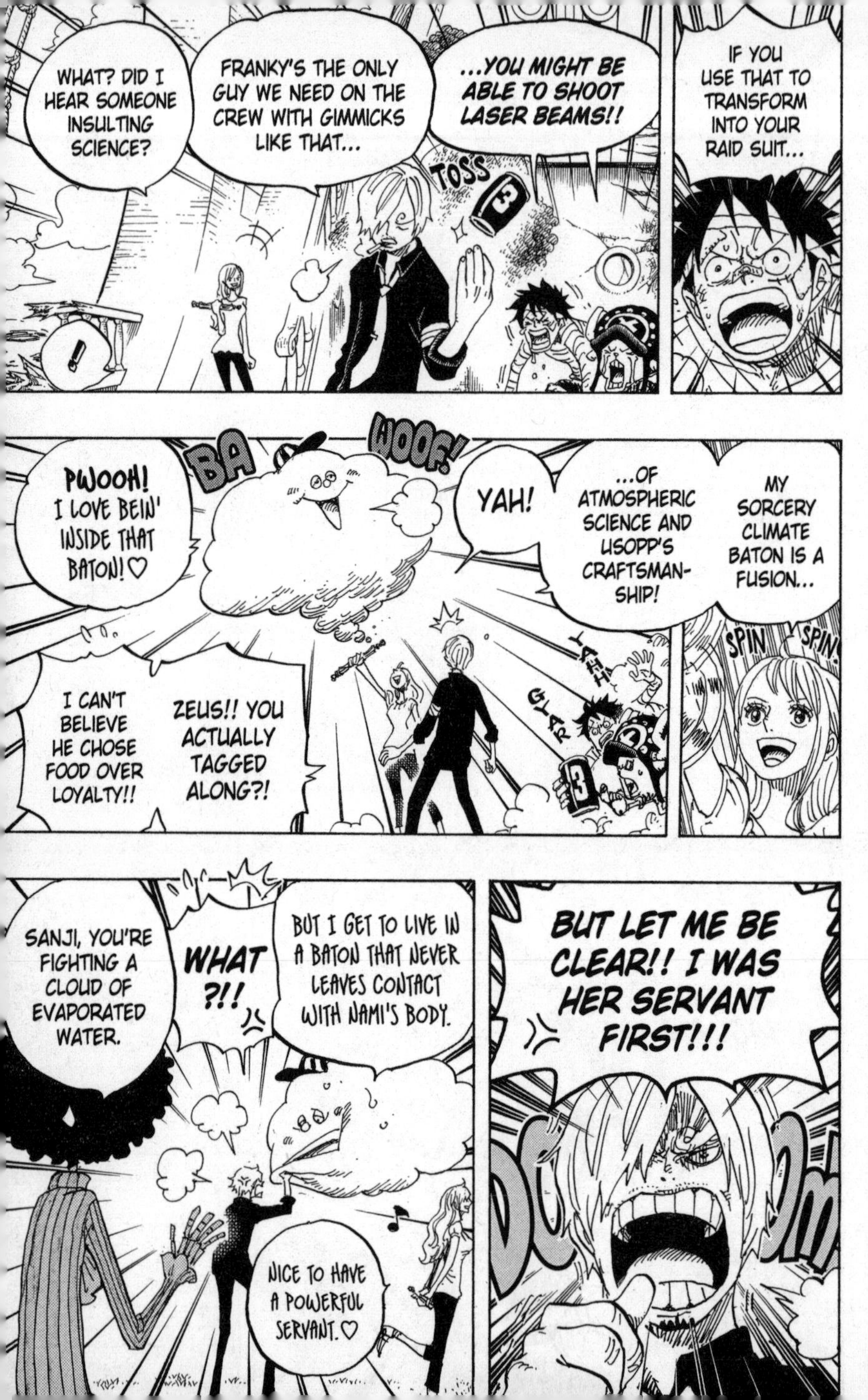
IF YOU USE THAT TO TRANSFORM INTO YOUR RAID SUIT...
...YOU MIGHT BE ABLE TO SHOOT LASER BEAMS!!
TOSS
FRANKY'S THE ONLY GUY WE NEED ON THE CREW WITH GIMMICKS LIKE THAT...
WHAT? DID I HEAR SOMEONE INSULTING SCIENCE?
MY SORCERY CLIMATE BATON IS A FUSION...
...OF ATMOSPHERIC SCIENCE AND USOPP'S CRAFTSMAN-SHIP!
SPIN SPIN
YAH!
WOOF!
BA
PWOOH! I LOVE BEIN' INSIDE THAT BATON!♡
YAHH
GYAR
ZEUS!! YOU ACTUALLY TAGGED ALONG?!
I CAN'T BELIEVE HE CHOSE FOOD OVER LOYALTY!!
BUT LET ME BE CLEAR!! I WAS HER SERVANT FIRST!!!
BUT I GET TO LIVE IN A BATON THAT NEVER LEAVES CONTACT WITH NAMI'S BODY.
WHAT?!!
SANJI, YOU'RE FIGHTING A CLOUD OF EVAPORATED WATER.
NICE TO HAVE A POWERFUL SERVANT.♡

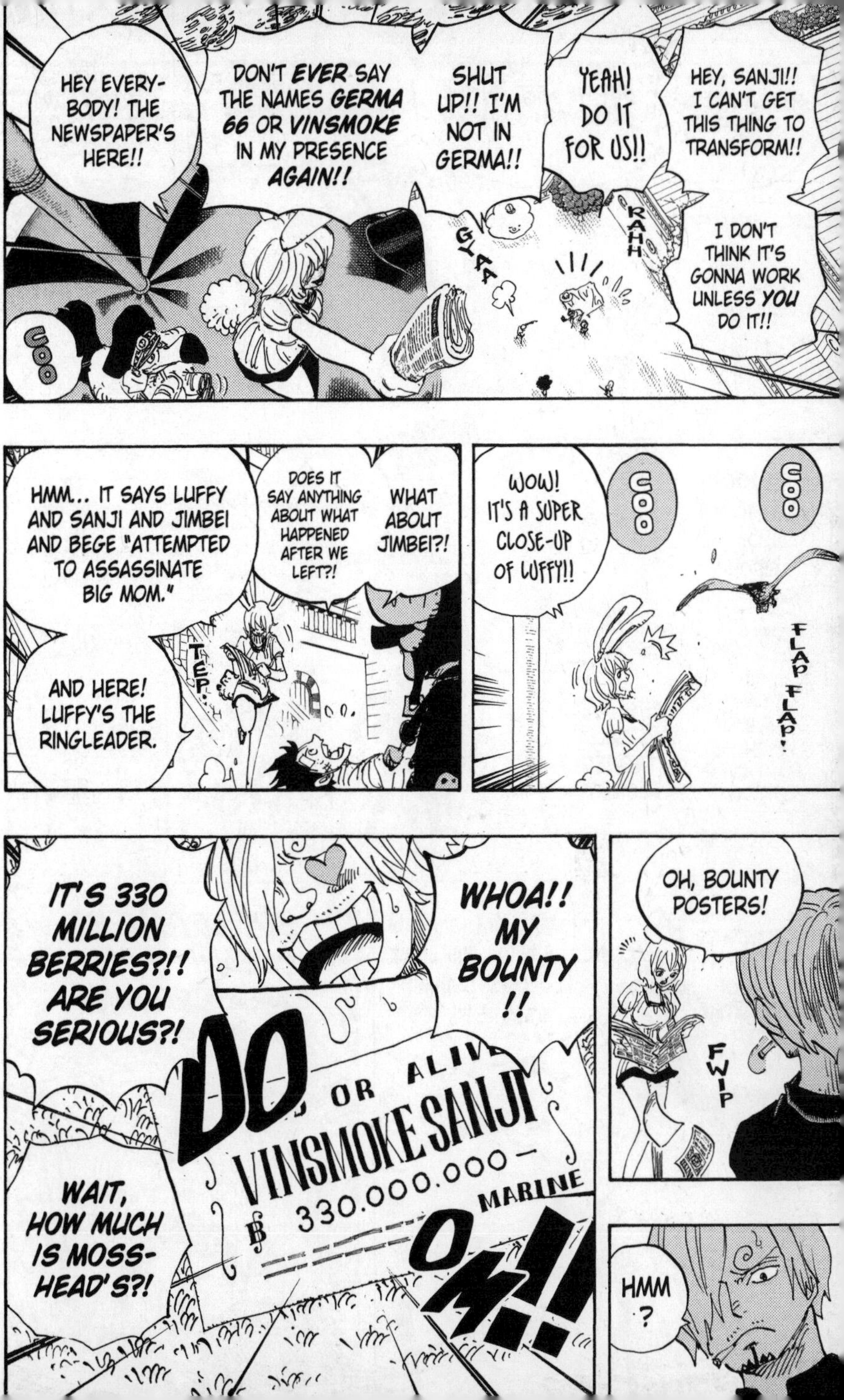
HEY, SANJI!! I CAN'T GET THIS THING TO TRANSFORM!!
I DON'T THINK IT'S GONNA WORK UNLESS YOU DO IT!!
YEAH! DO IT FOR US!!
RAHH
SHUT UP!! I'M NOT IN GERMA!!
GYAA
DON'T EVER SAY THE NAMES GERMA 66 OR VINSMOKE IN MY PRESENCE AGAIN!!
HEY EVERYBODY! THE NEWSPAPER'S HERE!!
COO
COO
FLAP FLAP
COO
WOW! IT'S A SUPER CLOSE-UP OF LUFFY!!
WHAT ABOUT JIMBEI?!
DOES IT SAY ANYTHING ABOUT WHAT HAPPENED AFTER WE LEFT?!
HMM... IT SAYS LUFFY AND SANJI AND JIMBEI AND BEGE "ATTEMPTED TO ASSASSINATE BIG MOM."
AND HERE! LUFFY'S THE RINGLEADER.
TEP
OH, BOUNTY POSTERS!
FWIP
HMM?
WHOA!! MY BOUNTY!!
IT'S 330 MILLION BERRIES?!! ARE YOU SERIOUS?!
OR ALIV
VINSMOKE SANJI
B 330.000.000-
MARINE
WAIT, HOW MUCH IS MOSS-HEAD'S?!
DOOM!!

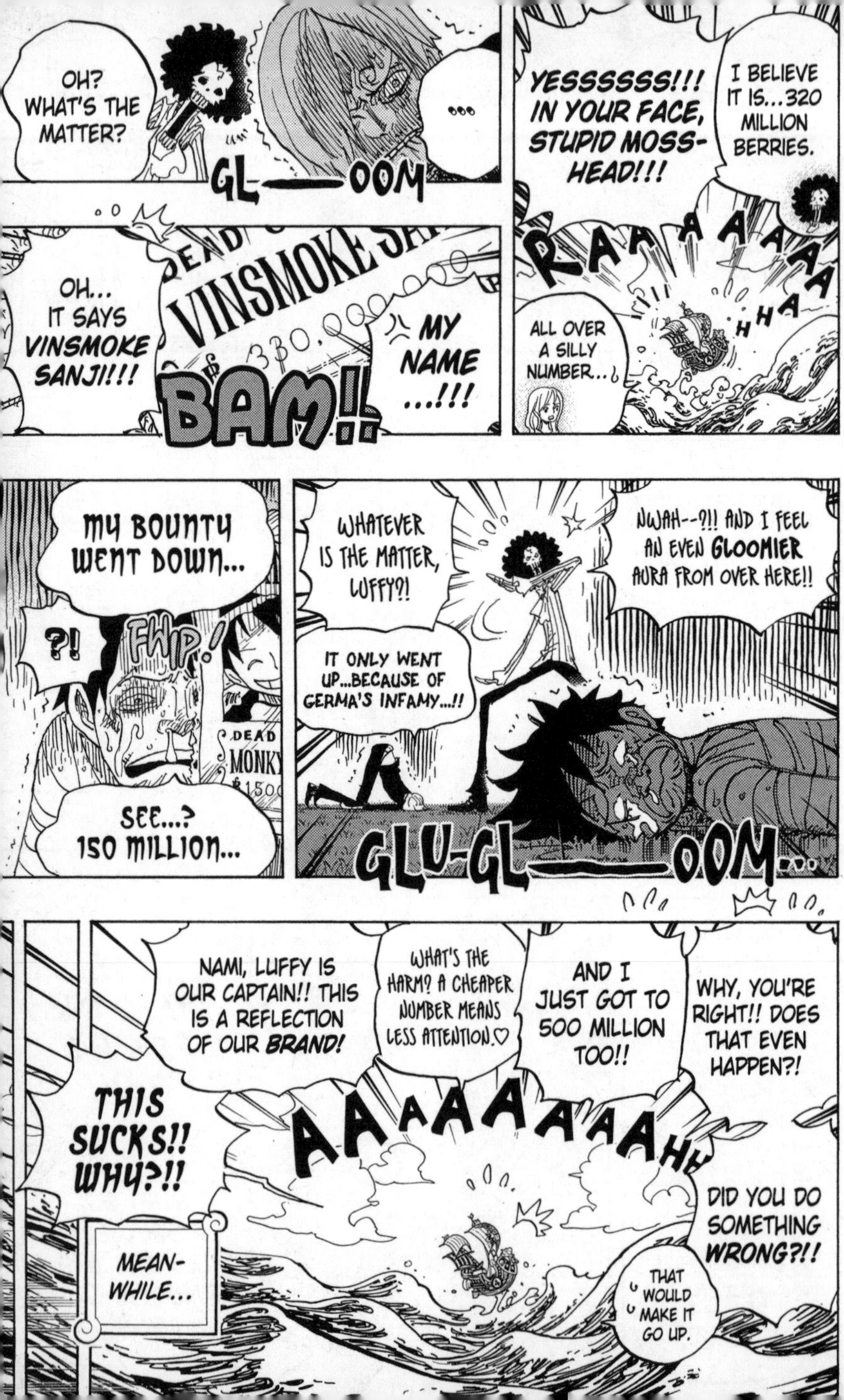
I BELIEVE IT IS...320 MILLION BERRIES.
YESSSSSS!!! IN YOUR FACE, STUPID MOSS-HEAD!!!
RAAAAAAAHHH
ALL OVER A SILLY NUMBER...
OH? WHAT'S THE MATTER?
...
GL—OOM
OH... IT SAYS VINSMOKE SANJI!!!
MY NAME ...!!!
BAM!!
NWAH--?!! AND I FEEL AN EVEN GLOOMIER AURA FROM OVER HERE!!
WHATEVER IS THE MATTER, LUFFY?!
IT ONLY WENT UP...BECAUSE OF GERMA'S INFAMY...!!
GLU-GL—OOM...
MY BOUNTY WENT DOWN...
?!
FWIP!
DEAD
MONKEY
SEE...? 150 MILLION...
WHY, YOU'RE RIGHT!! DOES THAT EVEN HAPPEN?!
AND I JUST GOT TO 500 MILLION TOO!!
WHAT'S THE HARM? A CHEAPER NUMBER MEANS LESS ATTENTION.♡
NAMI, LUFFY IS OUR CAPTAIN!! THIS IS A REFLECTION OF OUR BRAND!
THIS SUCKS!! WHY?!!
AAAAAAAAAHH
DID YOU DO SOMETHING WRONG?!!
THAT WOULD MAKE IT GO UP.
MEAN-WHILE...

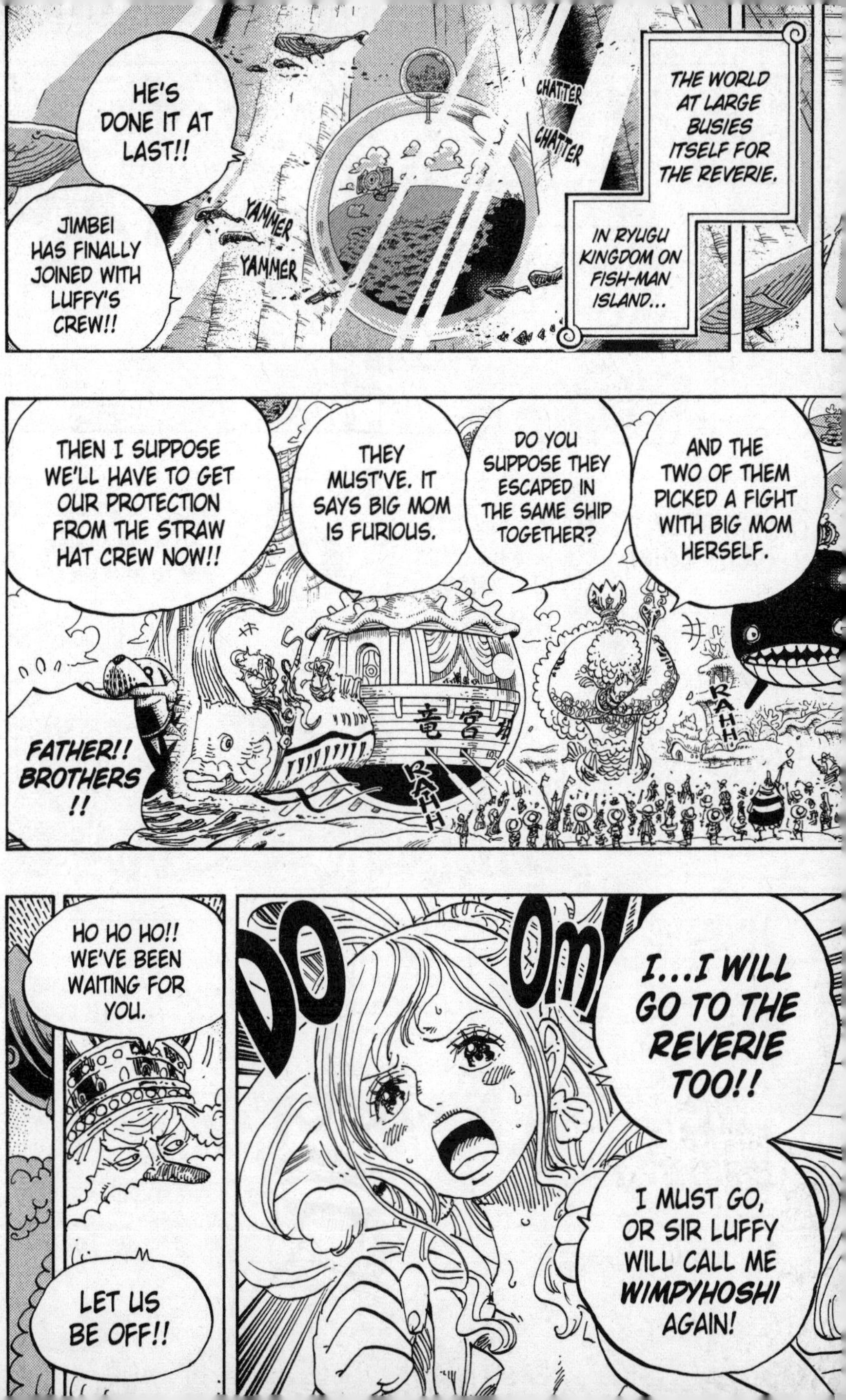
THE WORLD AT LARGE BUSIES ITSELF FOR THE REVERIE.
IN RYUGU KINGDOM ON FISH-MAN ISLAND...
CHATTER
CHATTER
YAMMER
YAMMER
HE'S DONE IT AT LAST!!
JIMBEI HAS FINALLY JOINED WITH LUFFY'S CREW!!
AND THE TWO OF THEM PICKED A FIGHT WITH BIG MOM HERSELF.
DO YOU SUPPOSE THEY ESCAPED IN THE SAME SHIP TOGETHER?
THEY MUST'VE. IT SAYS BIG MOM IS FURIOUS.
THEN I SUPPOSE WE'LL HAVE TO GET OUR PROTECTION FROM THE STRAW HAT CREW NOW!!
RAHH
RAHH
FATHER!! BROTHERS!!
DOOM!
I...I WILL GO TO THE REVERIE TOO!!
I MUST GO, OR SIR LUFFY WILL CALL ME *WIMPYHOSHI* AGAIN!
HO HO HO!! WE'VE BEEN WAITING FOR YOU.
LET US BE OFF!!

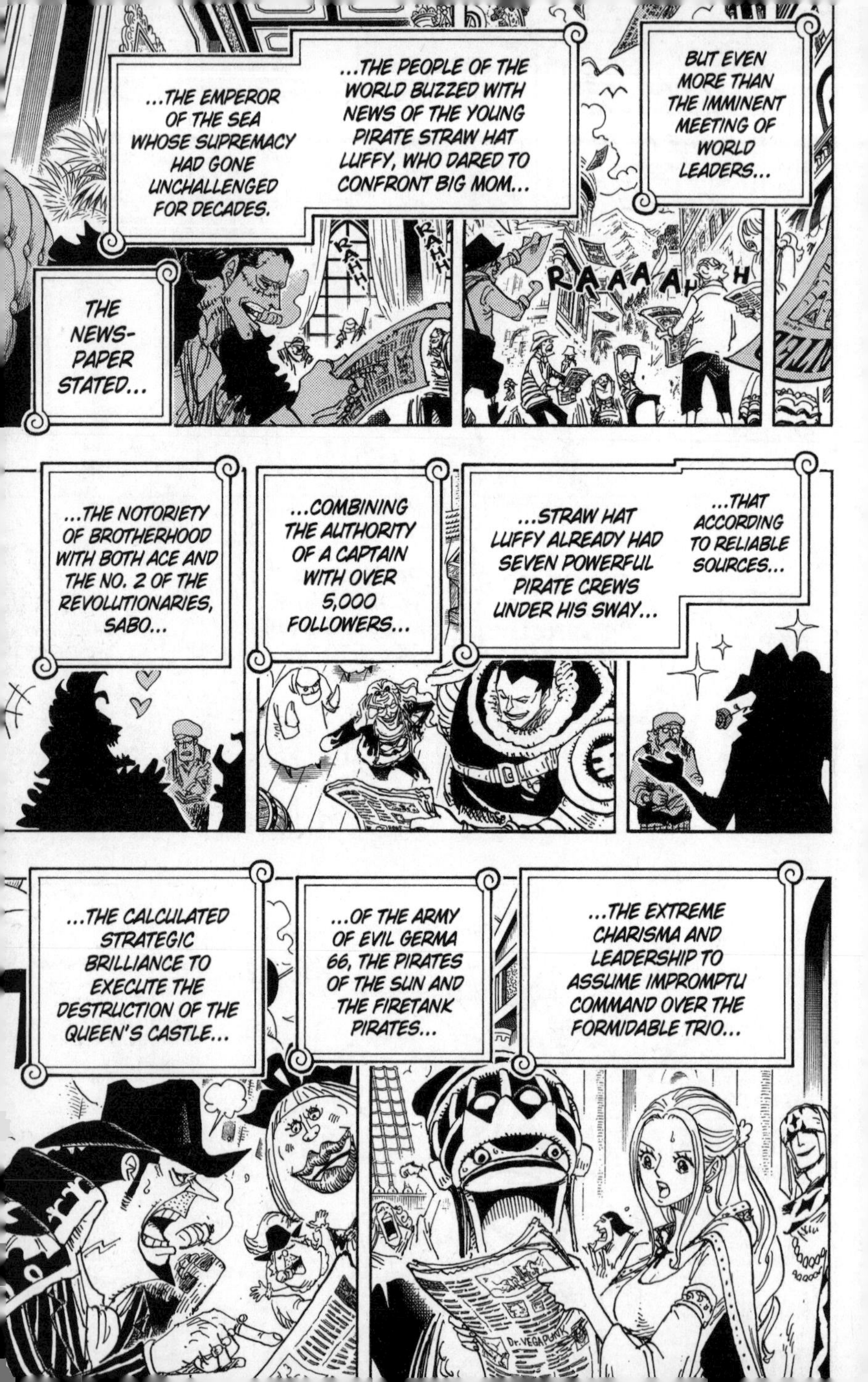
BUT EVEN MORE THAN THE IMMINENT MEETING OF WORLD LEADERS...
RAAAAAH
...THE PEOPLE OF THE WORLD BUZZED WITH NEWS OF THE YOUNG PIRATE STRAW HAT LUFFY, WHO DARED TO CONFRONT BIG MOM...
...THE EMPEROR OF THE SEA WHOSE SUPREMACY HAD GONE UNCHALLENGED FOR DECADES.
RAHH
RAHH
THE NEWS-PAPER STATED...
...THAT ACCORDING TO RELIABLE SOURCES...
...STRAW HAT LUFFY ALREADY HAD SEVEN POWERFUL PIRATE CREWS UNDER HIS SWAY...
...COMBINING THE AUTHORITY OF A CAPTAIN WITH OVER 5,000 FOLLOWERS...
...THE NOTORIETY OF BROTHERHOOD WITH BOTH ACE AND THE NO. 2 OF THE REVOLUTIONARIES, SABO...
...THE EXTREME CHARISMA AND LEADERSHIP TO ASSUME IMPROMPTU COMMAND OVER THE FORMIDABLE TRIO...
Dr. VEGAPUNK
...OF THE ARMY OF EVIL GERMA 66, THE PIRATES OF THE SUN AND THE FIRETANK PIRATES...
...THE CALCULATED STRATEGIC BRILLIANCE TO EXECUTE THE DESTRUCTION OF THE QUEEN'S CASTLE...

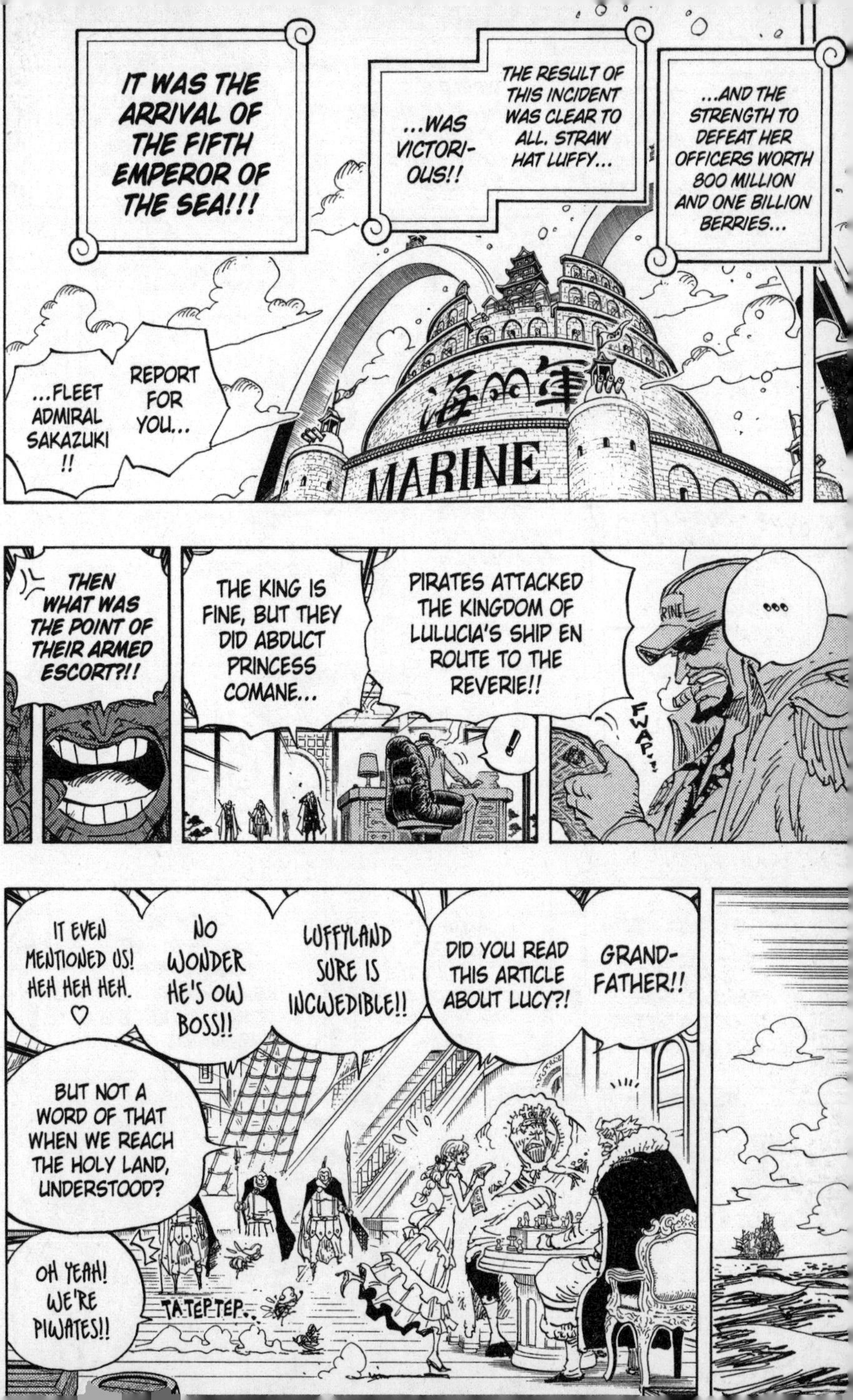
...AND THE STRENGTH TO DEFEAT HER OFFICERS WORTH 800 MILLION AND ONE BILLION BERRIES...
THE RESULT OF THIS INCIDENT WAS CLEAR TO ALL. STRAW HAT LUFFY...
...WAS VICTORIOUS!!
IT WAS THE ARRIVAL OF THE FIFTH EMPEROR OF THE SEA!!!
REPORT FOR YOU...
...FLEET ADMIRAL SAKAZUKI!!
MARINE
...
PIRATES ATTACKED THE KINGDOM OF LULUCIA'S SHIP EN ROUTE TO THE REVERIE!!
FWAP
!
THE KING IS FINE, BUT THEY DID ABDUCT PRINCESS COMANE...
THEN WHAT WAS THE POINT OF THEIR ARMED ESCORT?!!
GRAND-FATHER!!
DID YOU READ THIS ARTICLE ABOUT LUCY?!
LUFFYLAND SURE IS INCWEDIBLE!!
NO WONDER HE'S OW BOSS!!
IT EVEN MENTIONED US! HEH HEH HEH. ♡
BUT NOT A WORD OF THAT WHEN WE REACH THE HOLY LAND, UNDERSTOOD?
OH YEAH! WE'RE PIWATES!!
TA TEP TEP...

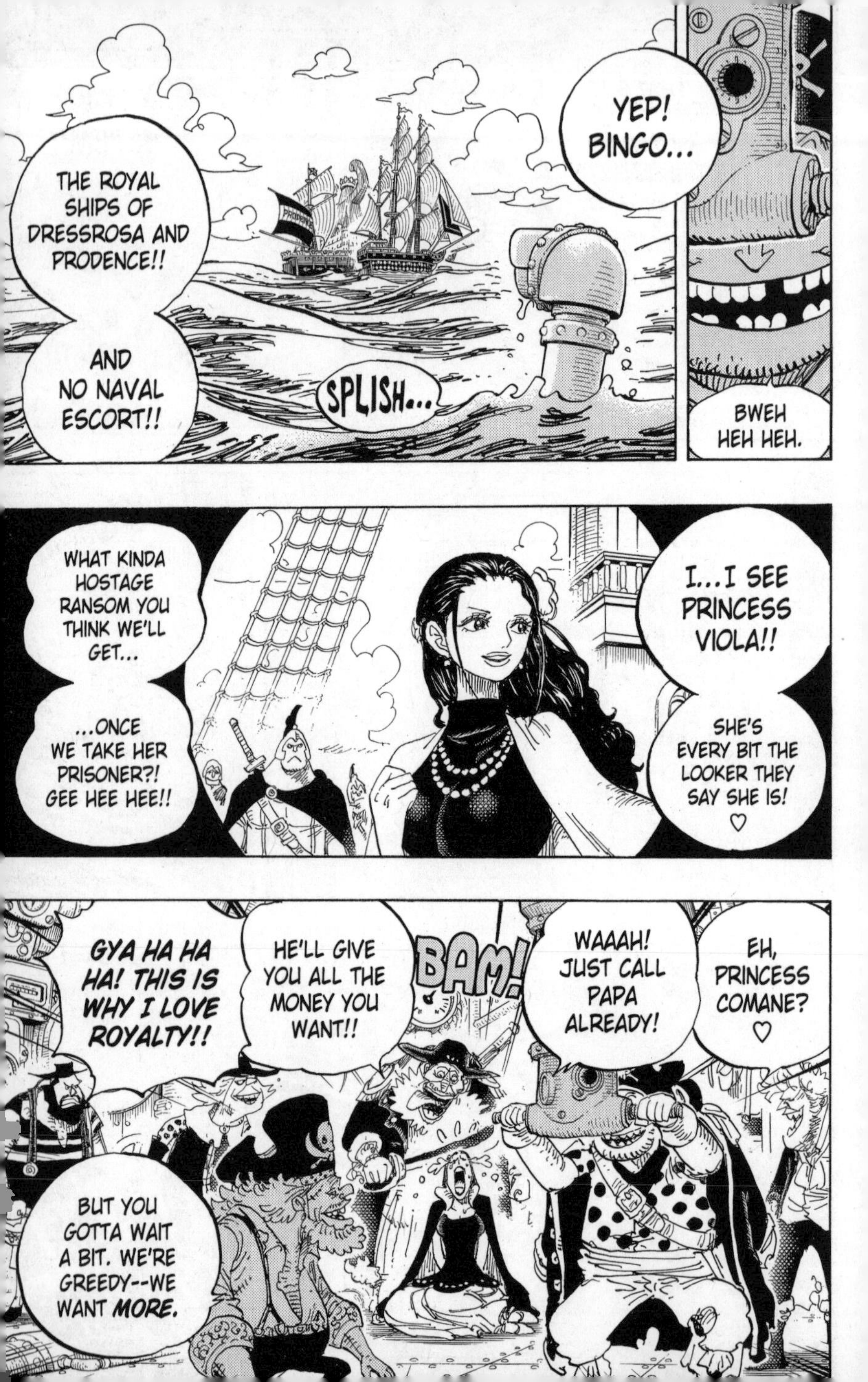
BWEH HEH HEH.
YEP! BINGO...
THE ROYAL SHIPS OF DRESSROSA AND PRODENCE!!
AND NO NAVAL ESCORT!!
SPLISH...
I...I SEE PRINCESS VIOLA!!
SHE'S EVERY BIT THE LOOKER THEY SAY SHE IS! ♡
WHAT KINDA HOSTAGE RANSOM YOU THINK WE'LL GET...
...ONCE WE TAKE HER PRISONER?! GEE HEE HEE!!
EH, PRINCESS COMANE? ♡
WAAAH! JUST CALL PAPA ALREADY!
BAM!
HE'LL GIVE YOU ALL THE MONEY YOU WANT!!
GYA HA HA HA! THIS IS WHY I LOVE ROYALTY!!
BUT YOU GOTTA WAIT A BIT. WE'RE GREEDY--WE WANT MORE.

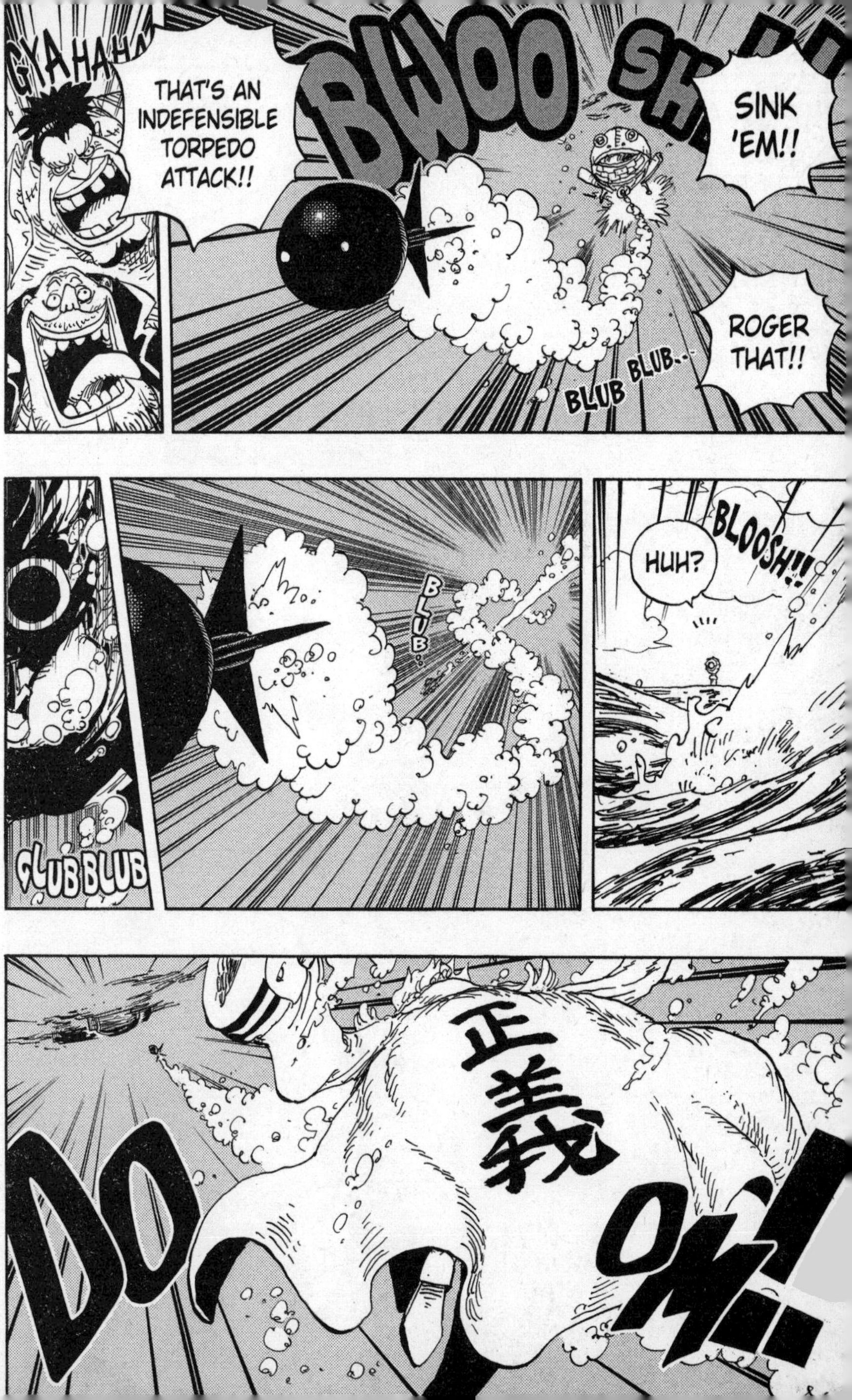
SINK 'EM!!
BWOO
ROGER THAT!!
BLUB BLUB...
GYA HA HA
THAT'S AN INDEFENSIBLE TORPEDO ATTACK!!
BLOOSH!!
HUH?
BLUB
GLUB BLUB
正義
DO
OM!!

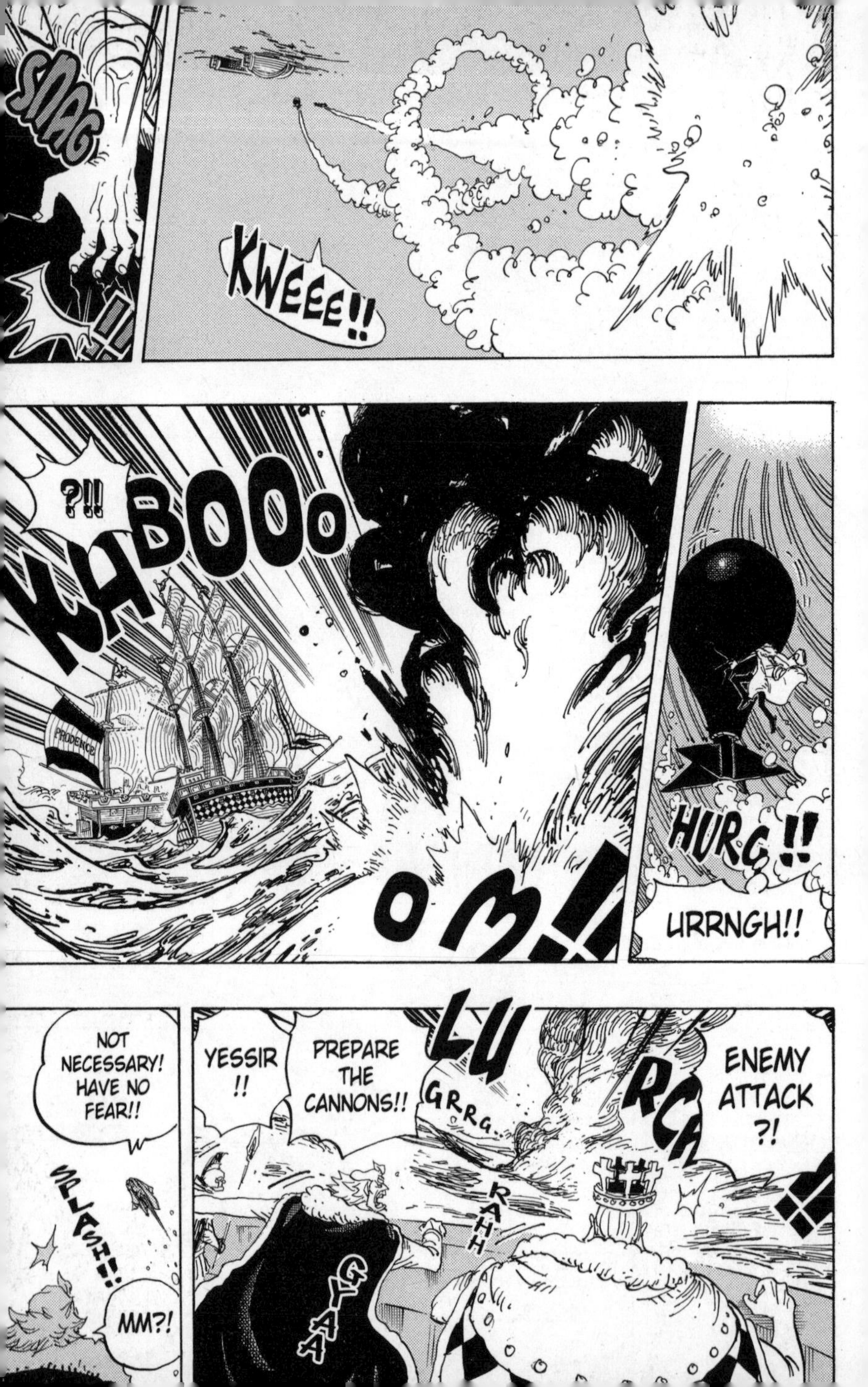
KWEEE!!
SNAG
HURG!!
URRNGH!!
?!!
KABOOoOOM!!
ENEMY ATTACK?!
LURCH!!
GRRG..
RAHH
PREPARE THE CANNONS!!
YESSIR!!
GYAA
NOT NECESSARY! HAVE NO FEAR!!
MM?!
SPLASH!!

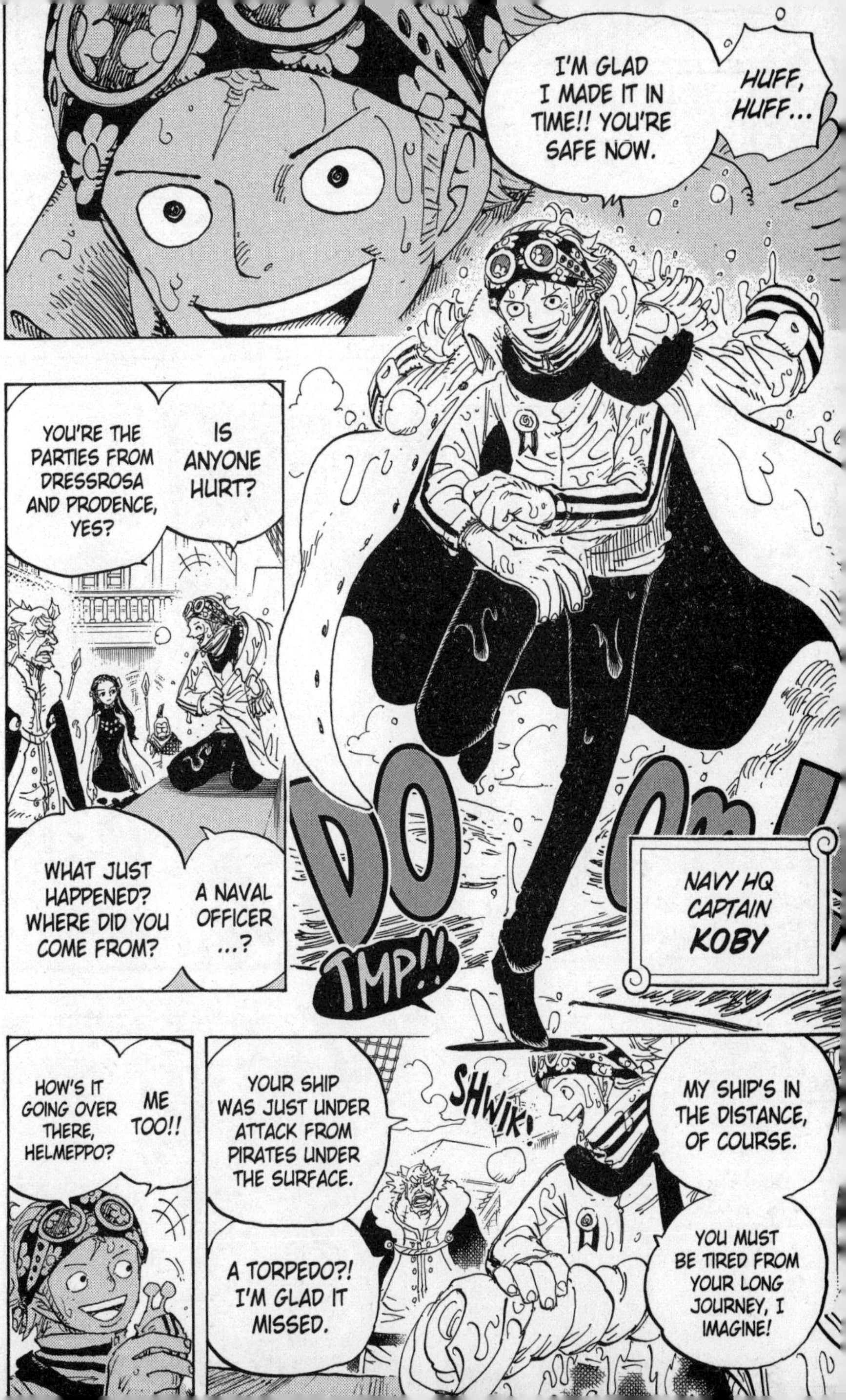
HUFF, HUFF...
I'M GLAD I MADE IT IN TIME!! YOU'RE SAFE NOW.
DO
TMP!!
NAVY HQ CAPTAIN KOBY
IS ANYONE HURT?
YOU'RE THE PARTIES FROM DRESSROSA AND PRODENCE, YES?
A NAVAL OFFICER ...?
WHAT JUST HAPPENED? WHERE DID YOU COME FROM?
SHWIK!
MY SHIP'S IN THE DISTANCE, OF COURSE.
YOU MUST BE TIRED FROM YOUR LONG JOURNEY, I IMAGINE!
YOUR SHIP WAS JUST UNDER ATTACK FROM PIRATES UNDER THE SURFACE.
A TORPEDO?! I'M GLAD IT MISSED.
ME TOO!!
HOW'S IT GOING OVER THERE, HELMEPPO?

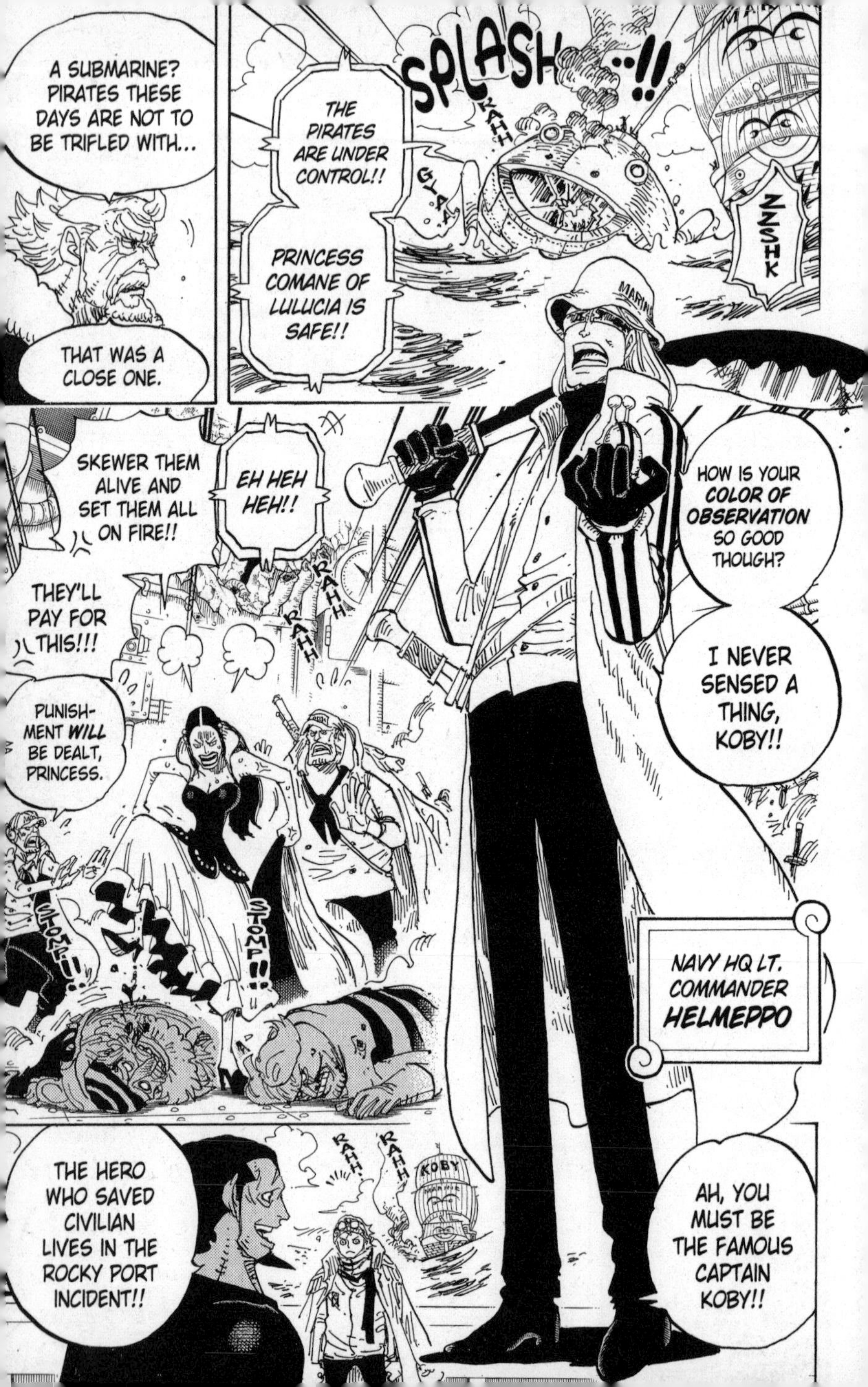
SPLASH...!!
RAHH
GYAA
ZZSHK
THE PIRATES ARE UNDER CONTROL!!
PRINCESS COMANE OF LULUCIA IS SAFE!!
A SUBMARINE? PIRATES THESE DAYS ARE NOT TO BE TRIFLED WITH...
THAT WAS A CLOSE ONE.
HOW IS YOUR COLOR OF OBSERVATION SO GOOD THOUGH?
I NEVER SENSED A THING, KOBY!!
NAVY HQ LT. COMMANDER HELMEPPO
EH HEH HEH!!
SKEWER THEM ALIVE AND SET THEM ALL ON FIRE!!
RAHH
RAHH
THEY'LL PAY FOR THIS!!!
PUNISHMENT WILL BE DEALT, PRINCESS.
STOMP!!
STOMP!!
AH, YOU MUST BE THE FAMOUS CAPTAIN KOBY!!
RAHH
RAHH
KOBY
THE HERO WHO SAVED CIVILIAN LIVES IN THE ROCKY PORT INCIDENT!!

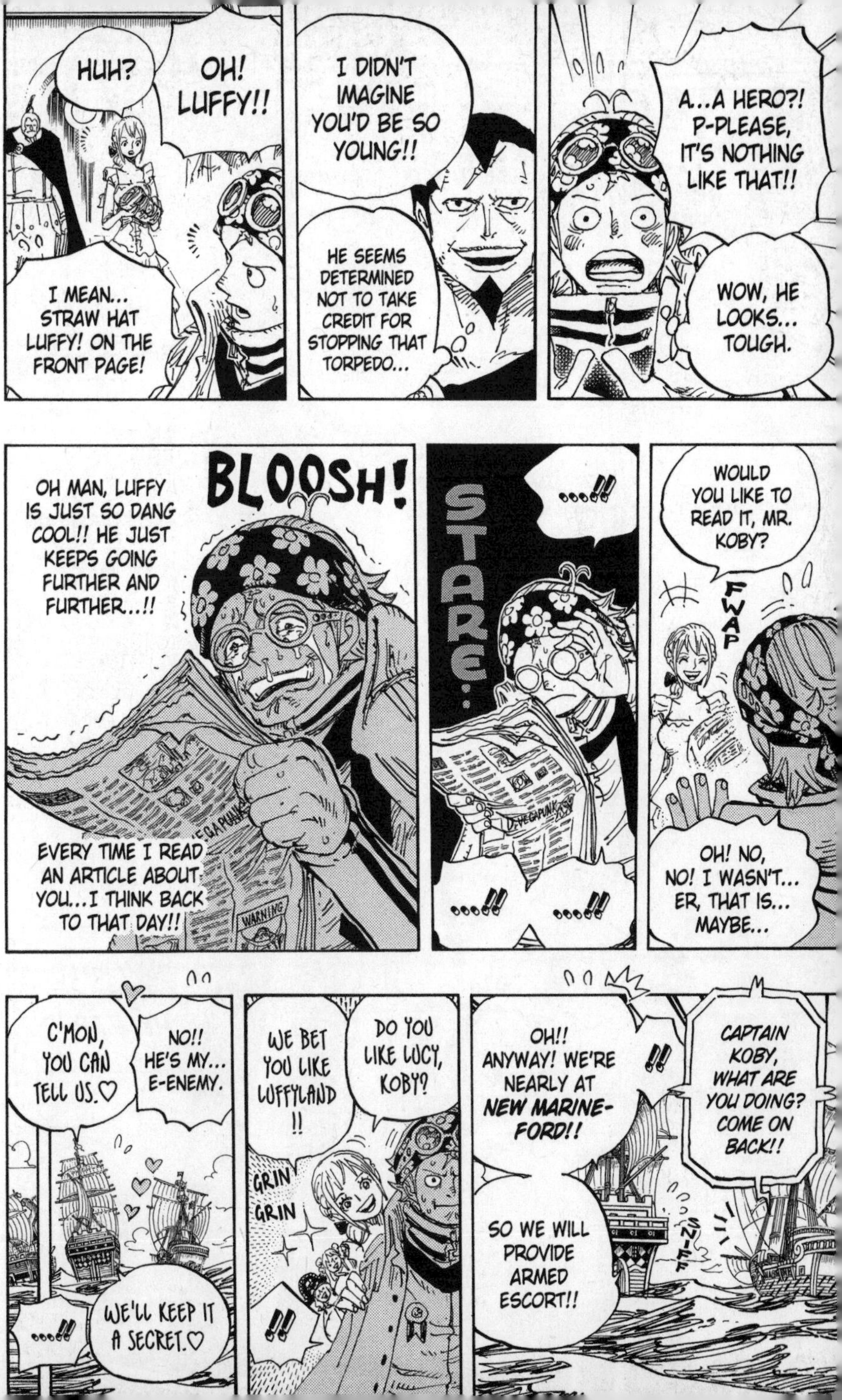
A...A HERO?! P-PLEASE, IT'S NOTHING LIKE THAT!!
WOW, HE LOOKS... TOUGH.
I DIDN'T IMAGINE YOU'D BE SO YOUNG!!
HE SEEMS DETERMINED NOT TO TAKE CREDIT FOR STOPPING THAT TORPEDO...
OH! LUFFY!!
HUH?
I MEAN... STRAW HAT LUFFY! ON THE FRONT PAGE!
WOULD YOU LIKE TO READ IT, MR. KOBY?
FWAP
OH! NO, NO! I WASN'T... ER, THAT IS... MAYBE...
STARE..
....!!
....!!
....!!
BLOOSH!
OH MAN, LUFFY IS JUST SO DANG COOL!! HE JUST KEEPS GOING FURTHER AND FURTHER...!!
EVERY TIME I READ AN ARTICLE ABOUT YOU...I THINK BACK TO THAT DAY!!
CAPTAIN KOBY, WHAT ARE YOU DOING? COME ON BACK!!
SNIFF
OH!! ANYWAY! WE'RE NEARLY AT NEW MARINE-FORD!!
!!
SO WE WILL PROVIDE ARMED ESCORT!!
DO YOU LIKE LUCY, KOBY?
WE BET YOU LIKE LUFFYLAND !!
GRIN GRIN
!!
NO!! HE'S MY... E-ENEMY.
C'MON, YOU CAN TELL US.♡
WE'LL KEEP IT A SECRET.♡
....!!

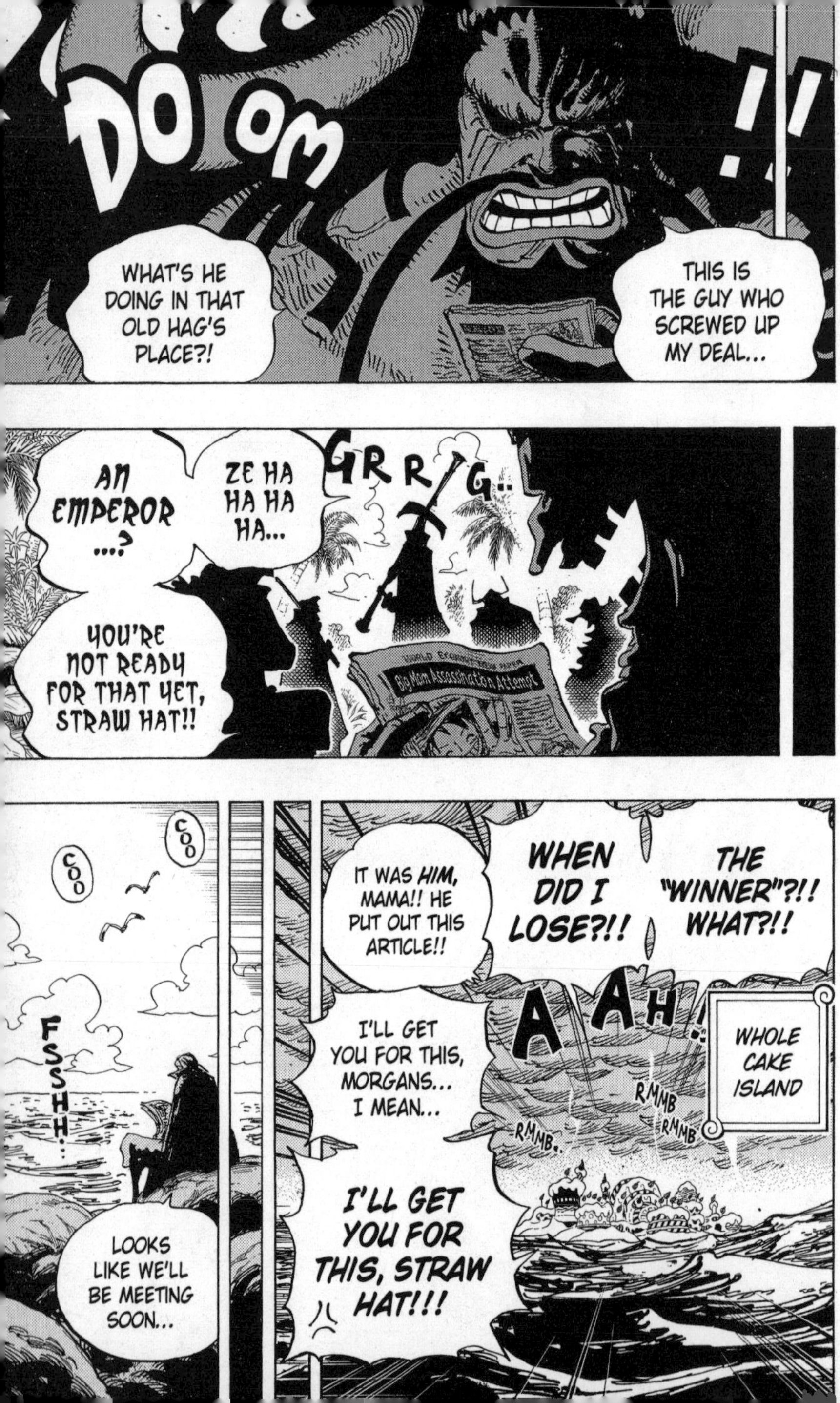
DOOM!!
THIS IS THE GUY WHO SCREWED UP MY DEAL...
WHAT'S HE DOING IN THAT OLD HAG'S PLACE?!
GRRRG..
Big Mom Assassination Attempt
ZE HA HA HA HA...
AN EMPEROR ...?
YOU'RE NOT READY FOR THAT YET, STRAW HAT!!
THE "WINNER"?!! WHAT?!!
WHEN DID I LOSE?!!
IT WAS HIM, MAMA!! HE PUT OUT THIS ARTICLE!!
AAH!!
WHOLE CAKE ISLAND
RMMB
RMMB
RMMB..
I'LL GET YOU FOR THIS, MORGANS... I MEAN...
I'LL GET YOU FOR THIS, STRAW HAT!!!
COO
COO
FSSHH...
LOOKS LIKE WE'LL BE MEETING SOON...

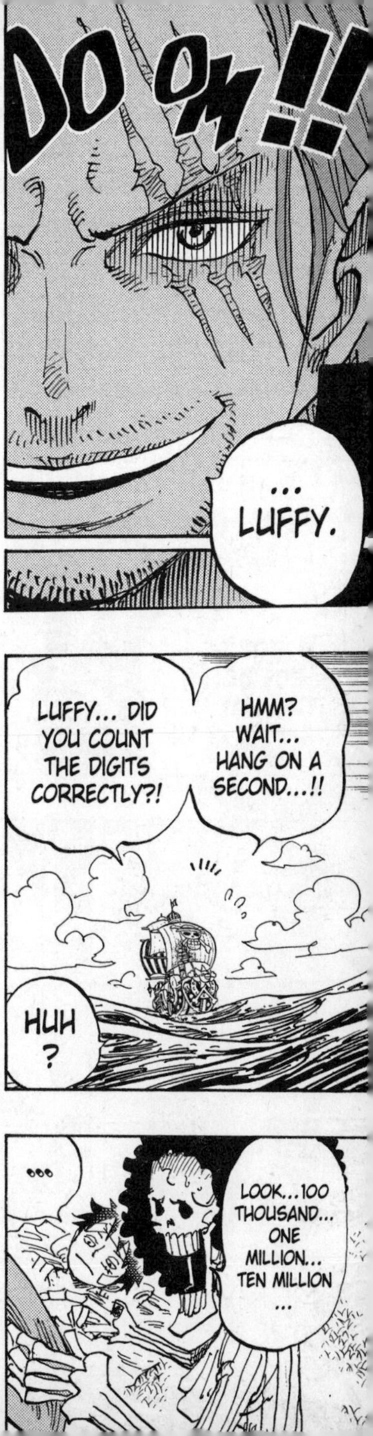
DOOM!!
... LUFFY.
HMM? WAIT... HANG ON A SECOND...!!
LUFFY... DID YOU COUNT THE DIGITS CORRECTLY?!
HUH?
LOOK...100 THOUSAND... ONE MILLION... TEN MILLION ...
...
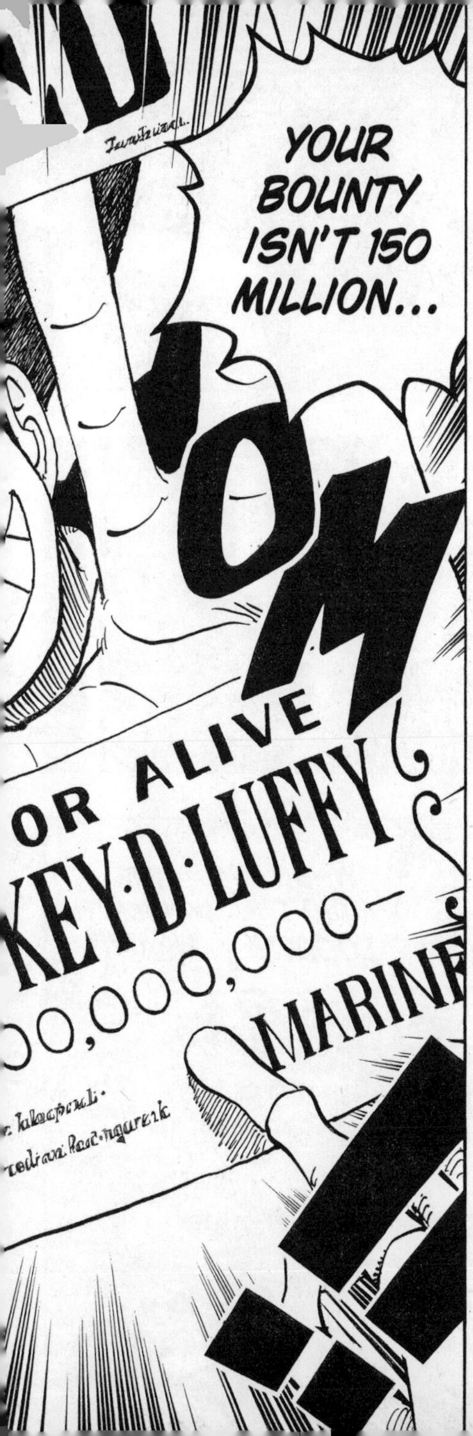
YOUR BOUNTY ISN'T 150 MILLION...
OM
OR ALIVE
KEY·D·LUFFY
00,000,000—
MARINE

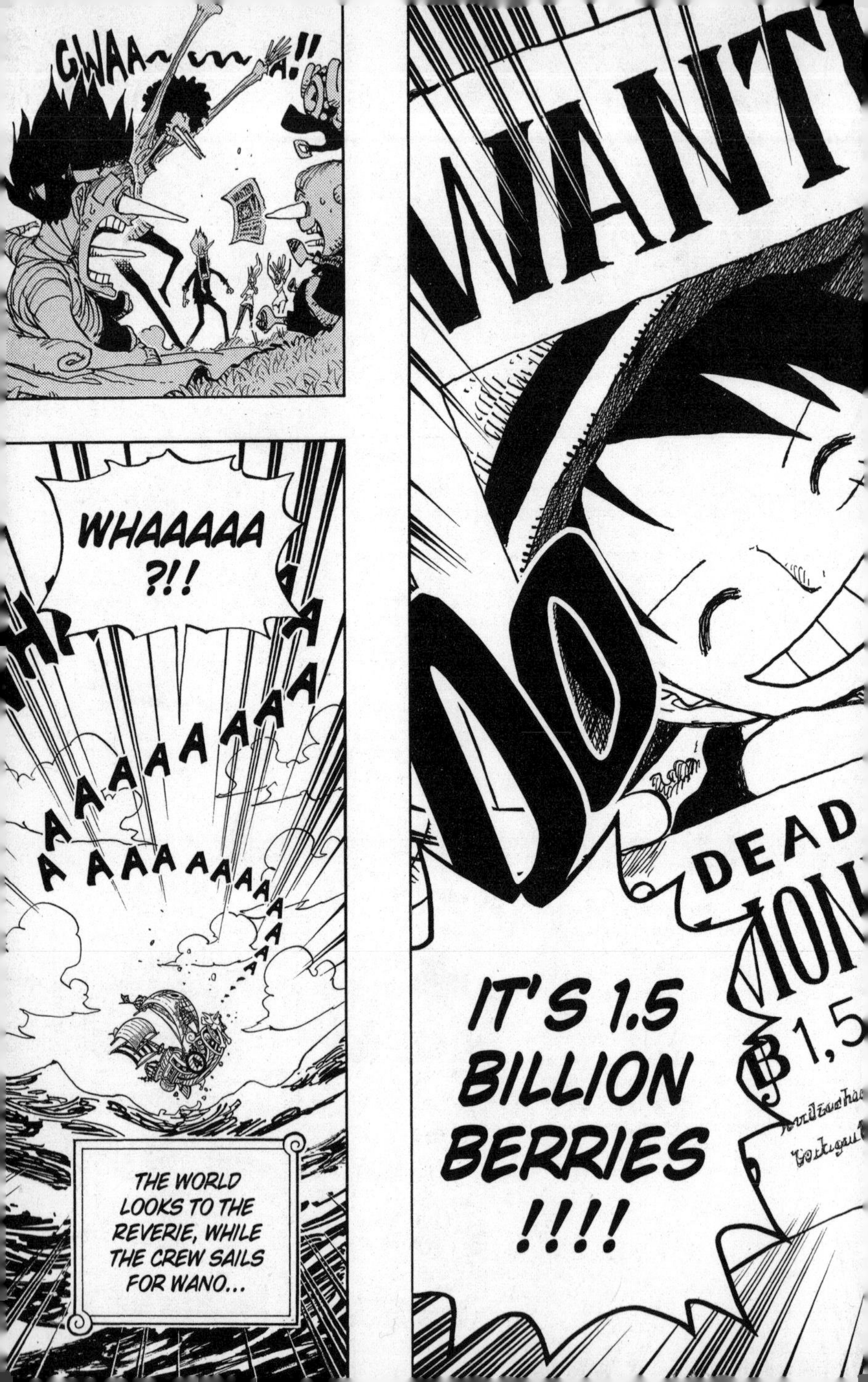
WANT
DO
DEAD
MON
฿1,5
IT'S 1.5 BILLION BERRIES !!!!
GWAA~~A!!
WHAAAAA ?!!
AAAAAAAAAAAAAAAAAAA
THE WORLD LOOKS TO THE REVERIE, WHILE THE CREW SAILS FOR WANO...

SBS Question Corner

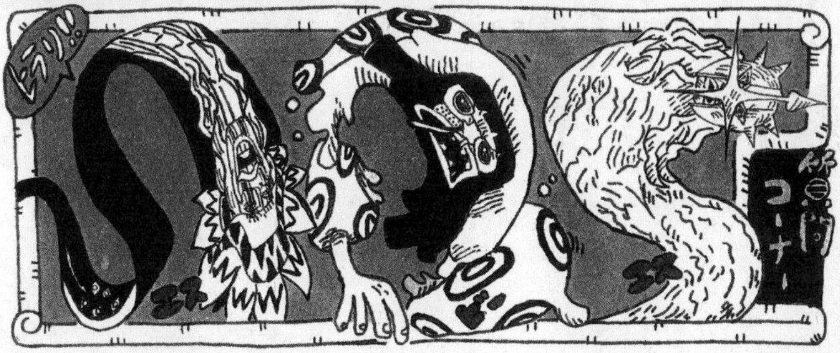

(Gamio, Osaka)

Q: Hello, Odacchi!! What's up with the crackling stuff at the end of General Cracker's hair? And how does he keep his cape on?

--MocchiMochi Donuts

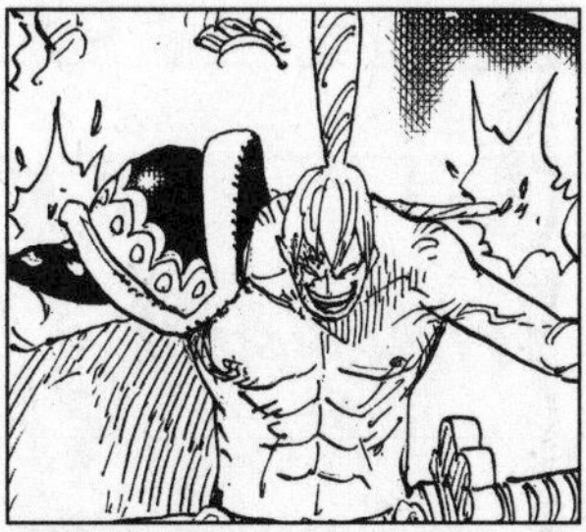

A: Well, his cape is simply attached by the spirit of his heart. The real issue is the crackling, right? As a matter of fact, even I was wondering what those things were as I drew them. Ha ha ha ha! When I was coming up with his design, I just kind of stumbled across that, and thought it was cool. My thought process was no deeper than, "That looks fine to me." If you wanted to make up a more rational reason after the fact, you could claim that the name Cracker gave me the idea of firecrackers. Do you suppose he'll explode eventually?

Q: Huh? What the…? *Baratie* looks bigger in chapter 902!!! I guess business is booming, huh?♡ Yesss!! I can't wait to tell Sanji!

--Chopa

A: Yes, that's right! This is the finished form of the *Baratie*, which was last seen being renovated on the cover of chapter 625! When you add in the connecting ships of Carne the Meat-Master and Patty the Patissier, all three together now represent the entirety of Baratie, the ocean-going restaurant.

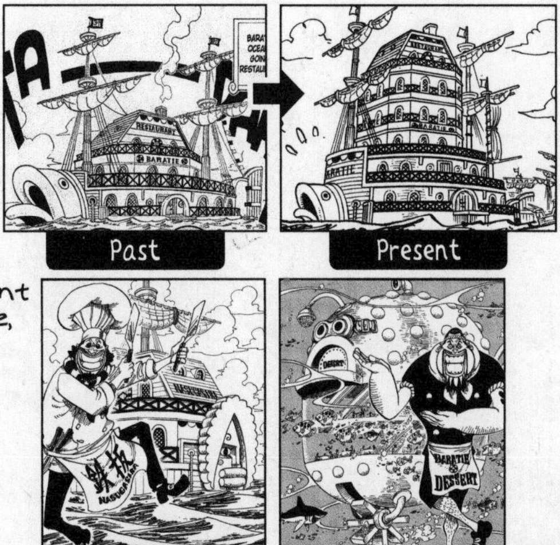
Past
Present
Carne
Patty

Chapter 904:

INTRODUCING THE REVOLUTIONARY ARMY CAPTAINS

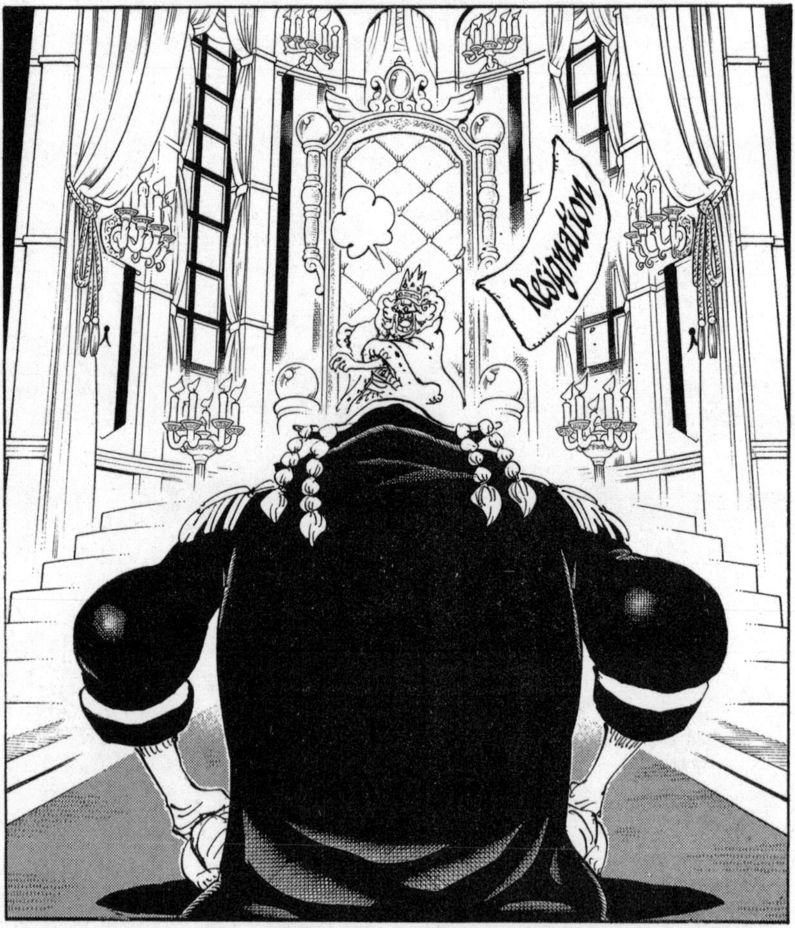
Resignation

THE SAGA OF THE SELF-PROCLAIMED STRAW HAT FLEET, VOL. 34, ORLUMBUS: "RETIRING FROM BEING THE PIONEER ADVENTURER OF THE STANDING KINGDOM"

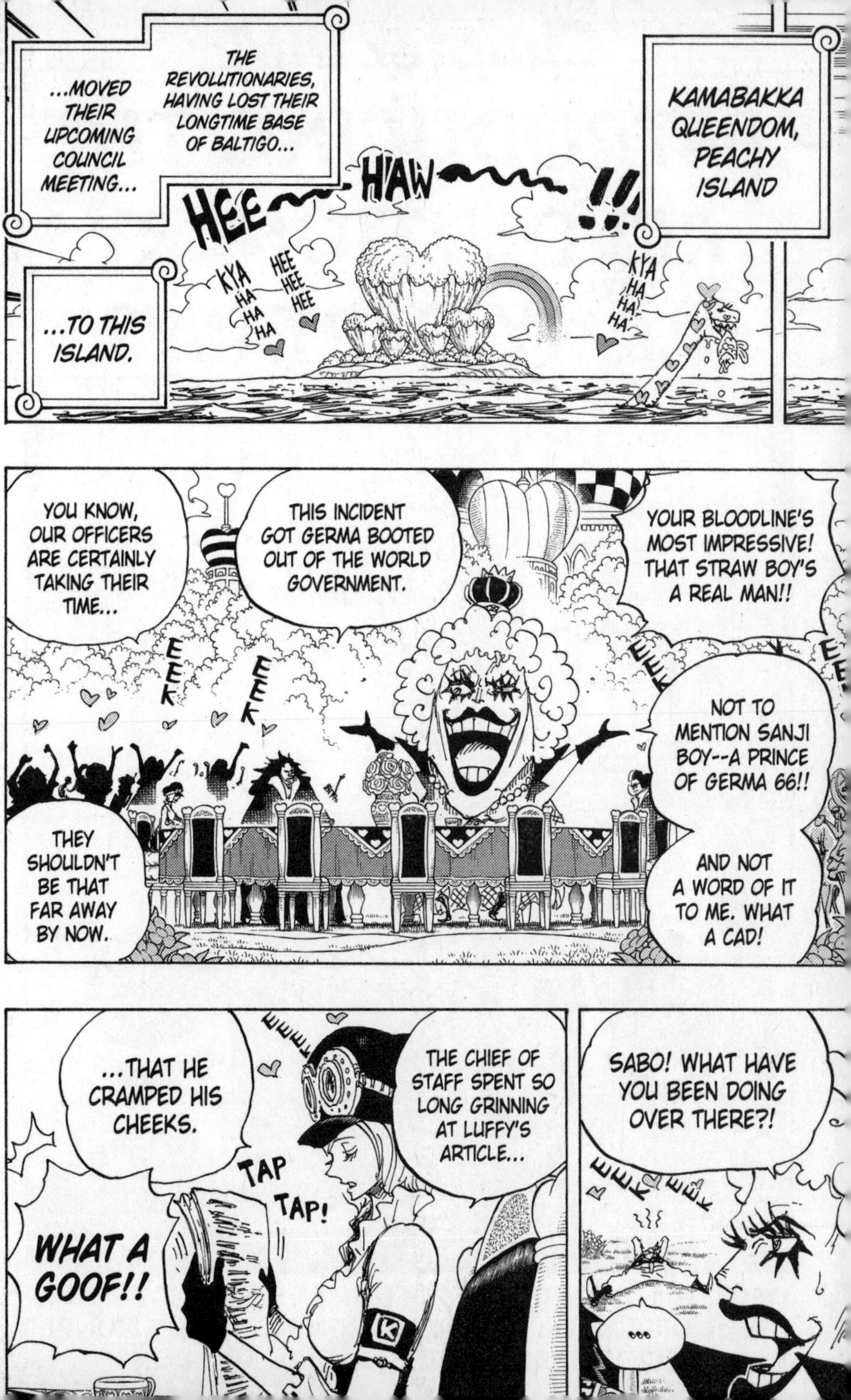
KAMABAKKA QUEENDOM, PEACHY ISLAND
THE REVOLUTIONARIES, HAVING LOST THEIR LONGTIME BASE OF BALTIGO...
...MOVED THEIR UPCOMING COUNCIL MEETING...
HEE~~HAW~~~!!
KYA HA HA HA
HEE HEE HEE
KYA HA HA! HA
...TO THIS ISLAND.
YOUR BLOODLINE'S MOST IMPRESSIVE! THAT STRAW BOY'S A REAL MAN!!
EEEK
NOT TO MENTION SANJI BOY--A PRINCE OF GERMA 66!!
AND NOT A WORD OF IT TO ME. WHAT A CAD!
THIS INCIDENT GOT GERMA BOOTED OUT OF THE WORLD GOVERNMENT.
EEK
EEK
YOU KNOW, OUR OFFICERS ARE CERTAINLY TAKING THEIR TIME...
THEY SHOULDN'T BE THAT FAR AWAY BY NOW.
SABO! WHAT HAVE YOU BEEN DOING OVER THERE?!
EEEK EEEK
THE CHIEF OF STAFF SPENT SO LONG GRINNING AT LUFFY'S ARTICLE...
EEEK
...THAT HE CRAMPED HIS CHEEKS.
TAP TAP!
WHAT A GOOF!!

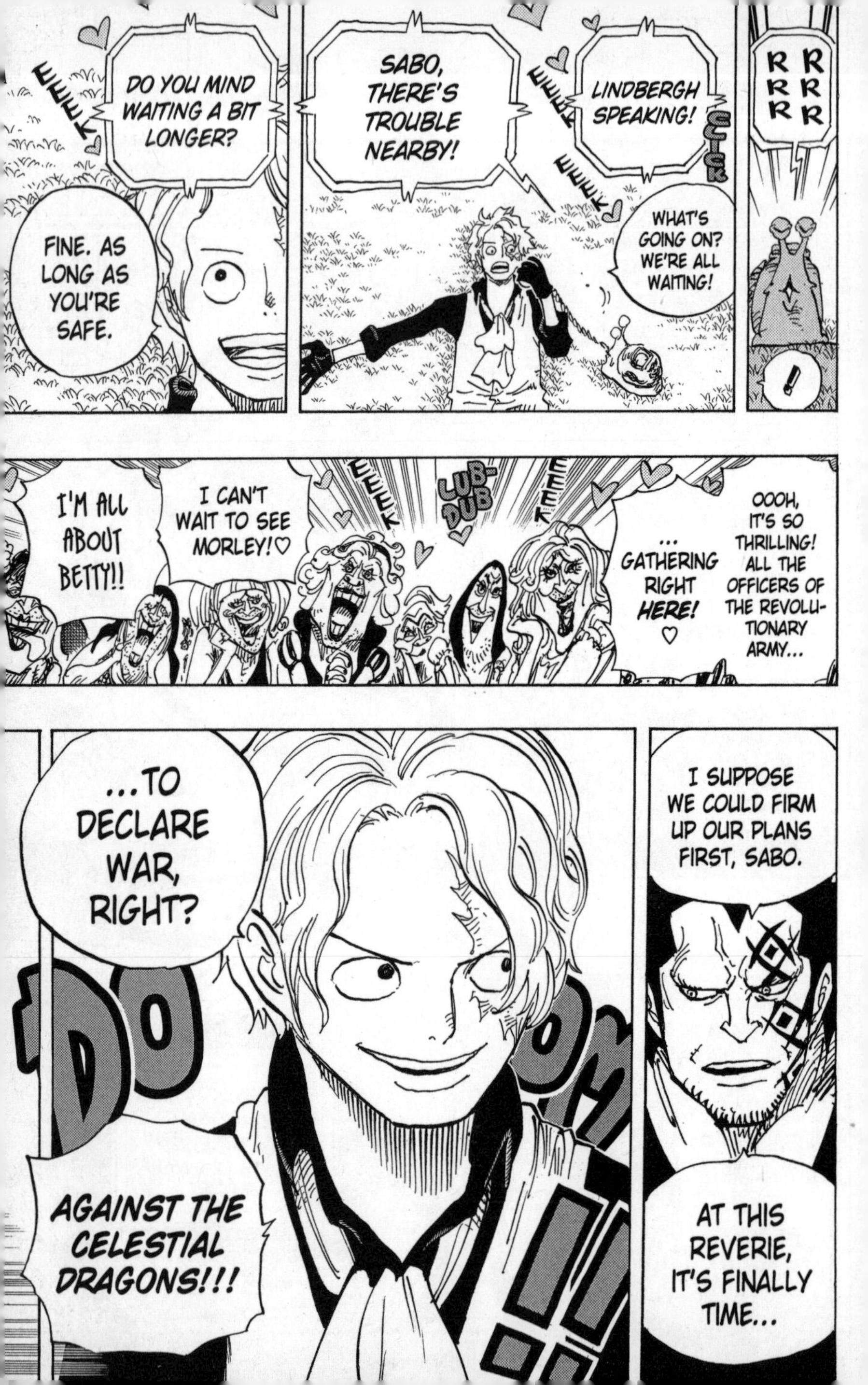
RRRRRR
!
LINDBERGH SPEAKING!
CLICK
EEEEK
WHAT'S GOING ON? WE'RE ALL WAITING!
SABO, THERE'S TROUBLE NEARBY!
EEEEK
DO YOU MIND WAITING A BIT LONGER?
EEEEK
FINE. AS LONG AS YOU'RE SAFE.
OOOH, IT'S SO THRILLING! ALL THE OFFICERS OF THE REVOLUTIONARY ARMY...
... GATHERING RIGHT HERE! ♡
EEEEK
LUB-DUB
EEEEK
I CAN'T WAIT TO SEE MORLEY!♡
I'M ALL ABOUT BETTY!!
I SUPPOSE WE COULD FIRM UP OUR PLANS FIRST, SABO.
AT THIS REVERIE, IT'S FINALLY TIME...
...TO DECLARE WAR, RIGHT?
DOOM
AGAINST THE CELESTIAL DRAGONS!!!

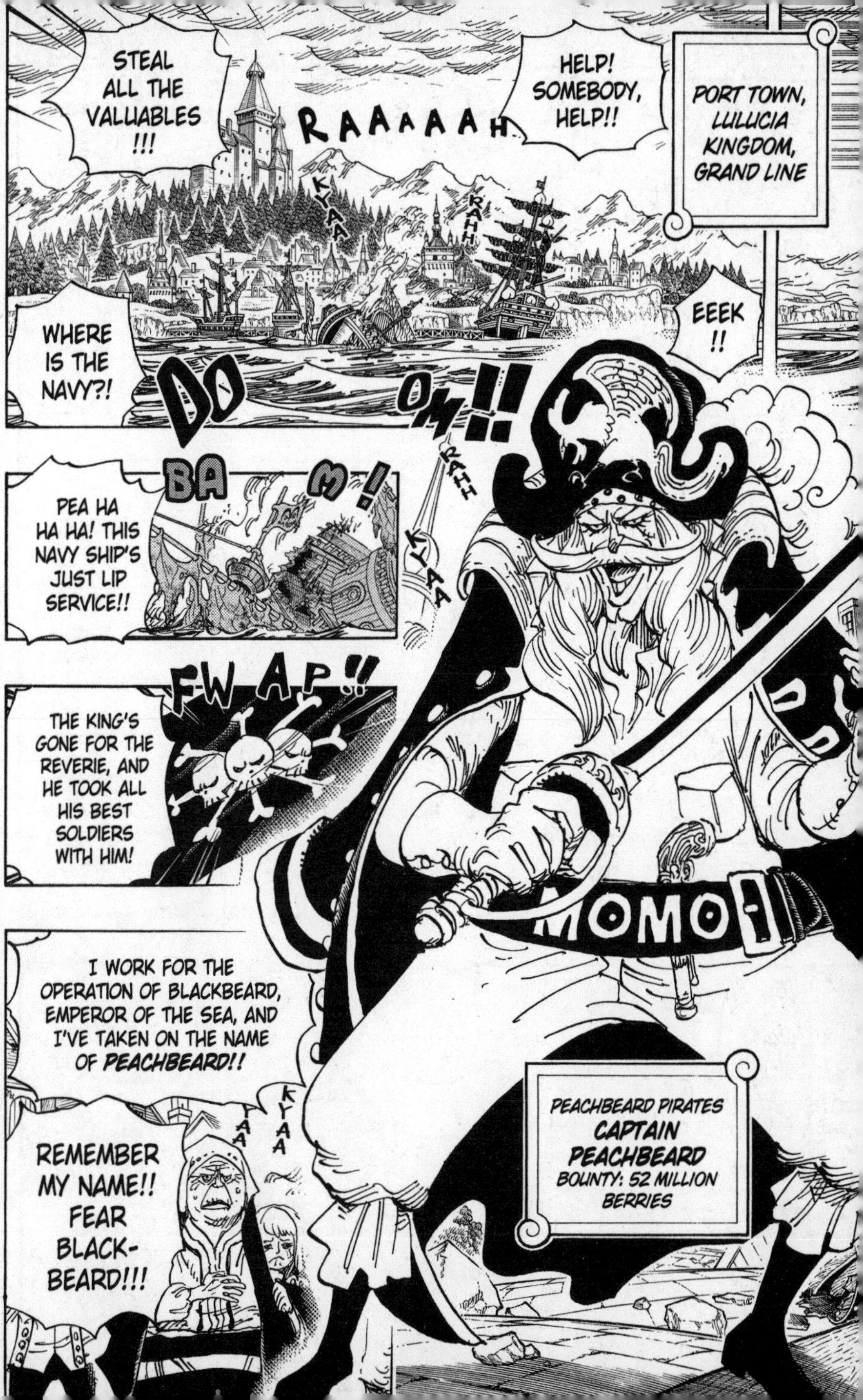
PORT TOWN, LULUCIA KINGDOM, GRAND LINE
HELP! SOMEBODY, HELP!!
RAAAAAH
STEAL ALL THE VALUABLES!!!
RAHH
KYAA
EEEK!!
DOOM!!
WHERE IS THE NAVY?!
RAHH
KYAA
BAM!
PEA HA HA HA! THIS NAVY SHIP'S JUST LIP SERVICE!!
FWAP!!
THE KING'S GONE FOR THE REVERIE, AND HE TOOK ALL HIS BEST SOLDIERS WITH HIM!
MOMO
PEACHBEARD PIRATES CAPTAIN PEACHBEARD BOUNTY: 52 MILLION BERRIES
I WORK FOR THE OPERATION OF BLACKBEARD, EMPEROR OF THE SEA, AND I'VE TAKEN ON THE NAME OF PEACHBEARD!!
KYAA
AA
REMEMBER MY NAME!! FEAR BLACK-BEARD!!!

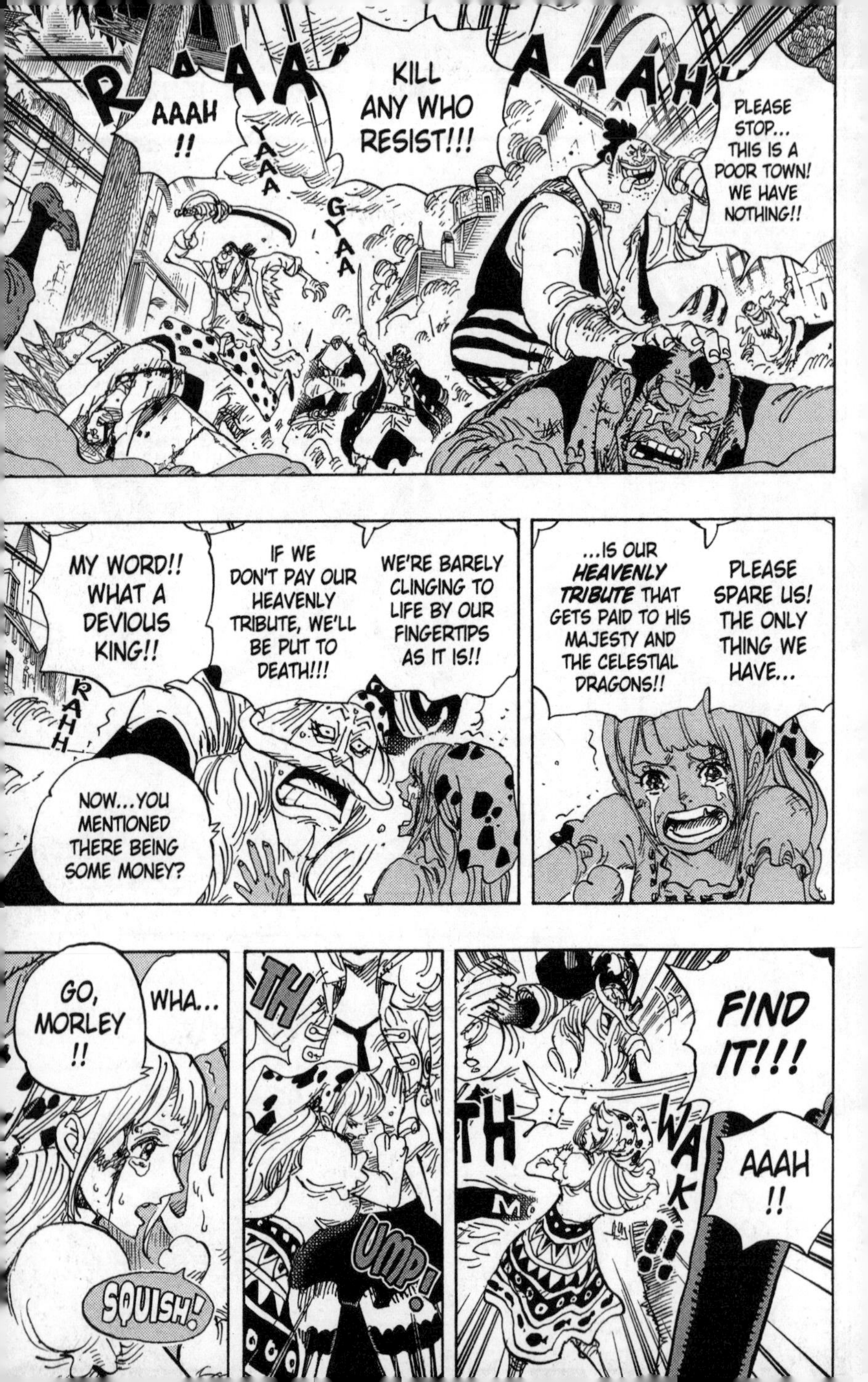
PLEASE STOP... THIS IS A POOR TOWN! WE HAVE NOTHING!!
KILL ANY WHO RESIST!!!
AAAH !!
YAAA
GYAA
RAAAAAAAH
PLEASE SPARE US! THE ONLY THING WE HAVE...
...IS OUR *HEAVENLY TRIBUTE* THAT GETS PAID TO HIS MAJESTY AND THE CELESTIAL DRAGONS!!
WE'RE BARELY CLINGING TO LIFE BY OUR FINGERTIPS AS IT IS!!
IF WE DON'T PAY OUR HEAVENLY TRIBUTE, WE'LL BE PUT TO DEATH!!!
MY WORD!! WHAT A DEVIOUS KING!!
RAHH
NOW...YOU MENTIONED THERE BEING SOME MONEY?
FIND IT!!!
AAAH !!
WAK!!
TH
M
TH
UMP!
WHA...
GO, MORLEY !!
SQUISH!

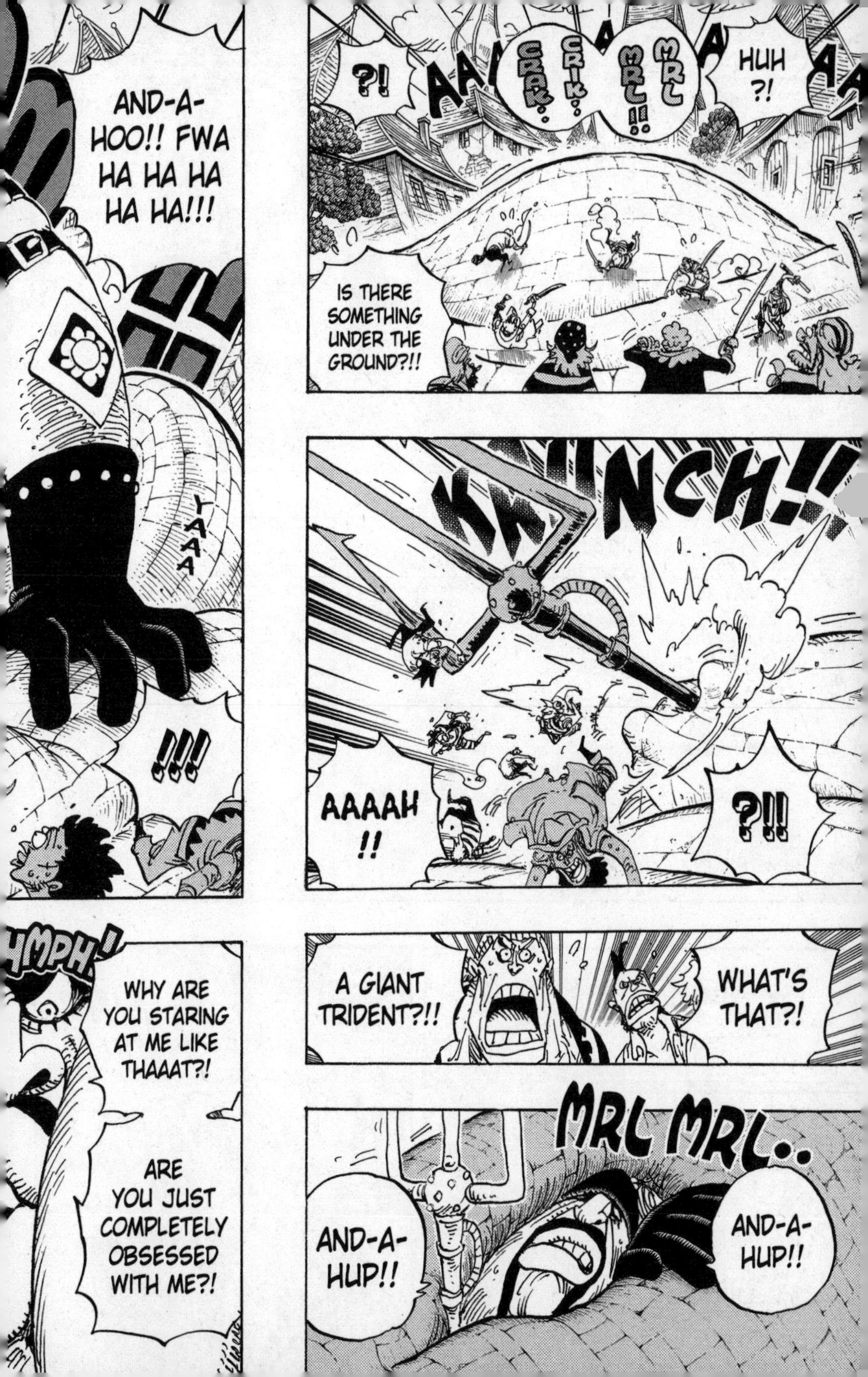
HUH ?!
MRL MRL
MRL MRL!!
CRIK.
CRRK.
?!
IS THERE SOMETHING UNDER THE GROUND?!!
?!!
AAAAH !!
AND-A-HOO!! FWA HA HA HA HA HA!!!
YAAAA
!!!
WHAT'S THAT?!
A GIANT TRIDENT?!!
MRL MRL..
AND-A-HUP!!
AND-A-HUP!!
HMPH!
WHY ARE YOU STARING AT ME LIKE THAAAT?!
ARE YOU JUST COMPLETELY OBSESSED WITH ME?!

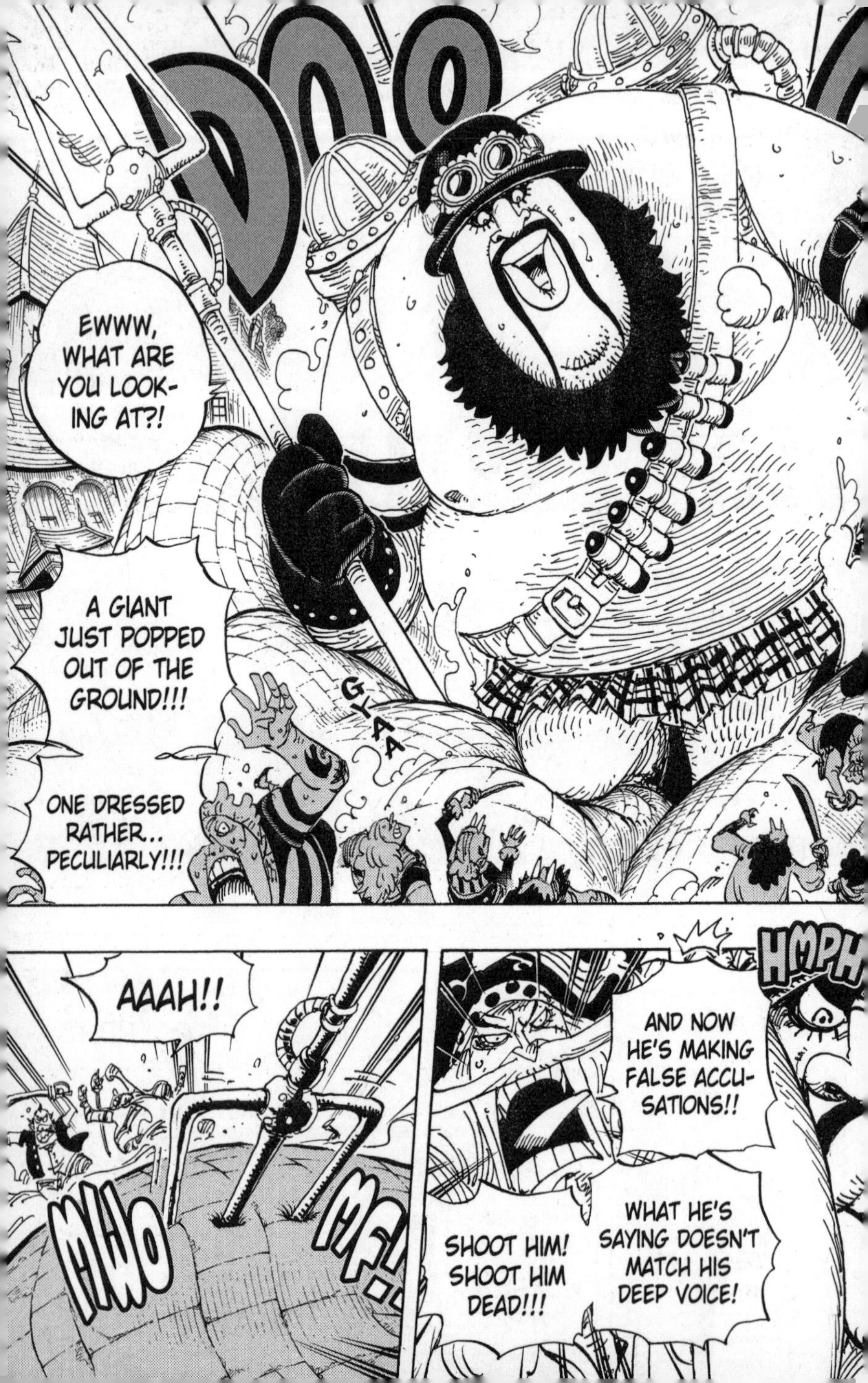
EWWW, WHAT ARE YOU LOOKING AT?!
A GIANT JUST POPPED OUT OF THE GROUND!!!
GYAA
ONE DRESSED RATHER.. PECULIARLY!!!
HMPH
AND NOW HE'S MAKING FALSE ACCUSATIONS!!
WHAT HE'S SAYING DOESN'T MATCH HIS DEEP VOICE!
SHOOT HIM! SHOOT HIM DEAD!!!
AAAH!!

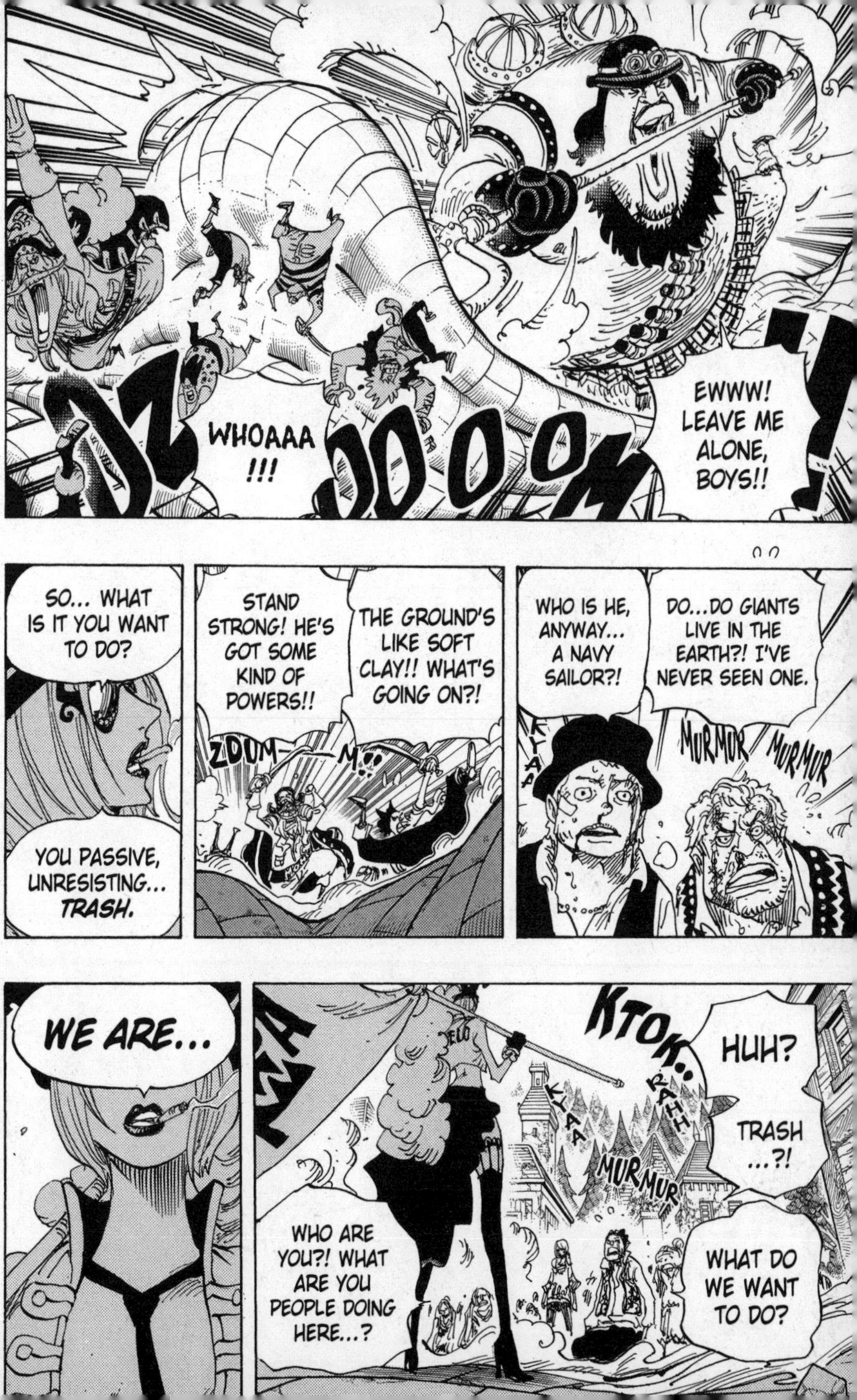

EWWW! LEAVE ME ALONE, BOYS!!
WHOAAA!!!
DO...DO GIANTS LIVE IN THE EARTH?! I'VE NEVER SEEN ONE.
WHO IS HE, ANYWAY... A NAVY SAILOR?!
MURMUR MURMUR
THE GROUND'S LIKE SOFT CLAY!! WHAT'S GOING ON?!
STAND STRONG! HE'S GOT SOME KIND OF POWERS!!
ZDOOM--M!!
SO... WHAT IS IT YOU WANT TO DO?
YOU PASSIVE, UNRESISTING... *TRASH.*
KTOK...
HUH?
TRASH...?!
RAHH
KYAA
MURMUR
WHAT DO WE WANT TO DO?
WHO ARE YOU?! WHAT ARE YOU PEOPLE DOING HERE...?
WE ARE...

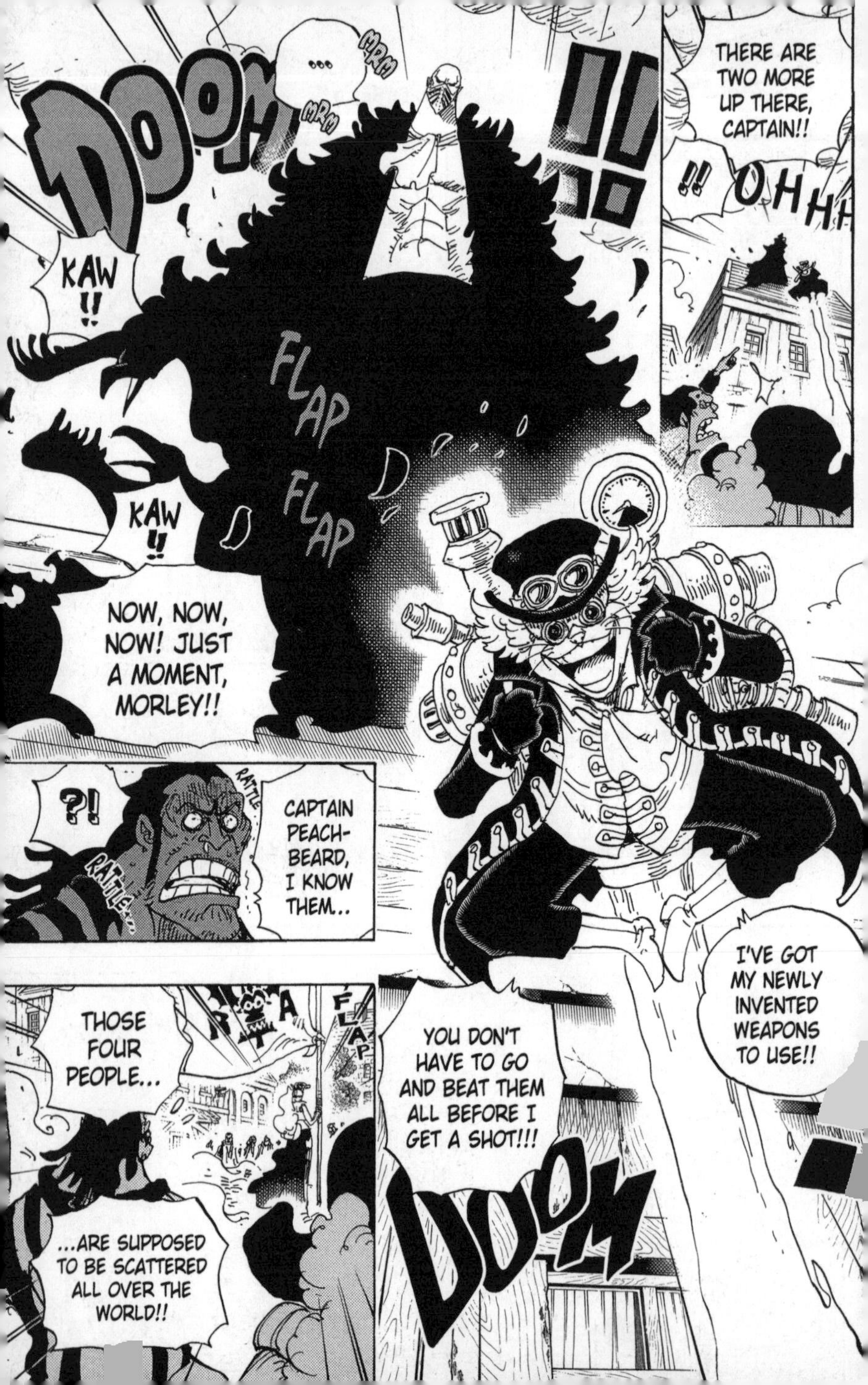
THERE ARE TWO MORE UP THERE, CAPTAIN!!
!! OHHH
!!
DOOM
...
MRM
MRM
KAW !!
FLAP
FLAP
KAW !!
NOW, NOW, NOW! JUST A MOMENT, MORLEY!!
YOU DON'T HAVE TO GO AND BEAT THEM ALL BEFORE I GET A SHOT!!!
I'VE GOT MY NEWLY INVENTED WEAPONS TO USE!!
DOOM
?!
RATTLE
RATTLE...
CAPTAIN PEACH-BEARD, I KNOW THEM...
FLAP
THOSE FOUR PEOPLE...
...ARE SUPPOSED TO BE SCATTERED ALL OVER THE WORLD!!

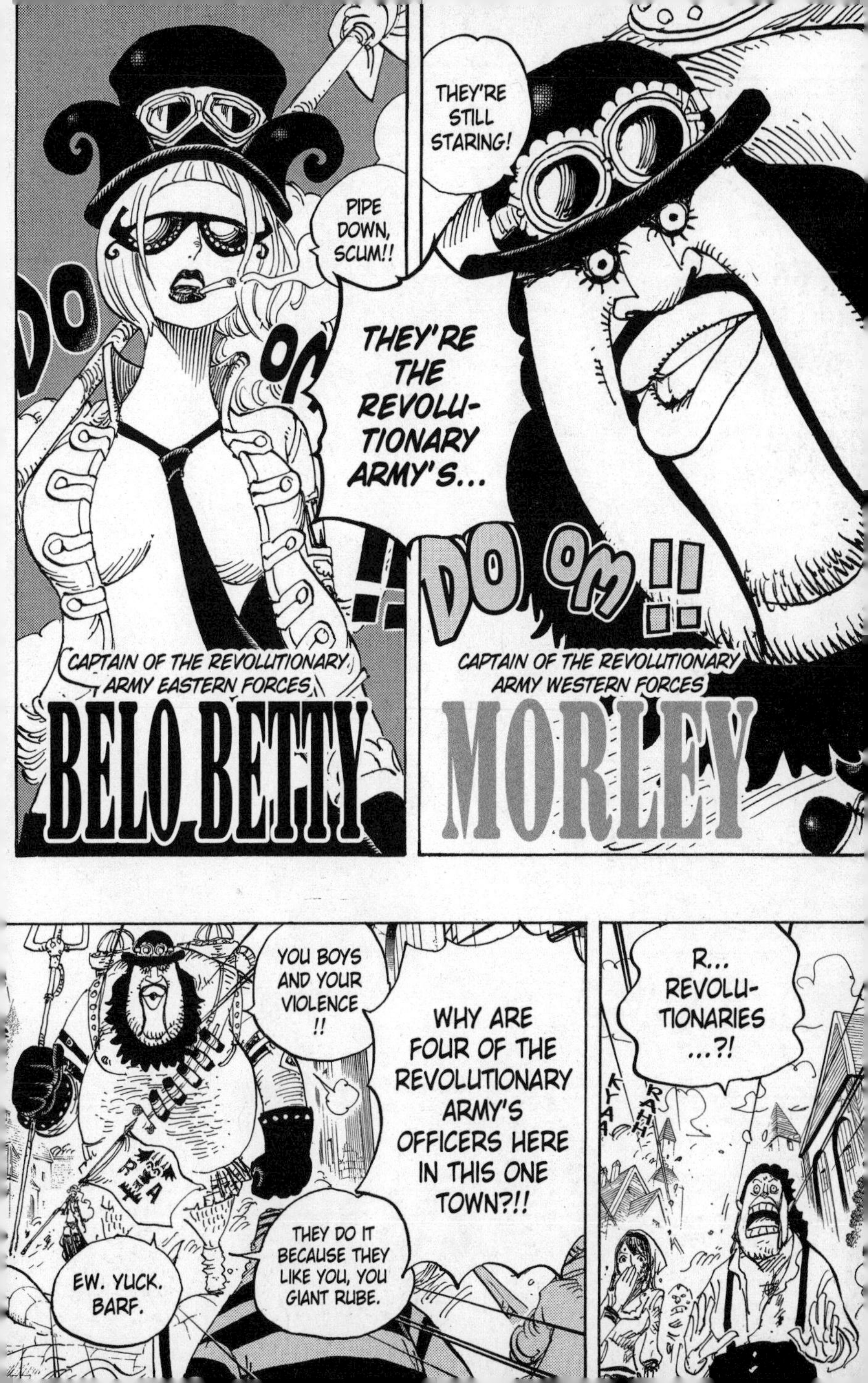
THEY'RE STILL STARING!
PIPE DOWN, SCUM!!
THEY'RE THE REVOLUTIONARY ARMY'S...
DOOM!!
CAPTAIN OF THE REVOLUTIONARY ARMY WESTERN FORCES
MORLEY
DOOM!!
CAPTAIN OF THE REVOLUTIONARY ARMY EASTERN FORCES
BELO BETTY
R... REVOLUTIONARIES ...?!
KYAA
RAHH
WHY ARE FOUR OF THE REVOLUTIONARY ARMY'S OFFICERS HERE IN THIS ONE TOWN?!!
YOU BOYS AND YOUR VIOLENCE !!
THEY DO IT BECAUSE THEY LIKE YOU, YOU GIANT RUBE.
EW. YUCK. BARF.

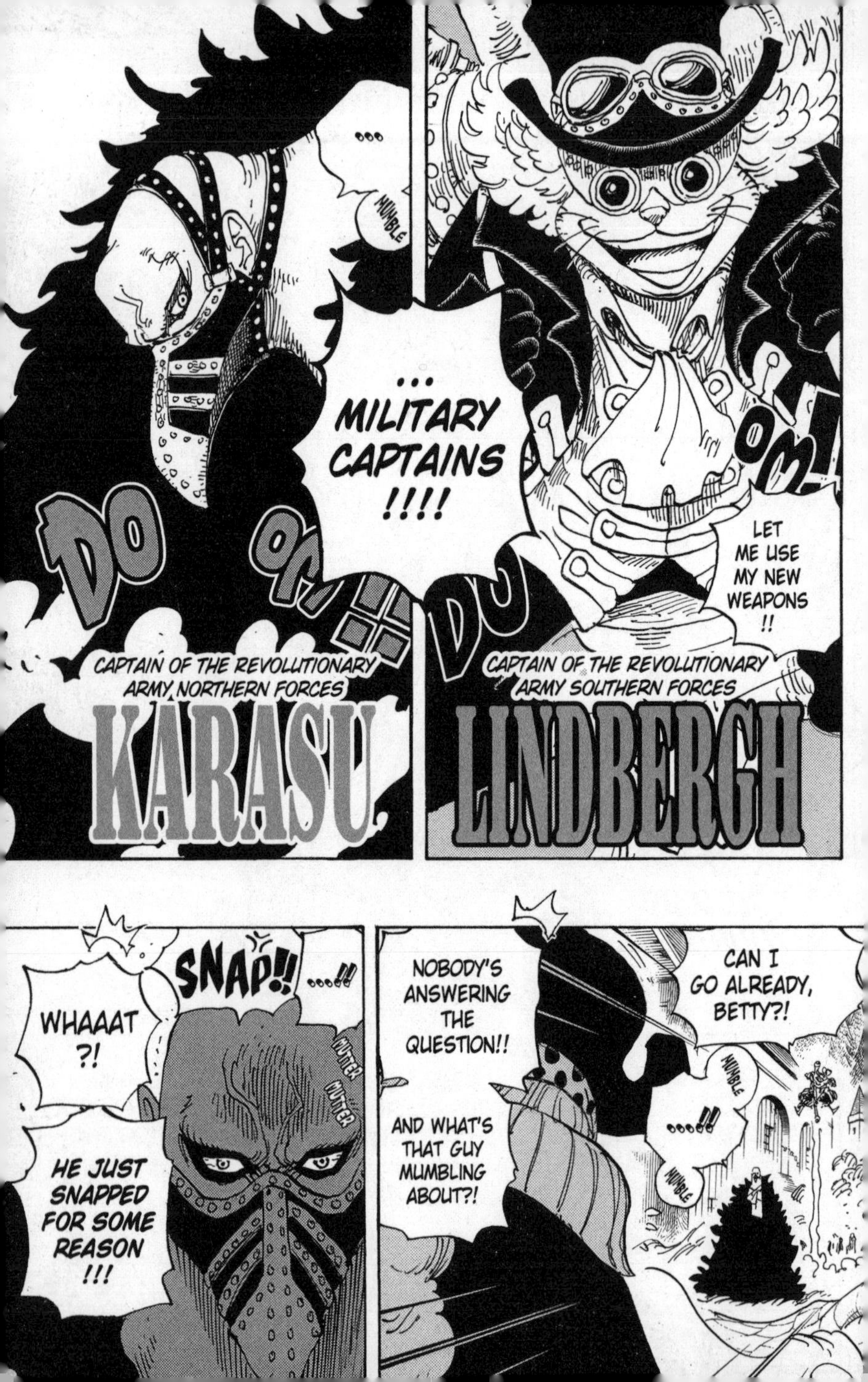
... MILITARY CAPTAINS !!!!
LET ME USE MY NEW WEAPONS !!
DO OM!!
CAPTAIN OF THE REVOLUTIONARY ARMY SOUTHERN FORCES
LINDBERGH
...
MUMBLE
DO OM!!
CAPTAIN OF THE REVOLUTIONARY ARMY NORTHERN FORCES
KARASU
CAN I GO ALREADY, BETTY?!
NOBODY'S ANSWERING THE QUESTION!!
AND WHAT'S THAT GUY MUMBLING ABOUT?!
MUMBLE
...!!
MUMBLE
SNAP!!
...!!
WHAAAT ?!
MUTTER
MUTTER
HE JUST SNAPPED FOR SOME REASON !!!

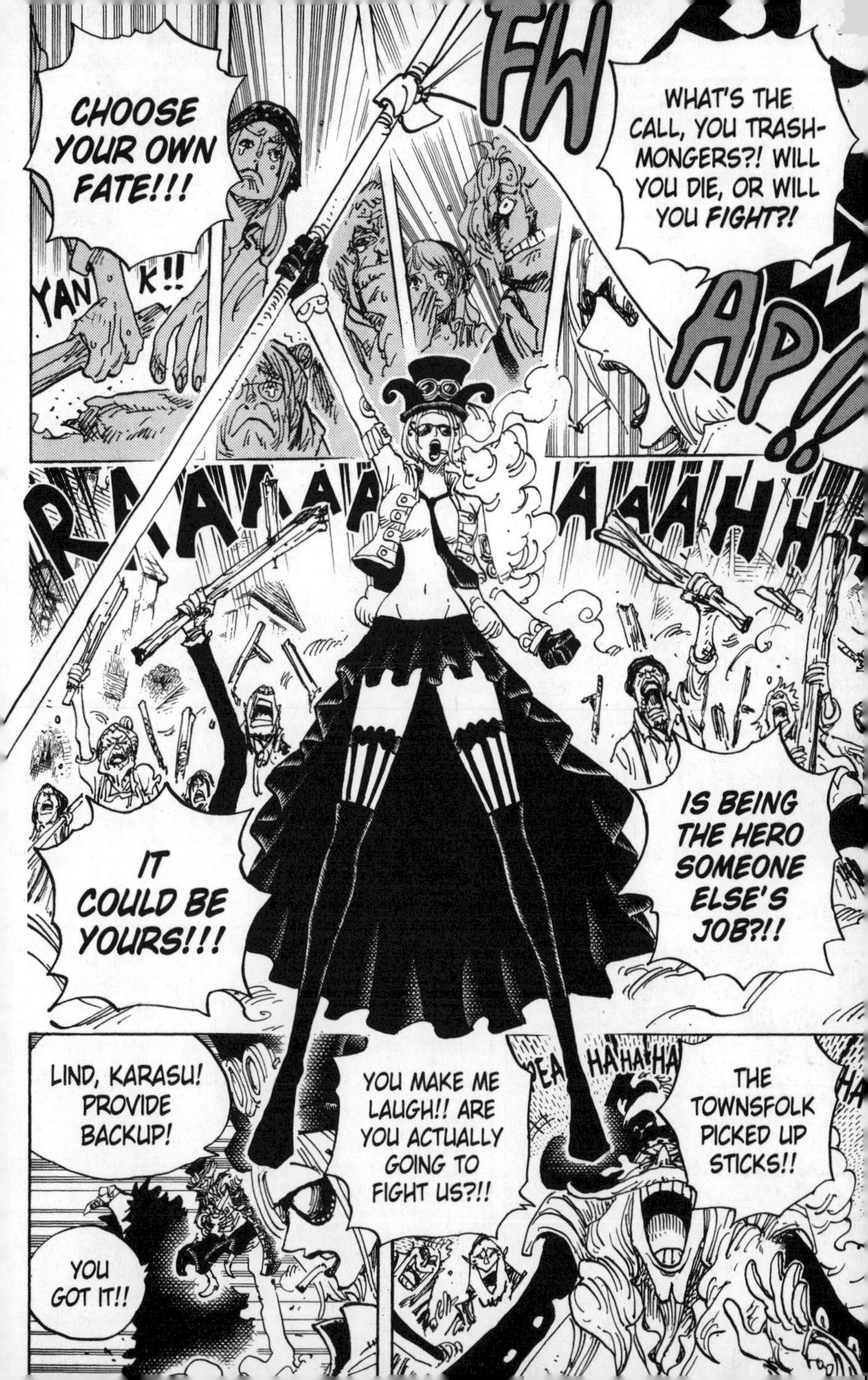
WHAT'S THE CALL, YOU TRASH-MONGERS?! WILL YOU DIE, OR WILL YOU FIGHT?!
FW AP!!
CHOOSE YOUR OWN FATE!!!
YAN K!!
RAAAAA AAAHH
IS BEING THE HERO SOMEONE ELSE'S JOB?!!
IT COULD BE YOURS!!!
THE TOWNSFOLK PICKED UP STICKS!!
DEA HA HA HA
YOU MAKE ME LAUGH!! ARE YOU ACTUALLY GOING TO FIGHT US?!!
LIND, KARASU! PROVIDE BACKUP!
YOU GOT IT!!

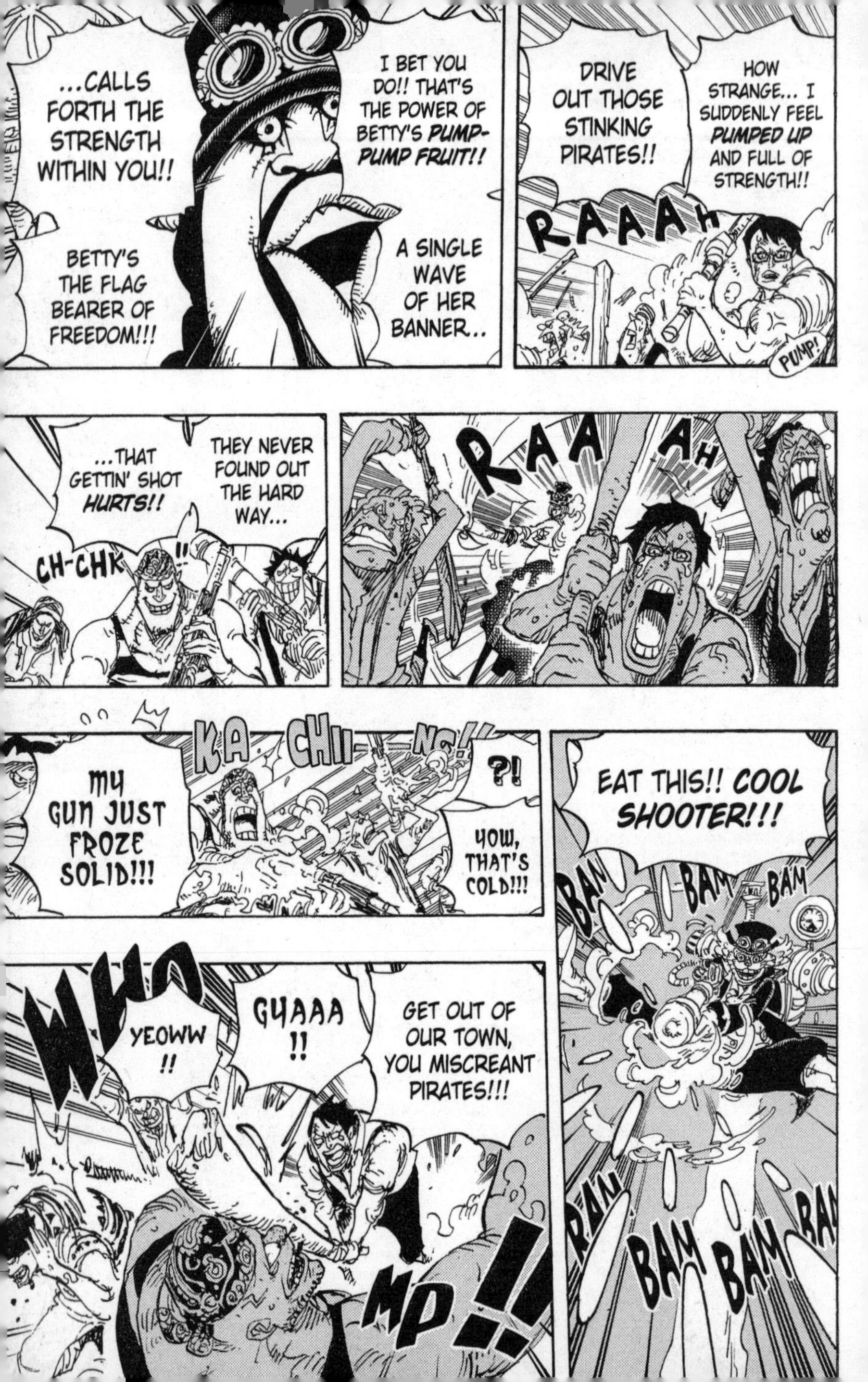
HOW STRANGE... I SUDDENLY FEEL *PUMPED UP* AND FULL OF STRENGTH!!
DRIVE OUT THOSE STINKING PIRATES!!
RAAAH
PUMP!
I BET YOU DO!! THAT'S THE POWER OF BETTY'S *PUMP-PUMP FRUIT!!*
...CALLS FORTH THE STRENGTH WITHIN YOU!!
A SINGLE WAVE OF HER BANNER...
BETTY'S THE FLAG BEARER OF FREEDOM!!!
RAAAAH
THEY NEVER FOUND OUT THE HARD WAY...
...THAT GETTIN' SHOT *HURTS!!*
CH-CHK
!!
EAT THIS!! *COOL SHOOTER!!!*
BAM BAM BAM
BAM BAM BAM
?!
YOW, THAT'S COLD!!!
KA-CHIIING!!
MY GUN JUST FROZE SOLID!!!
GET OUT OF OUR TOWN, YOU MISCREANT PIRATES!!!
GUAAA!!
YEOWW!!
WHOMP!!

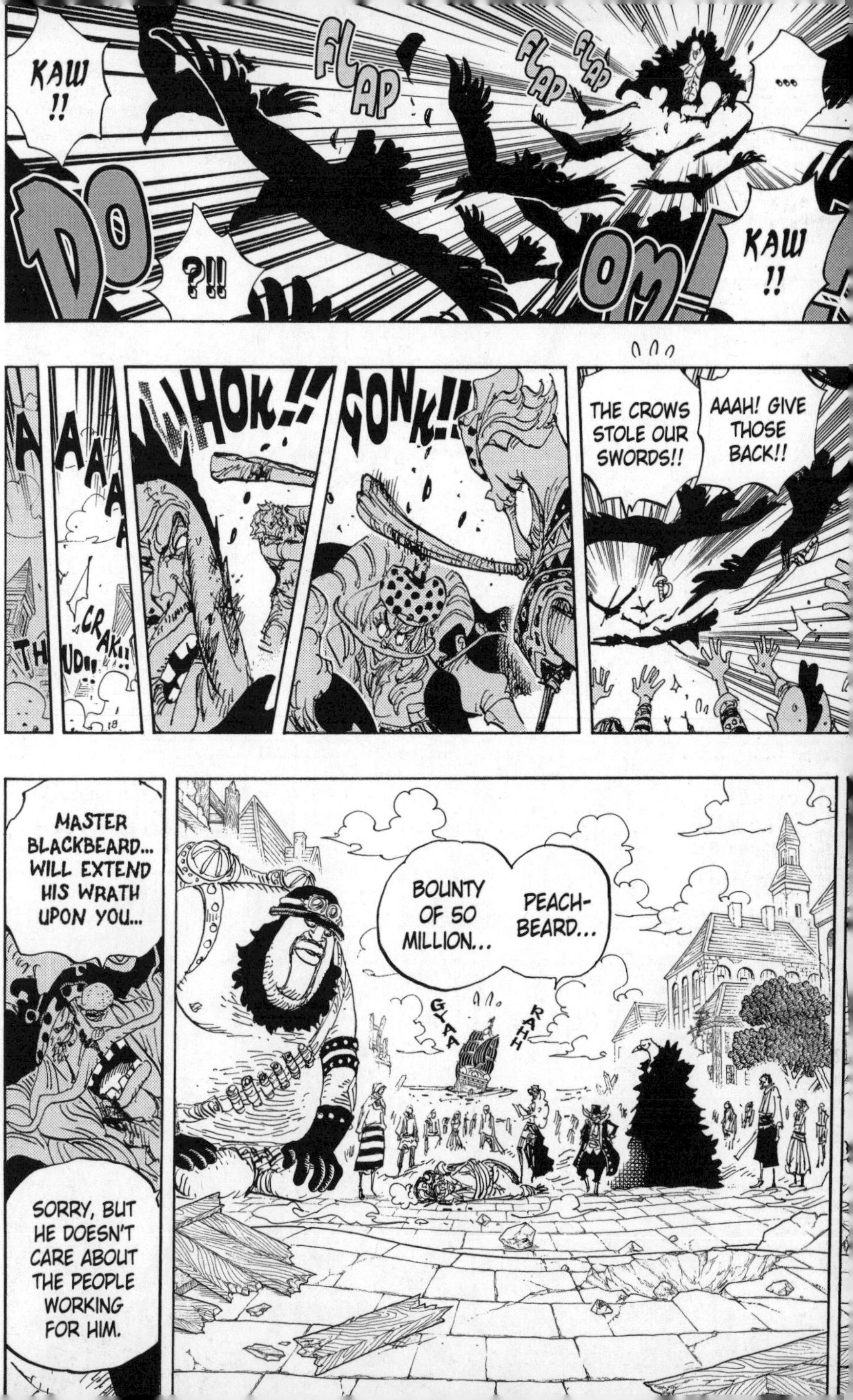

...
KAW !!
FLAP
FLAP
FLAP
DOOM!
?!!
KAW !!
AAAH! GIVE THOSE BACK!!
THE CROWS STOLE OUR SWORDS!!
GONK!!
WHOK!!
AAAA
CRAK!!
THUD!!
PEACH-BEARD...
BOUNTY OF 50 MILLION...
RAHH
GYAA
MASTER BLACKBEARD... WILL EXTEND HIS WRATH UPON YOU...
SORRY, BUT HE DOESN'T CARE ABOUT THE PEOPLE WORKING FOR HIM.

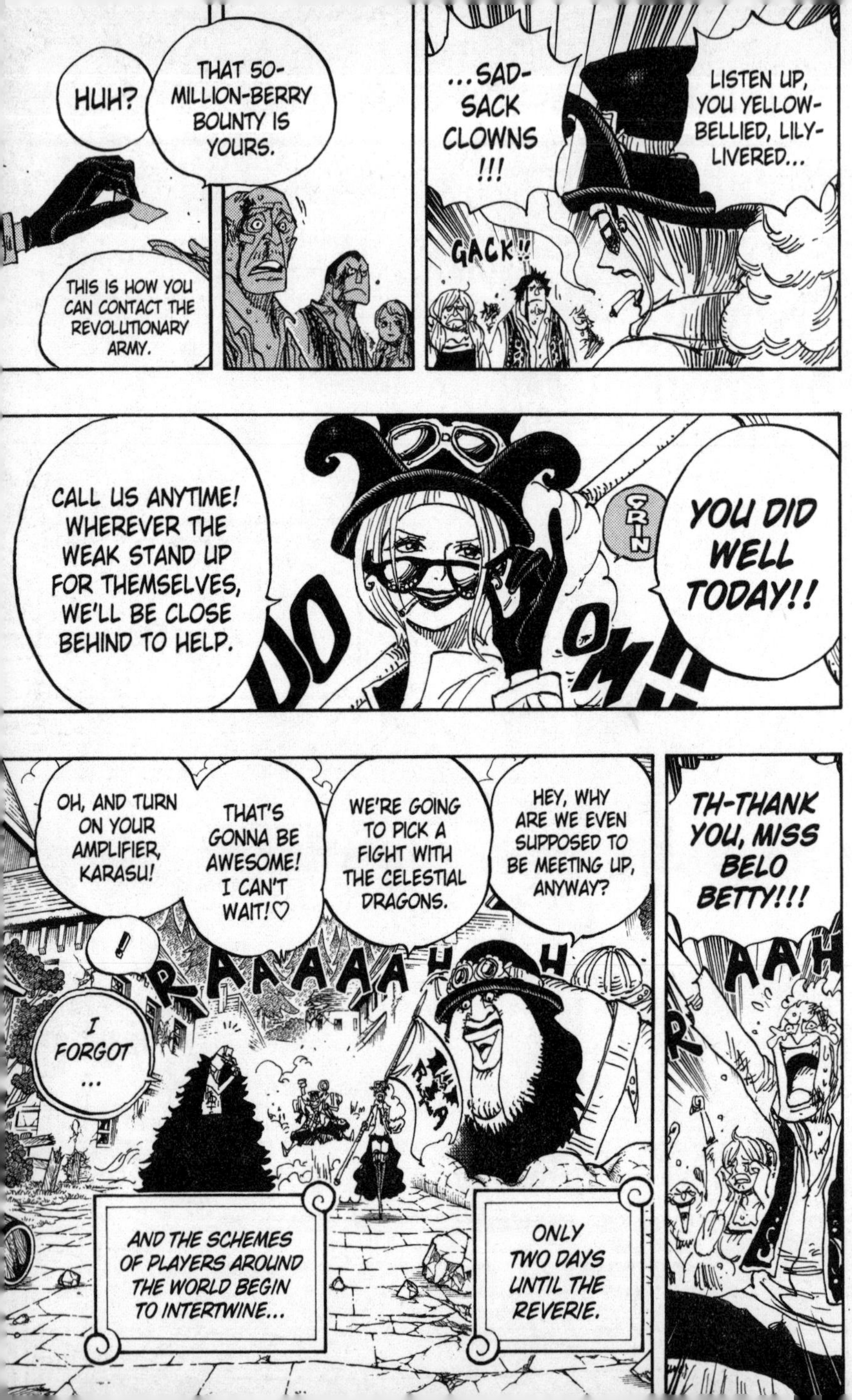
LISTEN UP, YOU YELLOW-BELLIED, LILY-LIVERED...
...SAD-SACK CLOWNS!!!
GACK!!
THAT 50-MILLION-BERRY BOUNTY IS YOURS.
HUH?
THIS IS HOW YOU CAN CONTACT THE REVOLUTIONARY ARMY.
YOU DID WELL TODAY!!
GRIN
DOOM!!
CALL US ANYTIME! WHEREVER THE WEAK STAND UP FOR THEMSELVES, WE'LL BE CLOSE BEHIND TO HELP.
TH-THANK YOU, MISS BELO BETTY!!!
RAAH
HEY, WHY ARE WE EVEN SUPPOSED TO BE MEETING UP, ANYWAY?
WE'RE GOING TO PICK A FIGHT WITH THE CELESTIAL DRAGONS.
THAT'S GONNA BE AWESOME! I CAN'T WAIT!♡
OH, AND TURN ON YOUR AMPLIFIER, KARASU!
!
I FORGOT...
RAAAAAAH
ONLY TWO DAYS UNTIL THE REVERIE.
AND THE SCHEMES OF PLAYERS AROUND THE WORLD BEGIN TO INTERTWINE...

Reverie Arc
Voyage Record 1
East Blue: Koby-Meppo

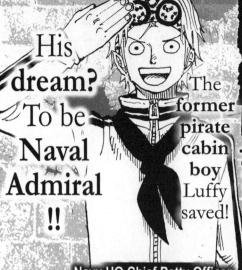

His dream? To be Naval Admiral!!

The former pirate cabin boy Luffy saved!

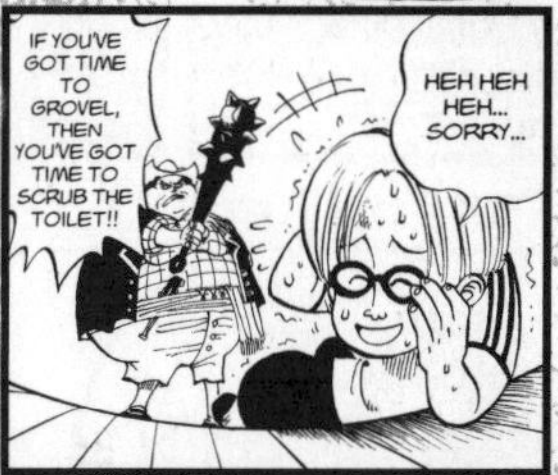
HEH HEH HEH... SORRY...
IF YOU'VE GOT TIME TO GROVEL, THEN YOU'VE GOT TIME TO SCRUB THE TOILET!!

➡ He got on a pirate ship by accident, and served as cabin boy for two years.

Navy HQ Chief Petty Officer

Koby

⬆ A kindhearted crybaby sailor. He's shown great improvement since training under Garp, Luffy's grandfather. He even took part in the Paramount War.

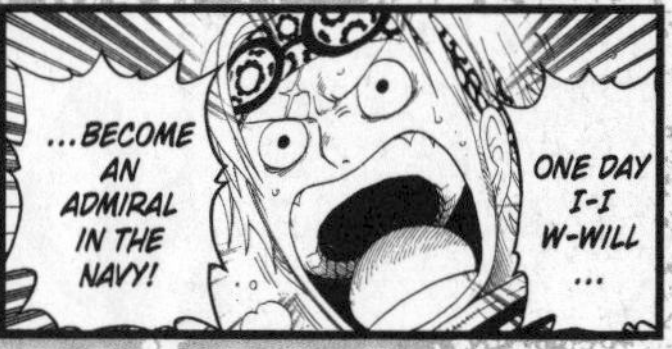
ONE DAY I-I W-WILL ...
...BECOME AN ADMIRAL IN THE NAVY!

⬆ He declares that he will one day be the Navy's greatest weapon and capture Luffy himself!!

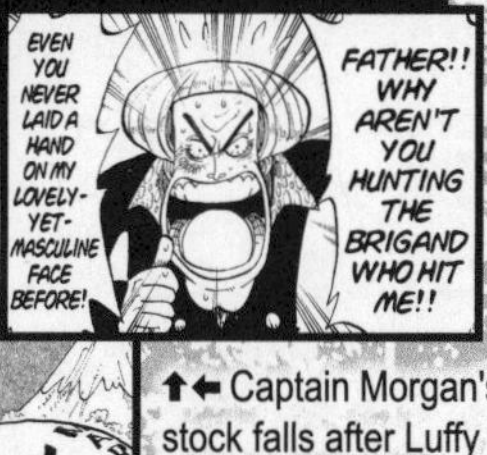
FATHER!! WHY AREN'T YOU HUNTING THE BRIGAND WHO HIT ME!!
EVEN YOU NEVER LAID A HAND ON MY LOVELY-YET-MASCULINE FACE BEFORE!

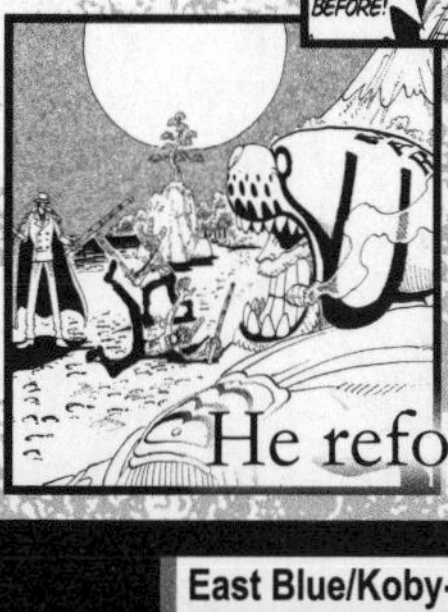

⬆⬅ Captain Morgan's stock falls after Luffy beats him. Helmeppo joins the Navy too, starting his new life in boot camp.

Navy HQ Petty Officer

Helmeppo

➡ A fighter who uses kukri blades. His father is former Navy Captain Morgan, and in his past, he abused that privilege to his own ends.

The **pampered son** who fell to earth!

He reforms himself as **Koby's partner!!**

*Current as of September 2018.

East Blue/Koby-Meppo Background

Luffy saves Koby from the ship of the lady pirate Alvida, then heads to Shells Town after hearing about the swordsman Zolo. The townspeople there quake in fear of Navy Captain Morgan's iron rule. Luffy frees Zolo so they can tackle Morgan and son!!

Volume 1

Reverie Arc
Voyage Record 2
Celestial Dragons & Nobles

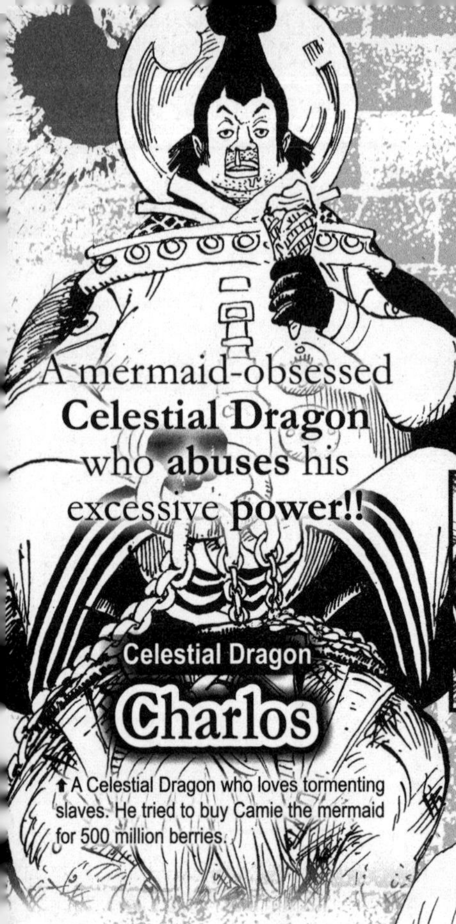

A mermaid-obsessed **Celestial Dragon** who **abuses** his excessive **power!!**

Celestial Dragon

Charlos

⬆ A Celestial Dragon who loves tormenting slaves. He tried to buy Camie the mermaid for 500 million berries.

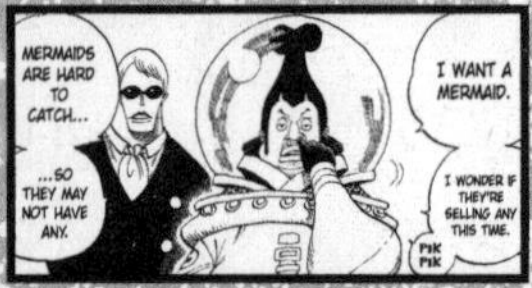
I WANT A MERMAID.
I WONDER IF THEY'RE SELLING ANY THIS TIME.
PIK PIK
MERMAIDS ARE HARD TO CATCH...
...SO THEY MAY NOT HAVE ANY.

➡ He wanted to have fun by setting piranhas to hunt a mermaid.

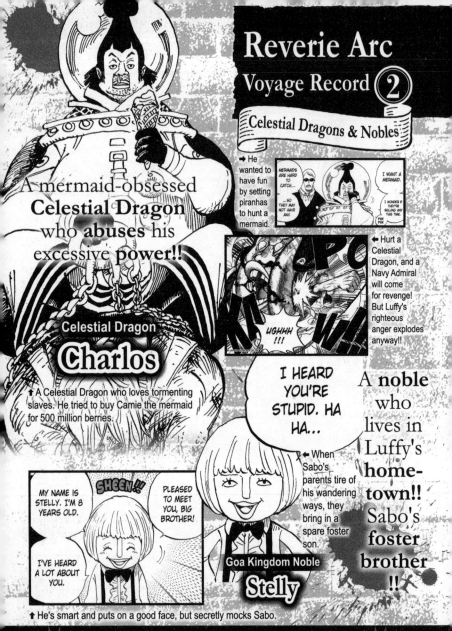

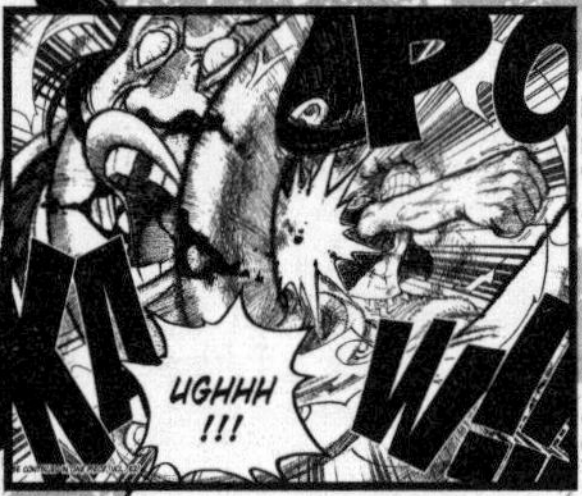
UGHHH !!!

⬅ Hurt a Celestial Dragon, and a Navy Admiral will come for revenge! But Luffy's righteous anger explodes anyway!!

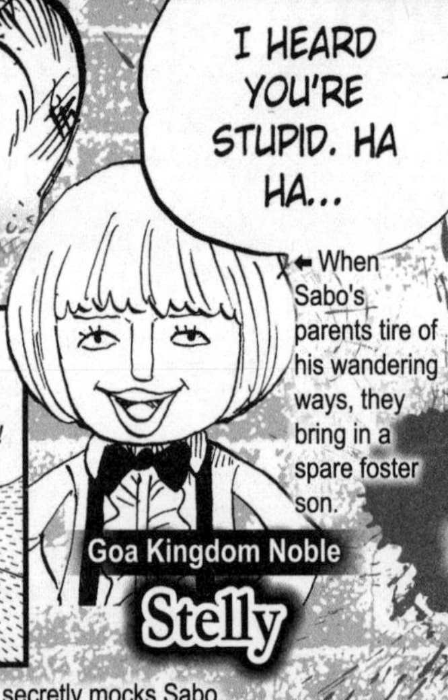
I HEARD YOU'RE STUPID. HA HA...

A **noble** who lives in Luffy's **home-town!!** Sabo's **foster brother!!**

⬅ When Sabo's parents tire of his wandering ways, they bring in a spare foster son.

Goa Kingdom Noble

Stelly

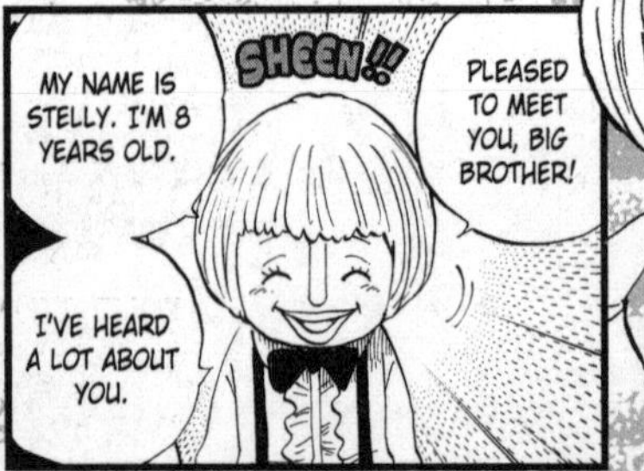
PLEASED TO MEET YOU, BIG BROTHER!
SHEEN!!
MY NAME IS STELLY. I'M 8 YEARS OLD.
I'VE HEARD A LOT ABOUT YOU.

⬆ He's smart and puts on a good face, but secretly mocks Sabo.

Volume 59-60

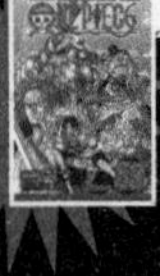

The Three Brothers Background

Garp forces young Luffy to live on Mt. Corvo. In those harsh conditions, he meets Ace and Sabo, and the three come to form a brotherly bond.

Sabaody Background

The crew disembarks at Sabaody Archipelago to prepare for the New World. This is where they witness the cruelty of the Celestial Dragons who possess the world's supreme authority!

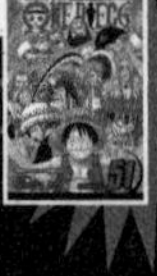

Volume 51-53

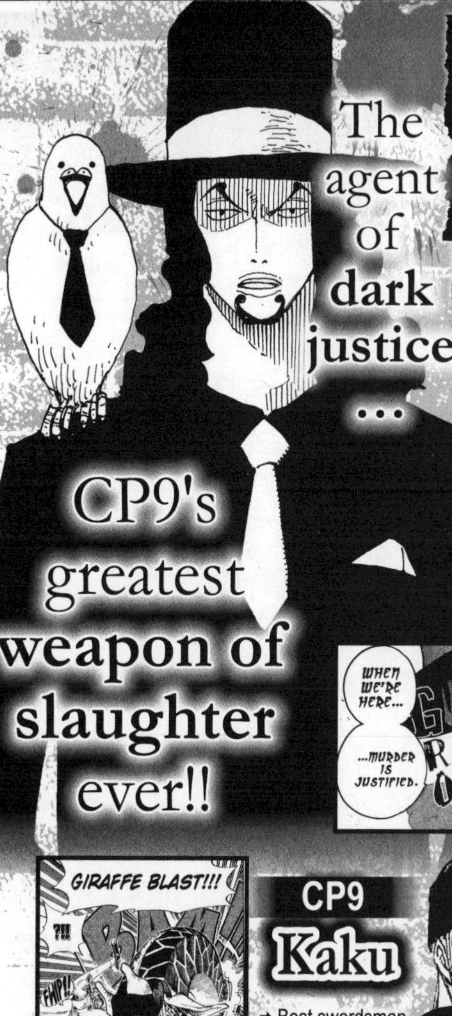

The agent of dark justice...

Reverie Arc
Voyage Record 3
Water Seven

CP9 (World Government Undercover Intelligence Agency, Cipher Pol No. 9)

Rob Lucci

⬆ A cold, unfeeling killer who believes weakness is a sin, and sacrifices whatever is necessary for the sake of his justice!

CP9's greatest weapon of slaughter ever!!

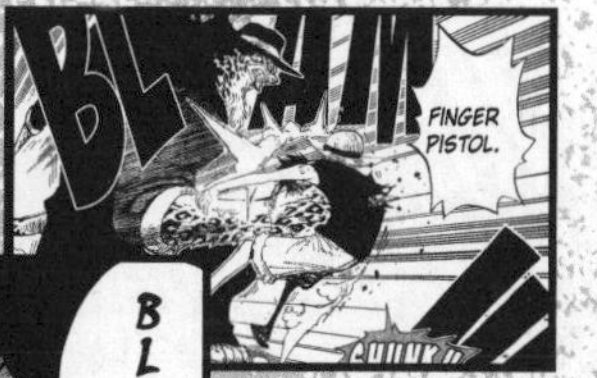
FINGER PISTOL.

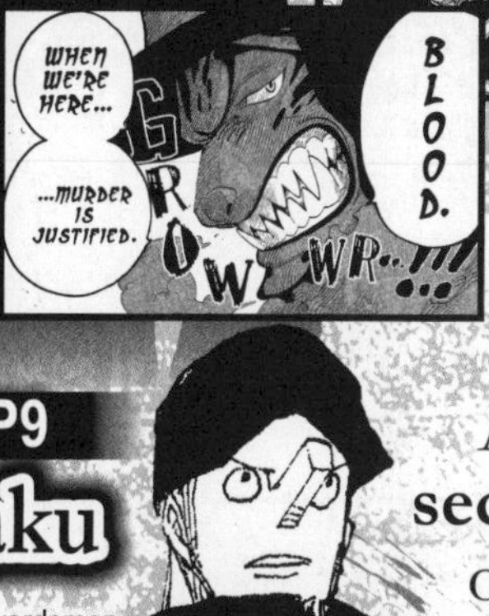
BLOOD.
WHEN WE'RE HERE...
...MURDER IS JUSTIFIED.

⬅⬆ He seeks blood! His loyalty to the World Government's justice is not for loyalty, but so that he can kill!!!

Another **secret agent** on Water Seven!! The wielder of the **Four Sword Style!!**

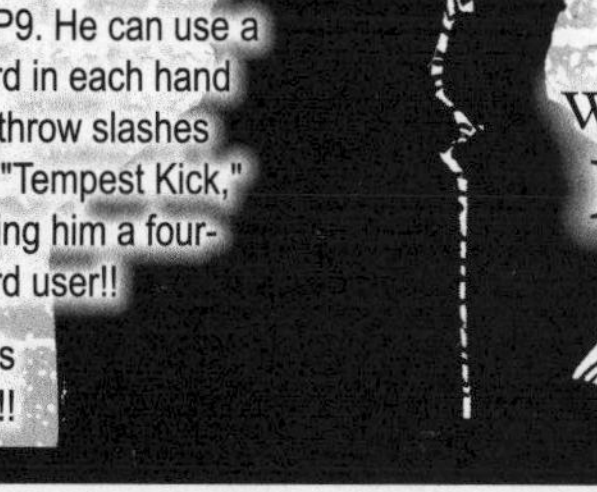

CP9

Kaku

➡ Best swordsman in CP9. He can use a sword in each hand and throw slashes with "Tempest Kick," making him a four-sword user!!

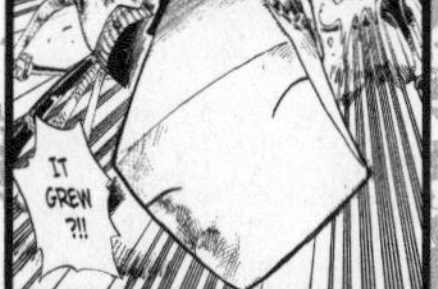
GIRAFFE BLAST!!!
?!!
FWIP!!
IT GREW ?!!

⬆ The Ox-Ox Fruit Giraffe Model is bizarre but holds explosive power!!

Water Seven Background

The Straw Hats try to save Robin from the World Government, but they can't beat CP9 and their mastery of the Six Powers. In order to take back their crewmate, Luffy and his friends will declare war on the World Government!!

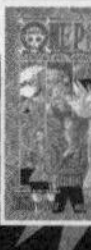

Volume 34-45

Reverie Arc
Voyage Record 4
Drum Kingdom

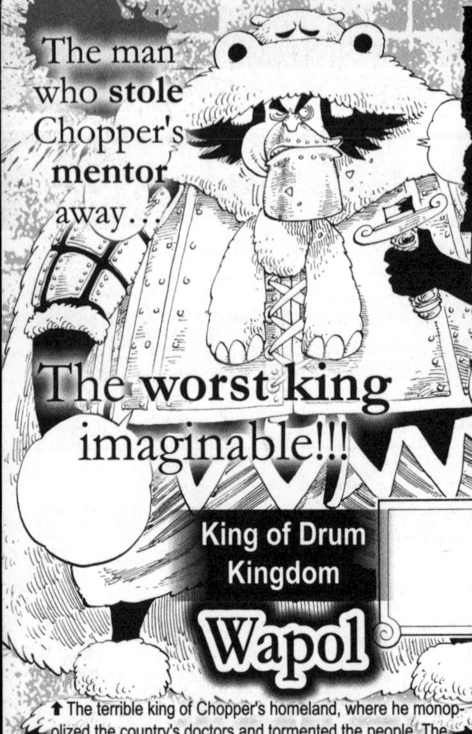

The man who **stole** Chopper's **mentor** away...

The **worst king** imaginable!!!

King of Drum Kingdom

Wapol

⬆ The terrible king of Chopper's homeland, where he monopolized the country's doctors and tormented the people. The very man who set a trap for Dr. Hiriluk, Chopper's mentor.

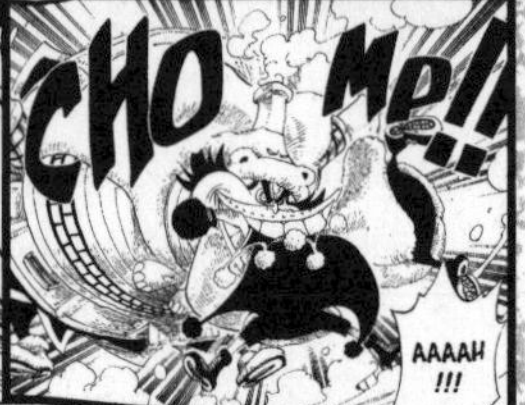

CHOMP!!
AAAAH !!!

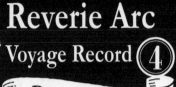

⬅ He uses the Munch-Munch Fruit to incorporate anything he eats into his body!!

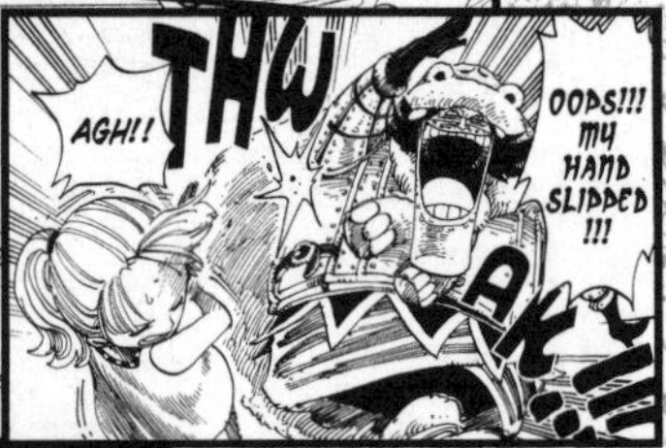

OOPS!!! MY HAND SLIPPED !!!
AGH!!
THWACK!!!

⬆ He also attacked Vivi at a Reverie in the past.

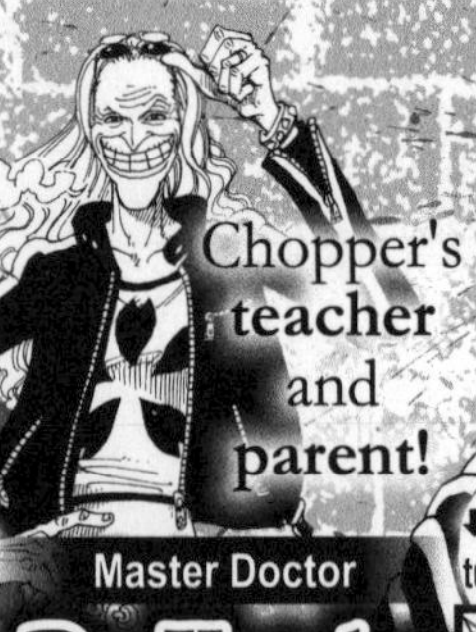

Chopper's **teacher** and **parent**!

The **incredible doctor** also nicknamed a **witch!!**

⬇ She taught him that you cannot save people with kindness alone.

Master Doctor

Dr. Kureha

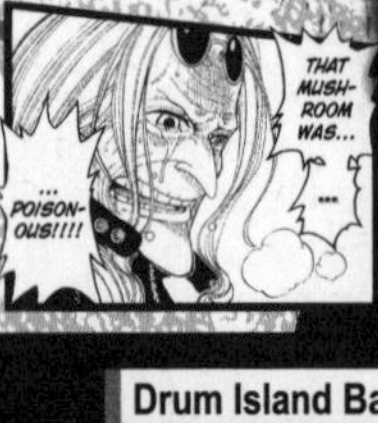

THAT MUSH-ROOM WAS...
...
...POISON-OUS!!!!

⬆ Infamous for charging way too much for medical treatment. But she cured Nami, and her skill is for real.

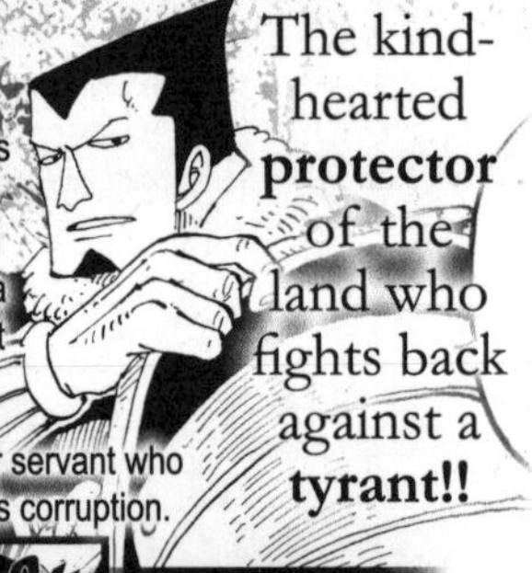

The kind-hearted **protector** of the land who fights back against a **tyrant!!**

➡ Owner of the Ox-Ox Fruit, Bison model. As a servant, he believed Wapol could develop a conscience, but to no avail.

⬇ Wapol's former servant who turned against his corruption.

Drum Island Civilian Guard Leader

Dalton

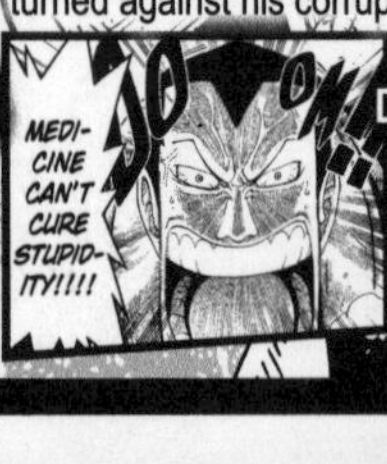

MEDI-CINE CAN'T CURE STUPID-ITY!!!!

Drum Island Background

On the way to Alabasta, Nami comes down with a prehistoric illness. In order to get her cured as soon as possible, the crew's search for a doctor brings them to Drum Kingdom. Unfortunately, Wapol took all the doctors with him and left the country without any medical help!!

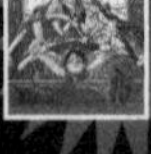

Volume 15-17

Reverie Arc Voyage Record 5

Alabasta

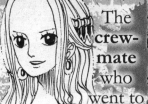

The crewmate who went to sea...

...and became **part of the team** in order to save her **country**!!

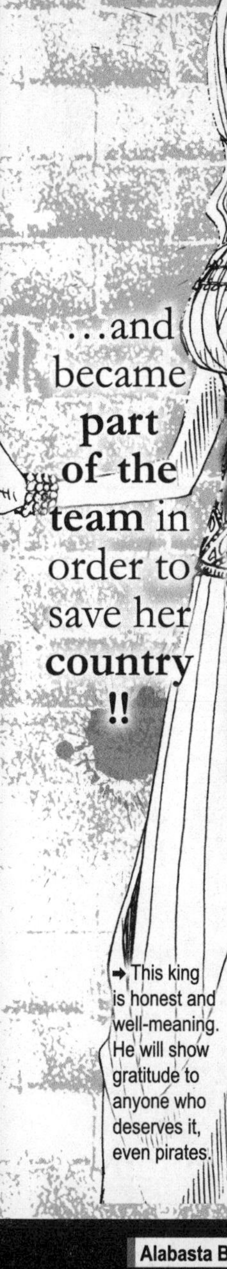

Princess of Alabasta

Nefeltari Vivi

⬆ The princess who infiltrated Baroque Works in order to stop Crocodile's conspiracy! She keeps her experience as a pirate a secret from the public.

➡ A tearful farewell from the Straw Hats!!

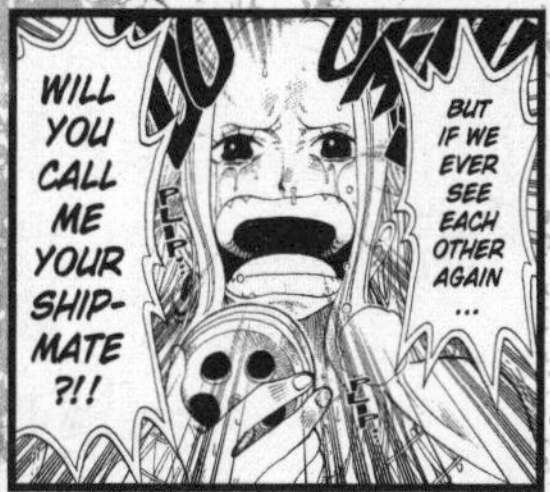
BUT IF WE EVER SEE EACH OTHER AGAIN ...
WILL YOU CALL ME YOUR SHIP-MATE ?!!
PLIP
PLIP

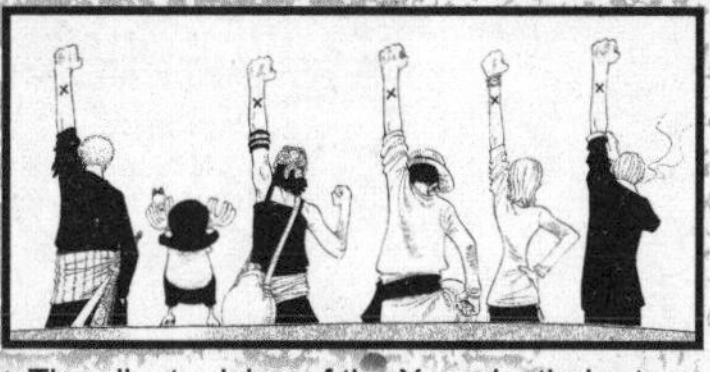

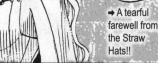

⬆ The silent raising of the X marks their eternal connection!

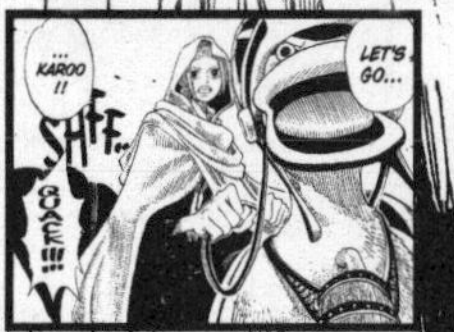
LET'S GO...
... KAROO !!
SHFF..
QUACK!!!

⬆ Vivi's partner Karoo. He's a supersonic duck with incredible speed!

The **wise ruler** who loves his **country** and **people**...

...and **guards** the secret of the **ancient weapon**!!

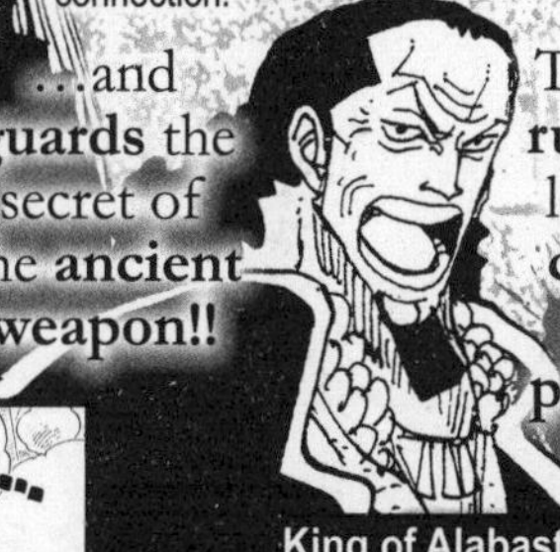

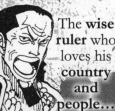

➡ This king is honest and well-meaning. He will show gratitude to anyone who deserves it, even pirates.

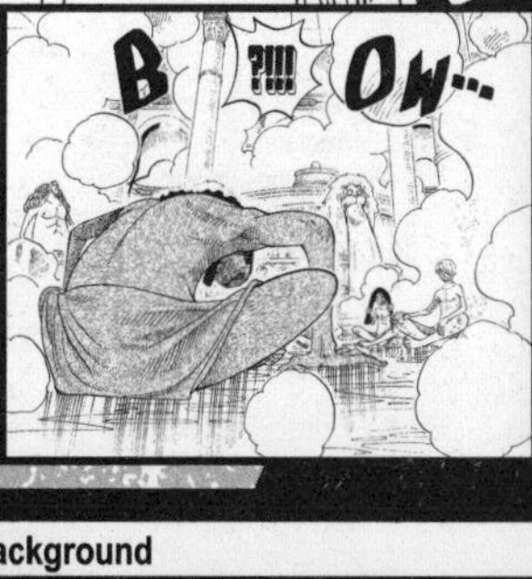
B
?!!!
OW...

King of Alabasta

Nefeltari Cobra

⬆ Vivi's father. He is concerned about the conversation he had with Robin in front of the Ponegliff, and is suspicious of the World Government.

Alabasta Background

In his search for military power, Crocodile set his sights on the ancient weapon Pluton, which slumbers in Alabasta. Vivi detects his plot in motion, but despairs at her lack of strength to stop him. Then the Straw Hat Crew pledges to help take down Crocodile!!

Volume 18-23

Reverie Arc

Voyage Record 6

Fish-man Island

She seeks to live under the **"Sun"** to honor the **wishes** of her **late mother!**

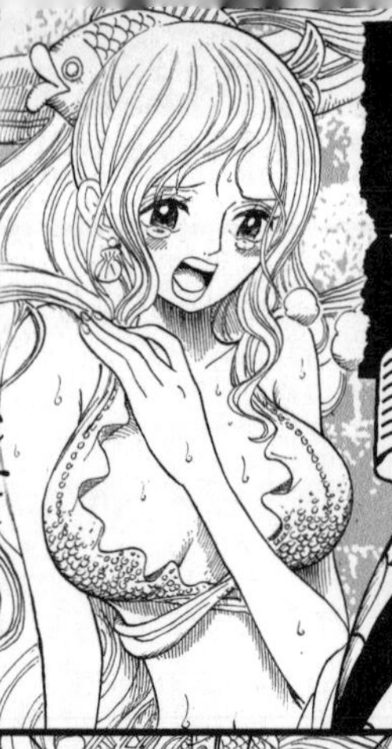

Princess of Ryugu Kingdom

Shirahoshi

A giant smelt mermaid, daughter of Neptune. She's quick to tears, but grows quickly after meeting Luffy. Now she's coming to the surface for the Reverie!!

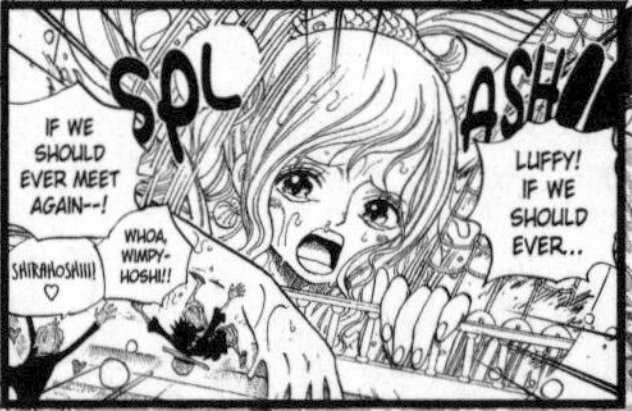
SPLASH!
IF WE SHOULD EVER MEET AGAIN--!
LUFFY! IF WE SHOULD EVER...
WHOA, WIMPY-HOSHI!!
SHIRAHOSHI!!! ♡

⬆ After Luffy saved Fish-man Island, she made a promise with him to go on a walk in a forest when they reunite.

Fish-man Island's **benevolent leader**...

...who seeks **amity** between human and fish-man!!

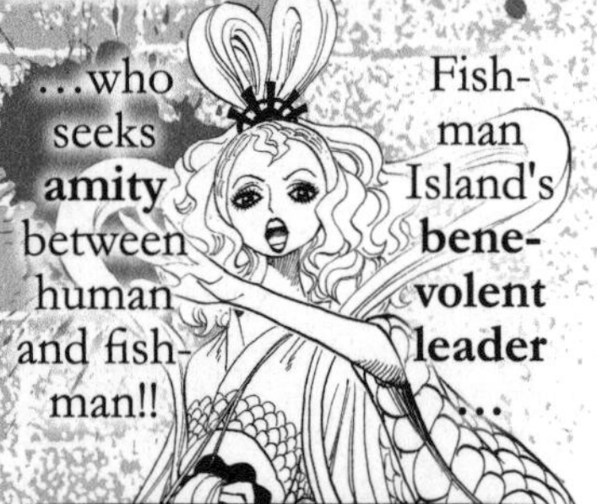

Late Queen of Ryugu Kingdom

Otohime

Shirahoshi's mother, who risked her life seeking understanding with humankind. She was felled by an assassin before her wish could come true.

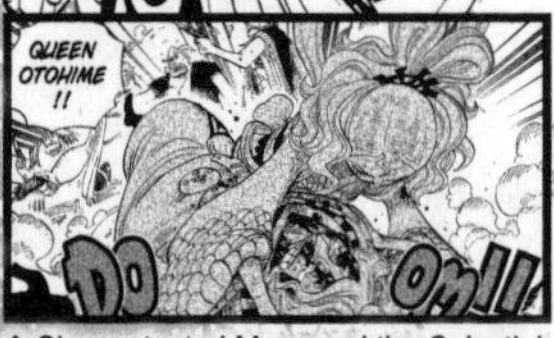
QUEEN OTOHIME !!
DOOM!!

⬆ She protected Myosgard the Celestial Dragon with her own body when his abused slaves struck back.

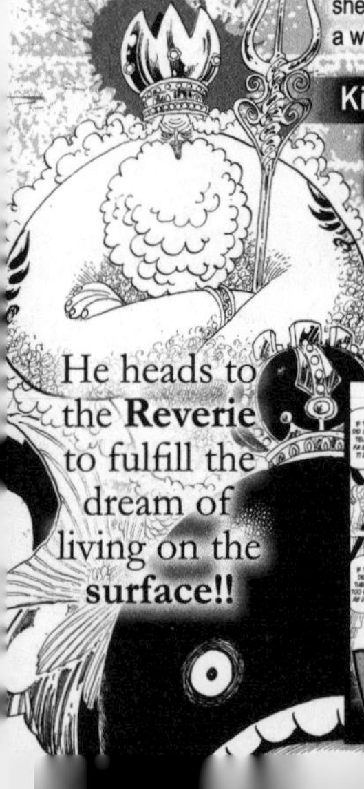

King of Ryugu Kingdom

Neptune

King of Fish-man Island. He's attending the Reverie to bring about the dream of his late wife: a world in which fish-men can live under the sun.

He heads to the **Reverie** to fulfill the dream of living on the **surface!!**

⬅ Neptune's three sons are going along to protect their sister Shirahoshi!!

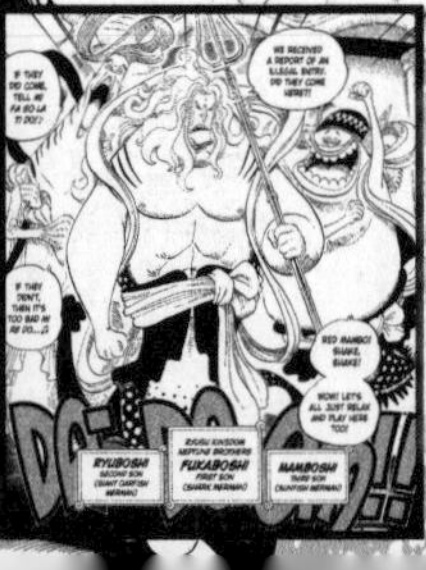
RYUBOSHI
FUKABOSHI

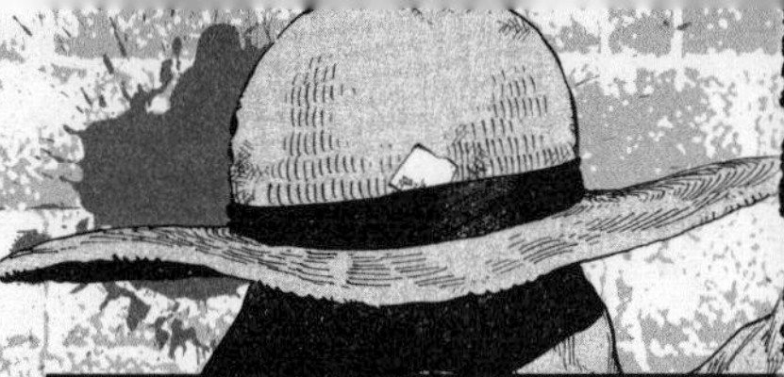

Reverie Arc

Voyage Record 7

The Straw Hat's Travels

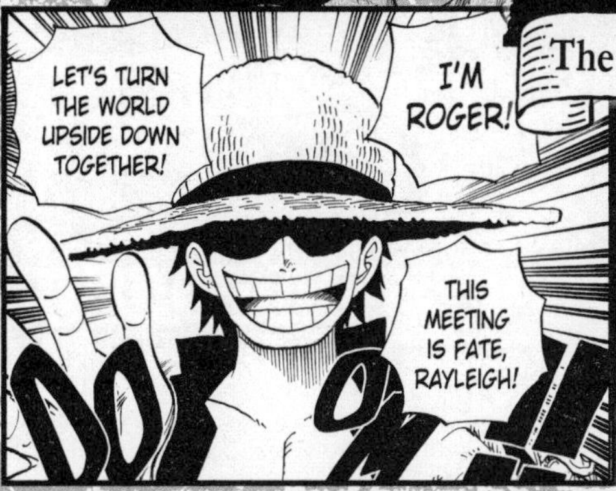

I'M ROGER!
LET'S TURN THE WORLD UPSIDE DOWN TOGETHER!
THIS MEETING IS FATE, RAYLEIGH!

King of the Pirates

Gol D. Roger

⬅ At the time that the King of the Pirates Roger met his right-hand man, Rayleigh, he was wearing a simple straw hat.

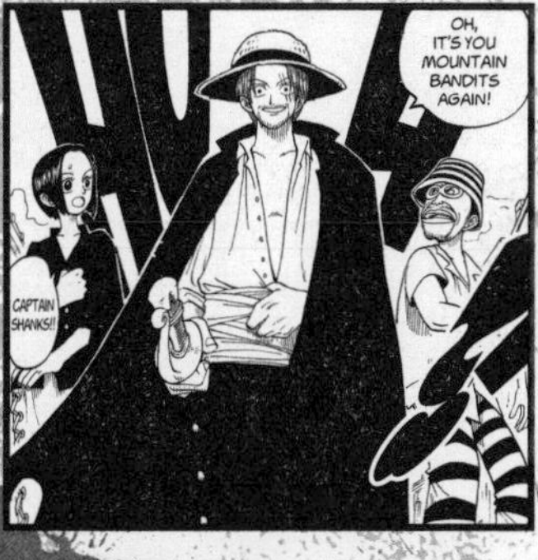

OH, IT'S YOU MOUNTAIN BANDITS AGAIN!
CAPTAIN SHANKS!!

⬅ Shanks wore the straw hat ever since he was a cabin boy on Roger's ship.

Emperor of the Sea

Shanks

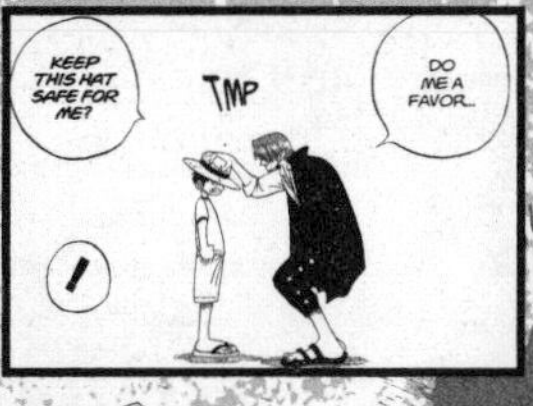

DO ME A FAVOR...
KEEP THIS HAT SAFE FOR ME?
TMP

➡ In Windmill Village in the East Blue, Shanks passed down his straw hat to the next generation, a boy named Luffy!!

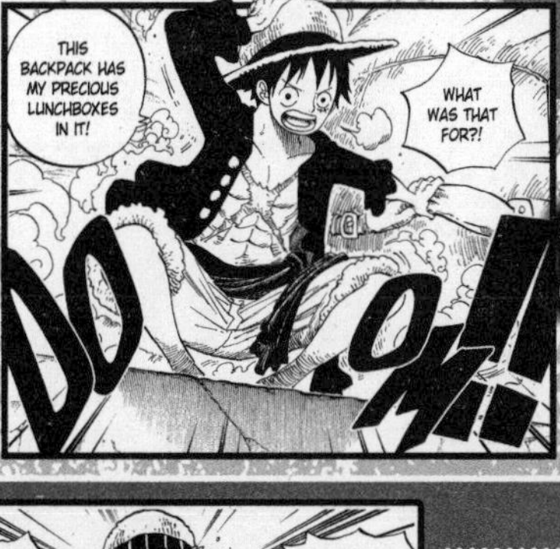

WHAT WAS THAT FOR?!
THIS BACKPACK HAS MY PRECIOUS LUNCHBOXES IN IT!

And now...

Worst Generation

Monkey D. Luffy

⬅ Luffy never lets the straw hat Shanks gave him leave his side. Now his pirate moniker is "Straw Hat"!! The hat has become Luffy's trademark.

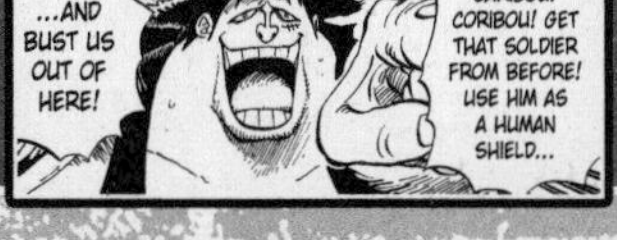

CARIBOU! CORIBOU! GET THAT SOLDIER FROM BEFORE! USE HIM AS A HUMAN SHIELD...
...AND BUST US OUT OF HERE!

A Straw Hat Pirate Side Story...?

There's another pirates who's worn a straw hat aside from these three. He's Demaro Black, aka. Fake Luffy. He fooled many pirates and navy sailors, and it seems that the straw hat was doing most of the heavy lifting!

Chapter 905:
WHAT A BEAUTIFUL WORLD

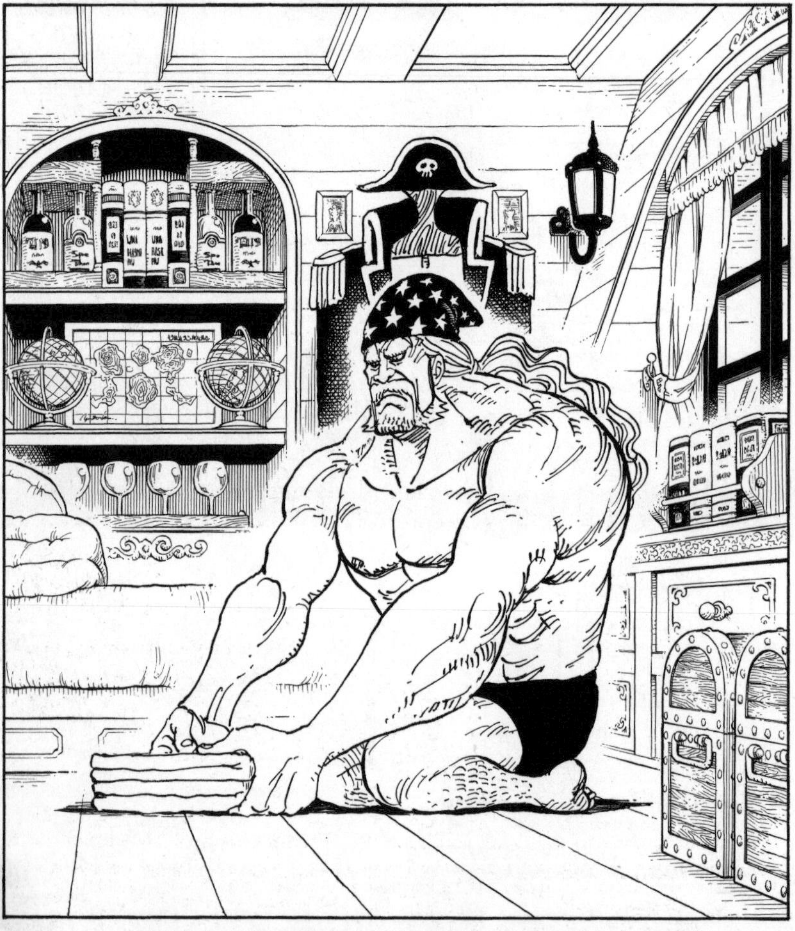

THE SAGA OF THE SELF-PROCLAIMED STRAW HAT FLEET, VOL. 35, ORLUMBUS: "THE PIRATE LIFE, 6:00 A.M.: FOLDING PAJAMAS"

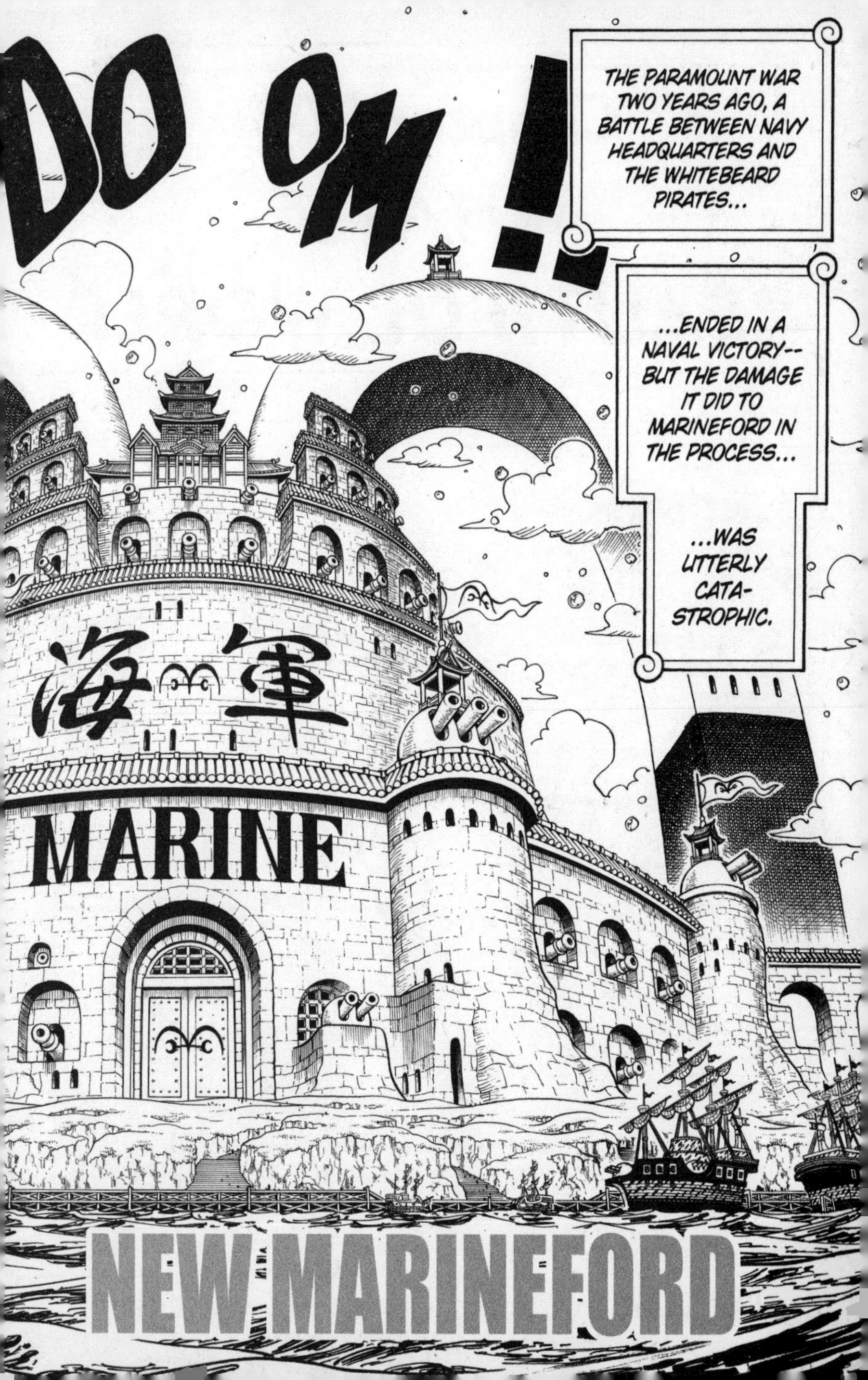
THE PARAMOUNT WAR TWO YEARS AGO, A BATTLE BETWEEN NAVY HEADQUARTERS AND THE WHITEBEARD PIRATES...
DO OM!!
...ENDED IN A NAVAL VICTORY--BUT THE DAMAGE IT DID TO MARINEFORD IN THE PROCESS...
...WAS UTTERLY CATA-STROPHIC.
海軍
MARINE
NEW MARINEFORD

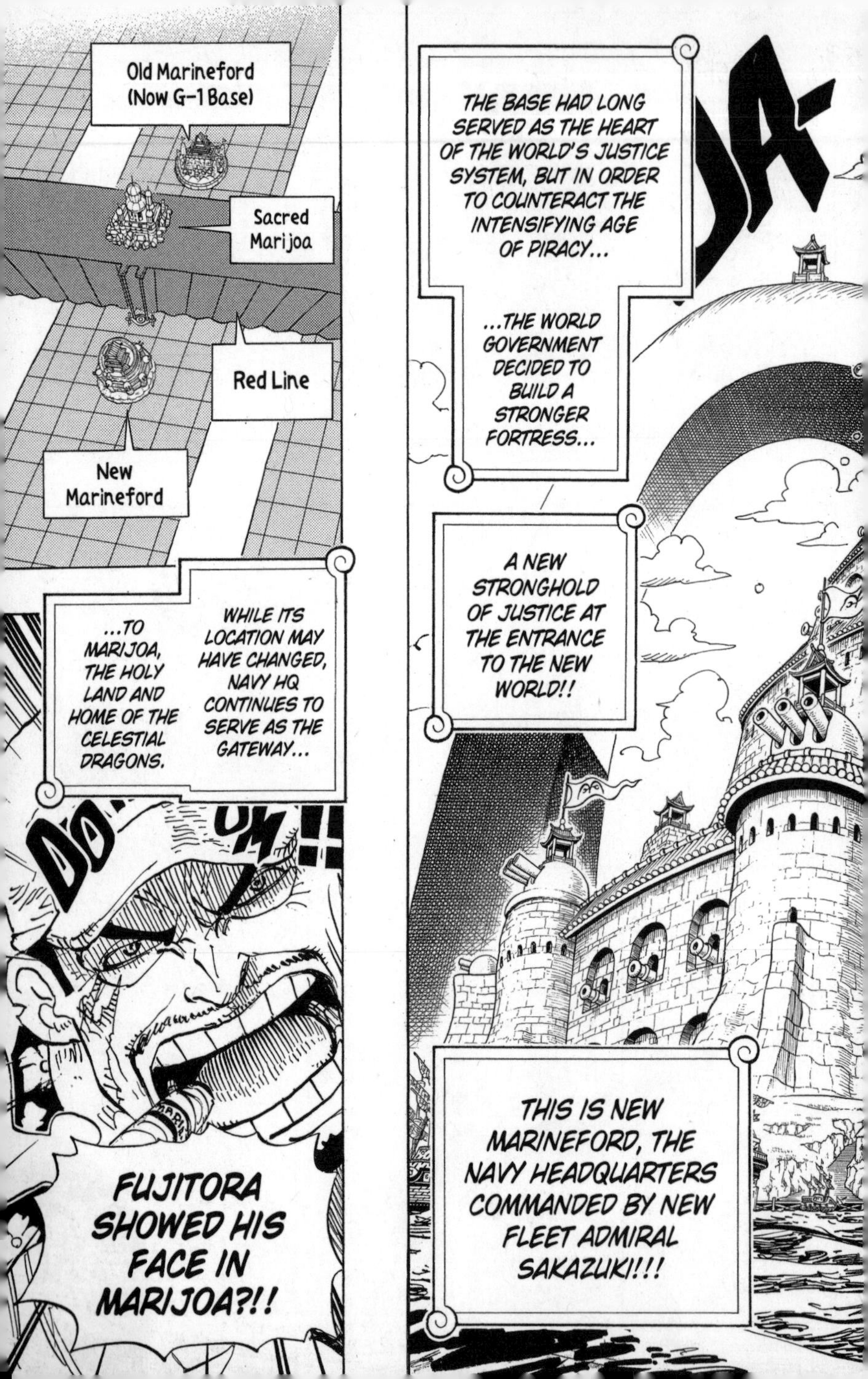
DA-
THE BASE HAD LONG SERVED AS THE HEART OF THE WORLD'S JUSTICE SYSTEM, BUT IN ORDER TO COUNTERACT THE INTENSIFYING AGE OF PIRACY...
...THE WORLD GOVERNMENT DECIDED TO BUILD A STRONGER FORTRESS...
A NEW STRONGHOLD OF JUSTICE AT THE ENTRANCE TO THE NEW WORLD!!
THIS IS NEW MARINEFORD, THE NAVY HEADQUARTERS COMMANDED BY NEW FLEET ADMIRAL SAKAZUKI!!!
Old Marineford (Now G-1 Base)
Sacred Marijoa
Red Line
New Marineford
WHILE ITS LOCATION MAY HAVE CHANGED, NAVY HQ CONTINUES TO SERVE AS THE GATEWAY...
...TO MARIJOA, THE HOLY LAND AND HOME OF THE CELESTIAL DRAGONS.
DO
UM!!
FUJITORA SHOWED HIS FACE IN MARIJOA?!!

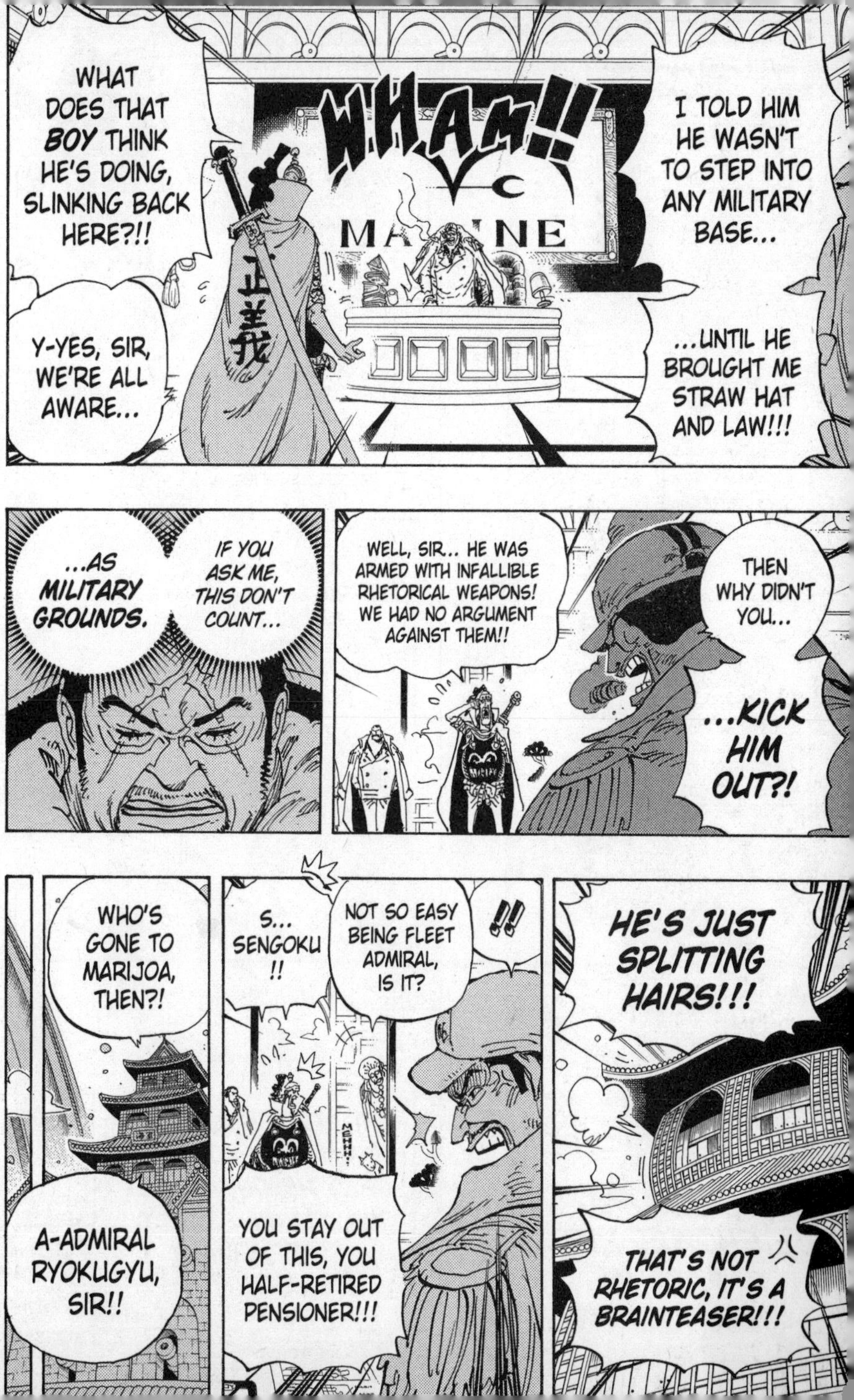
WHAM!!
WHAT DOES THAT BOY THINK HE'S DOING, SLINKING BACK HERE?!!
I TOLD HIM HE WASN'T TO STEP INTO ANY MILITARY BASE...
...UNTIL HE BROUGHT ME STRAW HAT AND LAW!!!
Y-YES, SIR, WE'RE ALL AWARE...
THEN WHY DIDN'T YOU...
...KICK HIM OUT?!
WELL, SIR... HE WAS ARMED WITH INFALLIBLE RHETORICAL WEAPONS! WE HAD NO ARGUMENT AGAINST THEM!!
IF YOU ASK ME, THIS DON'T COUNT...
...AS MILITARY GROUNDS.
HE'S JUST SPLITTING HAIRS!!!
THAT'S NOT RHETORIC, IT'S A BRAINTEASER!!!
!!
NOT SO EASY BEING FLEET ADMIRAL, IS IT?
S... SENGOKU!!
YOU STAY OUT OF THIS, YOU HALF-RETIRED PENSIONER!!!
MEHHH
WHO'S GONE TO MARIJOA, THEN?!
A-ADMIRAL RYOKUGYU, SIR!!

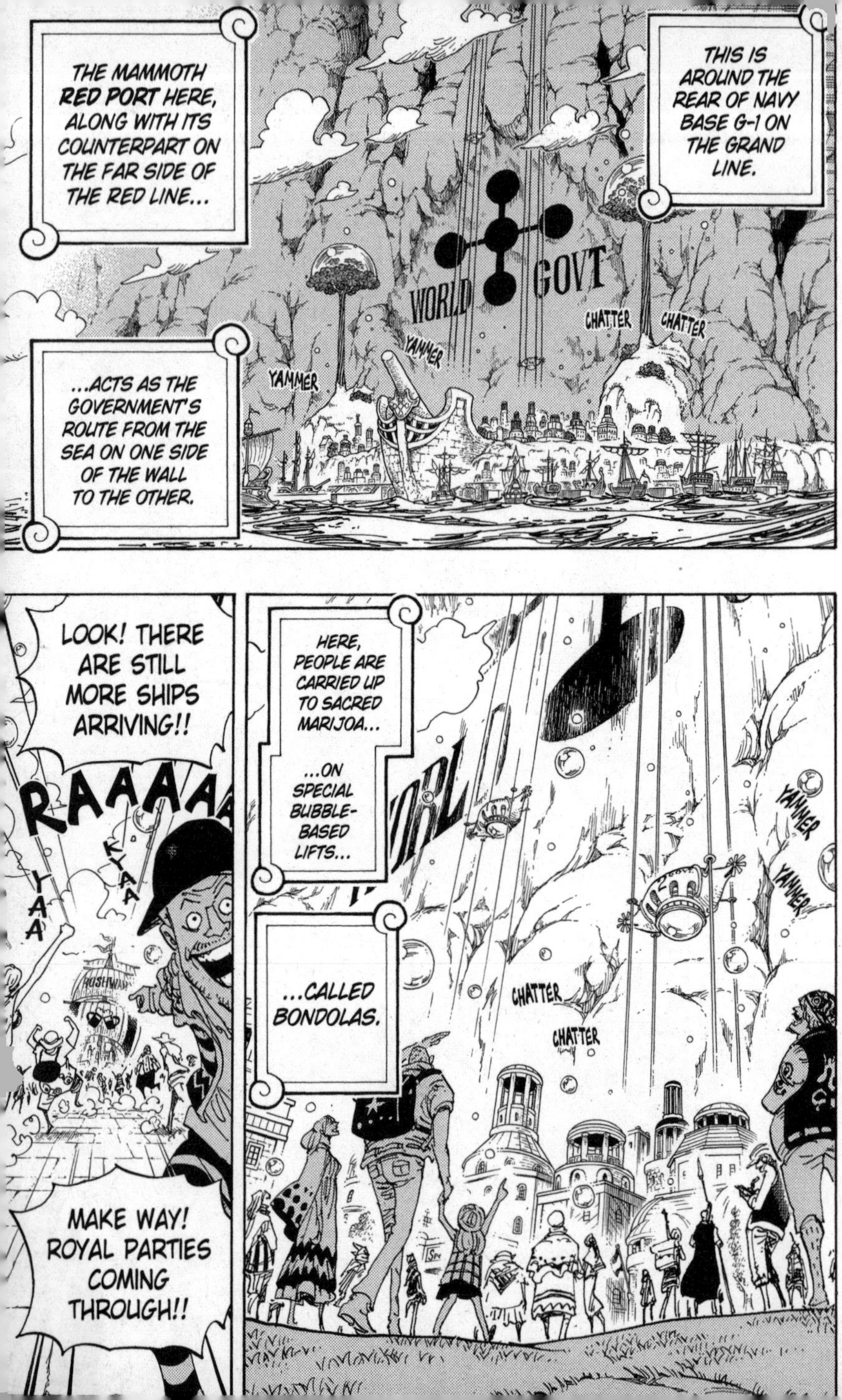
THIS IS AROUND THE REAR OF NAVY BASE G-1 ON THE GRAND LINE.
THE MAMMOTH **RED PORT** HERE, ALONG WITH ITS COUNTERPART ON THE FAR SIDE OF THE RED LINE...
WORLD GOVT
CHATTER
CHATTER
YAMMER
YAMMER
...ACTS AS THE GOVERNMENT'S ROUTE FROM THE SEA ON ONE SIDE OF THE WALL TO THE OTHER.
YAMMER
YAMMER
HERE, PEOPLE ARE CARRIED UP TO SACRED MARIJOA...
...ON SPECIAL BUBBLE-BASED LIFTS...
...CALLED BONDOLAS.
CHATTER
CHATTER
LOOK! THERE ARE STILL MORE SHIPS ARRIVING!!
RAAAAA
KYAA
YAA
MAKE WAY! ROYAL PARTIES COMING THROUGH!!

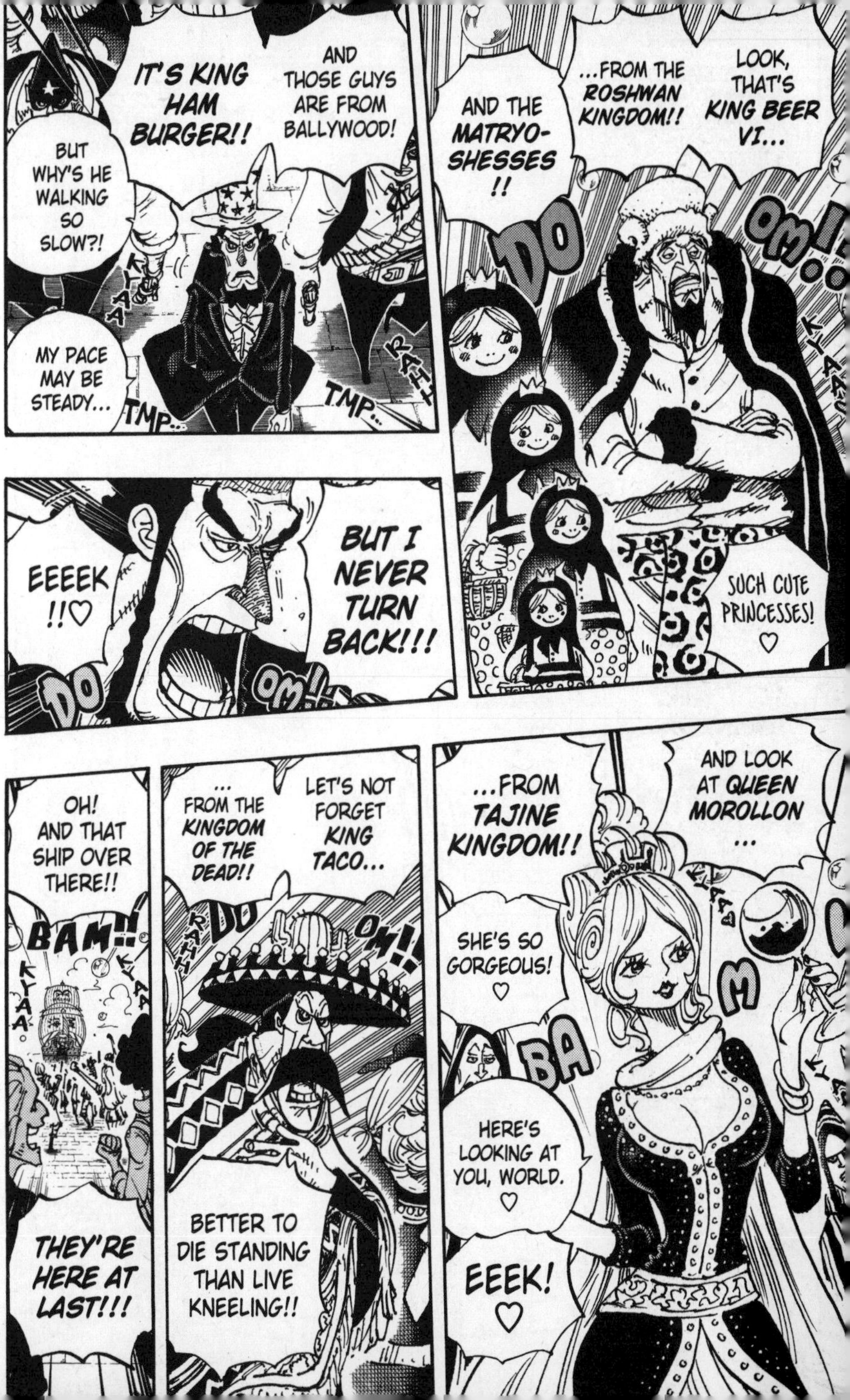
LOOK, THAT'S KING BEER VI...
...FROM THE ROSHWAN KINGDOM!!
AND THE MATRYOSHESSES!!
DOOM!!
KYAA
SUCH CUTE PRINCESSES! ♡
AND THOSE GUYS ARE FROM BALLYWOOD!
IT'S KING HAM BURGER!!
BUT WHY'S HE WALKING SO SLOW?!
KYAA
RAHH
MY PACE MAY BE STEADY...
TMP..
TMP..
BUT I NEVER TURN BACK!!!
EEEEK!!♡
DOOM!!
AND LOOK AT QUEEN MOROLLON...
...FROM TAJINE KINGDOM!!
KYAA
SHE'S SO GORGEOUS! ♡
BAM
KYAA
HERE'S LOOKING AT YOU, WORLD. ♡
EEEK! ♡
LET'S NOT FORGET KING TACO...
...FROM THE KINGDOM OF THE DEAD!!
RAHH
DOOM!!
BETTER TO DIE STANDING THAN LIVE KNEELING!!
OH! AND THAT SHIP OVER THERE!!
BAM!!
KYAA
KYAA
THEY'RE HERE AT LAST!!!

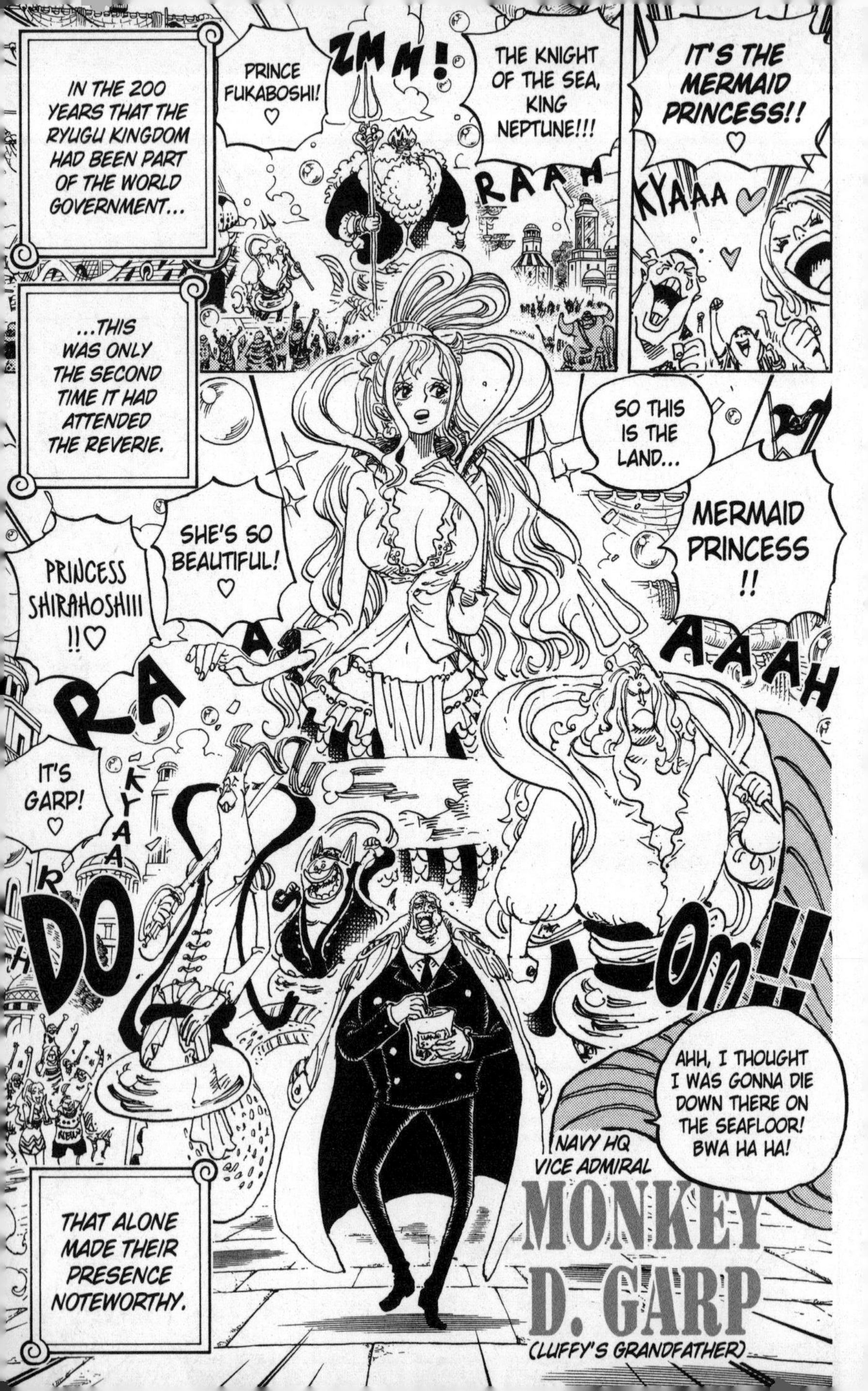
IT'S THE MERMAID PRINCESS!! ♡
KYAAA
THE KNIGHT OF THE SEA, KING NEPTUNE!!!
ZMM!
PRINCE FUKABOSHI! ♡
RAAH
IN THE 200 YEARS THAT THE RYUGU KINGDOM HAD BEEN PART OF THE WORLD GOVERNMENT...
...THIS WAS ONLY THE SECOND TIME IT HAD ATTENDED THE REVERIE.
SO THIS IS THE LAND...
MERMAID PRINCESS!!
AAAH
SHE'S SO BEAUTIFUL! ♡
PRINCESS SHIRAHOSHIII!! ♡
RAA
IT'S GARP! ♡
KYAAA
DOOM!!
AHH, I THOUGHT I WAS GONNA DIE DOWN THERE ON THE SEAFLOOR! BWA HA HA!
NAVY HQ VICE ADMIRAL
MONKEY D. GARP
(LUFFY'S GRANDFATHER)
THAT ALONE MADE THEIR PRESENCE NOTEWORTHY.

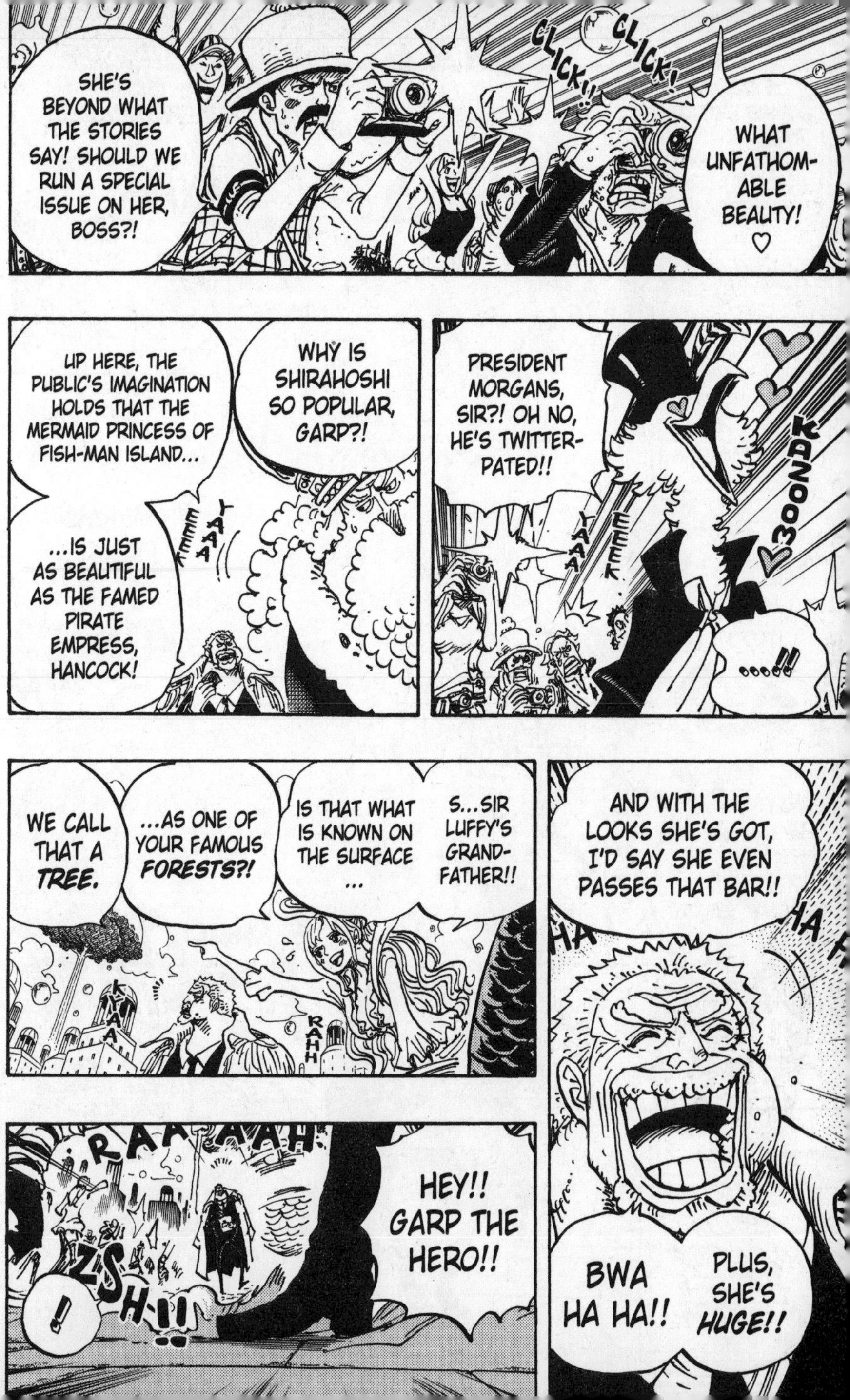
WHAT UNFATHOMABLE BEAUTY! ♡
CLICK!
CLICK!!
SHE'S BEYOND WHAT THE STORIES SAY! SHOULD WE RUN A SPECIAL ISSUE ON HER, BOSS?!
PRESIDENT MORGANS, SIR?! OH NO, HE'S TWITTER-PATED!!
KDOOOM
YAAA
EEEK
...!!
WHY IS SHIRAHOSHI SO POPULAR, GARP?!
UP HERE, THE PUBLIC'S IMAGINATION HOLDS THAT THE MERMAID PRINCESS OF FISH-MAN ISLAND...
...IS JUST AS BEAUTIFUL AS THE FAMED PIRATE EMPRESS, HANCOCK!
YAAA
EEEK
AND WITH THE LOOKS SHE'S GOT, I'D SAY SHE EVEN PASSES THAT BAR!!
HA
HA
PLUS, SHE'S HUGE!!
BWA HA HA!!
S...SIR LUFFY'S GRAND-FATHER!!
IS THAT WHAT IS KNOWN ON THE SURFACE ...
...AS ONE OF YOUR FAMOUS FORESTS?!
WE CALL THAT A TREE.
KYAAA
RAHH
HEY!! GARP THE HERO!!
RAAAAAH
ZSH!!
!

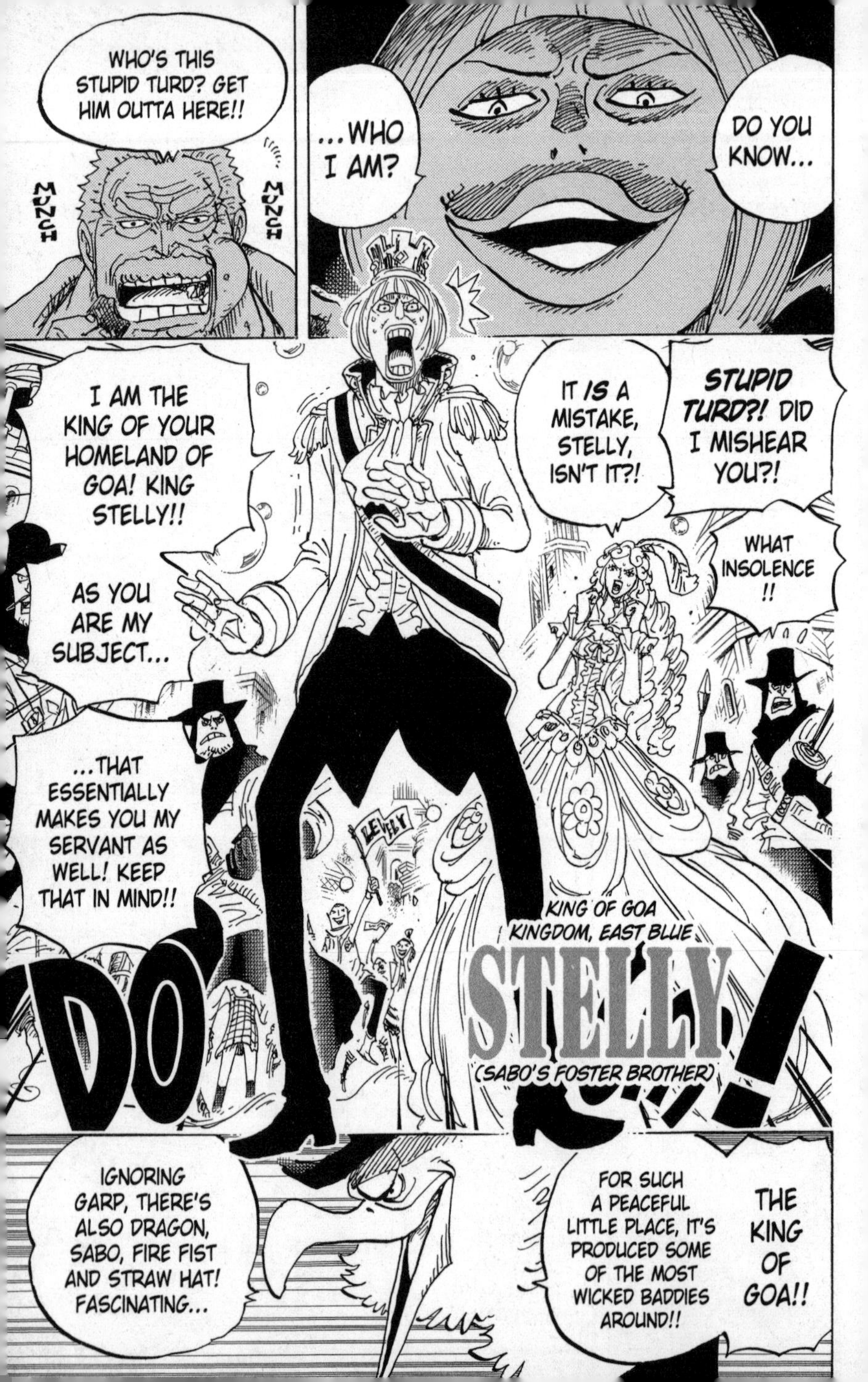
DO YOU KNOW...
...WHO I AM?
WHO'S THIS STUPID TURD? GET HIM OUTTA HERE!!
MUNCH
MUNCH
STUPID TURD?! DID I MISHEAR YOU?!
IT IS A MISTAKE, STELLY, ISN'T IT?!
WHAT INSOLENCE!!
I AM THE KING OF YOUR HOMELAND OF GOA! KING STELLY!!
AS YOU ARE MY SUBJECT...
...THAT ESSENTIALLY MAKES YOU MY SERVANT AS WELL! KEEP THAT IN MIND!!
KING OF GOA KINGDOM, EAST BLUE
STELLY
(SABO'S FOSTER BROTHER)
DO-!
THE KING OF GOA!!
FOR SUCH A PEACEFUL LITTLE PLACE, IT'S PRODUCED SOME OF THE MOST WICKED BADDIES AROUND!!
IGNORING GARP, THERE'S ALSO DRAGON, SABO, FIRE FIST AND STRAW HAT! FASCINATING...

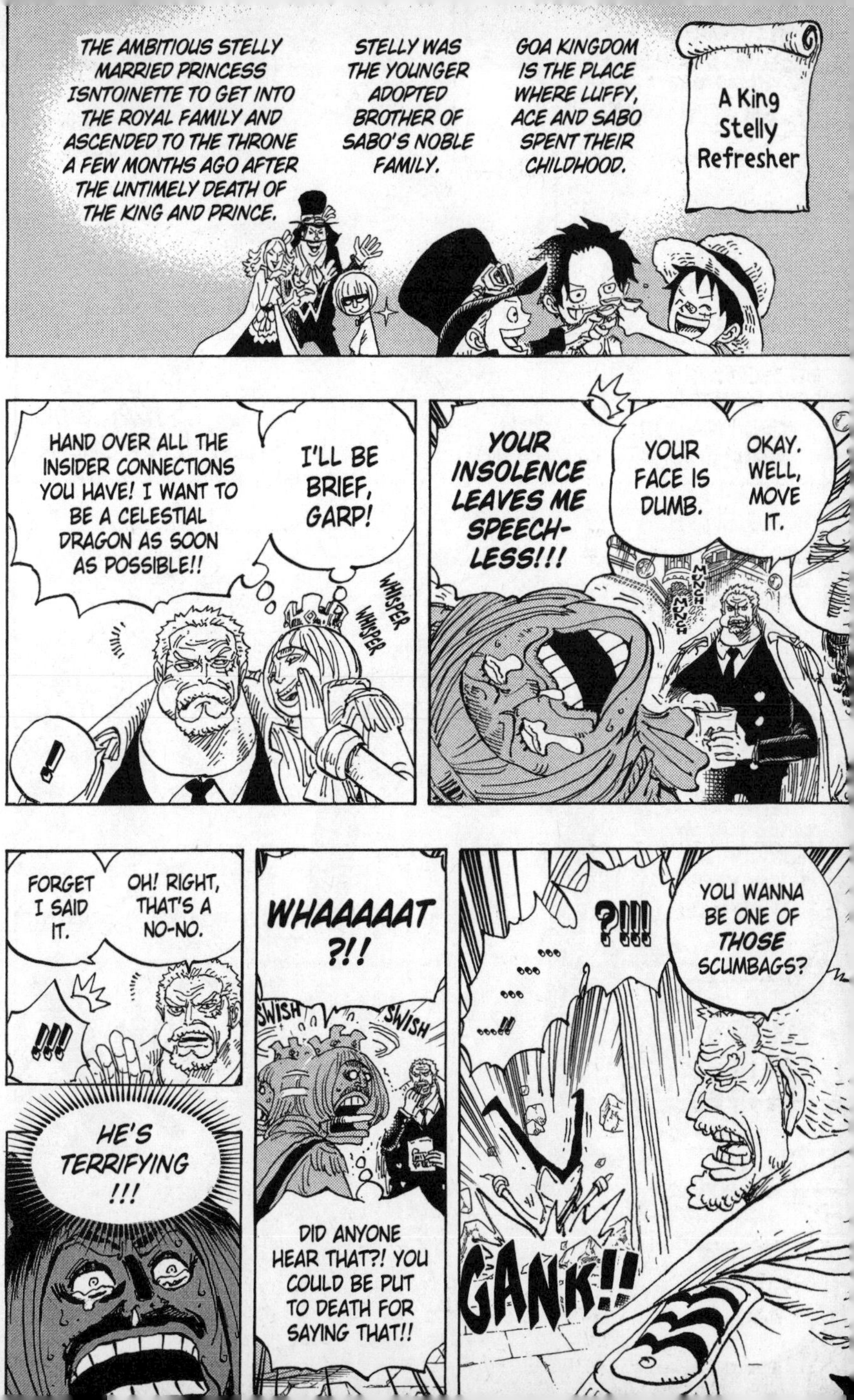
A King Stelly Refresher
GOA KINGDOM IS THE PLACE WHERE LUFFY, ACE AND SABO SPENT THEIR CHILDHOOD.
STELLY WAS THE YOUNGER ADOPTED BROTHER OF SABO'S NOBLE FAMILY.
THE AMBITIOUS STELLY MARRIED PRINCESS ISNTOINETTE TO GET INTO THE ROYAL FAMILY AND ASCENDED TO THE THRONE A FEW MONTHS AGO AFTER THE UNTIMELY DEATH OF THE KING AND PRINCE.
OKAY. WELL, MOVE IT.
YOUR FACE IS DUMB.
YOUR INSOLENCE LEAVES ME SPEECH-LESS!!!
MUNCH
MUNCH
I'LL BE BRIEF, GARP!
HAND OVER ALL THE INSIDER CONNECTIONS YOU HAVE! I WANT TO BE A CELESTIAL DRAGON AS SOON AS POSSIBLE!!
WHISPER
WHISPER
!
YOU WANNA BE ONE OF THOSE SCUMBAGS?
?!!!
...
...
...
...!!
GANK!!
WHAAAAAT?!!
SWISH
SWISH
DID ANYONE HEAR THAT?! YOU COULD BE PUT TO DEATH FOR SAYING THAT!!
OH! RIGHT, THAT'S A NO-NO.
FORGET I SAID IT.
!!!
HE'S TERRIFYING!!!

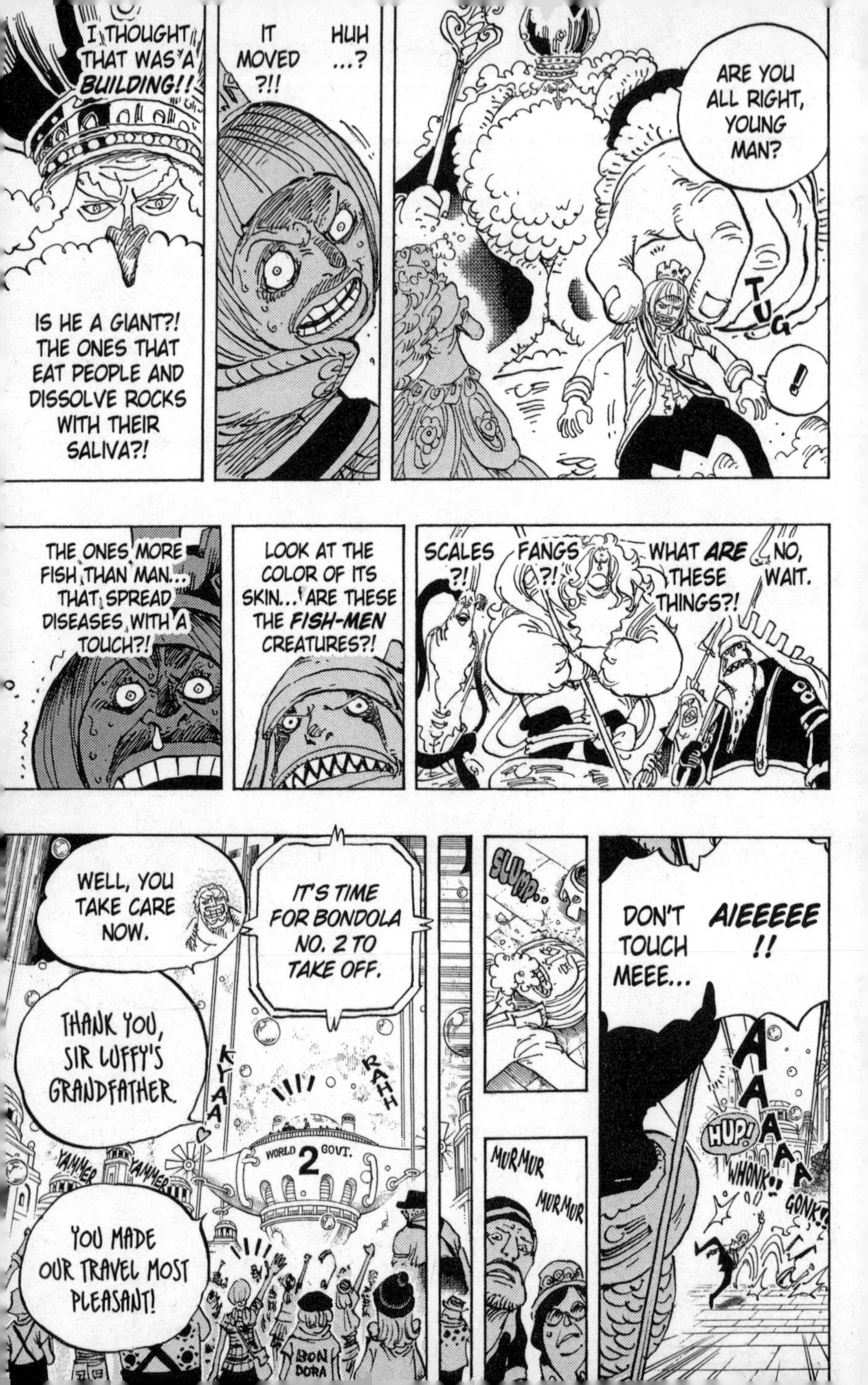
ARE YOU ALL RIGHT, YOUNG MAN?
TUG
!
HUH ...?
IT MOVED ?!!
I THOUGHT THAT WAS A BUILDING!!
IS HE A GIANT?! THE ONES THAT EAT PEOPLE AND DISSOLVE ROCKS WITH THEIR SALIVA?!
NO, WAIT.
WHAT ARE THESE THINGS?!
FANGS ?!
SCALES ?!
LOOK AT THE COLOR OF ITS SKIN... ARE THESE THE FISH-MEN CREATURES?!
THE ONES MORE FISH THAN MAN... THAT SPREAD DISEASES WITH A TOUCH?!
AIEEEEE !!
DON'T TOUCH MEEE...
AAAAAA
HUP!
WHONK!!
GONK!!
SLUMP..
MURMUR
MURMUR
IT'S TIME FOR BONDOLA NO. 2 TO TAKE OFF.
WELL, YOU TAKE CARE NOW.
THANK YOU, SIR LUFFY'S GRANDFATHER.
KYAA
RAHH
WORLD GOVT.
2
YAMMER
YAMMER
YOU MADE OUR TRAVEL MOST PLEASANT!
BON DORA

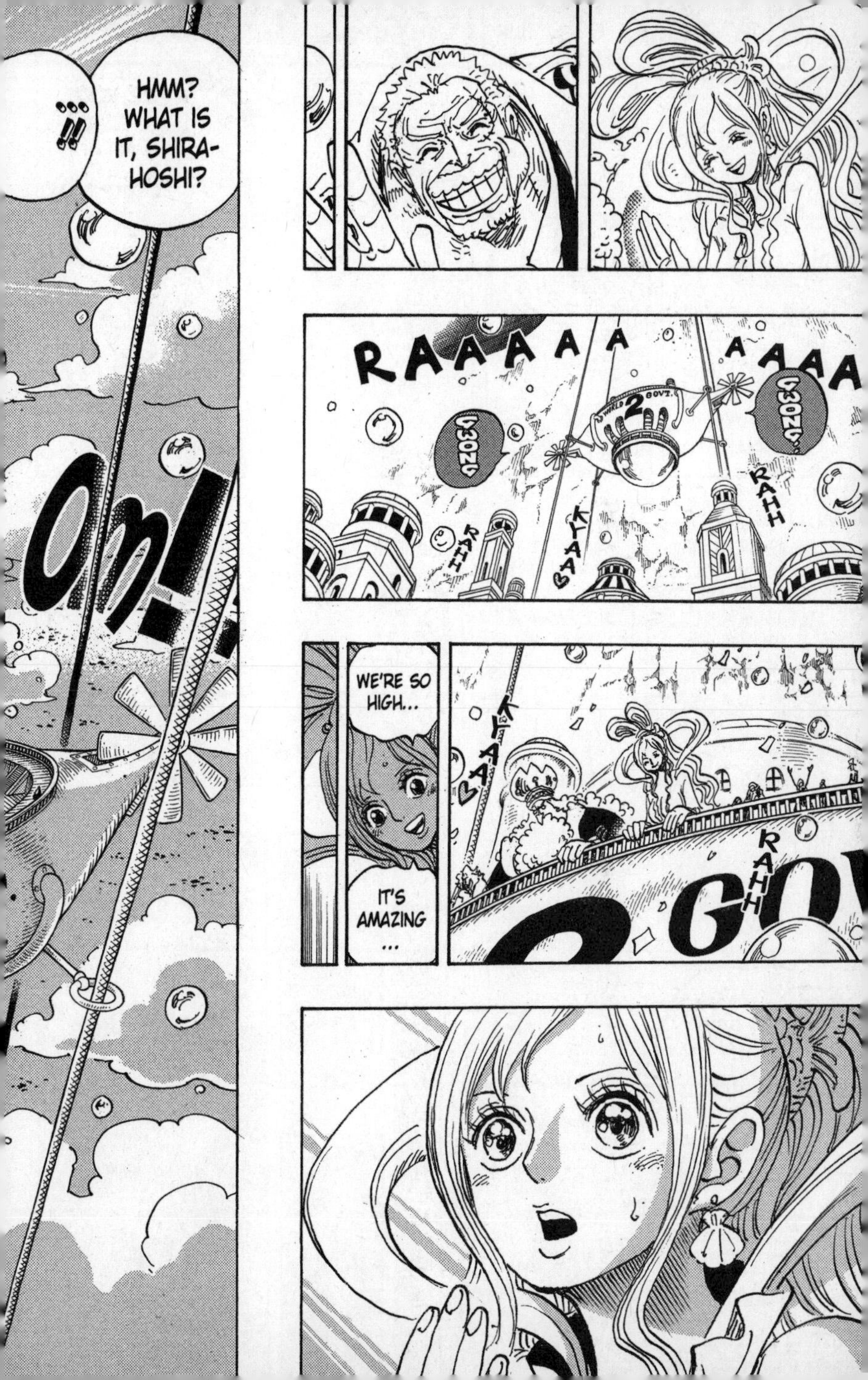
RAAAAAA AAAA
GWONG
RAHH
KYAA
GWONG
RAHH
KYAA
RAHH
WE'RE SO HIGH...
IT'S AMAZING...
HMM? WHAT IS IT, SHIRA-HOSHI?
...!!
OH!!

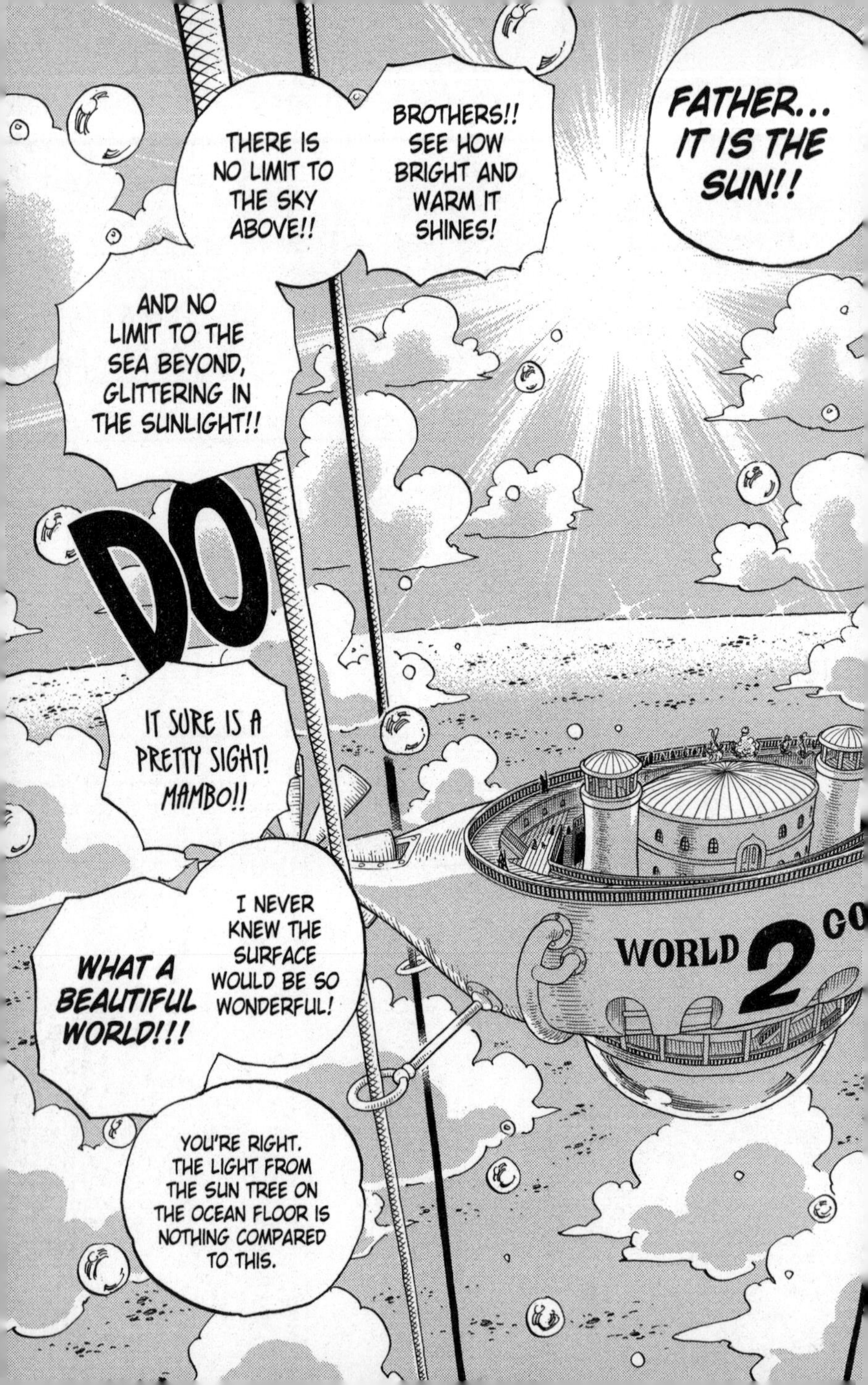
FATHER... IT IS THE SUN!!
BROTHERS!! SEE HOW BRIGHT AND WARM IT SHINES!
THERE IS NO LIMIT TO THE SKY ABOVE!!
AND NO LIMIT TO THE SEA BEYOND, GLITTERING IN THE SUNLIGHT!!
DO
IT SURE IS A PRETTY SIGHT! MAMBO!!
WORLD 2
I NEVER KNEW THE SURFACE WOULD BE SO WONDERFUL!
WHAT A BEAUTIFUL WORLD!!!
YOU'RE RIGHT. THE LIGHT FROM THE SUN TREE ON THE OCEAN FLOOR IS NOTHING COMPARED TO THIS.

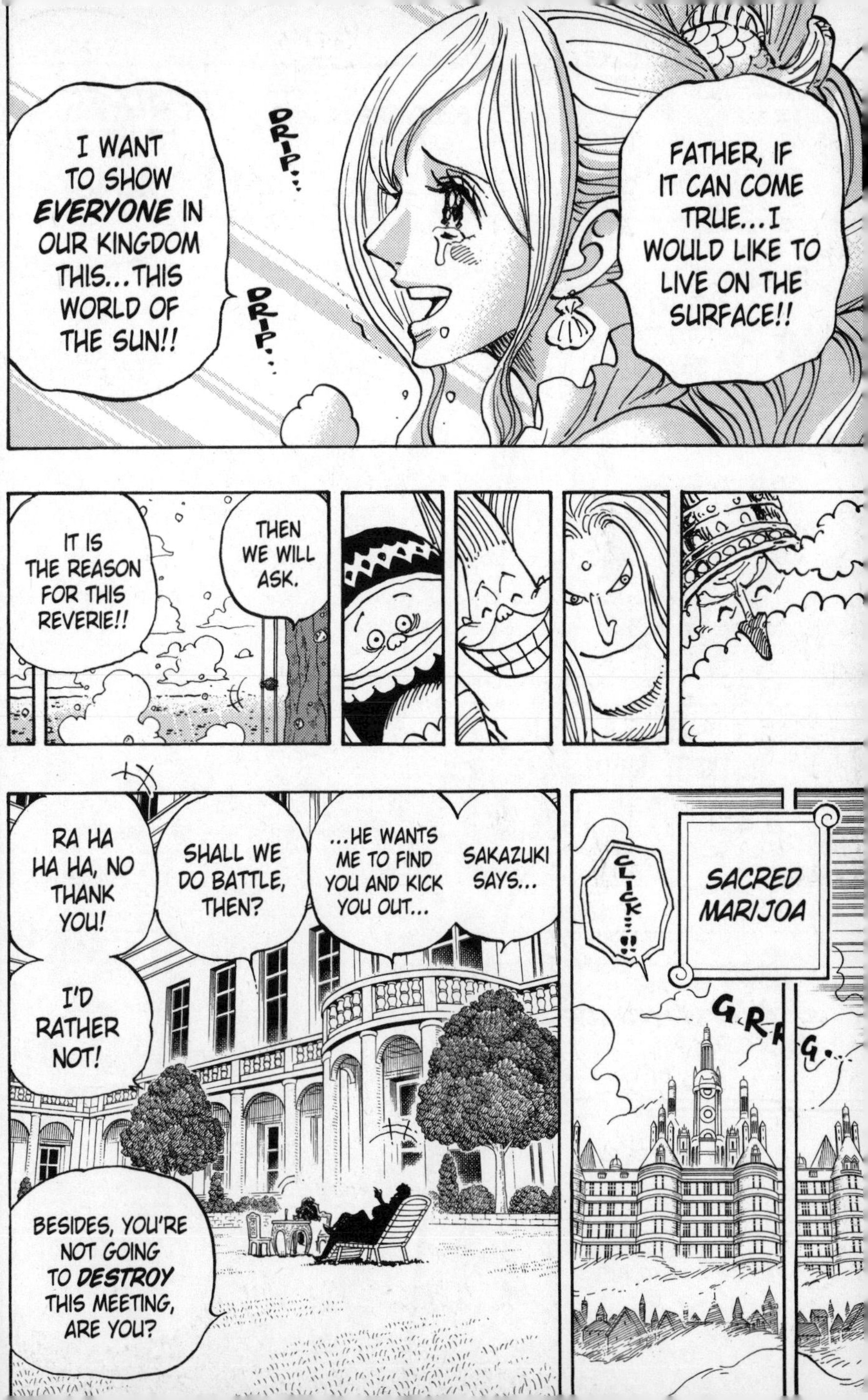
FATHER, IF IT CAN COME TRUE...I WOULD LIKE TO LIVE ON THE SURFACE!!
DRIP...
DRIP...
I WANT TO SHOW *EVERYONE* IN OUR KINGDOM THIS...THIS WORLD OF THE SUN!!
THEN WE WILL ASK.
IT IS THE REASON FOR THIS REVERIE!!
SACRED MARIJOA
CLICK..!!
GRRG...
SAKAZUKI SAYS...
...HE WANTS ME TO FIND YOU AND KICK YOU OUT...
SHALL WE DO BATTLE, THEN?
RA HA HA HA, NO THANK YOU!
I'D RATHER NOT!
BESIDES, YOU'RE NOT GOING TO *DESTROY* THIS MEETING, ARE YOU?

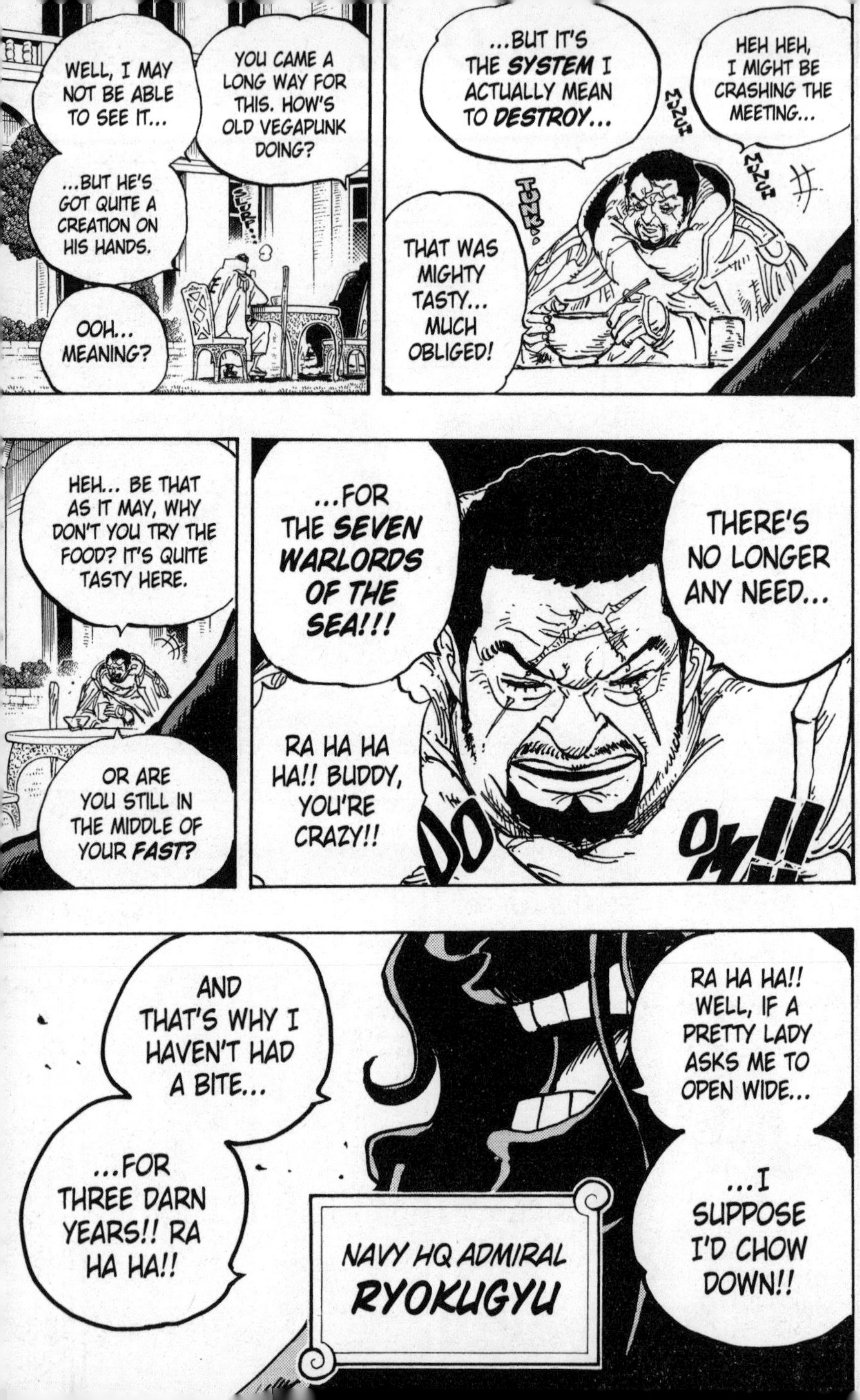
HEH HEH, I MIGHT BE CRASHING THE MEETING...
MUNCH
MUNCH
...BUT IT'S THE SYSTEM I ACTUALLY MEAN TO DESTROY...
TUNK
THAT WAS MIGHTY TASTY... MUCH OBLIGED!
YOU CAME A LONG WAY FOR THIS. HOW'S OLD VEGAPUNK DOING?
WELL, I MAY NOT BE ABLE TO SEE IT...
...BUT HE'S GOT QUITE A CREATION ON HIS HANDS.
SLURP...
OOH... MEANING?
THERE'S NO LONGER ANY NEED...
...FOR THE SEVEN WARLORDS OF THE SEA!!!
RA HA HA HA!! BUDDY, YOU'RE CRAZY!!
DOOM!!
HEH... BE THAT AS IT MAY, WHY DON'T YOU TRY THE FOOD? IT'S QUITE TASTY HERE.
OR ARE YOU STILL IN THE MIDDLE OF YOUR FAST?
RA HA HA!! WELL, IF A PRETTY LADY ASKS ME TO OPEN WIDE...
...I SUPPOSE I'D CHOW DOWN!!
AND THAT'S WHY I HAVEN'T HAD A BITE...
...FOR THREE DARN YEARS!! RA HA HA!!
NAVY HQ ADMIRAL
RYOKUGYU

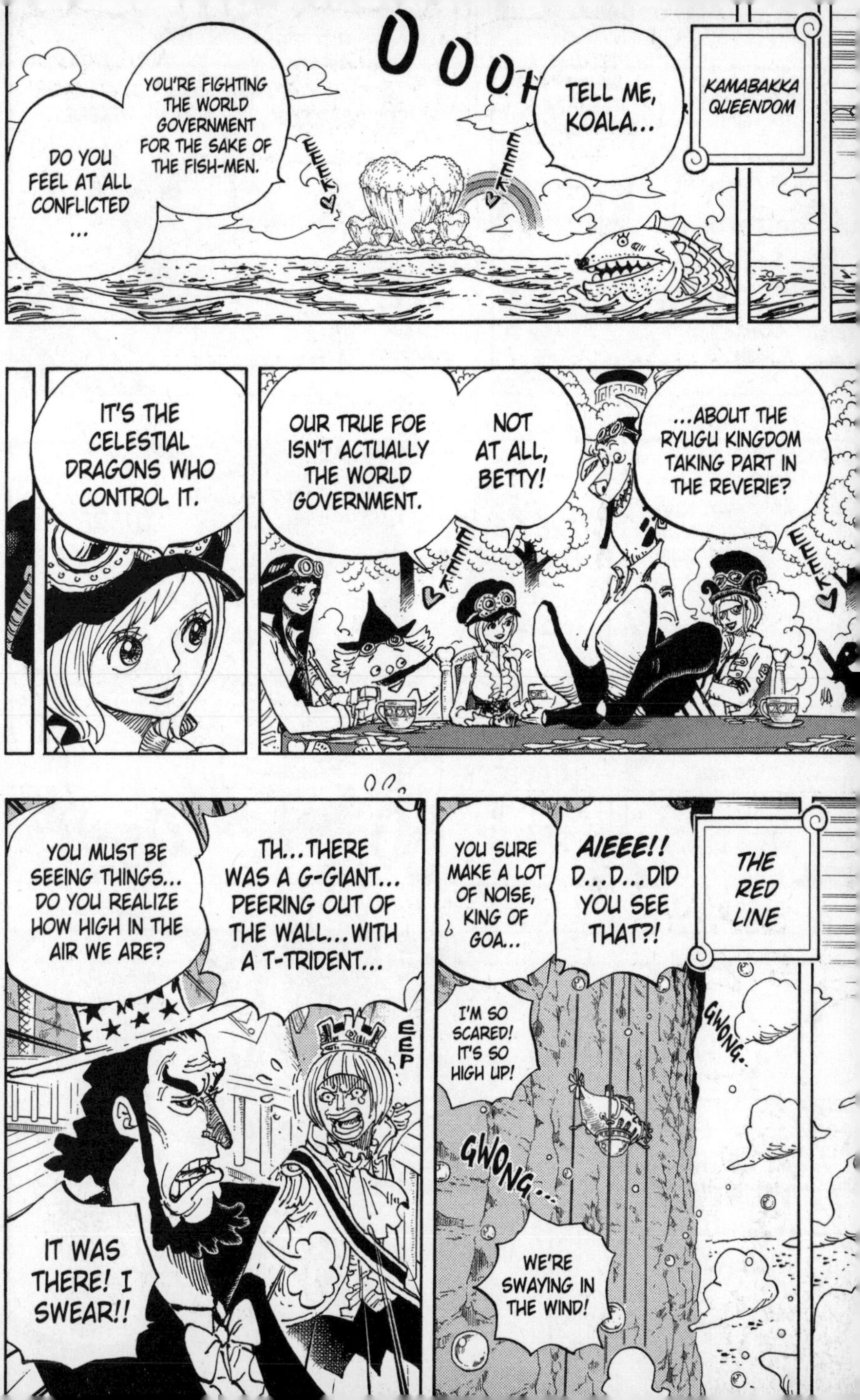
KAMABAKKA QUEENDOM
TELL ME, KOALA...
OOOH
EEEK♥
EEEK♥
YOU'RE FIGHTING THE WORLD GOVERNMENT FOR THE SAKE OF THE FISH-MEN.
DO YOU FEEL AT ALL CONFLICTED ...
...ABOUT THE RYUGU KINGDOM TAKING PART IN THE REVERIE?
EEEK♥
NOT AT ALL, BETTY!
OUR TRUE FOE ISN'T ACTUALLY THE WORLD GOVERNMENT.
EEEK♥
IT'S THE CELESTIAL DRAGONS WHO CONTROL IT.
THE RED LINE
AIEEE!! D...D...DID YOU SEE THAT?!
YOU SURE MAKE A LOT OF NOISE, KING OF GOA...
GWONG..
I'M SO SCARED! IT'S SO HIGH UP!
GWONG...
WE'RE SWAYING IN THE WIND!
TH...THERE WAS A G-GIANT... PEERING OUT OF THE WALL...WITH A T-TRIDENT...
EEP
YOU MUST BE SEEING THINGS... DO YOU REALIZE HOW HIGH IN THE AIR WE ARE?
IT WAS THERE! I SWEAR!!

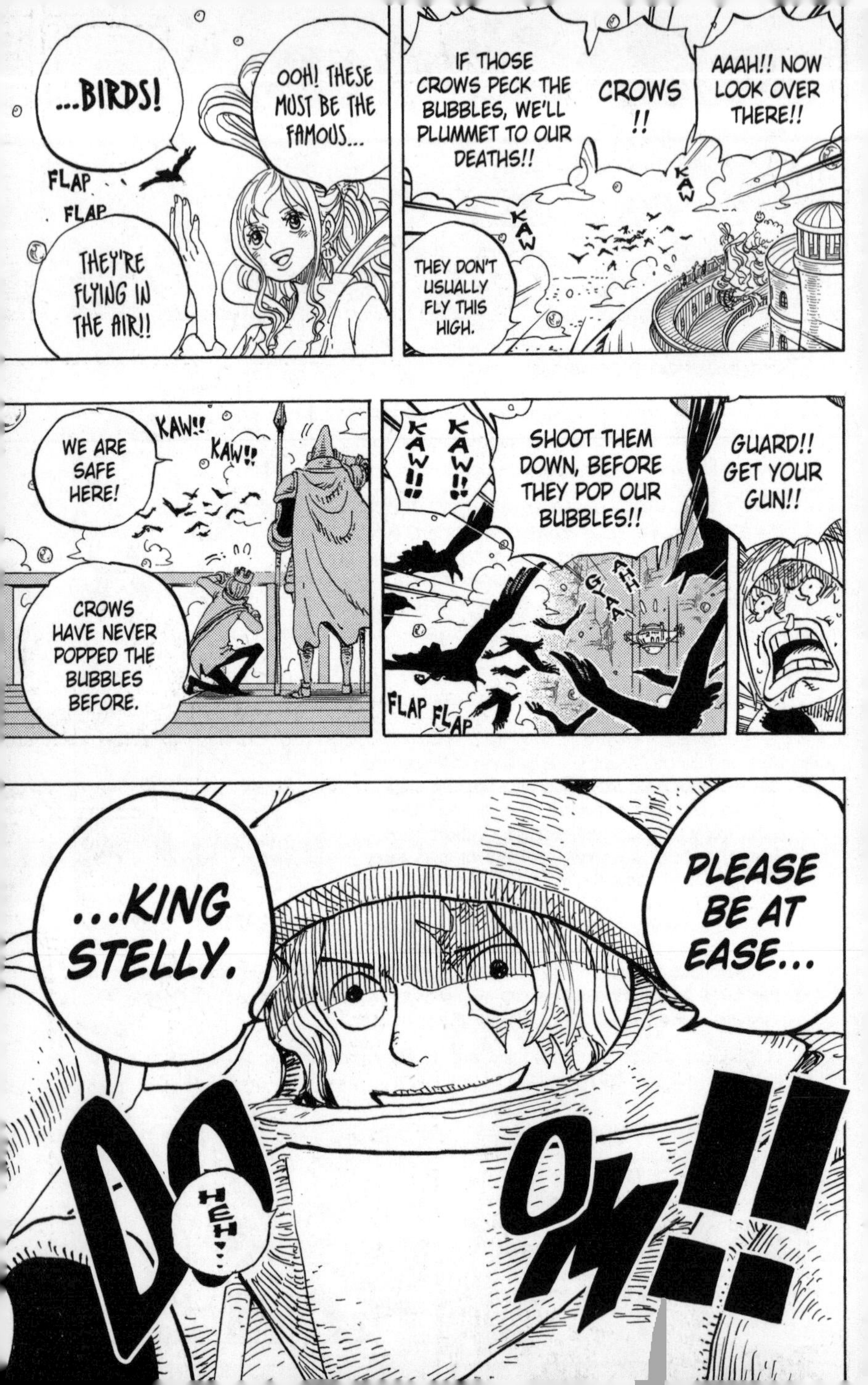
AAAH!! NOW LOOK OVER THERE!!
CROWS !!
IF THOSE CROWS PECK THE BUBBLES, WE'LL PLUMMET TO OUR DEATHS!!
KAW
KAW
THEY DON'T USUALLY FLY THIS HIGH.
OOH! THESE MUST BE THE FAMOUS...
...BIRDS!
FLAP
FLAP
THEY'RE FLYING IN THE AIR!!
GUARD!! GET YOUR GUN!!
SHOOT THEM DOWN, BEFORE THEY POP OUR BUBBLES!!
KAW!!
KAW!!
AHH
GYAA
FLAP FLAP
KAW!!
KAW!!
WE ARE SAFE HERE!
CROWS HAVE NEVER POPPED THE BUBBLES BEFORE.
PLEASE BE AT EASE...
...KING STELLY.
DOON!!
HEH...

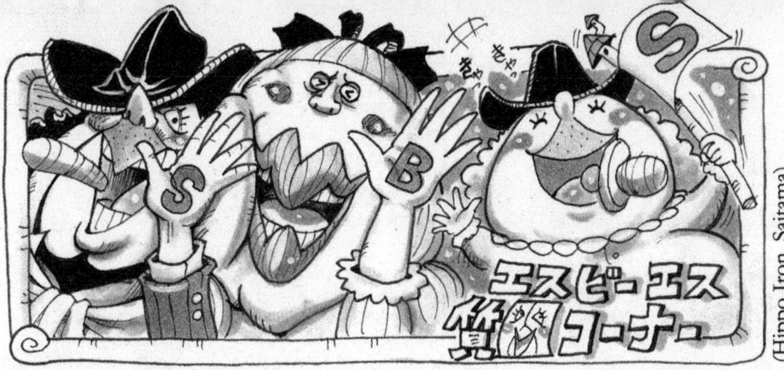

エスビーエス
質問コーナー

(Hippo Iron, Saitama)

SBS Question Corner

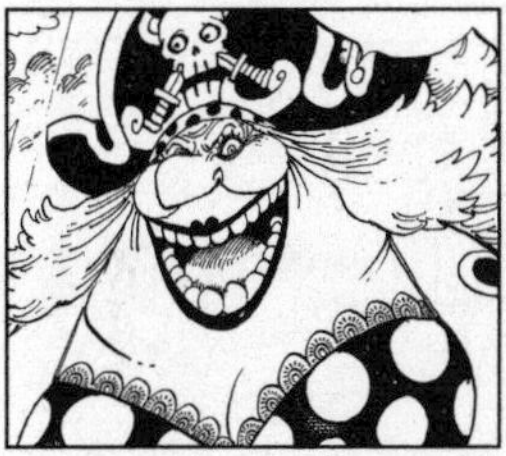

Q: Hello, Oda Sensei!! Big Mom sure has a bunch of ex-husbands. How does she handle that sort of thing? Do they have betrothal interviews?

--Big Mana

A: She's a pirate. She takes by force. And when she has her kid, she dumps them!! Her intent is to have children of a variety of races. She's a scary lady.

Q: If Big Mom has her hunger pangs and wants wedding cake again, what will happen to Totto Land? I can't imagine that anyone will be able to bake such a wedding cake again…

--Akibe

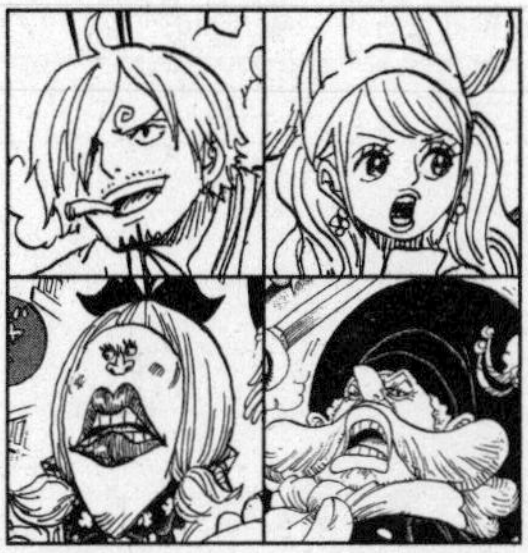

A: Good point! That's very kind of you to be concerned for Totto Land's well-being. Do you suppose they'll flee the country if disaster strikes? But the New World is a very treacherous sea. The family and citizens are largely protected by the menacing name of Big Mom. So even though danger might eventually strike, they can't help but stick close to her. This is a major concern for Totto Land, and part of what it means to live under a major power, perhaps! (Wow, what a serious answer.)

Q: Is the Gerd whom Big Mom lived with in her childhood the same person as the beautiful ship doctor Gerd from the New Giant Pirates on the cover of chapter 901?

--Assistant

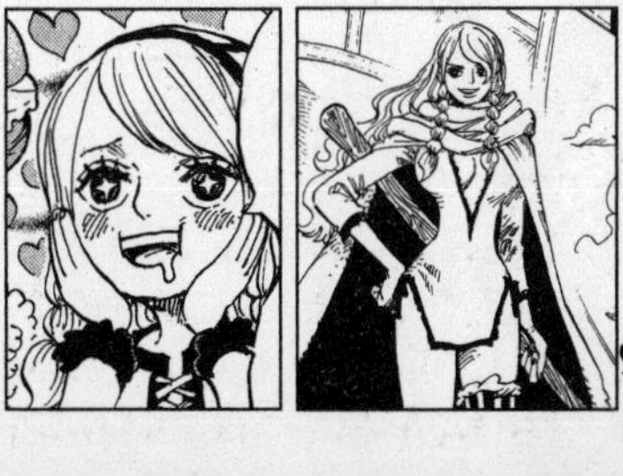

A: That's right. 63 years ago, Big Mom was five years old, and Gerd was 12. So now Big Mom is 68, and Gerd is 75. Since giants live to be 300 years old, she's still in the prime of her life.

Chapter 906:
SACRED MARIJOA

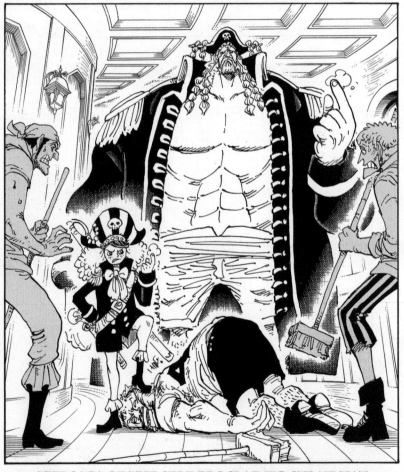

**THE SAGA OF THE SELF-PROCLAIMED STRAW HAT
FLEET, VOL. 36, ORLUMBUS: "10 A.M., CLEANING CHECK.
ORLUMBUS AND COLUMBUS--VERY FASTIDIOUS!"**

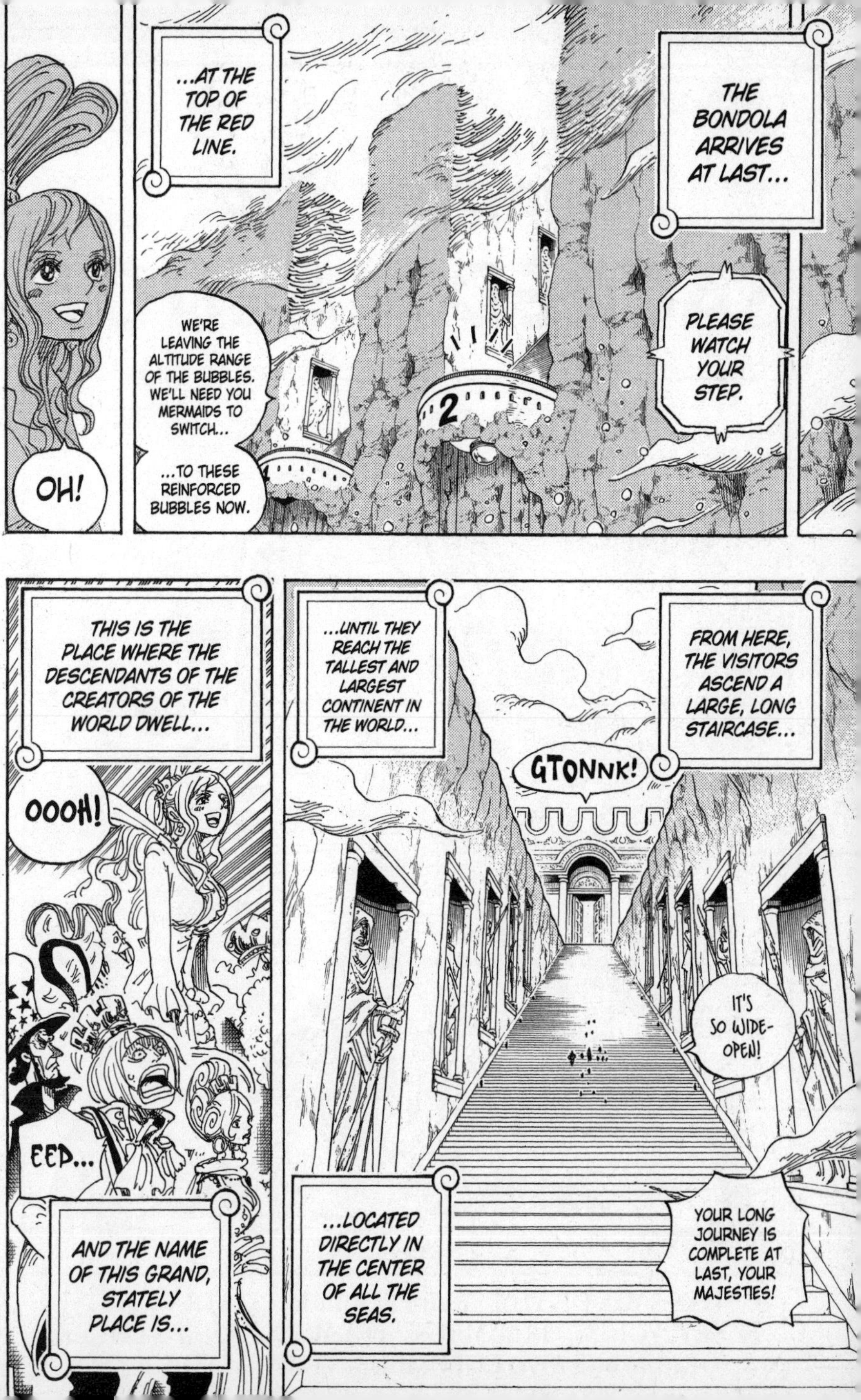
THE BONDOLA ARRIVES AT LAST...
PLEASE WATCH YOUR STEP.
...AT THE TOP OF THE RED LINE.
WE'RE LEAVING THE ALTITUDE RANGE OF THE BUBBLES. WE'LL NEED YOU MERMAIDS TO SWITCH...
...TO THESE REINFORCED BUBBLES NOW.
OH!
FROM HERE, THE VISITORS ASCEND A LARGE, LONG STAIRCASE...
GTONNK!
...UNTIL THEY REACH THE TALLEST AND LARGEST CONTINENT IN THE WORLD...
IT'S SO WIDE-OPEN!
YOUR LONG JOURNEY IS COMPLETE AT LAST, YOUR MAJESTIES!
...LOCATED DIRECTLY IN THE CENTER OF ALL THE SEAS.
THIS IS THE PLACE WHERE THE DESCENDANTS OF THE CREATORS OF THE WORLD DWELL...
OOOH!
EEP...
AND THE NAME OF THIS GRAND, STATELY PLACE IS...

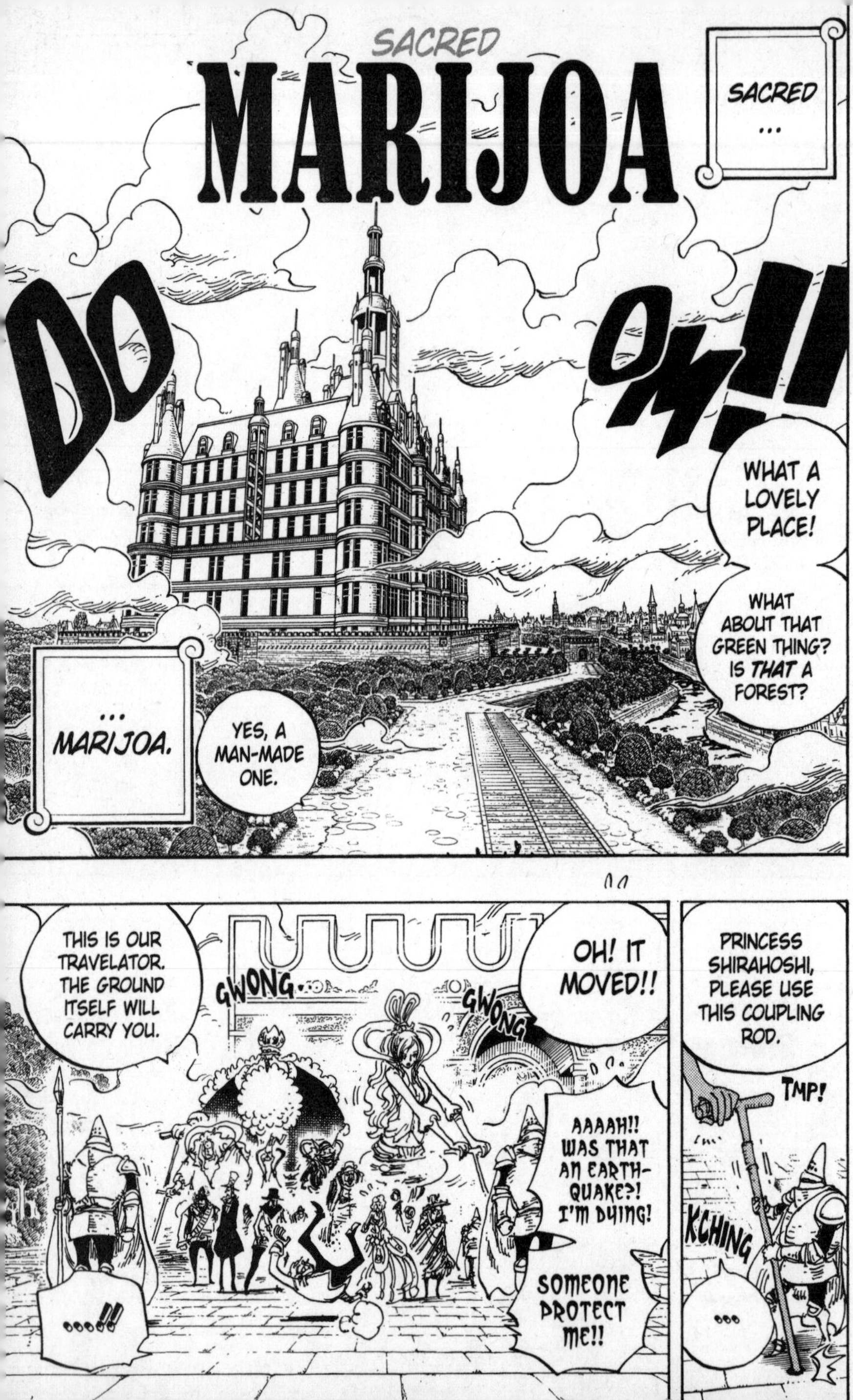
SACRED ...
SACRED
MARIJOA
DOON!!
WHAT A LOVELY PLACE!
WHAT ABOUT THAT GREEN THING? IS THAT A FOREST?
YES, A MAN-MADE ONE.
... MARIJOA.
PRINCESS SHIRAHOSHI, PLEASE USE THIS COUPLING ROD.
TMP!
KCHING
...
OH! IT MOVED!!
GWONG
GWONG
THIS IS OUR TRAVELATOR. THE GROUND ITSELF WILL CARRY YOU.
AAAAH!! WAS THAT AN EARTH-QUAKE?! I'M DYING!
SOMEONE PROTECT ME!!
....!!

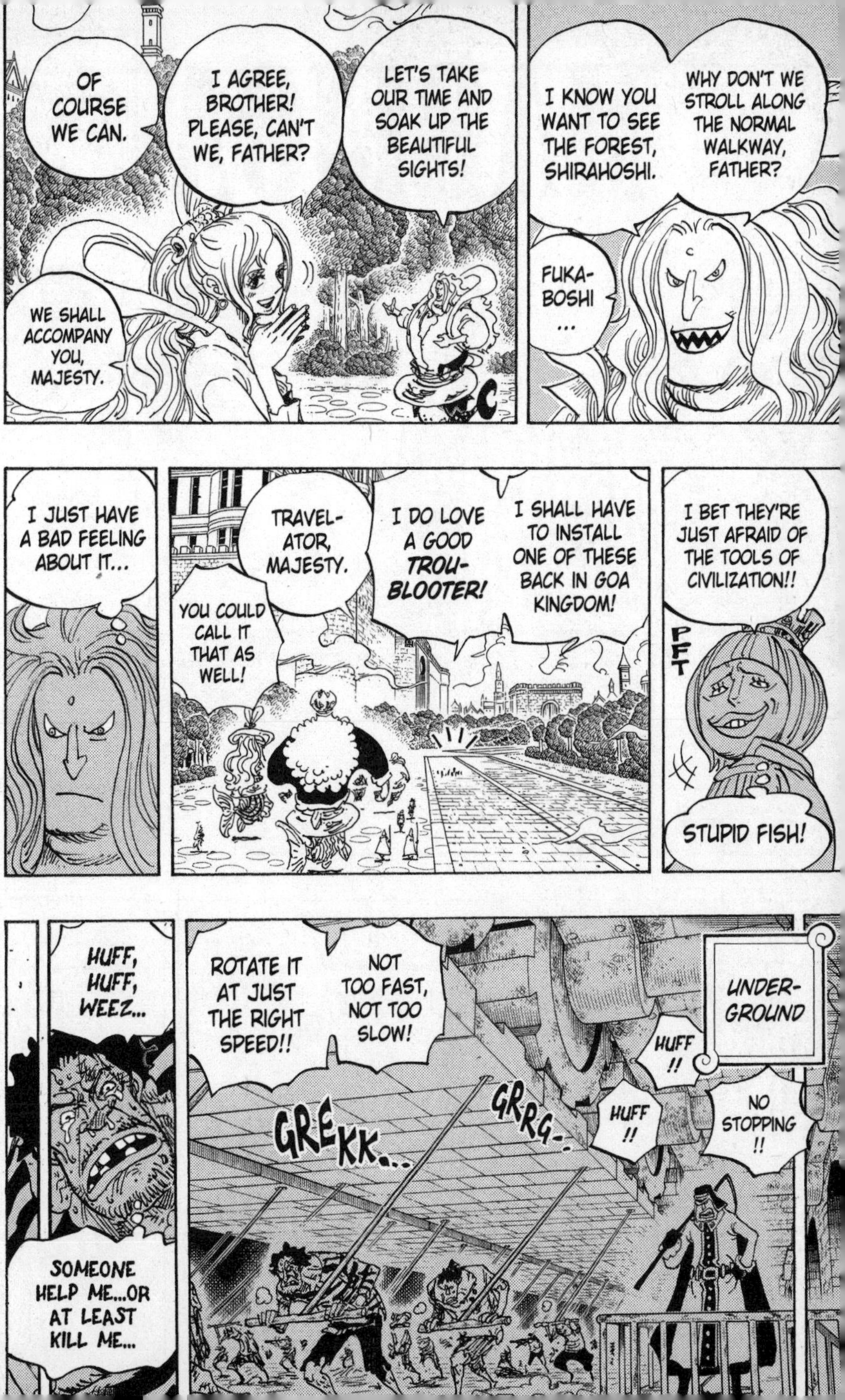
WHY DON'T WE STROLL ALONG THE NORMAL WALKWAY, FATHER?
I KNOW YOU WANT TO SEE THE FOREST, SHIRAHOSHI.
FUKA-BOSHI ...
LET'S TAKE OUR TIME AND SOAK UP THE BEAUTIFUL SIGHTS!
I AGREE, BROTHER! PLEASE, CAN'T WE, FATHER?
OF COURSE WE CAN.
WE SHALL ACCOMPANY YOU, MAJESTY.
I BET THEY'RE JUST AFRAID OF THE TOOLS OF CIVILIZATION!!
PFT
STUPID FISH!
I SHALL HAVE TO INSTALL ONE OF THESE BACK IN GOA KINGDOM!
I DO LOVE A GOOD TROU-BLOOTER!
TRAVEL-ATOR, MAJESTY.
YOU COULD CALL IT THAT AS WELL!
I JUST HAVE A BAD FEELING ABOUT IT...
UNDER-GROUND
HUFF !!
HUFF !!
NO STOPPING !!
GRRG...
NOT TOO FAST, NOT TOO SLOW!
ROTATE IT AT JUST THE RIGHT SPEED!!
GREKK...
HUFF, HUFF, WEEZ...
SOMEONE HELP ME...OR AT LEAST KILL ME...

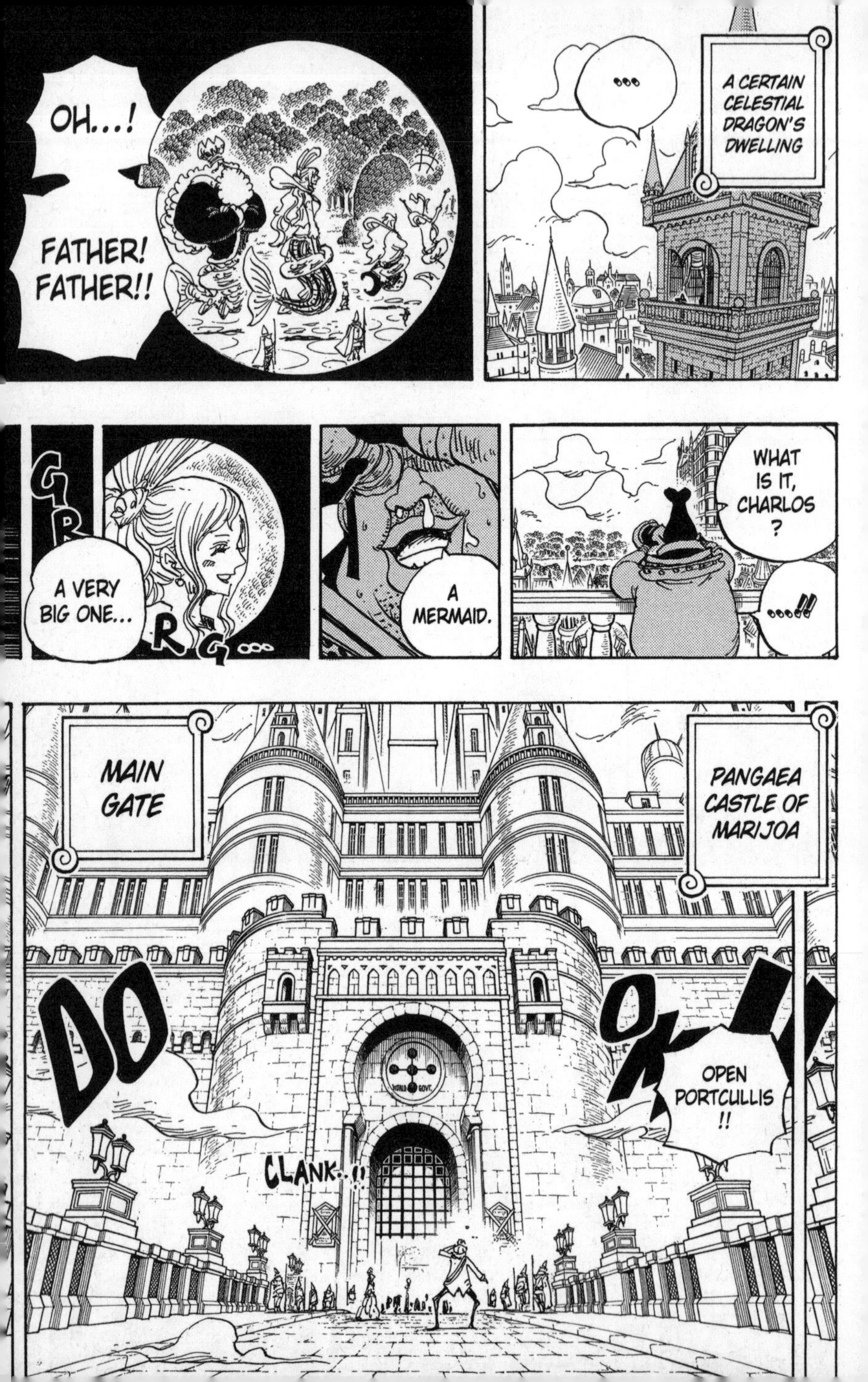
A CERTAIN CELESTIAL DRAGON'S DWELLING
...
OH...!
FATHER! FATHER!!
WHAT IS IT, CHARLOS ?
...!!
A MERMAID.
A VERY BIG ONE...
GR
RG...
PANGAEA CASTLE OF MARIJOA
MAIN GATE
DO
OPEN PORTCULLIS !!
WORLD GOVT.
CLANK..!!

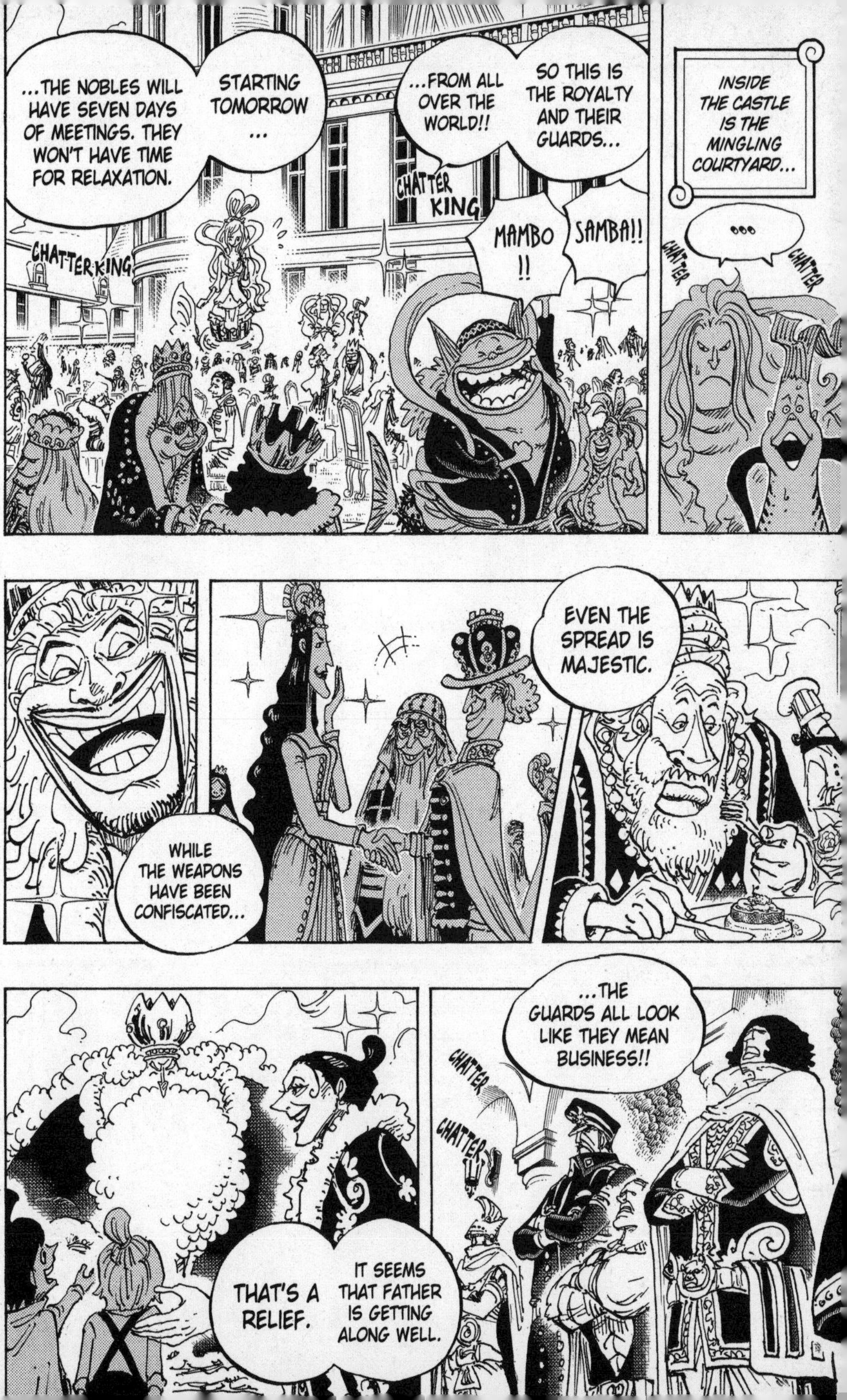
INSIDE THE CASTLE IS THE MINGLING COURTYARD...
CHATTER
...
CHATTER
SO THIS IS THE ROYALTY AND THEIR GUARDS...
...FROM ALL OVER THE WORLD!!
STARTING TOMORROW ...
...THE NOBLES WILL HAVE SEVEN DAYS OF MEETINGS. THEY WON'T HAVE TIME FOR RELAXATION.
CHATTER KING
SAMBA!!
MAMBO !!
CHATTER KING
EVEN THE SPREAD IS MAJESTIC.
WHILE THE WEAPONS HAVE BEEN CONFISCATED...
...THE GUARDS ALL LOOK LIKE THEY MEAN BUSINESS!!
CHATTER
CHATTER
IT SEEMS THAT FATHER IS GETTING ALONG WELL.
THAT'S A RELIEF.

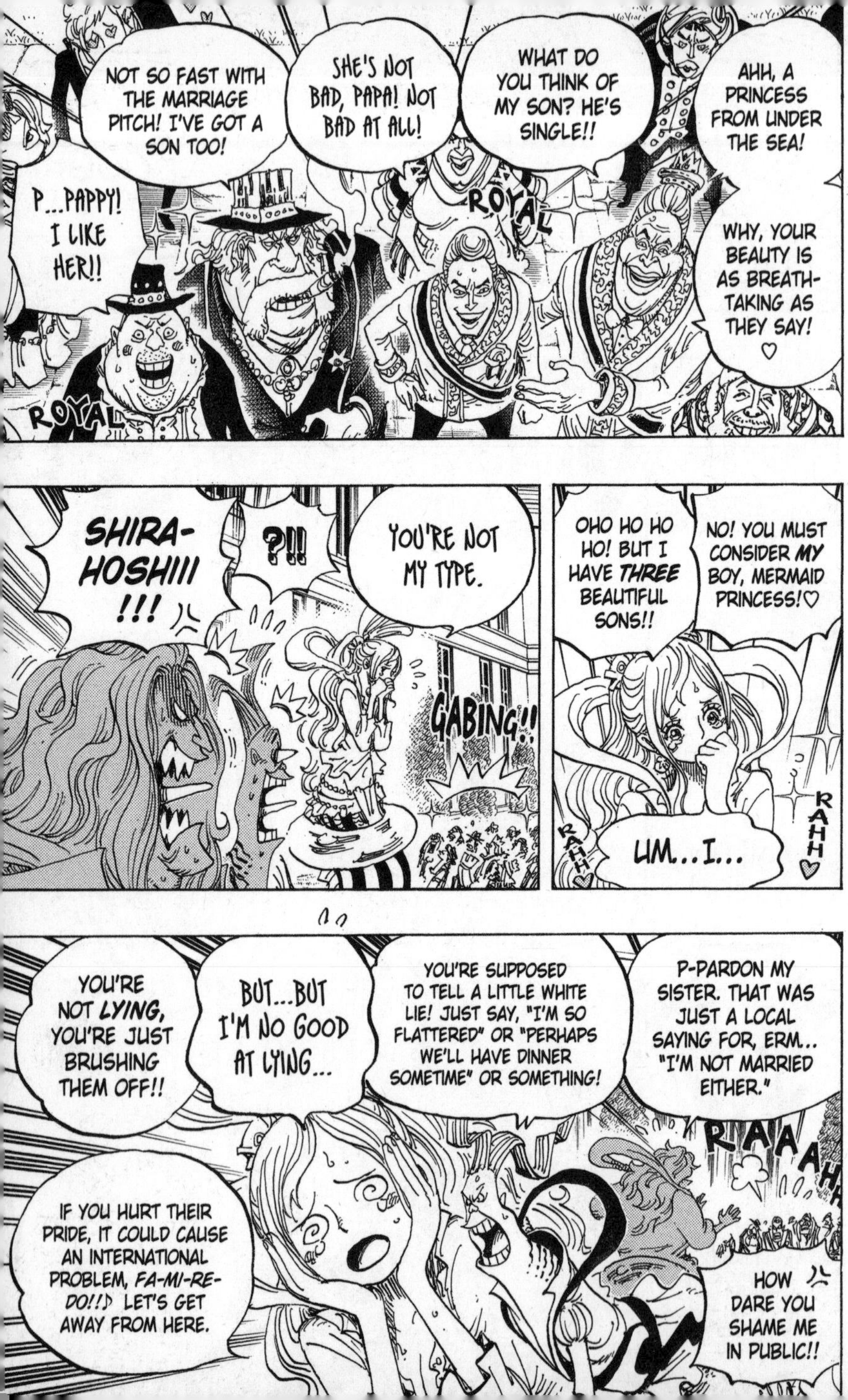
AHH, A PRINCESS FROM UNDER THE SEA!
WHY, YOUR BEAUTY IS AS BREATH-TAKING AS THEY SAY! ♡
WHAT DO YOU THINK OF MY SON? HE'S SINGLE!!
ROYAL
SHE'S NOT BAD, PAPA! NOT BAD AT ALL!
NOT SO FAST WITH THE MARRIAGE PITCH! I'VE GOT A SON TOO!
P...PAPPY! I LIKE HER!!
ROYAL
NO! YOU MUST CONSIDER *MY* BOY, MERMAID PRINCESS!♡
OHO HO HO HO! BUT I HAVE *THREE* BEAUTIFUL SONS!!
RAHH ♡
UM...I...
RAHH ♡
YOU'RE NOT MY TYPE.
GABING!!
?!!
SHIRA-HOSHIII !!!
P-PARDON MY SISTER. THAT WAS JUST A LOCAL SAYING FOR, ERM... "I'M NOT MARRIED EITHER."
RAAAAH
HOW DARE YOU SHAME ME IN PUBLIC!!
YOU'RE SUPPOSED TO TELL A LITTLE WHITE LIE! JUST SAY, "I'M SO FLATTERED" OR "PERHAPS WE'LL HAVE DINNER SOMETIME" OR SOMETHING!
BUT...BUT I'M NO GOOD AT LYING...
YOU'RE NOT *LYING*, YOU'RE JUST BRUSHING THEM OFF!!
IF YOU HURT THEIR PRIDE, IT COULD CAUSE AN INTERNATIONAL PROBLEM, *FA-MI-RE-DO!!*♪ LET'S GET AWAY FROM HERE.

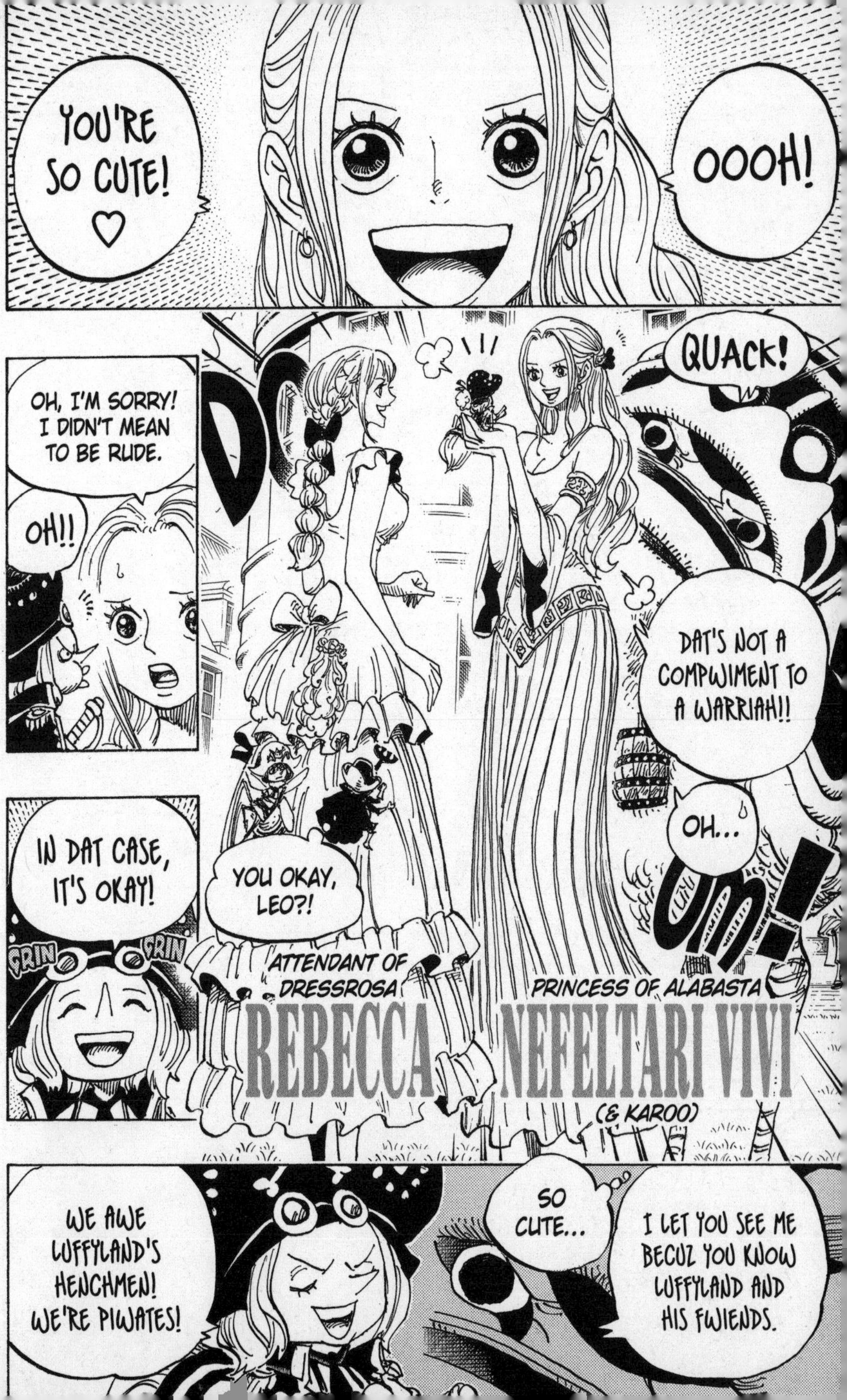
OOOH!
YOU'RE SO CUTE! ♡
QUACK!
DAT'S NOT A COMPWIMENT TO A WARRIAH!!
OH...
YOU OKAY, LEO?!
PRINCESS OF ALABASTA
NEFELTARI VIVI
(& KAROO)
ATTENDANT OF DRESSROSA
REBECCA
OH, I'M SORRY! I DIDN'T MEAN TO BE RUDE.
OH!!
IN DAT CASE, IT'S OKAY!
GRIN
GRIN
I LET YOU SEE ME BECUZ YOU KNOW LUFFYLAND AND HIS FWIENDS.
SO CUTE...
WE AWE LUFFYLAND'S HENCHMEN! WE'RE PIWATES!

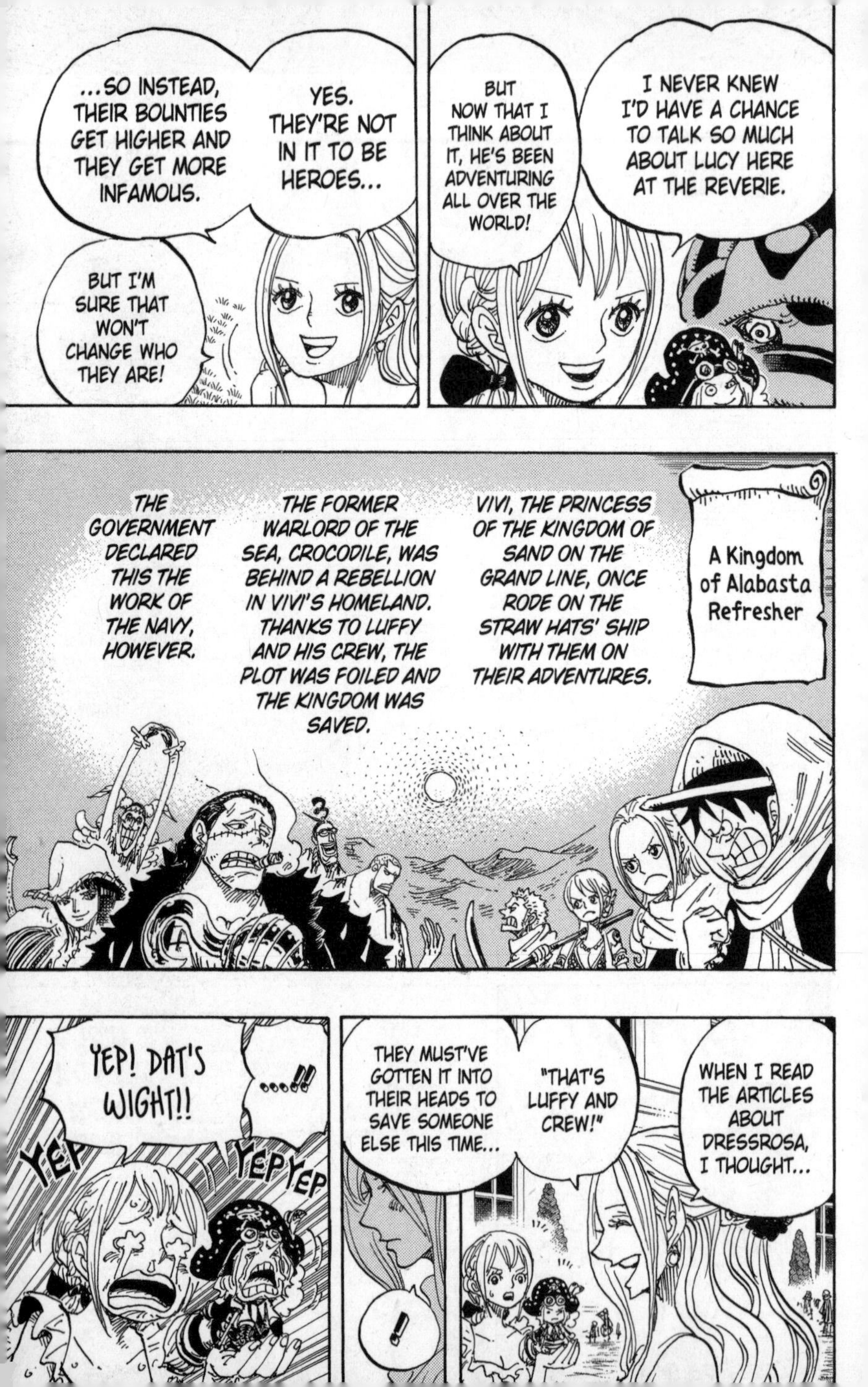
I NEVER KNEW I'D HAVE A CHANCE TO TALK SO MUCH ABOUT LUCY HERE AT THE REVERIE.
BUT NOW THAT I THINK ABOUT IT, HE'S BEEN ADVENTURING ALL OVER THE WORLD!
YES. THEY'RE NOT IN IT TO BE HEROES...
...SO INSTEAD, THEIR BOUNTIES GET HIGHER AND THEY GET MORE INFAMOUS.
BUT I'M SURE THAT WON'T CHANGE WHO THEY ARE!
A Kingdom of Alabasta Refresher
VIVI, THE PRINCESS OF THE KINGDOM OF SAND ON THE GRAND LINE, ONCE RODE ON THE STRAW HATS' SHIP WITH THEM ON THEIR ADVENTURES.
THE FORMER WARLORD OF THE SEA, CROCODILE, WAS BEHIND A REBELLION IN VIVI'S HOMELAND. THANKS TO LUFFY AND HIS CREW, THE PLOT WAS FOILED AND THE KINGDOM WAS SAVED.
THE GOVERNMENT DECLARED THIS THE WORK OF THE NAVY, HOWEVER.
WHEN I READ THE ARTICLES ABOUT DRESSROSA, I THOUGHT...
"THAT'S LUFFY AND CREW!"
THEY MUST'VE GOTTEN IT INTO THEIR HEADS TO SAVE SOMEONE ELSE THIS TIME...
!
...!!
YEP! DAT'S WIGHT!!
YEP
YEP YEP

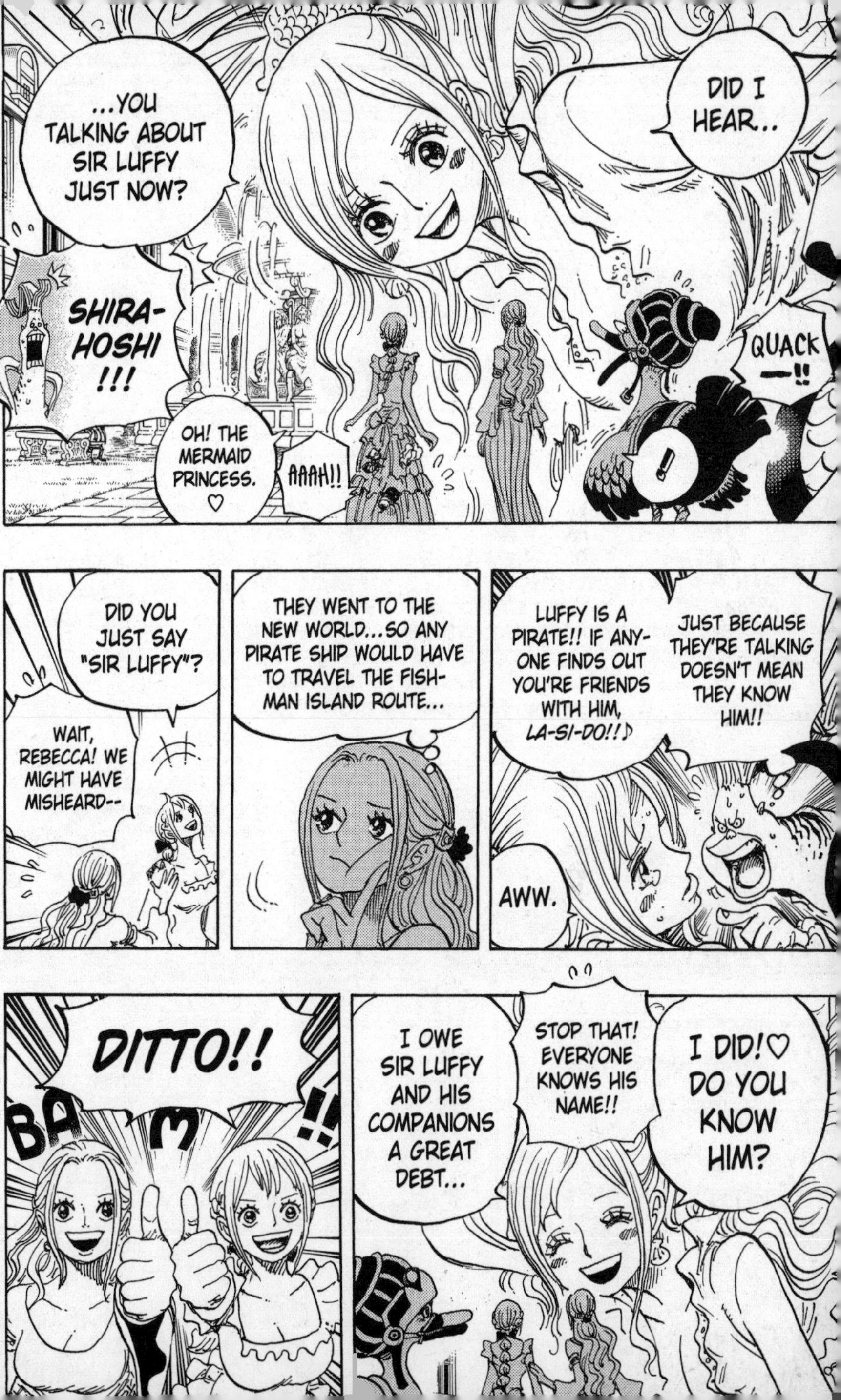
DID I HEAR...
...YOU TALKING ABOUT SIR LUFFY JUST NOW?
QUACK—!!
AAAH!!
OH! THE MERMAID PRINCESS. ♡
SHIRA-HOSHI!!!
JUST BECAUSE THEY'RE TALKING DOESN'T MEAN THEY KNOW HIM!!
LUFFY IS A PIRATE!! IF ANYONE FINDS OUT YOU'RE FRIENDS WITH HIM, LA-SI-DO!!♪
AWW.
THEY WENT TO THE NEW WORLD...SO ANY PIRATE SHIP WOULD HAVE TO TRAVEL THE FISH-MAN ISLAND ROUTE...
DID YOU JUST SAY "SIR LUFFY"?
WAIT, REBECCA! WE MIGHT HAVE MISHEARD--
I DID!♡ DO YOU KNOW HIM?
STOP THAT! EVERYONE KNOWS HIS NAME!!
I OWE SIR LUFFY AND HIS COMPANIONS A GREAT DEBT...
DITTO!!
BAM!!

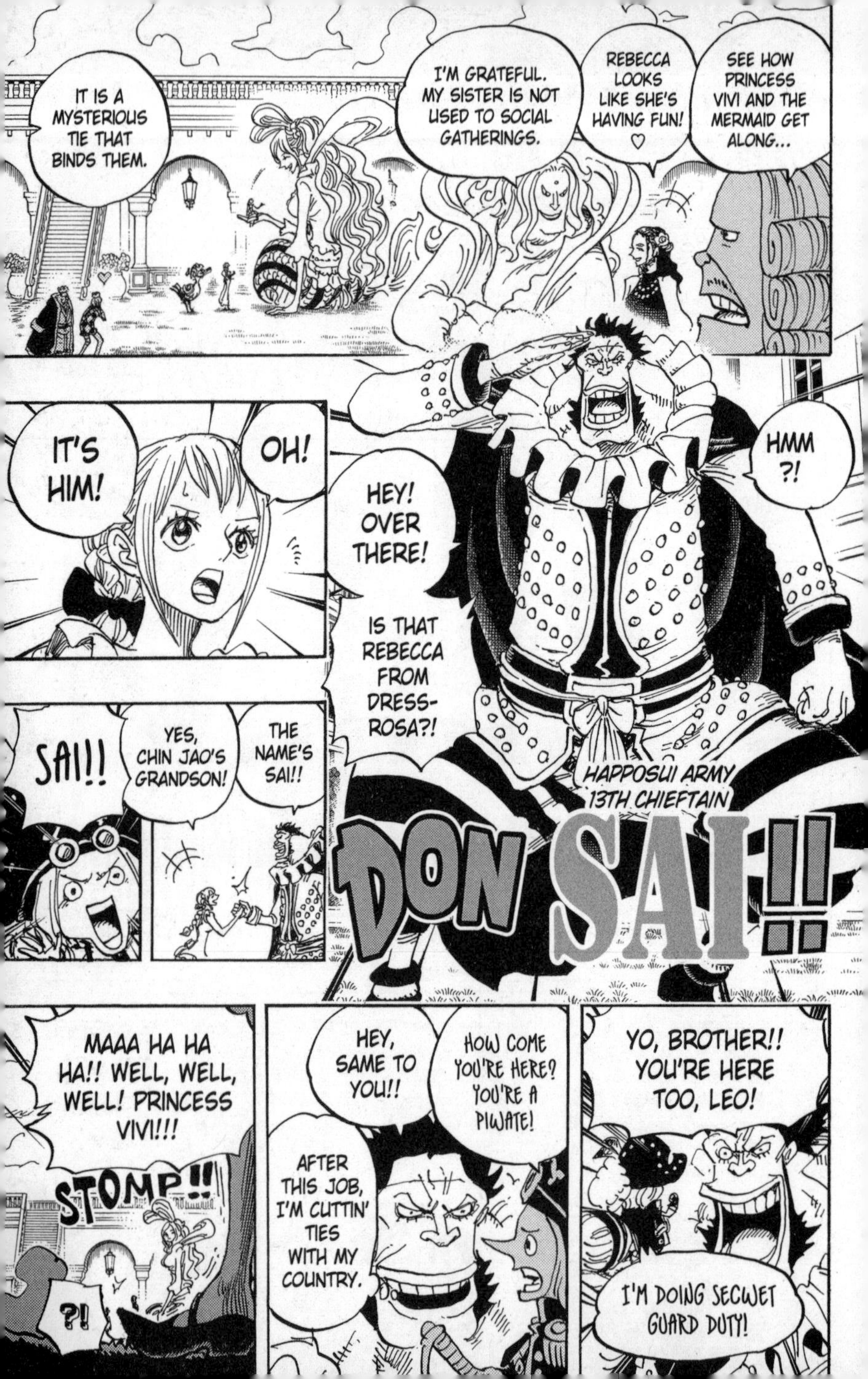
SEE HOW PRINCESS VIVI AND THE MERMAID GET ALONG...
REBECCA LOOKS LIKE SHE'S HAVING FUN! ♡
I'M GRATEFUL. MY SISTER IS NOT USED TO SOCIAL GATHERINGS.
IT IS A MYSTERIOUS TIE THAT BINDS THEM.
HMM ?!
HEY! OVER THERE!
IS THAT REBECCA FROM DRESS-ROSA?!
HAPPOSUI ARMY 13TH CHIEFTAIN
DON SAI!!
OH!
IT'S HIM!
THE NAME'S SAI!!
YES, CHIN JAO'S GRANDSON!
SAI!!
YO, BROTHER!! YOU'RE HERE TOO, LEO!
I'M DOING SECWET GUARD DUTY!
HOW COME YOU'RE HERE? YOU'RE A PIWATE!
HEY, SAME TO YOU!!
AFTER THIS JOB, I'M CUTTIN' TIES WITH MY COUNTRY.
MAAA HA HA HA!! WELL, WELL, WELL! PRINCESS VIVI!!!
STOMP!!
?!

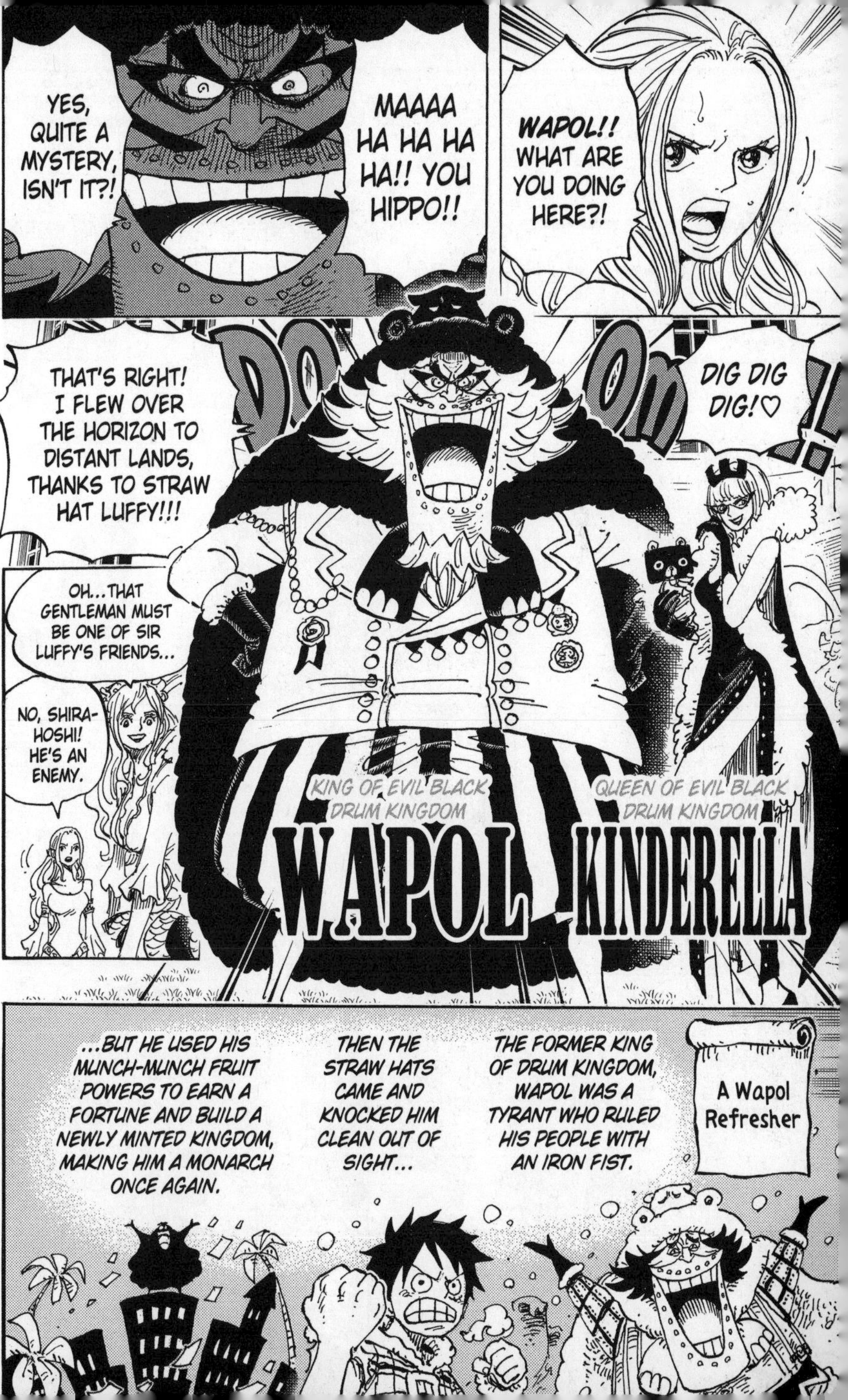
WAPOL!! WHAT ARE YOU DOING HERE?!
MAAAA HA HA HA HA!! YOU HIPPO!!
YES, QUITE A MYSTERY, ISN'T IT?!
DIG DIG DIG!♡
THAT'S RIGHT! I FLEW OVER THE HORIZON TO DISTANT LANDS, THANKS TO STRAW HAT LUFFY!!!
QUEEN OF EVIL BLACK DRUM KINGDOM
KINDERELLA
KING OF EVIL BLACK DRUM KINGDOM
WAPOL
OH...THAT GENTLEMAN MUST BE ONE OF SIR LUFFY'S FRIENDS...
NO, SHIRAHOSHI! HE'S AN ENEMY.
A Wapol Refresher
THE FORMER KING OF DRUM KINGDOM, WAPOL WAS A TYRANT WHO RULED HIS PEOPLE WITH AN IRON FIST.
THEN THE STRAW HATS CAME AND KNOCKED HIM CLEAN OUT OF SIGHT...
...BUT HE USED HIS MUNCH-MUNCH FRUIT POWERS TO EARN A FORTUNE AND BUILD A NEWLY MINTED KINGDOM, MAKING HIM A MONARCH ONCE AGAIN.

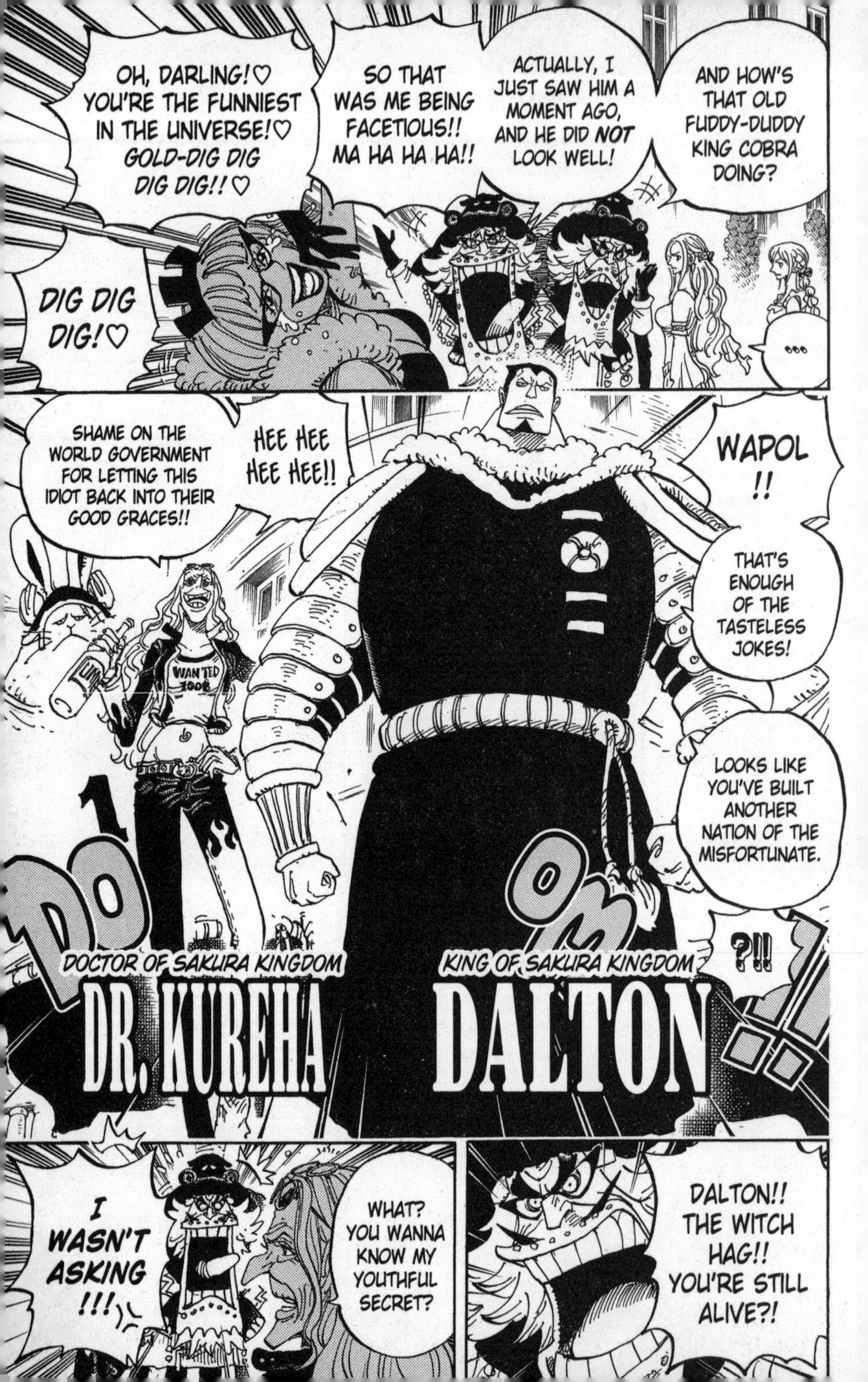
AND HOW'S THAT OLD FUDDY-DUDDY KING COBRA DOING?
ACTUALLY, I JUST SAW HIM A MOMENT AGO, AND HE DID NOT LOOK WELL!
SO THAT WAS ME BEING FACETIOUS!! MA HA HA HA!!
OH, DARLING!♡ YOU'RE THE FUNNIEST IN THE UNIVERSE!♡ GOLD-DIG DIG DIG DIG!!♡
...
DIG DIG DIG!♡
WAPOL !!
THAT'S ENOUGH OF THE TASTELESS JOKES!
LOOKS LIKE YOU'VE BUILT ANOTHER NATION OF THE MISFORTUNATE.
?!!
HEE HEE HEE HEE!!
SHAME ON THE WORLD GOVERNMENT FOR LETTING THIS IDIOT BACK INTO THEIR GOOD GRACES!!
DOOM
KING OF SAKURA KINGDOM
DALTON
DOCTOR OF SAKURA KINGDOM
DR. KUREHA
DALTON!! THE WITCH HAG!! YOU'RE STILL ALIVE?!
WHAT? YOU WANNA KNOW MY YOUTHFUL SECRET?
I WASN'T ASKING !!!

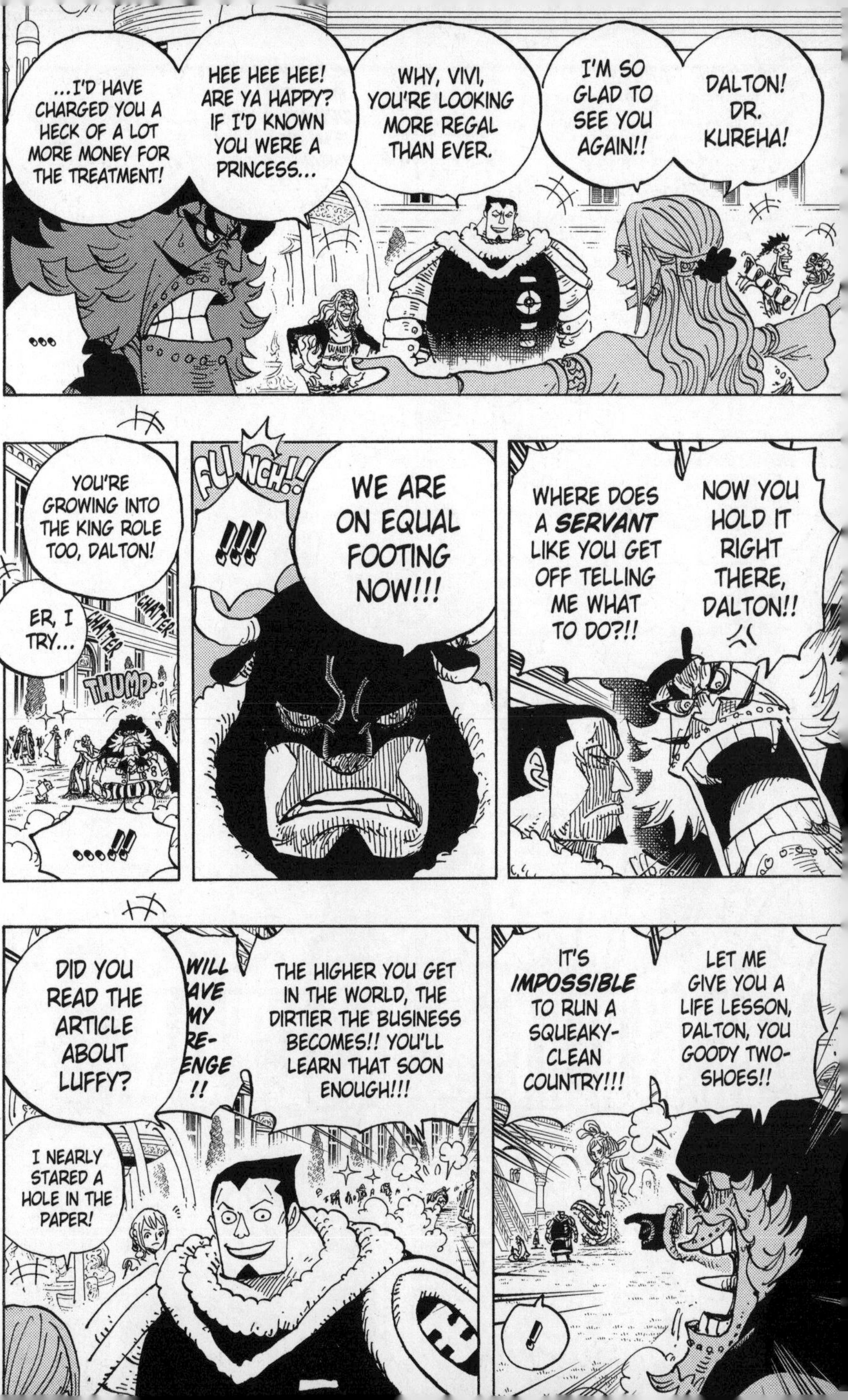
DALTON! DR. KUREHA!
I'M SO GLAD TO SEE YOU AGAIN!!
WHY, VIVI, YOU'RE LOOKING MORE REGAL THAN EVER.
HEE HEE HEE! ARE YA HAPPY? IF I'D KNOWN YOU WERE A PRINCESS...
...I'D HAVE CHARGED YOU A HECK OF A LOT MORE MONEY FOR THE TREATMENT!
...
NOW YOU HOLD IT RIGHT THERE, DALTON!!
WHERE DOES A SERVANT LIKE YOU GET OFF TELLING ME WHAT TO DO?!!
FLINCH!!
!!!
WE ARE ON EQUAL FOOTING NOW!!!
YOU'RE GROWING INTO THE KING ROLE TOO, DALTON!
ER, I TRY...
CHATTER
CHATTER
THUMP
....!!
LET ME GIVE YOU A LIFE LESSON, DALTON, YOU GOODY TWO-SHOES!!
IT'S IMPOSSIBLE TO RUN A SQUEAKY-CLEAN COUNTRY!!!
!
THE HIGHER YOU GET IN THE WORLD, THE DIRTIER THE BUSINESS BECOMES!! YOU'LL LEARN THAT SOON ENOUGH!!!
WILL AVE MY RE- ENGE !!
DID YOU READ THE ARTICLE ABOUT LUFFY?
I NEARLY STARED A HOLE IN THE PAPER!

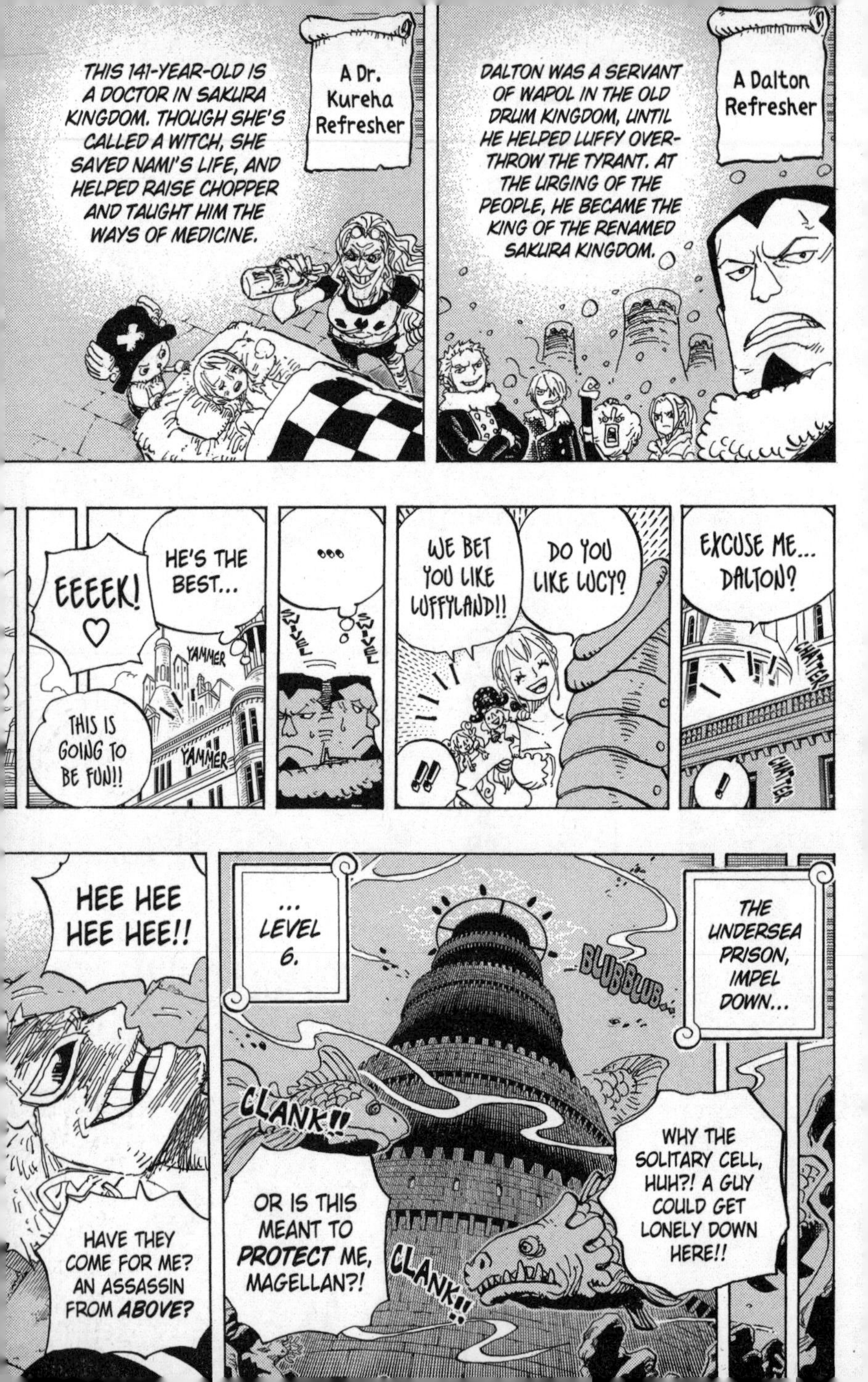
A Dalton Refresher
DALTON WAS A SERVANT OF WAPOL IN THE OLD DRUM KINGDOM, UNTIL HE HELPED LUFFY OVER-THROW THE TYRANT. AT THE URGING OF THE PEOPLE, HE BECAME THE KING OF THE RENAMED SAKURA KINGDOM.
A Dr. Kureha Refresher
THIS 141-YEAR-OLD IS A DOCTOR IN SAKURA KINGDOM. THOUGH SHE'S CALLED A WITCH, SHE SAVED NAMI'S LIFE, AND HELPED RAISE CHOPPER AND TAUGHT HIM THE WAYS OF MEDICINE.
EXCUSE ME... DALTON?
CHATTER
!
CHATTER
DO YOU LIKE LUCY?
WE BET YOU LIKE LUFFYLAND!!
!!
...
SWIVEL
SWIVEL
HE'S THE BEST...
EEEEK! ♥
YAMMER
YAMMER
THIS IS GOING TO BE FUN!!
THE UNDERSEA PRISON, IMPEL DOWN...
... LEVEL 6.
BLUB BLUB
CLANK!!
WHY THE SOLITARY CELL, HUH?! A GUY COULD GET LONELY DOWN HERE!!
OR IS THIS MEANT TO PROTECT ME, MAGELLAN?!
CLANK!!
HEE HEE HEE HEE!!
HAVE THEY COME FOR ME? AN ASSASSIN FROM ABOVE?

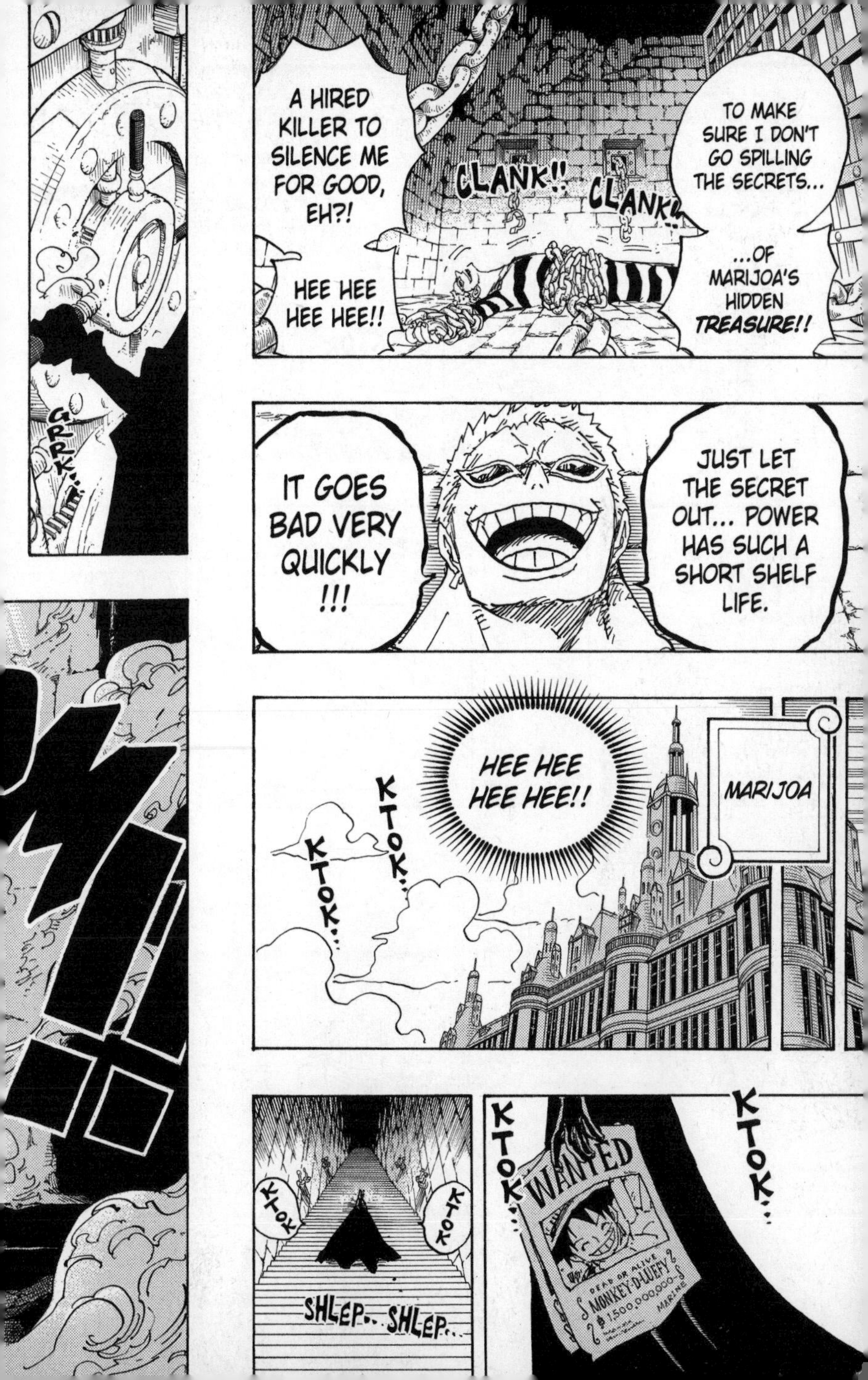
TO MAKE SURE I DON'T GO SPILLING THE SECRETS...
...OF MARIJOA'S HIDDEN *TREASURE!!*
CLANK!!
CLANK!!
A HIRED KILLER TO SILENCE ME FOR GOOD, EH?!
HEE HEE HEE HEE!!
JUST LET THE SECRET OUT... POWER HAS SUCH A SHORT SHELF LIFE.
IT GOES BAD VERY QUICKLY!!!
MARIJOA
HEE HEE HEE HEE!!
KTOK...
KTOK...
KTOK...
KTOK...
WANTED
DEAD OR ALIVE
MONKEY·D·LUFFY
1,500,000,000-
MARINE
KTOK
KTOK
SHLEP... SHLEP...
GRRK...

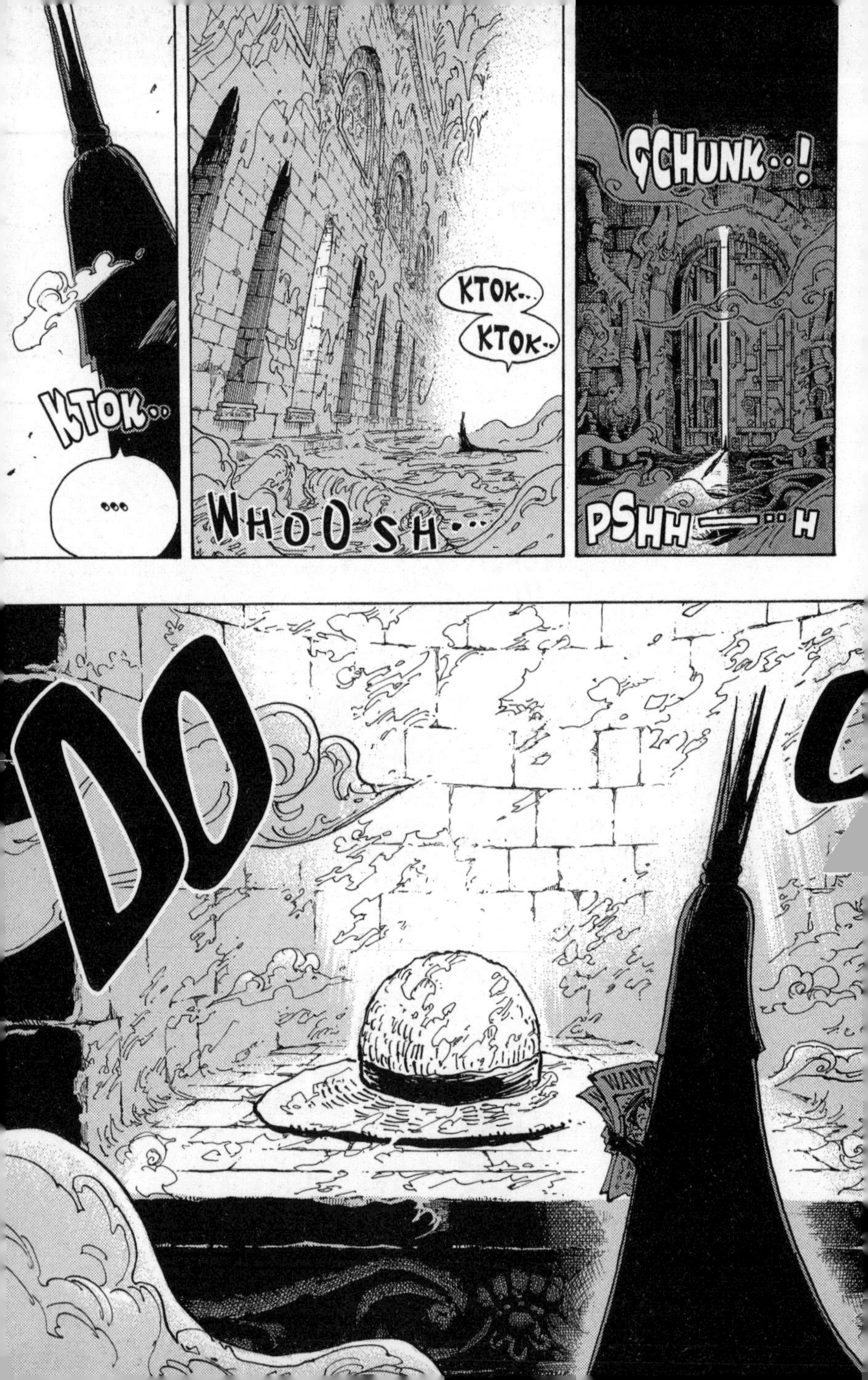
GCHUNK..!
PSHH—..H
KTOK...
KTOK..
WHOOSH..
KTOK..
...
DO

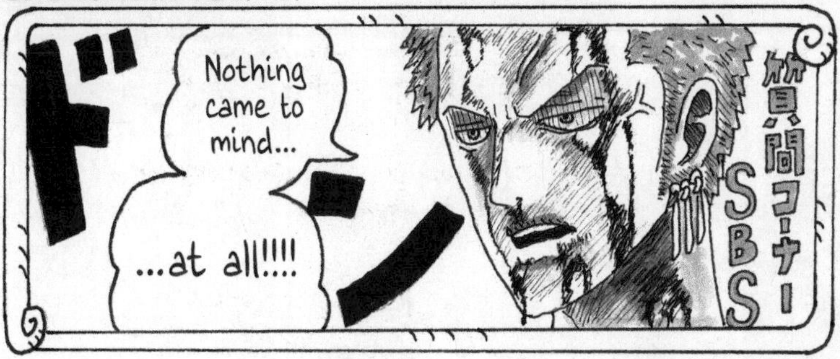
質問コーナー
SBS
Nothing came to mind...
...at all!!!!

(Masamichi Kobayashi, Gunma)

Q: So, that's Fire Atacchan in chapter 905, right? He's calling Morgans "Boss," so does that mean he's working as a photographer for the *World Economic Journal* now? Fire!!

--Match and Takeshi

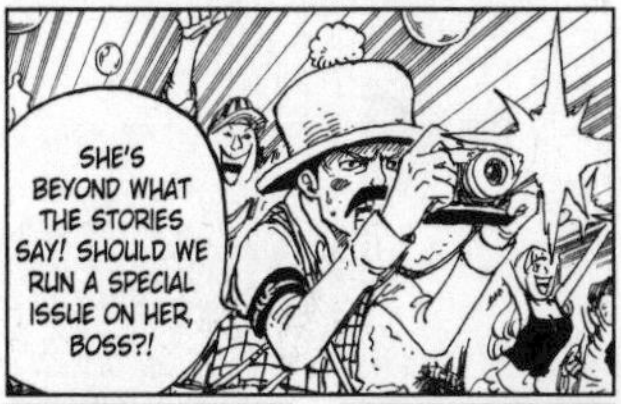
SHE'S BEYOND WHAT THE STORIES SAY! SHOULD WE RUN A SPECIAL ISSUE ON HER, BOSS?!

A: Yes, that's correct. He is the famous cameraman, Fire Atacchan. Long ago he was the head of the Navy's Photography Office, but after the 57th instance of him forgetting to remove the cap from his lens, he finally got fired. Morgans hired him after that. Now he takes aim with his cap-less camera for the WEJ and shouts his catchphrase, "Fire!"

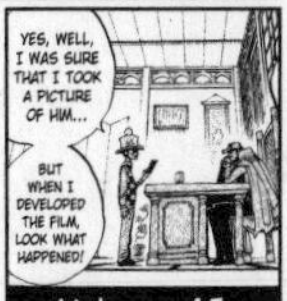
YES, WELL, I WAS SURE THAT I TOOK A PICTURE OF HIM...
BUT WHEN I DEVELOPED THE FILM, LOOK WHAT HAPPENED!
Volume 45

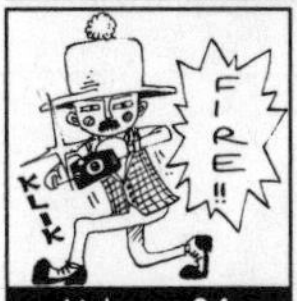
FIRE!!
KLIK
Volume 24

Q: Hello, Mr. Oda! So, Luffy uses his hat to cover Katakuri's mouth after he beat him in their fight! Both of them were so cool!! I think that if I ever happen across a naked sleeping Oda on the side of the road, I would use my hat to cover his "symbol of manhood"!!

--Neon

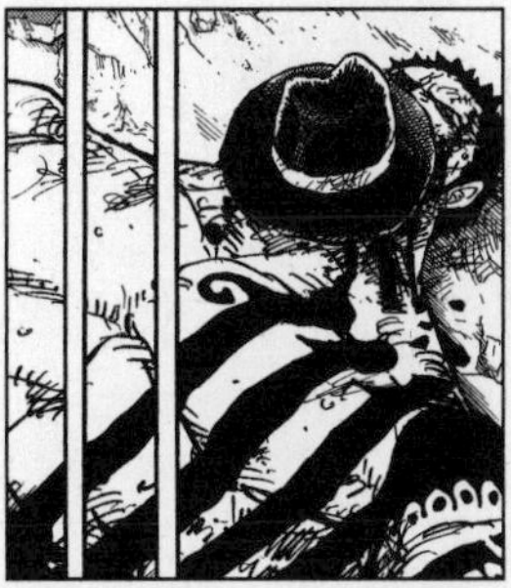

A: I understand how that goes. Every now and then, you spot a naked sleeping Oda on the side of the road. Thank you. But I have to ask, will that be enough? Can you cover my symbol of manhood **with a mere hat?!** (Yes, you can. I'll shut up now.)

Q: You always answer these dirty questions. Doesn't your wife get angry at you?

--Pigya

A: My wife will laugh at anything I do, so we're fine! Thank you for your concern about my family life!! Also, it's not my fault that the SBS is like this!!

Chapter 907:
THE EMPTY THRONE

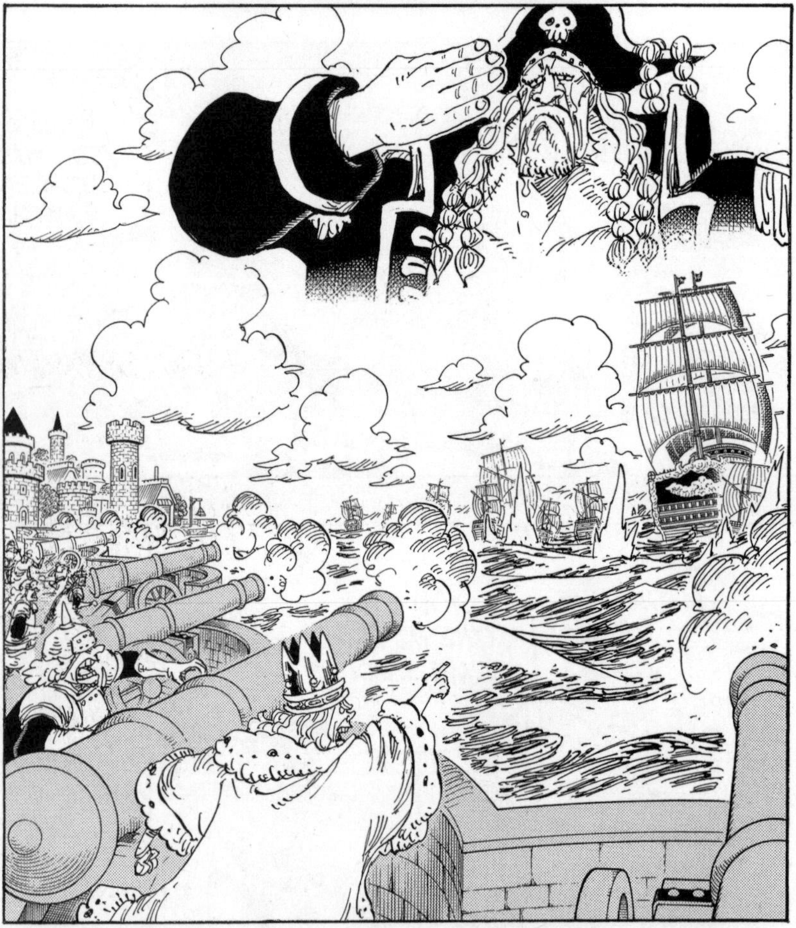

THE SAGA OF THE SELF-PROCLAIMED STRAW HAT FLEET, VOL. 37, ORLUMBUS: "STEALING A 56-SHIP FLEET IN A TEARFUL DEPARTURE: THANK YOU FOR EVERYTHING"

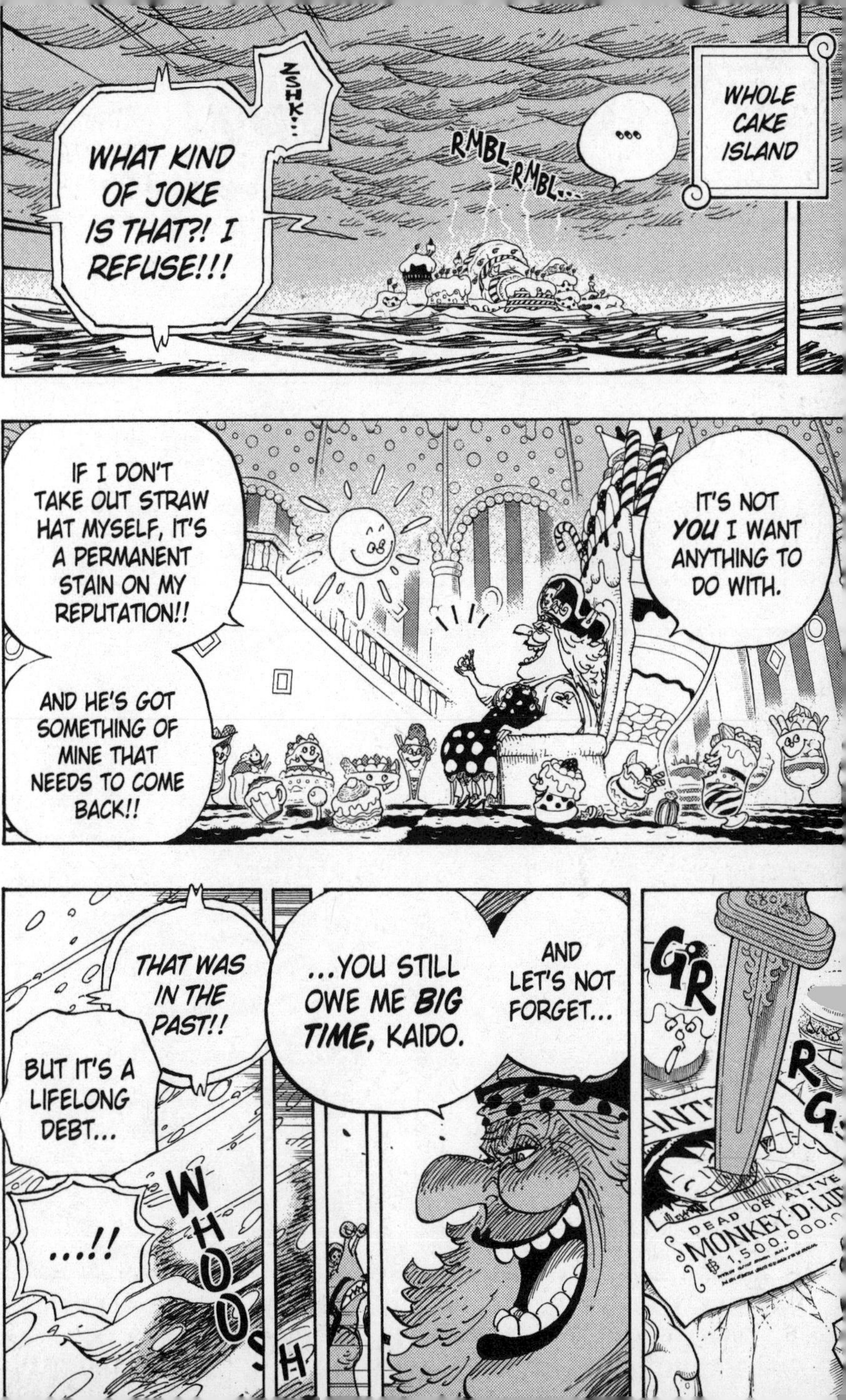
WHOLE CAKE ISLAND
...
RMBL RMBL...
ZSHK...
WHAT KIND OF JOKE IS THAT?! I REFUSE!!!
IT'S NOT **YOU** I WANT ANYTHING TO DO WITH.
IF I DON'T TAKE OUT STRAW HAT MYSELF, IT'S A PERMANENT STAIN ON MY REPUTATION!!
AND HE'S GOT SOMETHING OF MINE THAT NEEDS TO COME BACK!!
GR
RG
DEAD OR ALIVE
AND LET'S NOT FORGET...
...YOU STILL OWE ME **BIG TIME**, KAIDO.
THAT WAS IN THE PAST!!
BUT IT'S A LIFELONG DEBT...
WHOOSH
...!!

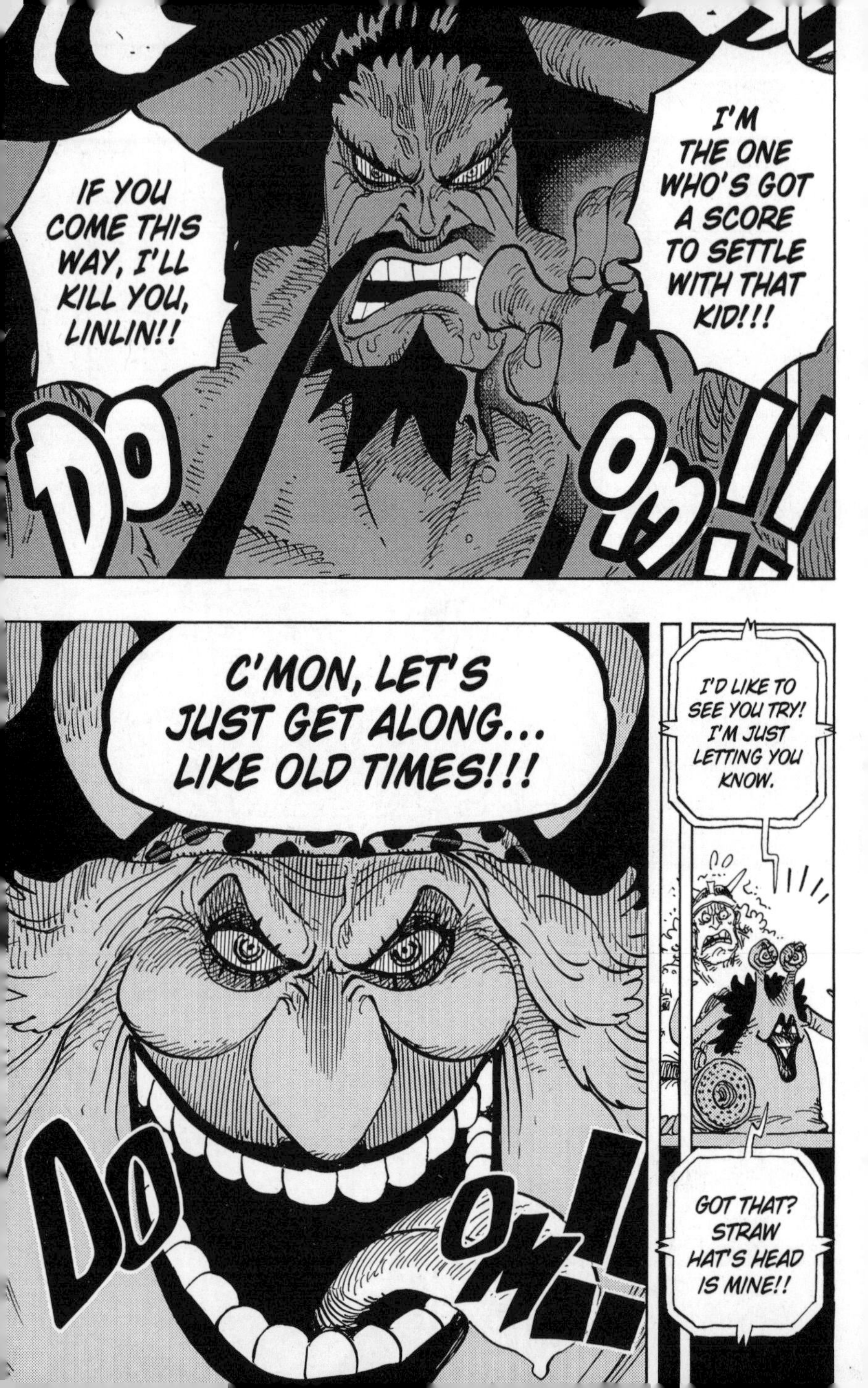
I'M THE ONE WHO'S GOT A SCORE TO SETTLE WITH THAT KID!!!
IF YOU COME THIS WAY, I'LL KILL YOU, LINLIN!!
DOOM!!
I'D LIKE TO SEE YOU TRY! I'M JUST LETTING YOU KNOW.
GOT THAT? STRAW HAT'S HEAD IS MINE!!
C'MON, LET'S JUST GET ALONG... LIKE OLD TIMES!!!
DOOM!!

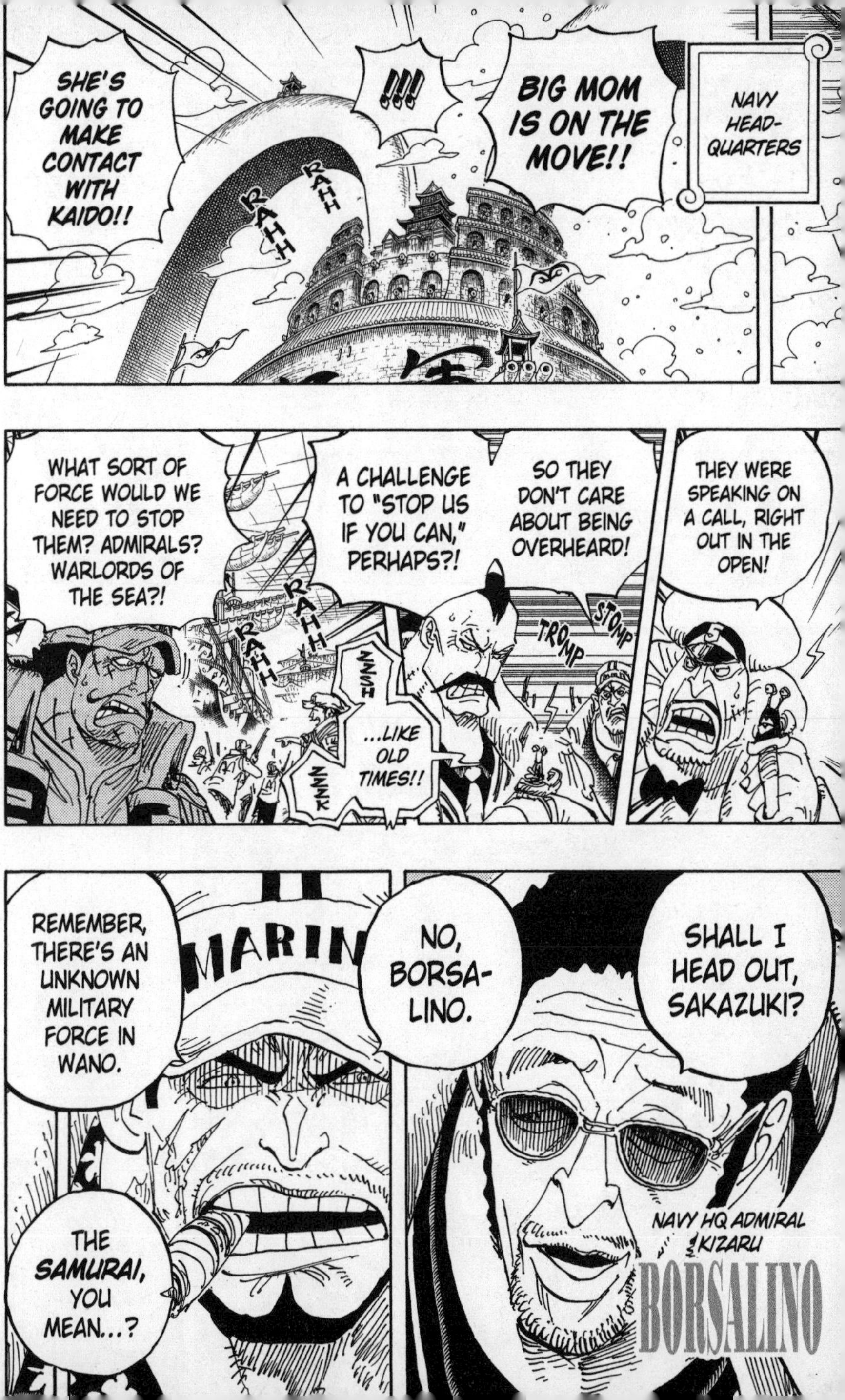
NAVY HEADQUARTERS
BIG MOM IS ON THE MOVE!!
!!!
SHE'S GOING TO MAKE CONTACT WITH KAIDO!!
RAHH RAHH
THEY WERE SPEAKING ON A CALL, RIGHT OUT IN THE OPEN!
SO THEY DON'T CARE ABOUT BEING OVERHEARD!
A CHALLENGE TO "STOP US IF YOU CAN," PERHAPS?!
WHAT SORT OF FORCE WOULD WE NEED TO STOP THEM? ADMIRALS? WARLORDS OF THE SEA?!
STOMP
TROMP
RAHH RAHH
ZZZSH
ZZZK
...LIKE OLD TIMES!!
SHALL I HEAD OUT, SAKAZUKI?
NAVY HQ ADMIRAL KIZARU
BORSALINO
NO, BORSALINO.
MARIN
REMEMBER, THERE'S AN UNKNOWN MILITARY FORCE IN WANO.
THE SAMURAI, YOU MEAN...?

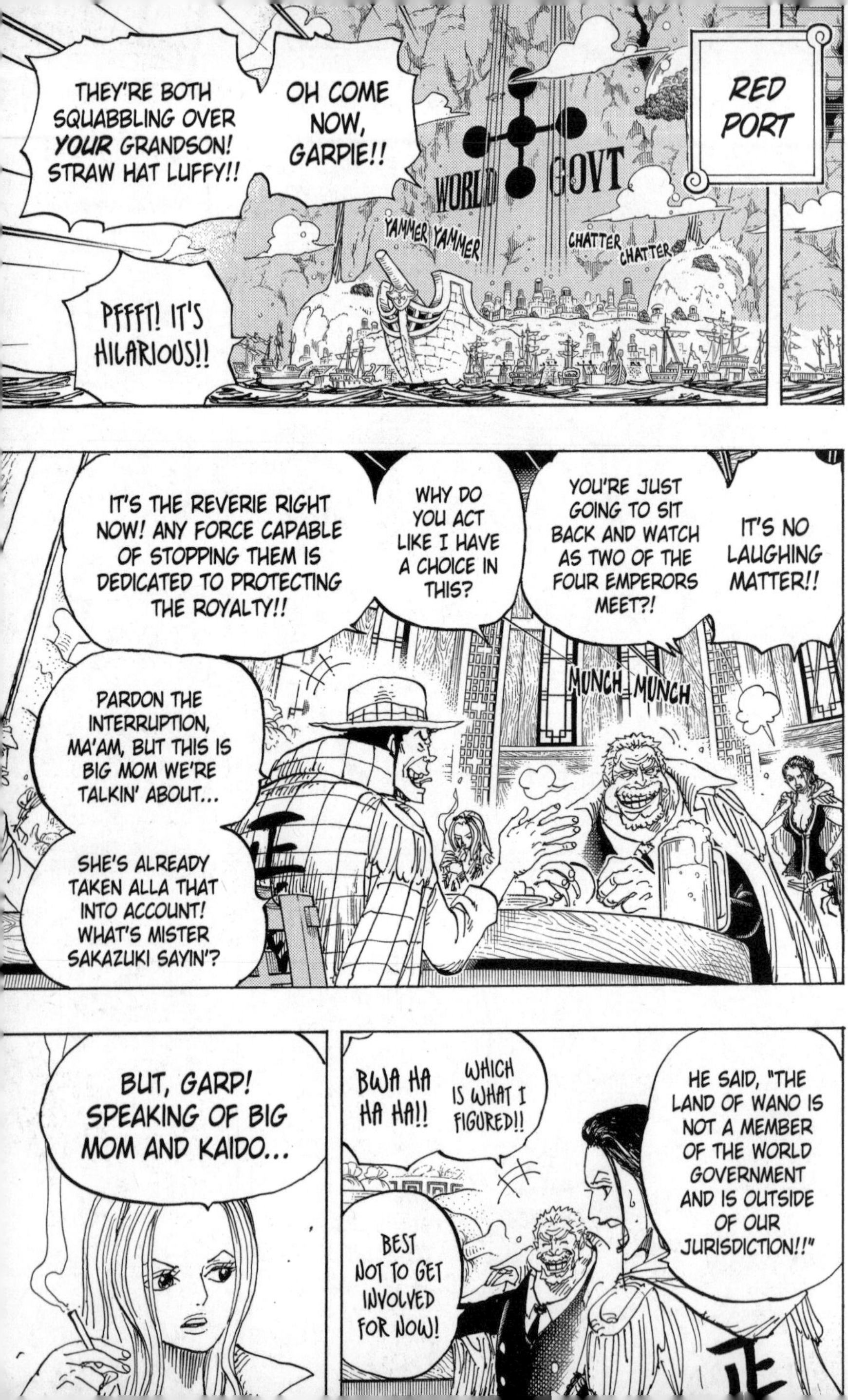
RED PORT
WORLD GOVT
CHATTER CHATTER
YAMMER YAMMER
OH COME NOW, GARPIE!!
THEY'RE BOTH SQUABBLING OVER YOUR GRANDSON! STRAW HAT LUFFY!!
PFFFT! IT'S HILARIOUS!!
IT'S NO LAUGHING MATTER!!
YOU'RE JUST GOING TO SIT BACK AND WATCH AS TWO OF THE FOUR EMPERORS MEET?!
WHY DO YOU ACT LIKE I HAVE A CHOICE IN THIS?
IT'S THE REVERIE RIGHT NOW! ANY FORCE CAPABLE OF STOPPING THEM IS DEDICATED TO PROTECTING THE ROYALTY!!
MUNCH MUNCH
PARDON THE INTERRUPTION, MA'AM, BUT THIS IS BIG MOM WE'RE TALKIN' ABOUT...
SHE'S ALREADY TAKEN ALLA THAT INTO ACCOUNT! WHAT'S MISTER SAKAZUKI SAYIN'?
HE SAID, "THE LAND OF WANO IS NOT A MEMBER OF THE WORLD GOVERNMENT AND IS OUTSIDE OF OUR JURISDICTION!!"
WHICH IS WHAT I FIGURED!!
BWA HA HA HA!!
BEST NOT TO GET INVOLVED FOR NOW!
BUT, GARP! SPEAKING OF BIG MOM AND KAIDO...

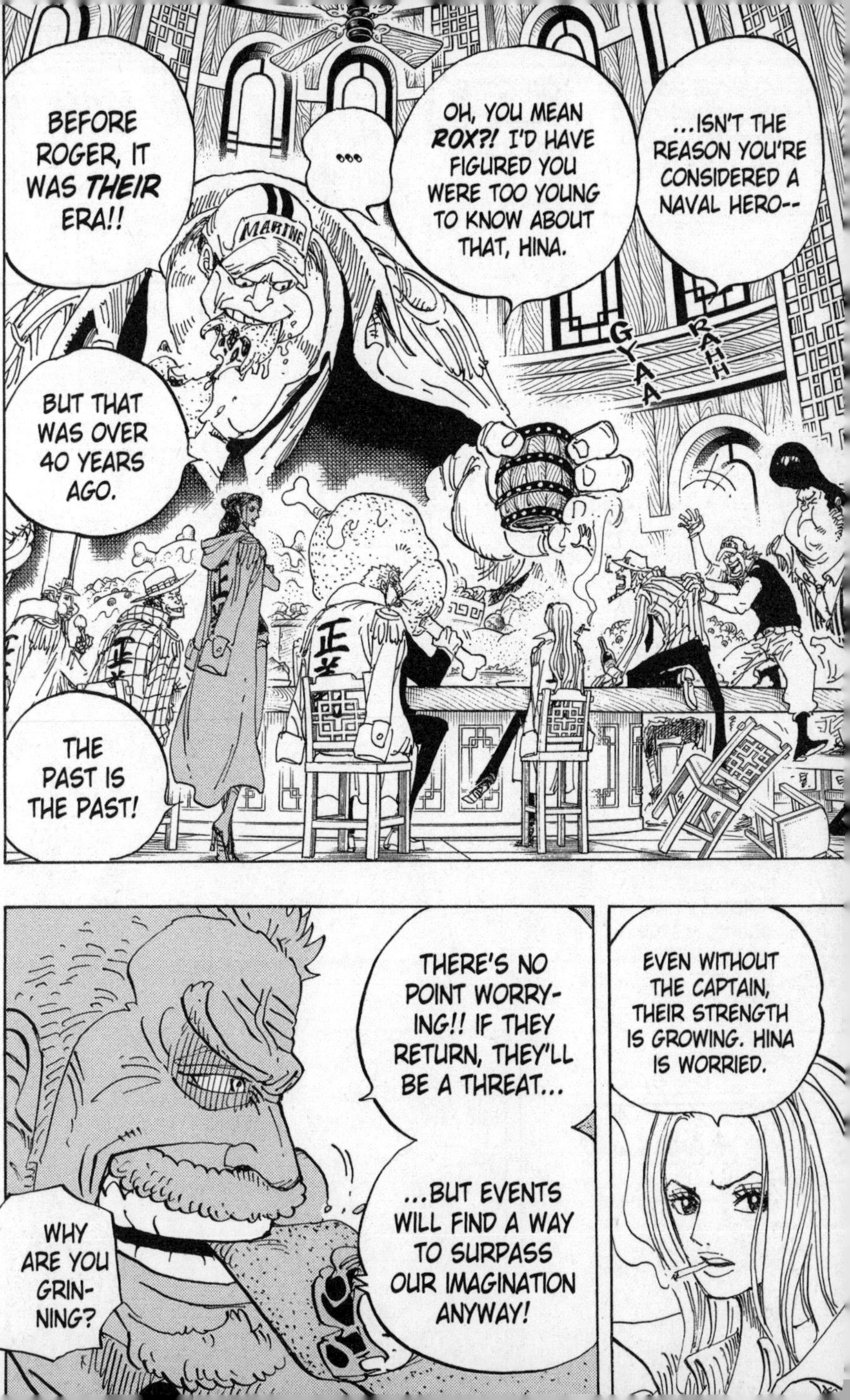
...ISN'T THE REASON YOU'RE CONSIDERED A NAVAL HERO--
OH, YOU MEAN ROX?! I'D HAVE FIGURED YOU WERE TOO YOUNG TO KNOW ABOUT THAT, HINA.
...
BEFORE ROGER, IT WAS THEIR ERA!!
MARINE
GYAA
RAHH
BUT THAT WAS OVER 40 YEARS AGO.
THE PAST IS THE PAST!
EVEN WITHOUT THE CAPTAIN, THEIR STRENGTH IS GROWING. HINA IS WORRIED.
THERE'S NO POINT WORRY-ING!! IF THEY RETURN, THEY'LL BE A THREAT...
...BUT EVENTS WILL FIND A WAY TO SURPASS OUR IMAGINATION ANYWAY!
WHY ARE YOU GRIN-NING?

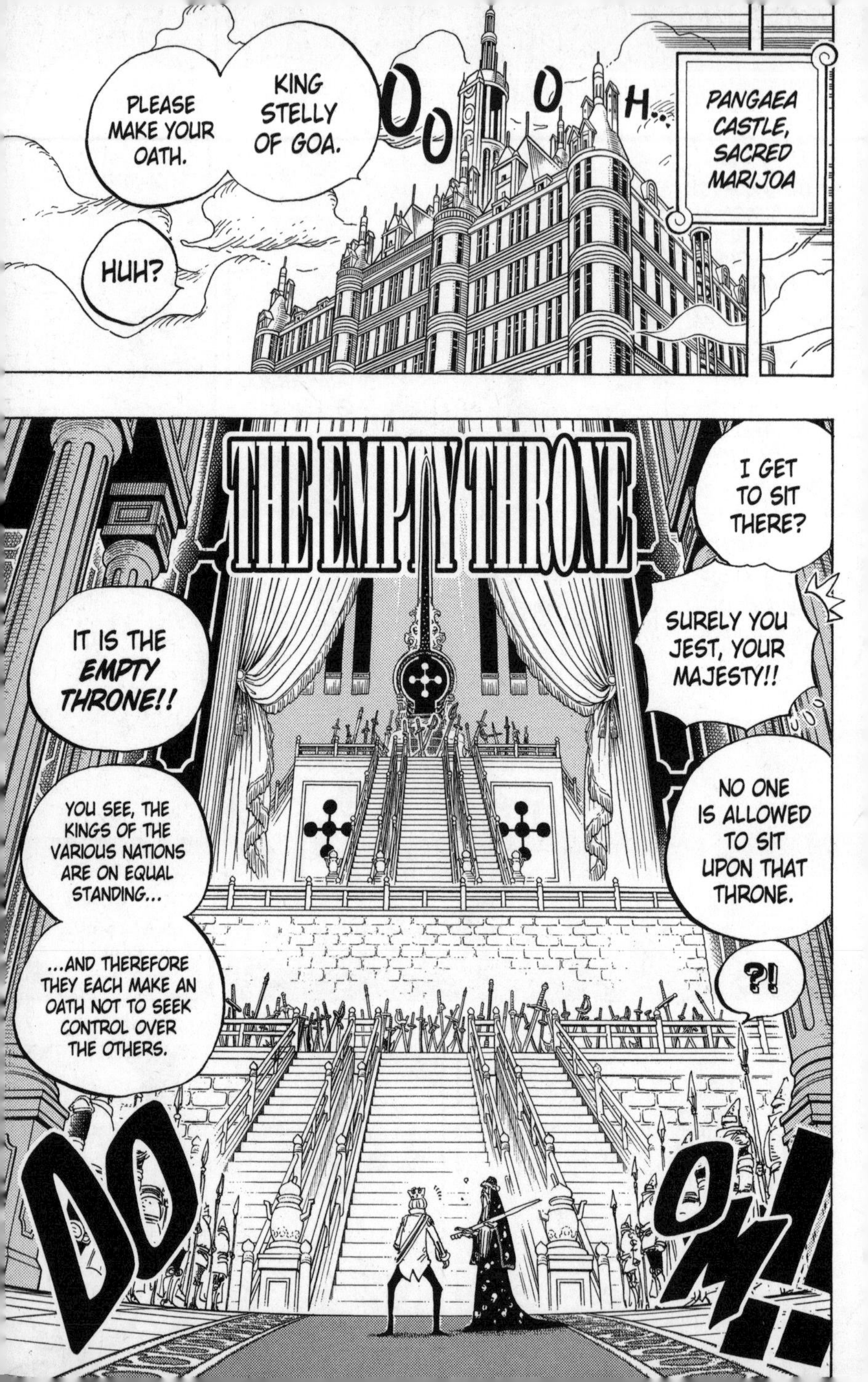
PANGAEA CASTLE, SACRED MARIJOA
OOOH...
KING STELLY OF GOA.
PLEASE MAKE YOUR OATH.
HUH?
THE EMPTY THRONE
I GET TO SIT THERE?
SURELY YOU JEST, YOUR MAJESTY!!
IT IS THE EMPTY THRONE!!
NO ONE IS ALLOWED TO SIT UPON THAT THRONE.
?!
YOU SEE, THE KINGS OF THE VARIOUS NATIONS ARE ON EQUAL STANDING...
...AND THEREFORE THEY EACH MAKE AN OATH NOT TO SEEK CONTROL OVER THE OTHERS.
DOOM!!

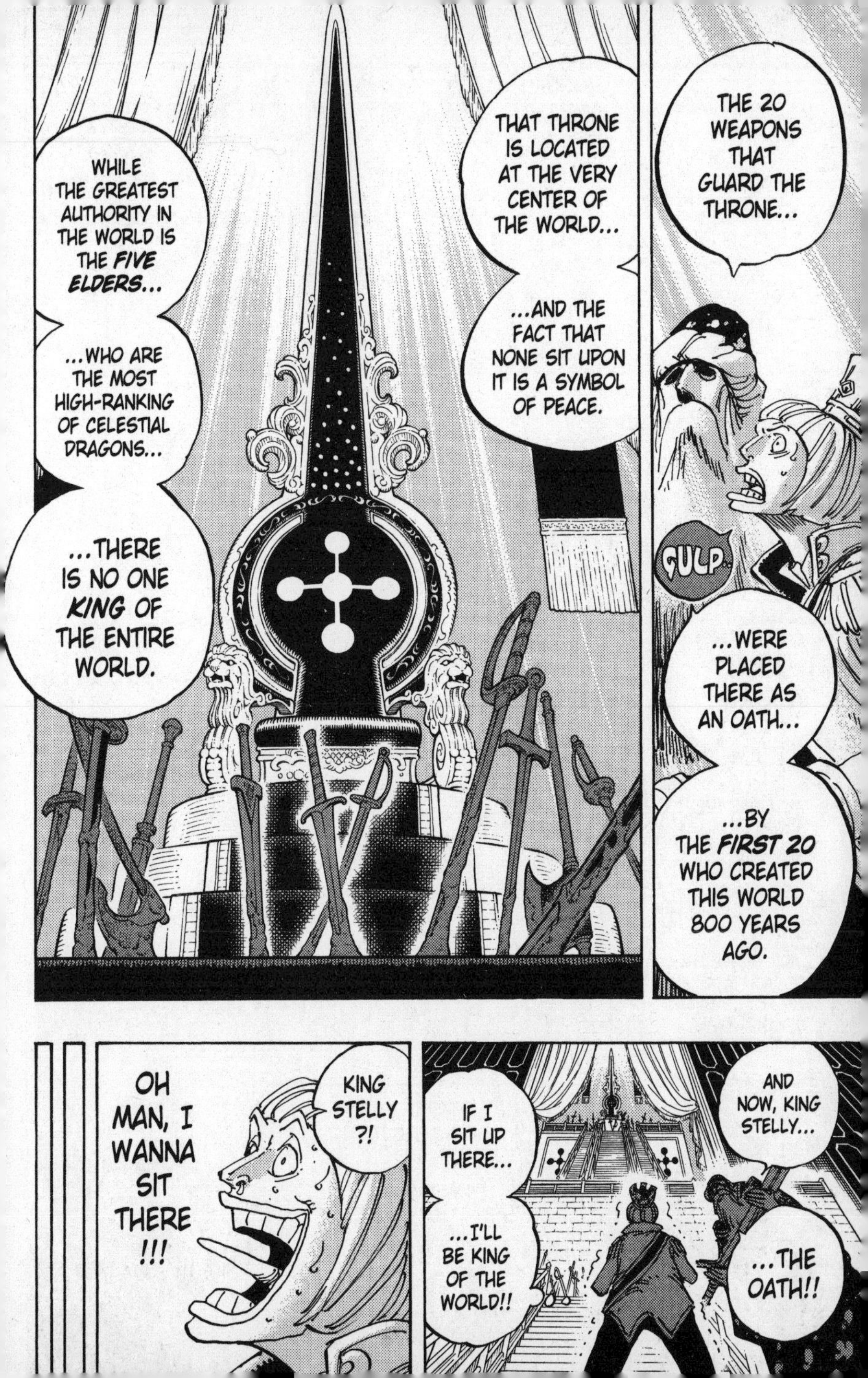

WHILE THE GREATEST AUTHORITY IN THE WORLD IS THE *FIVE ELDERS*...
...WHO ARE THE MOST HIGH-RANKING OF CELESTIAL DRAGONS...
...THERE IS NO ONE *KING* OF THE ENTIRE WORLD.
THAT THRONE IS LOCATED AT THE VERY CENTER OF THE WORLD...
...AND THE FACT THAT NONE SIT UPON IT IS A SYMBOL OF PEACE.
THE 20 WEAPONS THAT GUARD THE THRONE...
GULP..
...WERE PLACED THERE AS AN OATH...
...BY THE *FIRST 20* WHO CREATED THIS WORLD 800 YEARS AGO.
AND NOW, KING STELLY...
...THE OATH!!
IF I SIT UP THERE...
...I'LL BE KING OF THE WORLD!!
KING STELLY ?!
OH MAN, I WANNA SIT THERE !!!

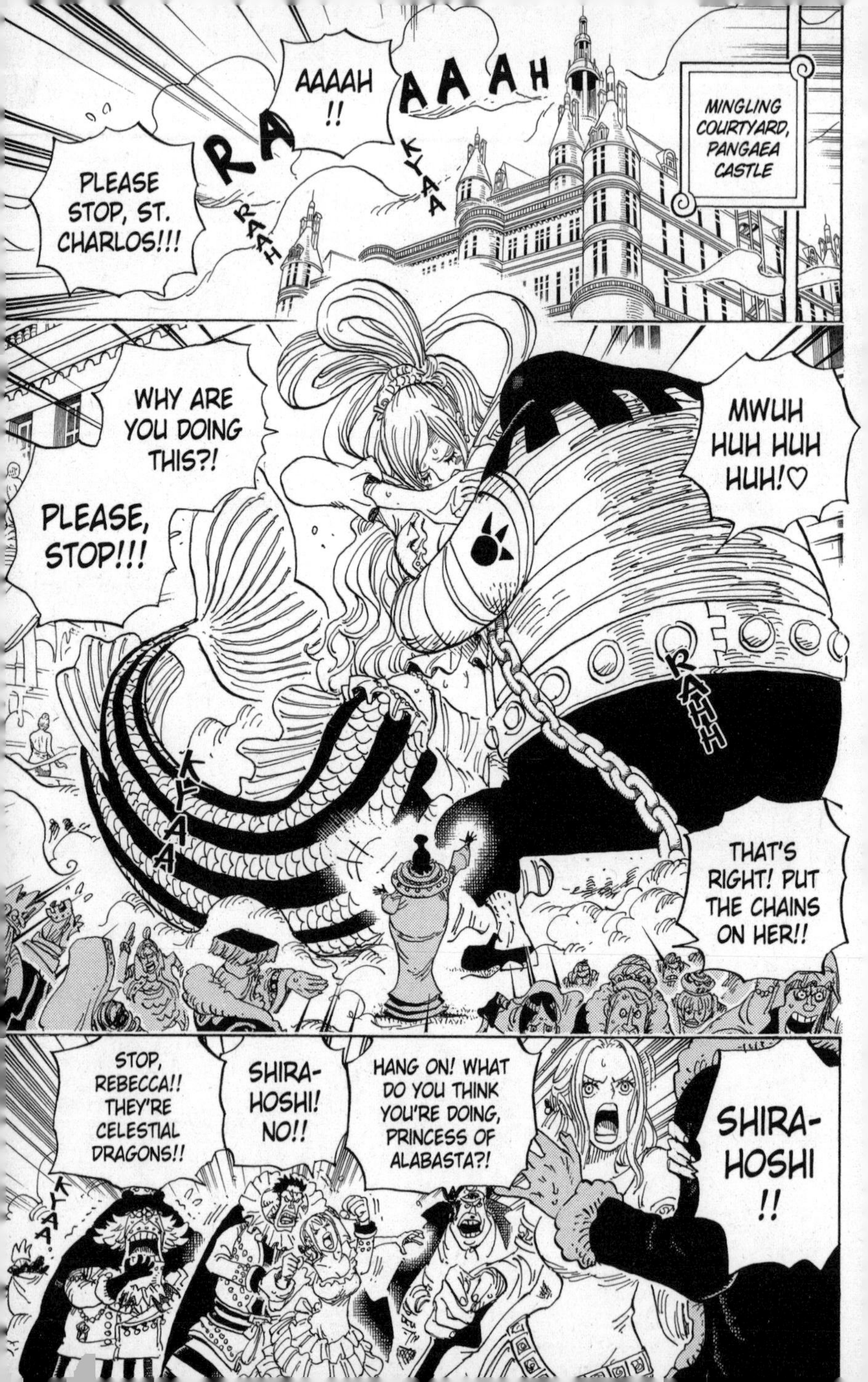
MINGLING COURTYARD, PANGAEA CASTLE
RAAAAH
AAAAH!!
KYAA
RAAH
PLEASE STOP, ST. CHARLOS!!!
MWUH HUH HUH HUH!♡
WHY ARE YOU DOING THIS?!
PLEASE, STOP!!!
RAHHH
KYAA
THAT'S RIGHT! PUT THE CHAINS ON HER!!
SHIRA-HOSHI!!
HANG ON! WHAT DO YOU THINK YOU'RE DOING, PRINCESS OF ALABASTA?!
SHIRA-HOSHI! NO!!
STOP, REBECCA!! THEY'RE CELESTIAL DRAGONS!!
KYAA

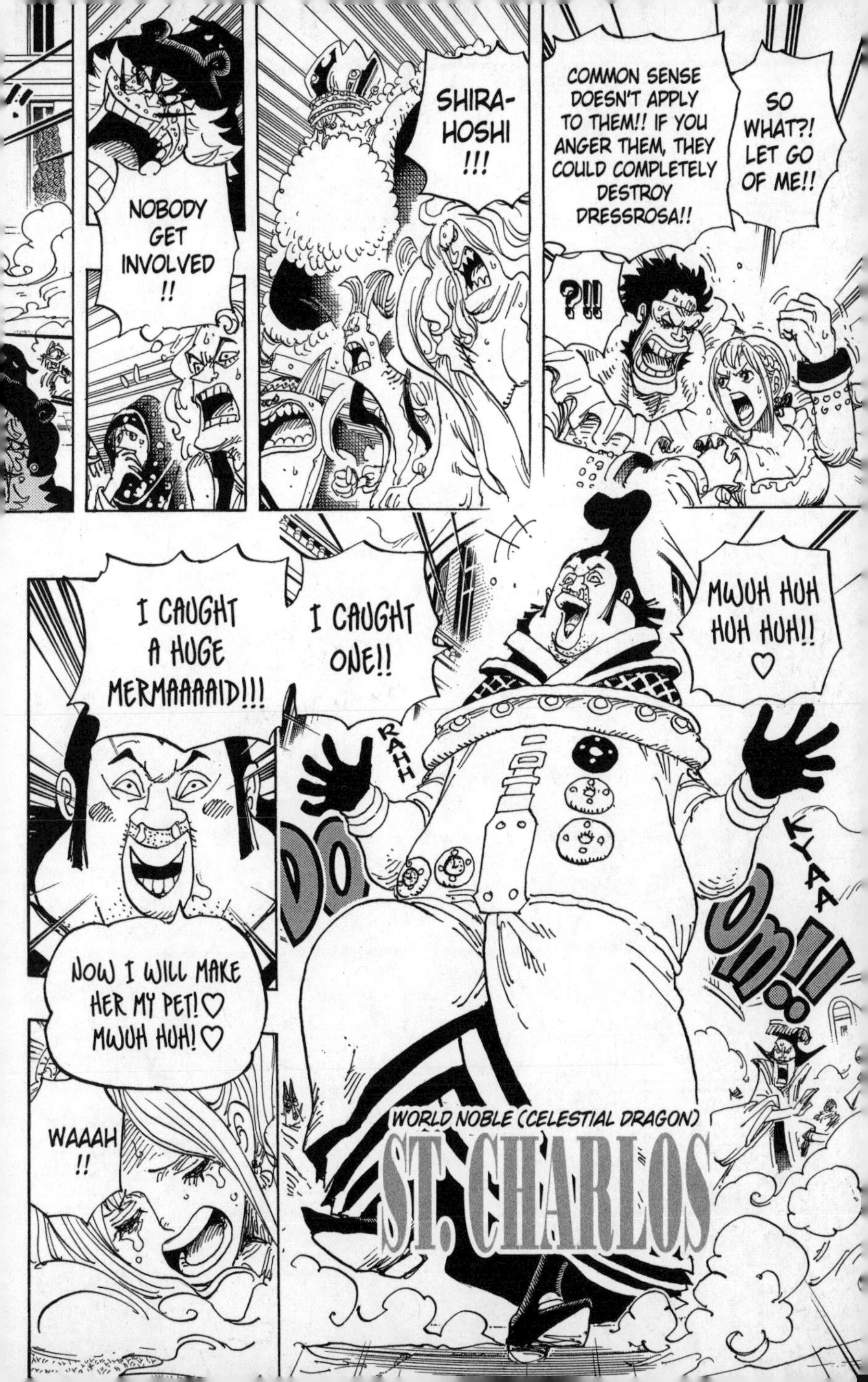
SO WHAT?! LET GO OF ME!!
COMMON SENSE DOESN'T APPLY TO THEM!! IF YOU ANGER THEM, THEY COULD COMPLETELY DESTROY DRESSROSA!!
?!!
SHIRA-HOSHI !!!
NOBODY GET INVOLVED !!
!!
MWUH HUH HUH HUH!! ♡
I CAUGHT ONE!!
RAHH
KYAA
DOOM!!
WORLD NOBLE (CELESTIAL DRAGON)
ST. CHARLOS
I CAUGHT A HUGE MERMAAAAID!!!
NOW I WILL MAKE HER MY PET! ♡ MWUH HUH! ♡
WAAAH !!

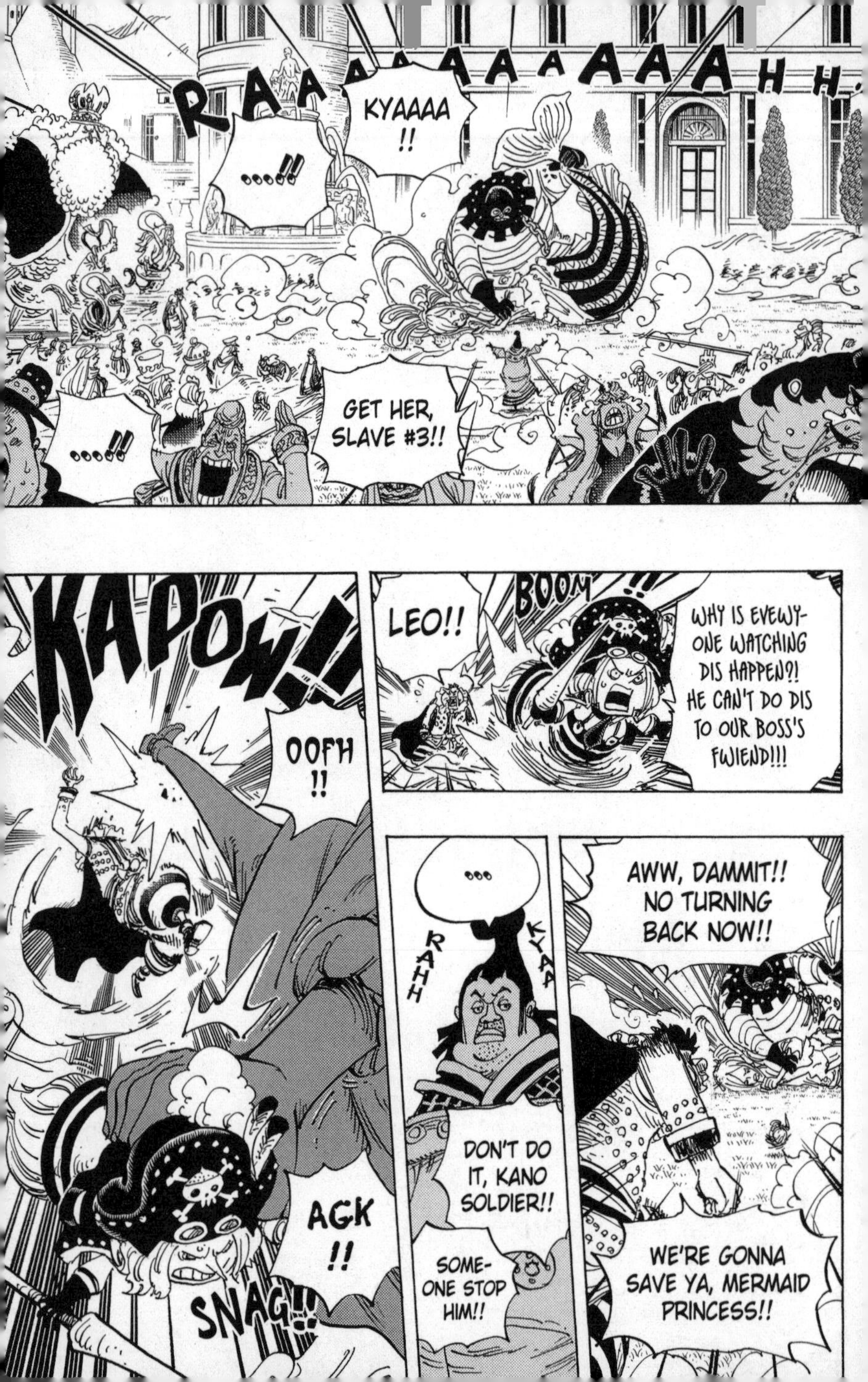
RAAAAAAAAAAAH.
KYAAAA !!
....!!
GET HER, SLAVE #3!!
....!!
WHY IS EVEWY-ONE WATCHING DIS HAPPEN?! HE CAN'T DO DIS TO OUR BOSS'S FWIEND!!!
BOOM!!
LEO!!
AWW, DAMMIT!! NO TURNING BACK NOW!!
WE'RE GONNA SAVE YA, MERMAID PRINCESS!!
...
KYAA
RAHH
DON'T DO IT, KANO SOLDIER!!
SOME-ONE STOP HIM!!
KAPOW!!
OOFH !!
AGK !!
SNAG!!

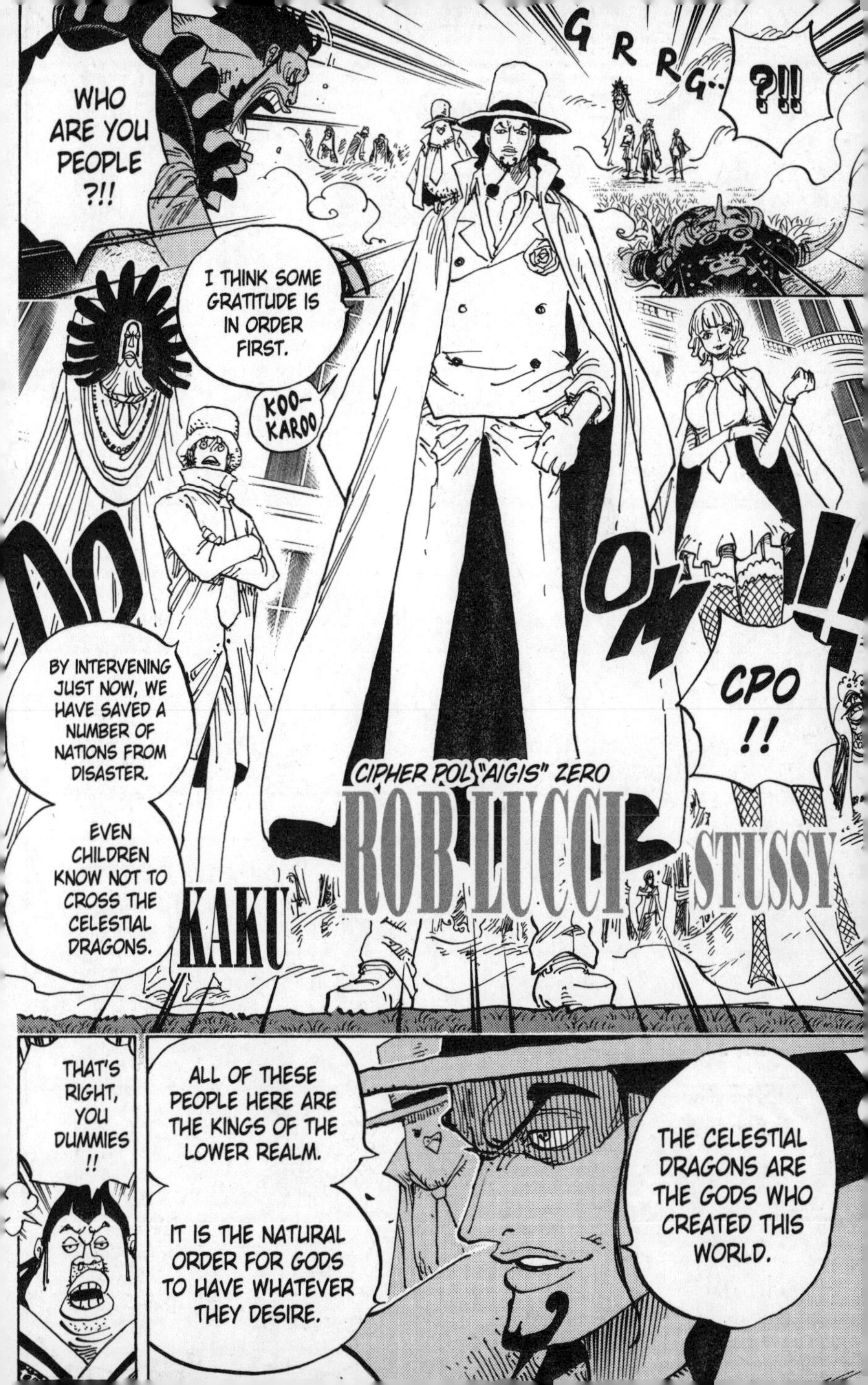
?!!
G R R G..
WHO ARE YOU PEOPLE ?!!
I THINK SOME GRATITUDE IS IN ORDER FIRST.
KOO-KAROO
DOOM!!
CPO !!
CIPHER POL "AIGIS" ZERO
STUSSY
ROB LUCCI
KAKU
BY INTERVENING JUST NOW, WE HAVE SAVED A NUMBER OF NATIONS FROM DISASTER.
EVEN CHILDREN KNOW NOT TO CROSS THE CELESTIAL DRAGONS.
THE CELESTIAL DRAGONS ARE THE GODS WHO CREATED THIS WORLD.
ALL OF THESE PEOPLE HERE ARE THE KINGS OF THE LOWER REALM.
IT IS THE NATURAL ORDER FOR GODS TO HAVE WHATEVER THEY DESIRE.
THAT'S RIGHT, YOU DUMMIES !!

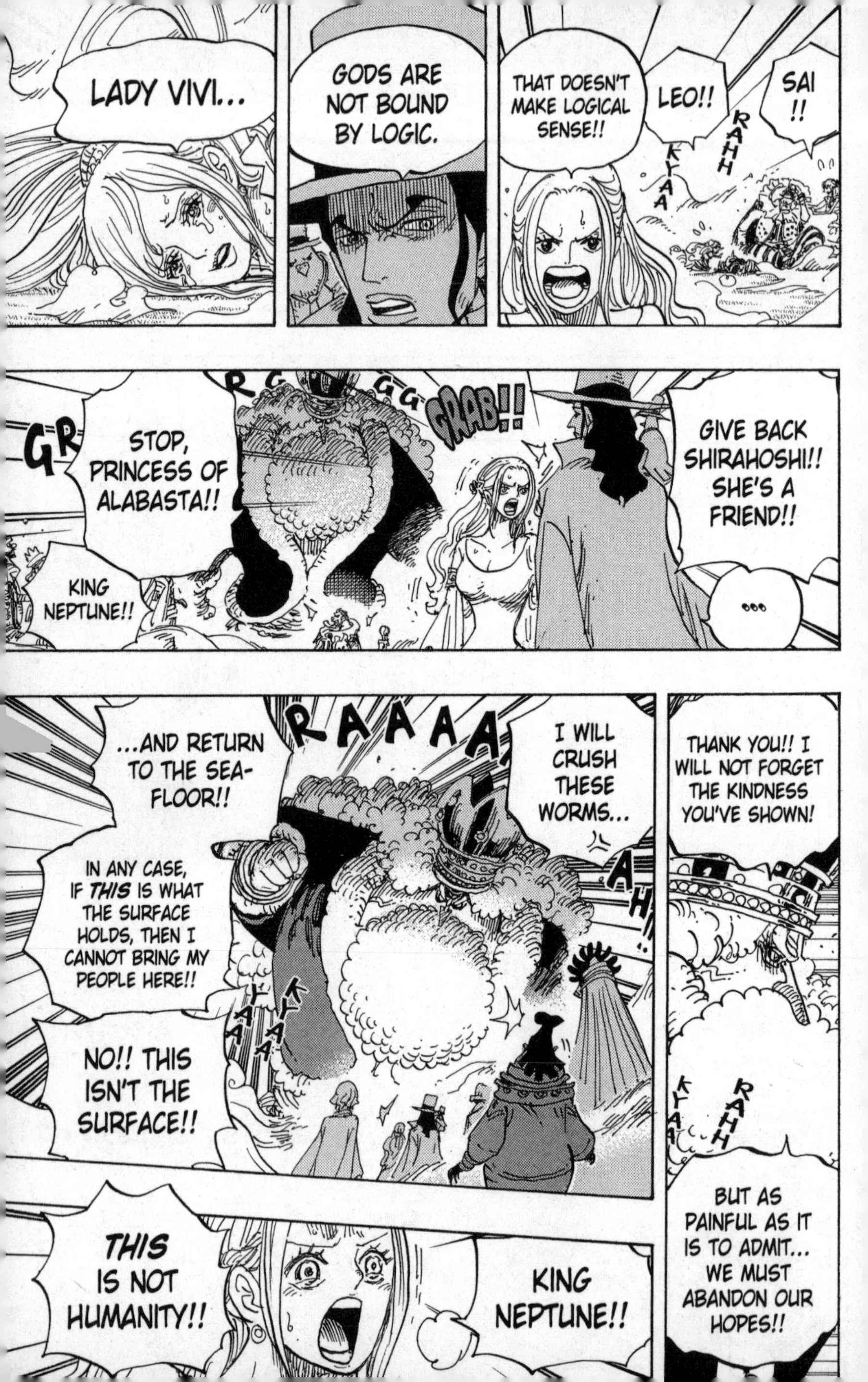
SAI !!
LEO!!
RAHH
KYAA
THAT DOESN'T MAKE LOGICAL SENSE!!
GODS ARE NOT BOUND BY LOGIC.
LADY VIVI...
GIVE BACK SHIRAHOSHI!! SHE'S A FRIEND!!
GRAB!!
...
GG
RG
STOP, PRINCESS OF ALABASTA!!
GR
KING NEPTUNE!!
THANK YOU!! I WILL NOT FORGET THE KINDNESS YOU'VE SHOWN!
RAHH
KYAA
BUT AS PAINFUL AS IT IS TO ADMIT... WE MUST ABANDON OUR HOPES!!
I WILL CRUSH THESE WORMS...
AH!!
RAAAAA
...AND RETURN TO THE SEA-FLOOR!!
IN ANY CASE, IF *THIS* IS WHAT THE SURFACE HOLDS, THEN I CANNOT BRING MY PEOPLE HERE!!
KYAA
KYAA
NO!! THIS ISN'T THE SURFACE!!
KING NEPTUNE!!
THIS IS NOT HUMANITY!!

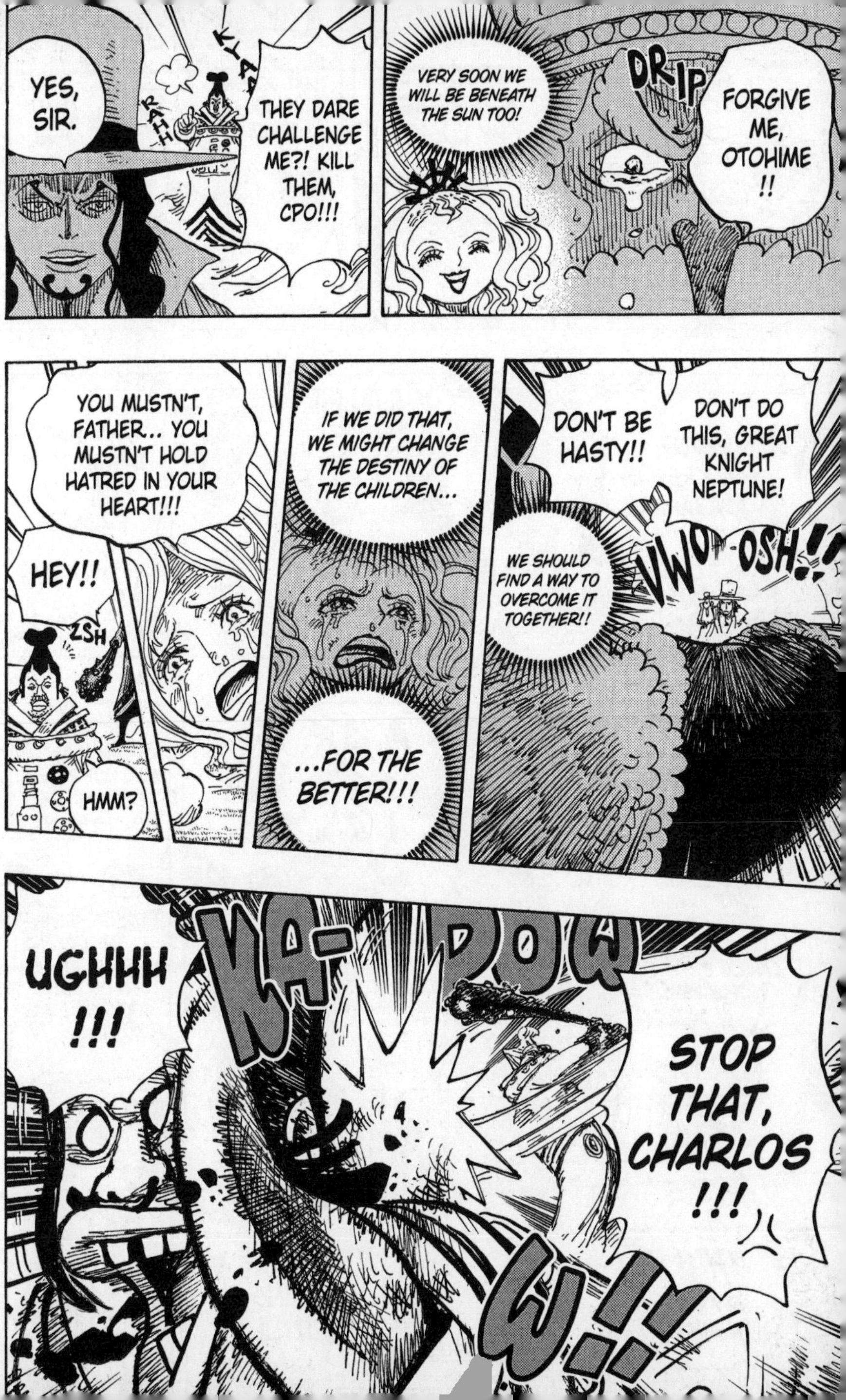
DRIP
FORGIVE ME, OTOHIME !!
VERY SOON WE WILL BE BENEATH THE SUN TOO!
KYAA
THEY DARE CHALLENGE ME?! KILL THEM, CPO!!!
RAHH
YES, SIR.
DON'T DO THIS, GREAT KNIGHT NEPTUNE!
DON'T BE HASTY!!
WE SHOULD FIND A WAY TO OVERCOME IT TOGETHER!!
VWO-OSH!!
IF WE DID THAT, WE MIGHT CHANGE THE DESTINY OF THE CHILDREN...
...FOR THE BETTER!!!
YOU MUSTN'T, FATHER... YOU MUSTN'T HOLD HATRED IN YOUR HEART!!!
HEY!!
ZSH
HMM?
STOP THAT, CHARLOS !!!
KA-DOOW!!
UGHHH !!!

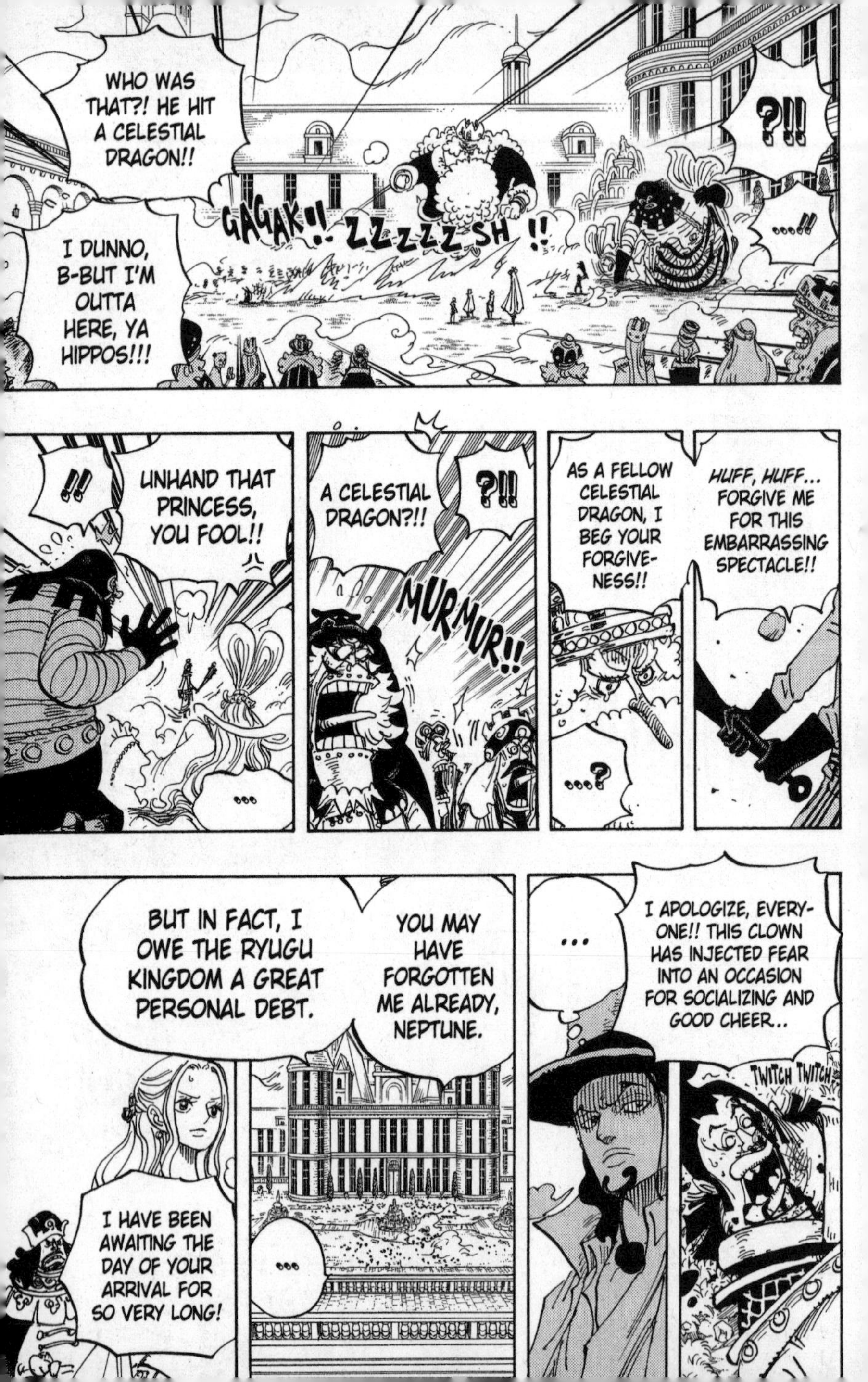
?!!
...!!
WHO WAS THAT?! HE HIT A CELESTIAL DRAGON!!
GAGAK!!
ZZZZZSH!!
I DUNNO, B-BUT I'M OUTTA HERE, YA HIPPOS!!!
HUFF, HUFF... FORGIVE ME FOR THIS EMBARRASSING SPECTACLE!!
AS A FELLOW CELESTIAL DRAGON, I BEG YOUR FORGIVE-NESS!!
...?
?!!
A CELESTIAL DRAGON?!!
MURMUR!!
!!
UNHAND THAT PRINCESS, YOU FOOL!!
...
I APOLOGIZE, EVERY-ONE!! THIS CLOWN HAS INJECTED FEAR INTO AN OCCASION FOR SOCIALIZING AND GOOD CHEER..
...
TWITCH TWITCH
YOU MAY HAVE FORGOTTEN ME ALREADY, NEPTUNE.
BUT IN FACT, I OWE THE RYUGU KINGDOM A GREAT PERSONAL DEBT.
...
I HAVE BEEN AWAITING THE DAY OF YOUR ARRIVAL FOR SO VERY LONG!

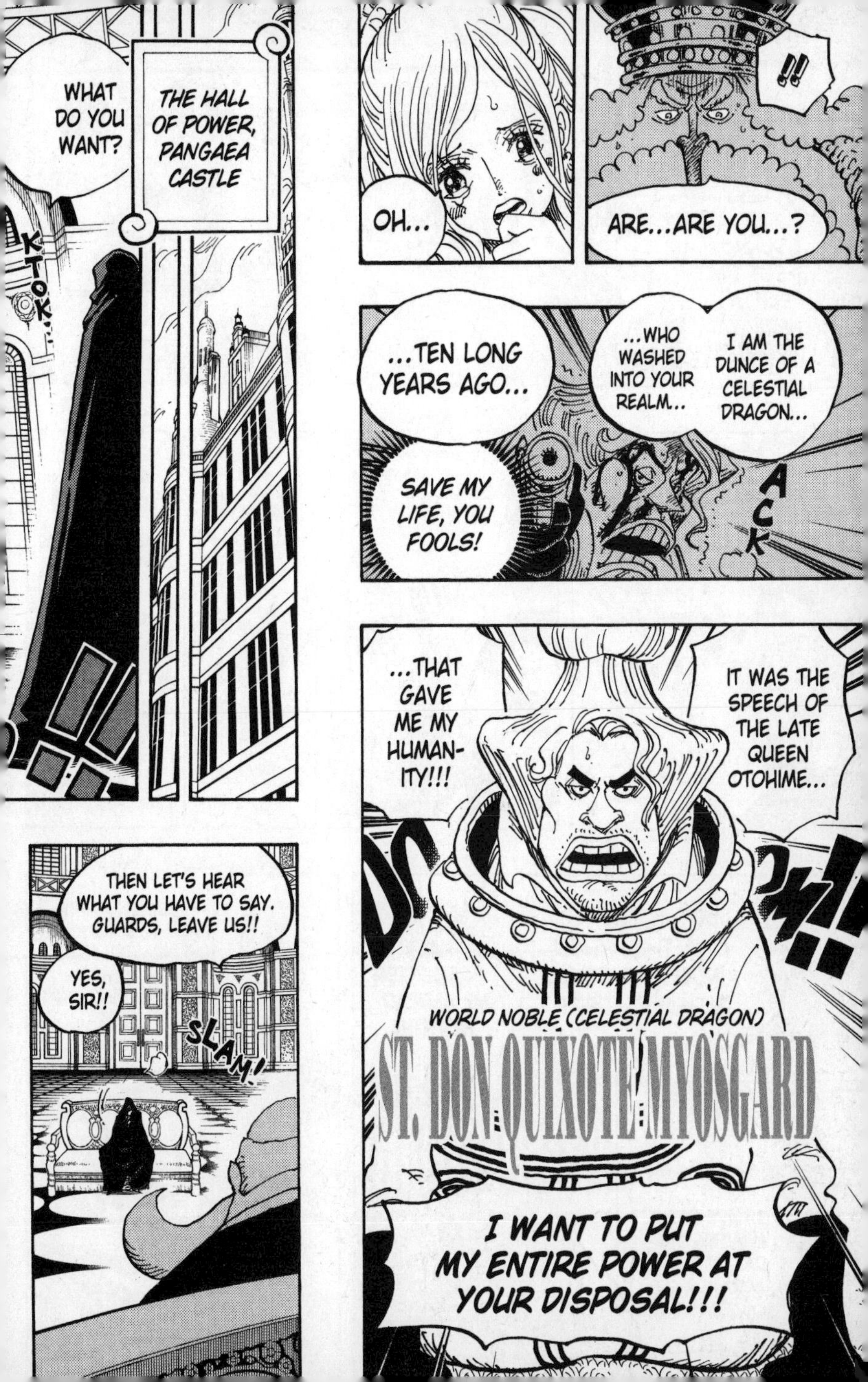
!!
ARE...ARE YOU...?
OH...
I AM THE DUNCE OF A CELESTIAL DRAGON...
...WHO WASHED INTO YOUR REALM...
...TEN LONG YEARS AGO...
SAVE MY LIFE, YOU FOOLS!
ACK
IT WAS THE SPEECH OF THE LATE QUEEN OTOHIME...
...THAT GAVE ME MY HUMANITY!!!
WORLD NOBLE (CELESTIAL DRAGON)
ST. DON QUIXOTE MYOSGARD
I WANT TO PUT MY ENTIRE POWER AT YOUR DISPOSAL!!!
THE HALL OF POWER, PANGAEA CASTLE
WHAT DO YOU WANT?
KTOK
THEN LET'S HEAR WHAT YOU HAVE TO SAY. GUARDS, LEAVE US!!
YES, SIR!!
SLAM!

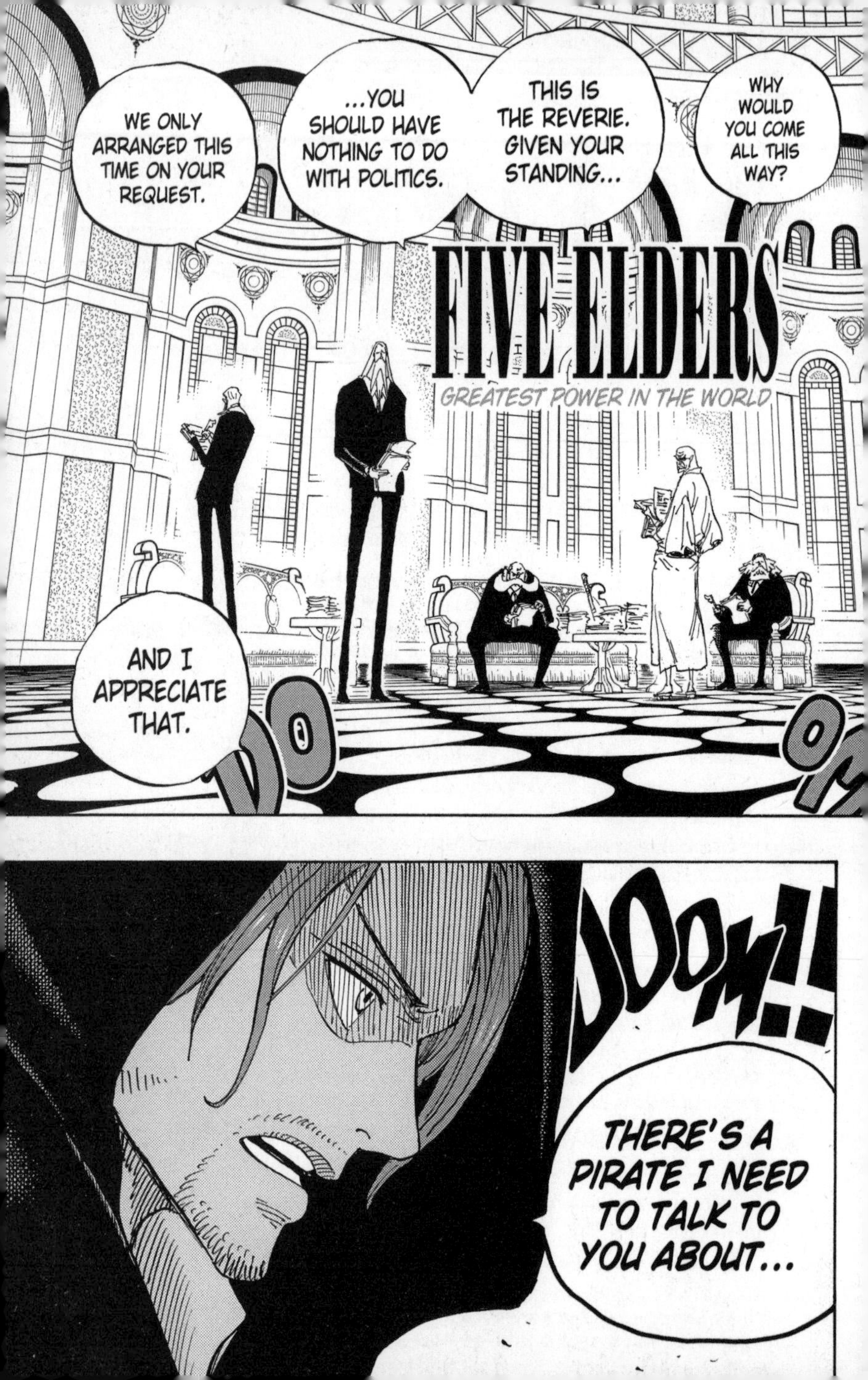
WHY WOULD YOU COME ALL THIS WAY?
THIS IS THE REVERIE. GIVEN YOUR STANDING...
...YOU SHOULD HAVE NOTHING TO DO WITH POLITICS.
WE ONLY ARRANGED THIS TIME ON YOUR REQUEST.
FIVE ELDERS
GREATEST POWER IN THE WORLD
AND I APPRECIATE THAT.
DOOM!!
THERE'S A PIRATE I NEED TO TALK TO YOU ABOUT...

SBS

(Takashi Mori (Chief), Tochigi)

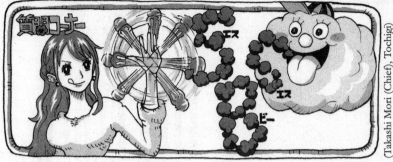

Q: In chapter 847, Perospero called Nami his little candy when she was covered in syrup. Does that mean he licked her after that? I can't do anything until I find out the answer! Please draw Perospero licking Nami! Please!!

--Woman Who Wants to Be an Author

KUH-KUH-KUH! WHY, MY LITTLE CANDY...
...YOU LOOK SO SWEET!♪
LICK
ELDEST SON OF, CHARLOTTE
PEROSPERO

A: Okay. No!! I was like, what perverted old man sent this request...and it's a girl!! Why are the dirty jokes so dirty this time?! The SBS is meant to be a place for a wholesome author and wholesome boys and girls to interact. Would you mind not tarnishing its good name?!

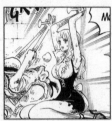

Q: Oda-Oda-Odacchi! I just got the bestest idea!! You know how *fugu* is a very delicious fish, but it's extremely poisonous? Well, as long as you have Reiju to suck out the poison afterward, you get both a tasty meal, and a… (tee heehee). Isn't that two birds with one stone?!

--Totally Pure 25-year-old

DOWN THE HATCH.♡
SMOOO

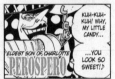

A: Ah, I see! Well, I hope you eat that fugu, get poisoned, and then find out that Reiju is busy and she can't show up to help you!!! You freak!!
(*Don't worry, fugu prepared at a restaurant is safe.)

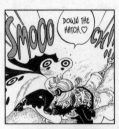

Q: When I hear the words "pirate," "40 years ago," and "Garp," I can't help but be put in mind of Shakky. Is there any connection between Shakky and this mysterious "Rox"?

--*World Economic Journal* Intern

SHAKKY USED TO BE A PIRATE.
THAT WAS 40 YEARS AGO. I'VE WASHED MY HANDS OF IT NOW.
FORTY YEARS? HOW OLD ARE YOU?

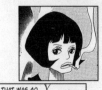

A: Oof...! Why would you remember something that happened 40 volumes ago? I...I have no idea what you mean! D...doo-de-doo-de-doo...♪

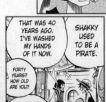

Chapter 908:
THE REVERIE BEGINS

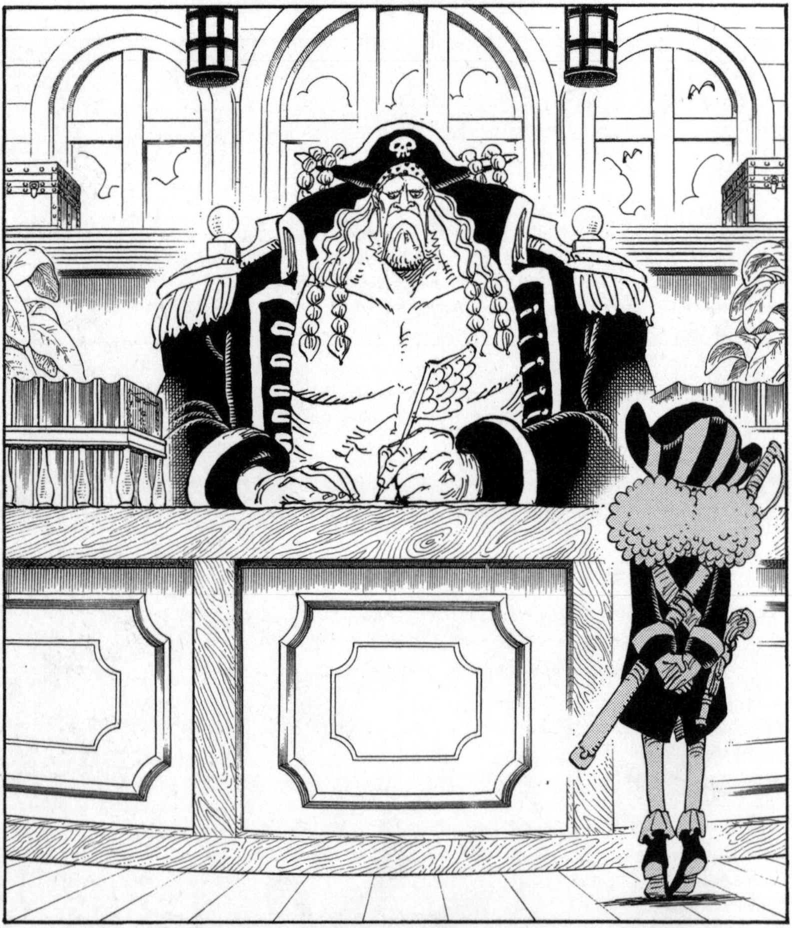

THE SAGA OF THE SELF-PROCLAIMED STRAW HAT FLEET, VOL. 38, ORLUMBUS: "3 P.M.: PLANNING CHART FOR PIRATING ACTIVITIES"

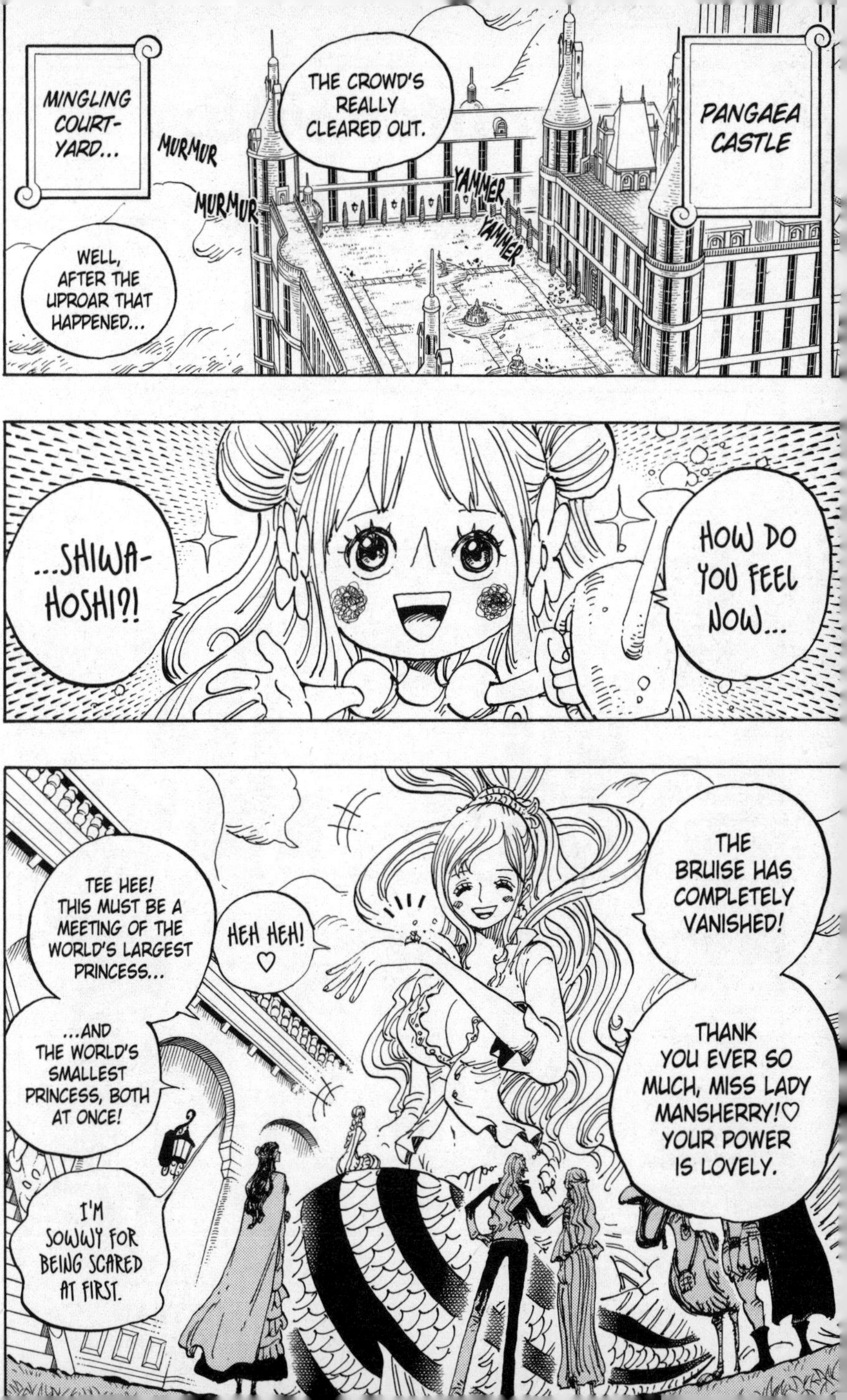
PANGAEA CASTLE
YAMMER
YAMMER
THE CROWD'S REALLY CLEARED OUT.
MINGLING COURT-YARD...
MURMUR
MURMUR
WELL, AFTER THE UPROAR THAT HAPPENED...
HOW DO YOU FEEL NOW...
...SHIWA-HOSHI?!
THE BRUISE HAS COMPLETELY VANISHED!
THANK YOU EVER SO MUCH, MISS LADY MANSHERRY!♡ YOUR POWER IS LOVELY.
HEH HEH! ♡
TEE HEE! THIS MUST BE A MEETING OF THE WORLD'S LARGEST PRINCESS...
...AND THE WORLD'S SMALLEST PRINCESS, BOTH AT ONCE!
I'M SOWWY FOR BEING SCARED AT FIRST.

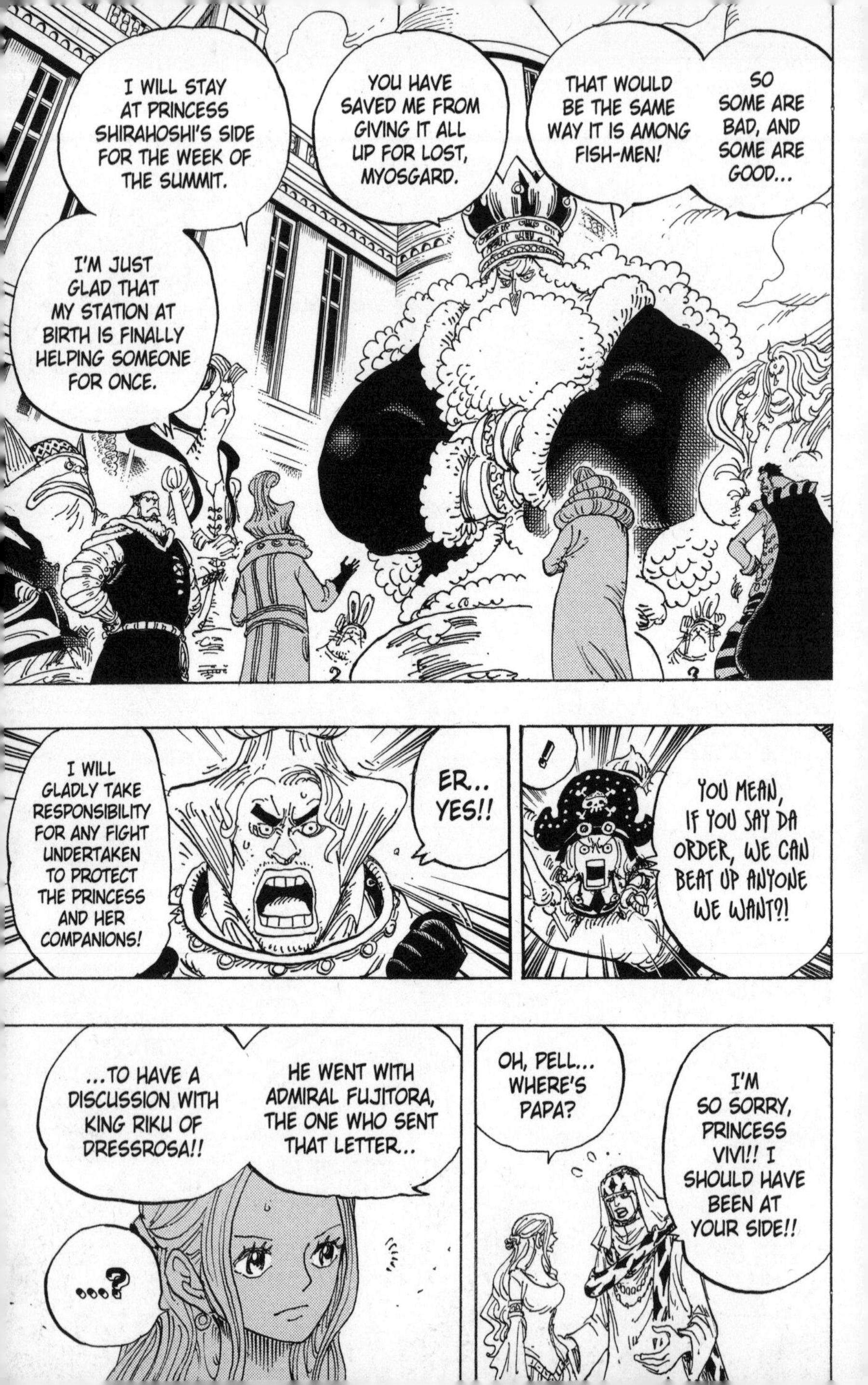
SO SOME ARE BAD, AND SOME ARE GOOD...
THAT WOULD BE THE SAME WAY IT IS AMONG FISH-MEN!
YOU HAVE SAVED ME FROM GIVING IT ALL UP FOR LOST, MYOSGARD.
I WILL STAY AT PRINCESS SHIRAHOSHI'S SIDE FOR THE WEEK OF THE SUMMIT.
I'M JUST GLAD THAT MY STATION AT BIRTH IS FINALLY HELPING SOMEONE FOR ONCE.
!
YOU MEAN, IF YOU SAY DA ORDER, WE CAN BEAT UP ANYONE WE WANT?!
ER... YES!!
I WILL GLADLY TAKE RESPONSIBILITY FOR ANY FIGHT UNDERTAKEN TO PROTECT THE PRINCESS AND HER COMPANIONS!
OH, PELL... WHERE'S PAPA?
I'M SO SORRY, PRINCESS VIVI!! I SHOULD HAVE BEEN AT YOUR SIDE!!
HE WENT WITH ADMIRAL FUJITORA, THE ONE WHO SENT THAT LETTER..
...TO HAVE A DISCUSSION WITH KING RIKU OF DRESSROSA!!
...?

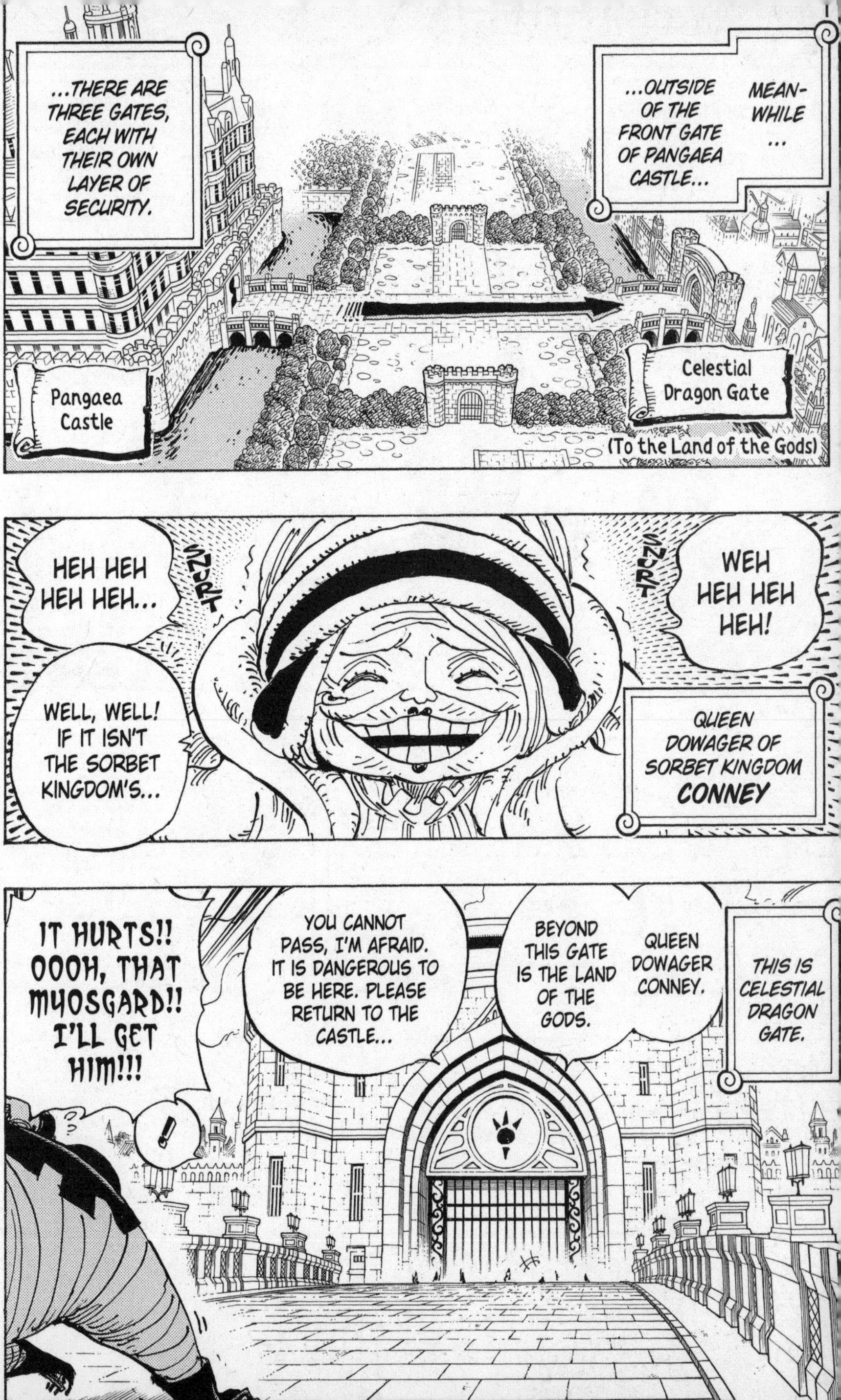

MEANWHILE...
...OUTSIDE OF THE FRONT GATE OF PANGAEA CASTLE...
...THERE ARE THREE GATES, EACH WITH THEIR OWN LAYER OF SECURITY.
Celestial Dragon Gate
(To the Land of the Gods)
Pangaea Castle
SNURT
WEH HEH HEH HEH!
QUEEN DOWAGER OF SORBET KINGDOM CONNEY
SNURT
HEH HEH HEH HEH...
WELL, WELL! IF IT ISN'T THE SORBET KINGDOM'S...
THIS IS CELESTIAL DRAGON GATE.
QUEEN DOWAGER CONNEY.
BEYOND THIS GATE IS THE LAND OF THE GODS.
YOU CANNOT PASS, I'M AFRAID. IT IS DANGEROUS TO BE HERE. PLEASE RETURN TO THE CASTLE...
IT HURTS!! OOOH, THAT MYOSGARD!! I'LL GET HIM!!!
!
??

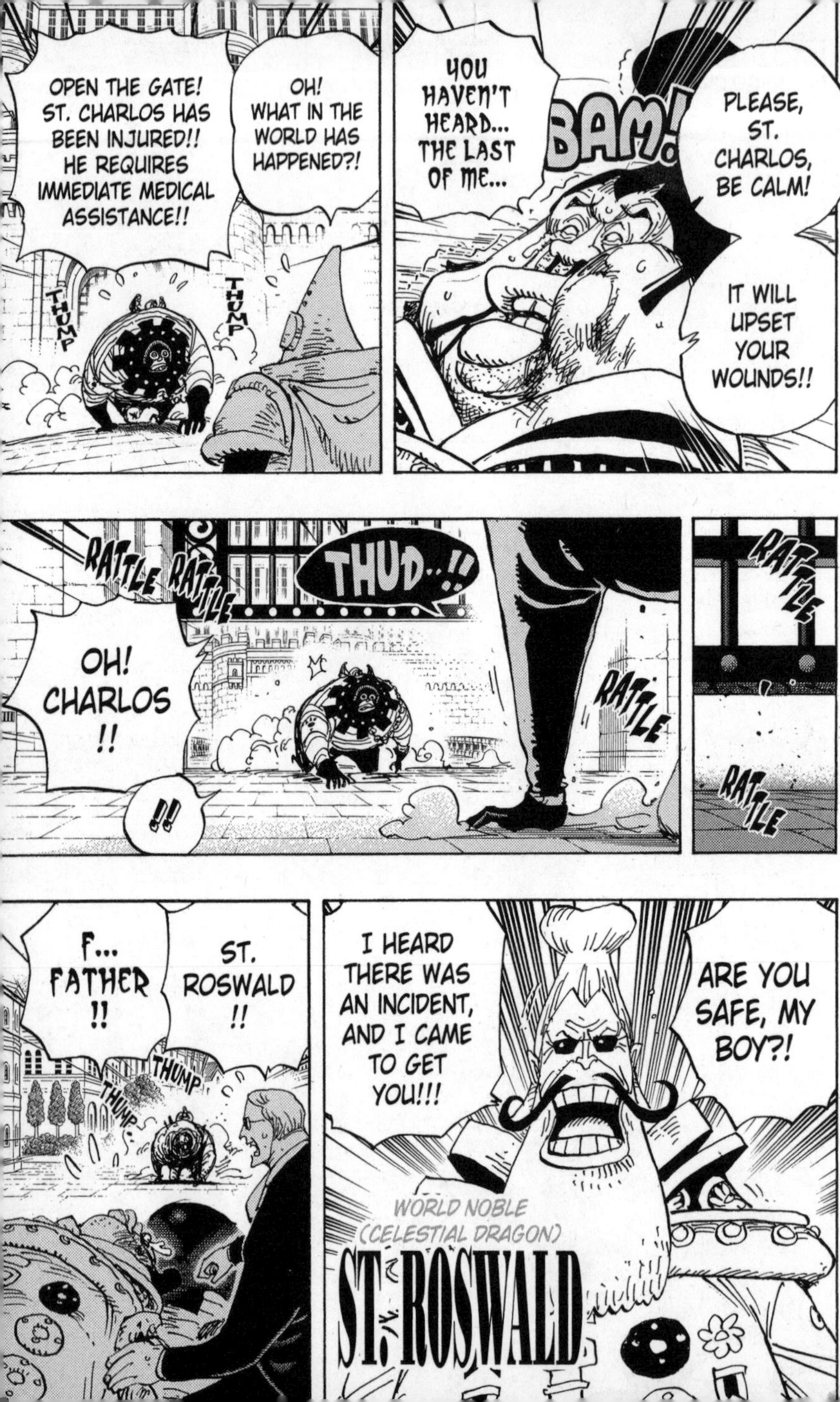
YOU HAVEN'T HEARD... THE LAST OF ME...
BAM!
PLEASE, ST. CHARLOS, BE CALM!
IT WILL UPSET YOUR WOUNDS!!
OH! WHAT IN THE WORLD HAS HAPPENED?!
OPEN THE GATE! ST. CHARLOS HAS BEEN INJURED!! HE REQUIRES IMMEDIATE MEDICAL ASSISTANCE!!
THUMP
THUMP
RATTLE
RATTLE
RATTLE
THUD..!!
RATTLE RATTLE
OH! CHARLOS !!
!!
ARE YOU SAFE, MY BOY?!
I HEARD THERE WAS AN INCIDENT, AND I CAME TO GET YOU!!!
WORLD NOBLE (CELESTIAL DRAGON)
ST. ROSWALD
ST. ROSWALD !!
F... FATHER !!
THUMP
THUMP

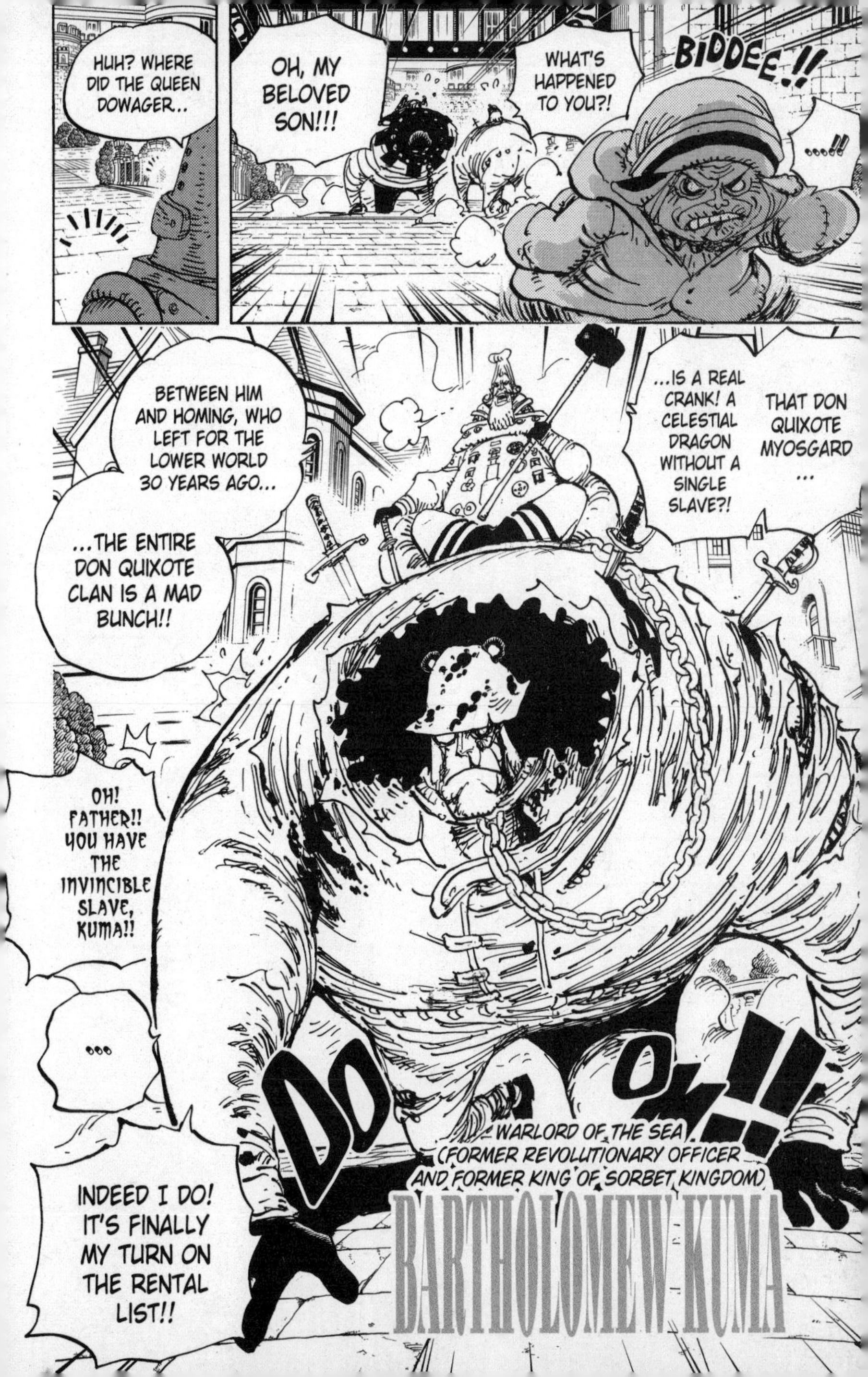
BIDDEE!!
....!!
WHAT'S HAPPENED TO YOU?!
OH, MY BELOVED SON!!!
HUH? WHERE DID THE QUEEN DOWAGER..
THAT DON QUIXOTE MYOSGARD ...
...IS A REAL CRANK! A CELESTIAL DRAGON WITHOUT A SINGLE SLAVE?!
BETWEEN HIM AND HOMING, WHO LEFT FOR THE LOWER WORLD 30 YEARS AGO...
...THE ENTIRE DON QUIXOTE CLAN IS A MAD BUNCH!!
DO O!!
WARLORD OF THE SEA (FORMER REVOLUTIONARY OFFICER AND FORMER KING OF SORBET KINGDOM)
BARTHOLOMEW KUMA
OH! FATHER!! YOU HAVE THE INVINCIBLE SLAVE, KUMA!!
...
INDEED I DO! IT'S FINALLY MY TURN ON THE RENTAL LIST!!

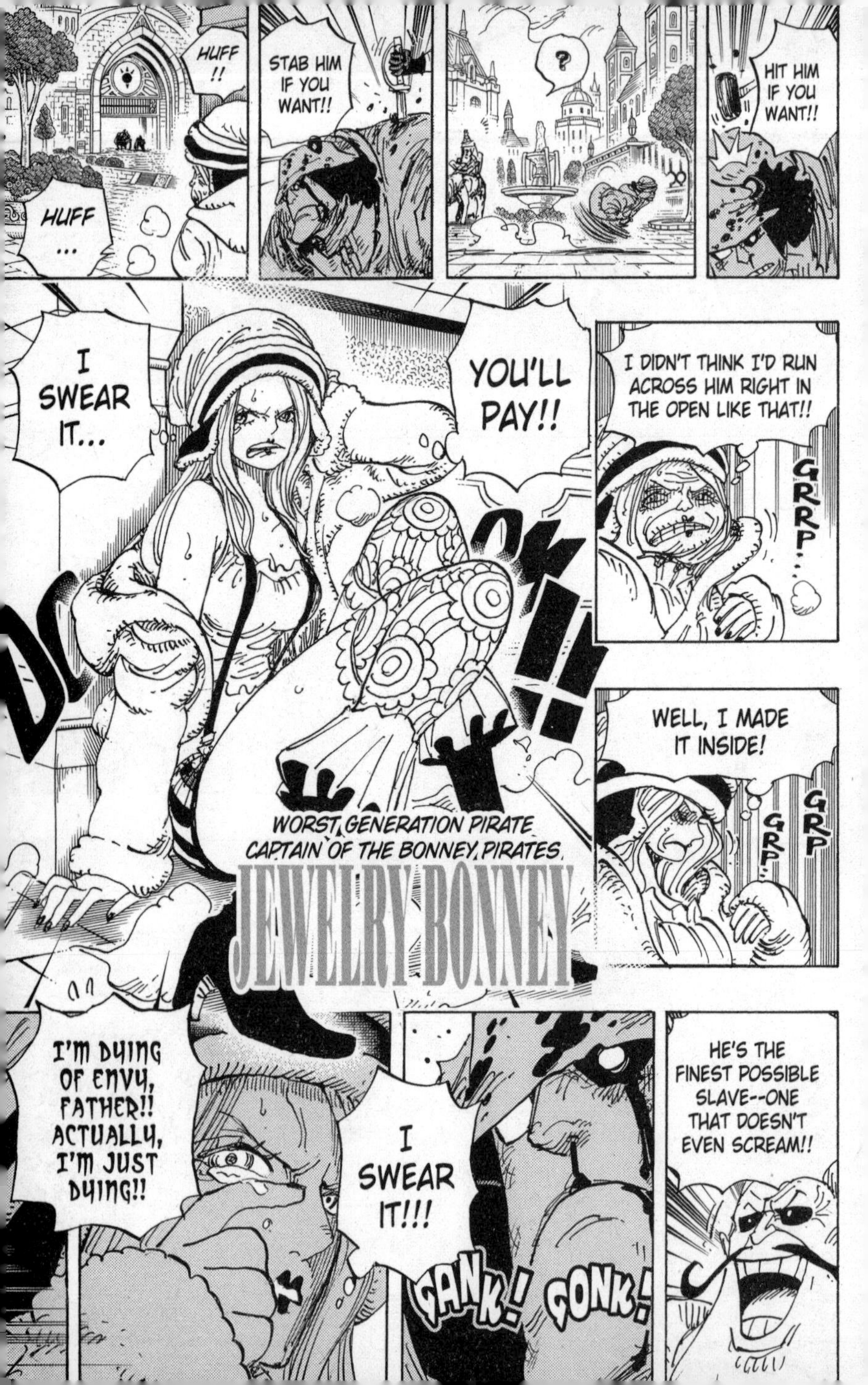
HIT HIM IF YOU WANT!!
?
STAB HIM IF YOU WANT!!
HUFF !!
HUFF ...
I DIDN'T THINK I'D RUN ACROSS HIM RIGHT IN THE OPEN LIKE THAT!!
GRRP...
WELL, I MADE IT INSIDE!
GRP GRP...
YOU'LL PAY!!
I SWEAR IT...
WORST GENERATION PIRATE
CAPTAIN OF THE BONNEY PIRATES
JEWELRY BONNEY
HE'S THE FINEST POSSIBLE SLAVE--ONE THAT DOESN'T EVEN SCREAM!!
GANK! GONK!
I SWEAR IT!!!
I'M DYING OF ENVY, FATHER!! ACTUALLY, I'M JUST DYING!!

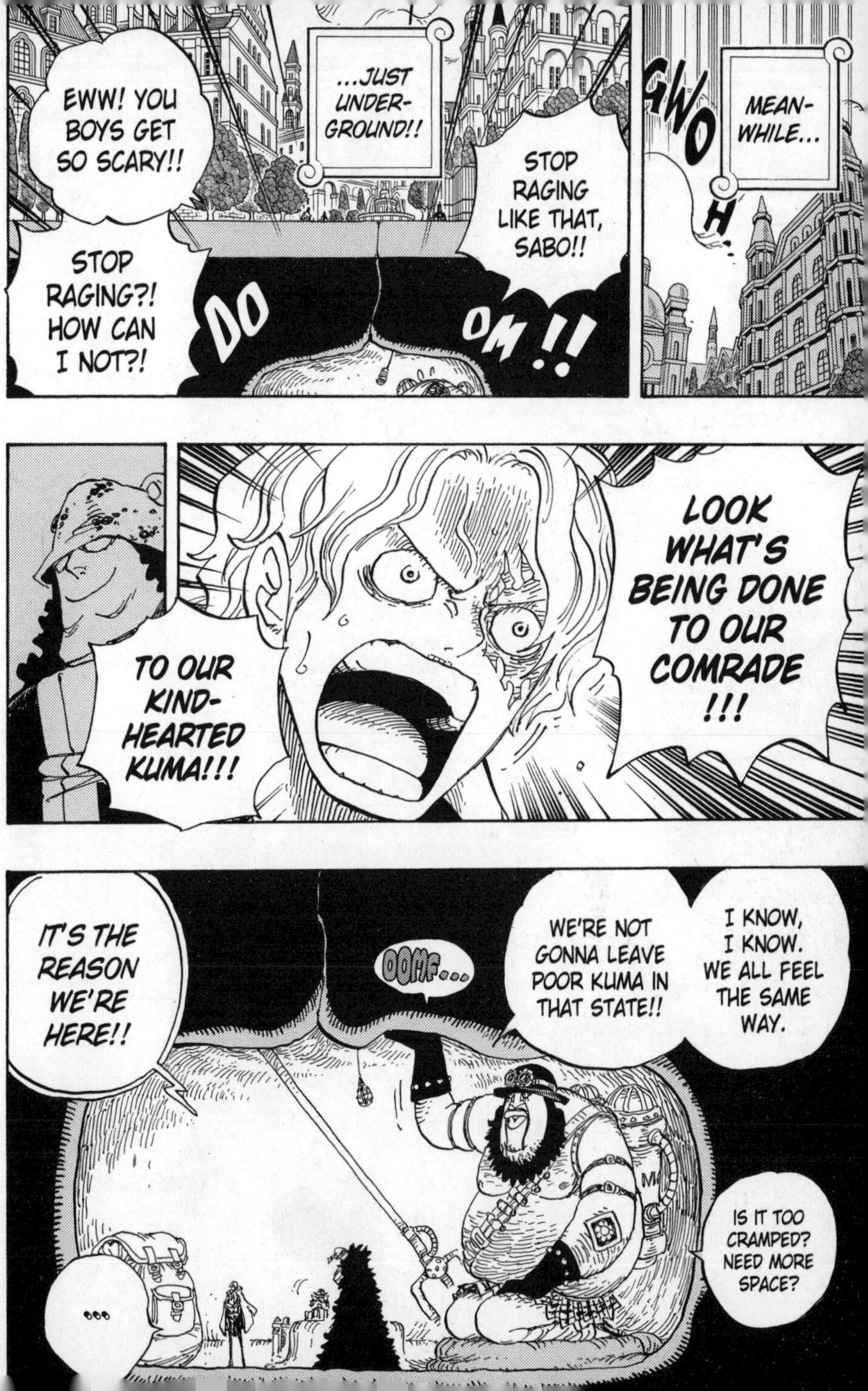
GWOH
MEAN-WHILE...
...JUST UNDER-GROUND!!
STOP RAGING LIKE THAT, SABO!!
DOOM!!
EWW! YOU BOYS GET SO SCARY!!
STOP RAGING?! HOW CAN I NOT?!
LOOK WHAT'S BEING DONE TO OUR COMRADE!!!
TO OUR KIND-HEARTED KUMA!!!
I KNOW, I KNOW. WE ALL FEEL THE SAME WAY.
WE'RE NOT GONNA LEAVE POOR KUMA IN THAT STATE!!
OOMF...
IT'S THE REASON WE'RE HERE!!
IS IT TOO CRAMPED? NEED MORE SPACE?
...

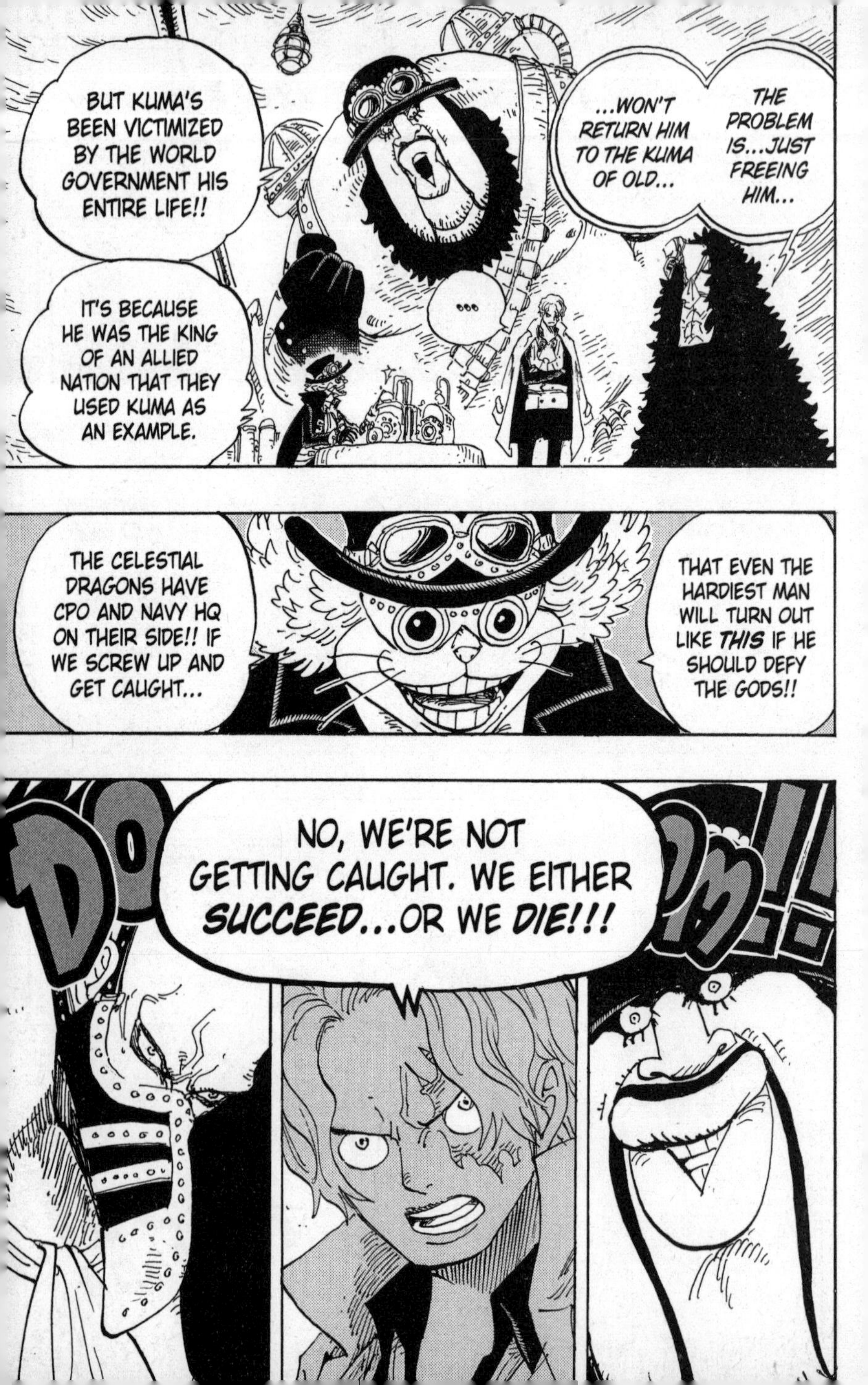
THE PROBLEM IS...JUST FREEING HIM...
...WON'T RETURN HIM TO THE KUMA OF OLD...
BUT KUMA'S BEEN VICTIMIZED BY THE WORLD GOVERNMENT HIS ENTIRE LIFE!!
...
IT'S BECAUSE HE WAS THE KING OF AN ALLIED NATION THAT THEY USED KUMA AS AN EXAMPLE.
THAT EVEN THE HARDIEST MAN WILL TURN OUT LIKE *THIS* IF HE SHOULD DEFY THE GODS!!
THE CELESTIAL DRAGONS HAVE CPO AND NAVY HQ ON THEIR SIDE!! IF WE SCREW UP AND GET CAUGHT...
DOOM!!
NO, WE'RE NOT GETTING CAUGHT. WE EITHER *SUCCEED*...OR WE *DIE!!!*
...

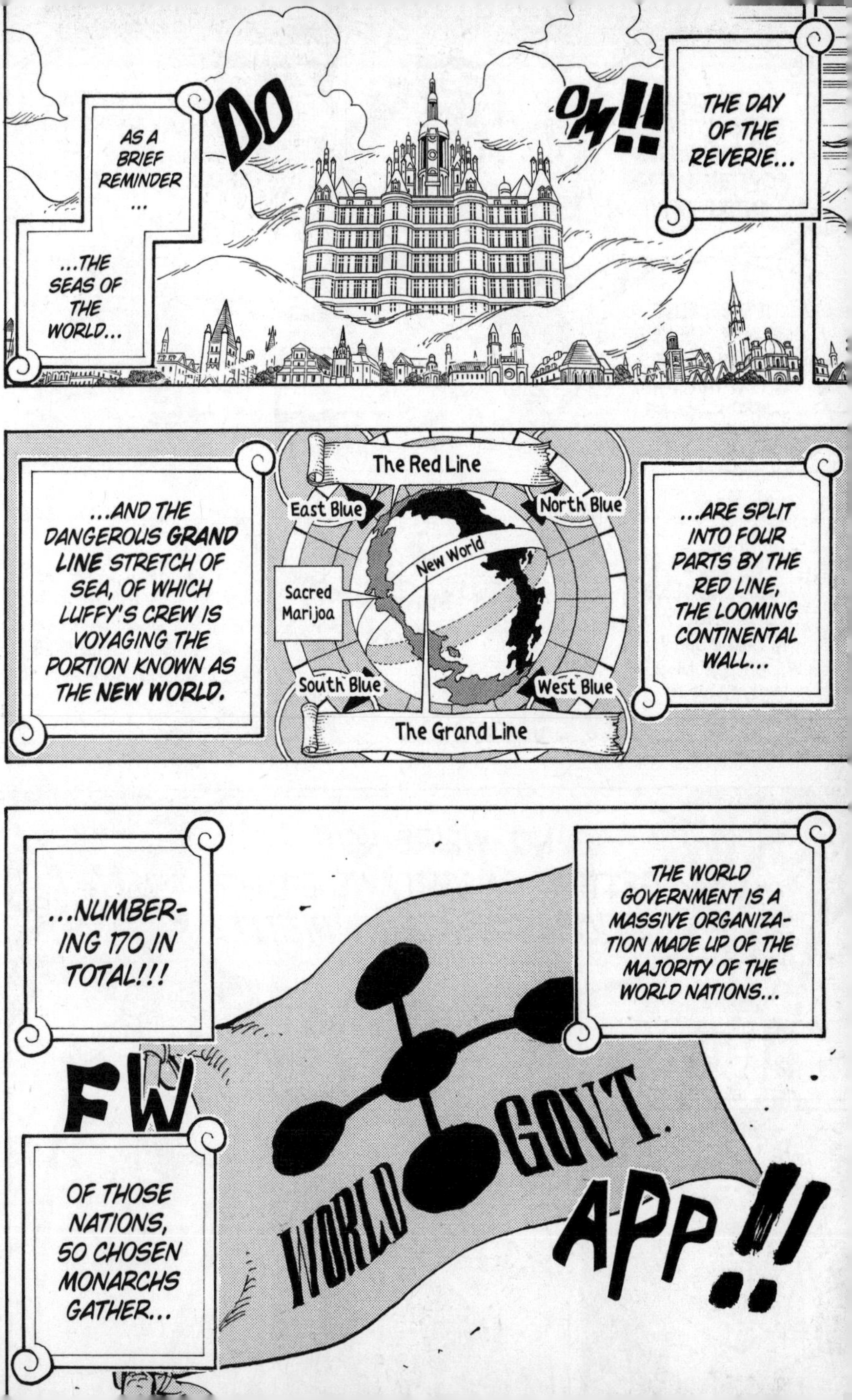
THE DAY OF THE REVERIE...
DOOM!!
AS A BRIEF REMINDER...
...THE SEAS OF THE WORLD...
...ARE SPLIT INTO FOUR PARTS BY THE RED LINE, THE LOOMING CONTINENTAL WALL...
The Red Line
North Blue
East Blue
New World
Sacred Marijoa
West Blue
South Blue
The Grand Line
...AND THE DANGEROUS GRAND LINE STRETCH OF SEA, OF WHICH LUFFY'S CREW IS VOYAGING THE PORTION KNOWN AS THE NEW WORLD.
THE WORLD GOVERNMENT IS A MASSIVE ORGANIZATION MADE UP OF THE MAJORITY OF THE WORLD NATIONS...
...NUMBERING 170 IN TOTAL!!!
FWAPP!!
WORLD GOVT.
OF THOSE NATIONS, 50 CHOSEN MONARCHS GATHER...

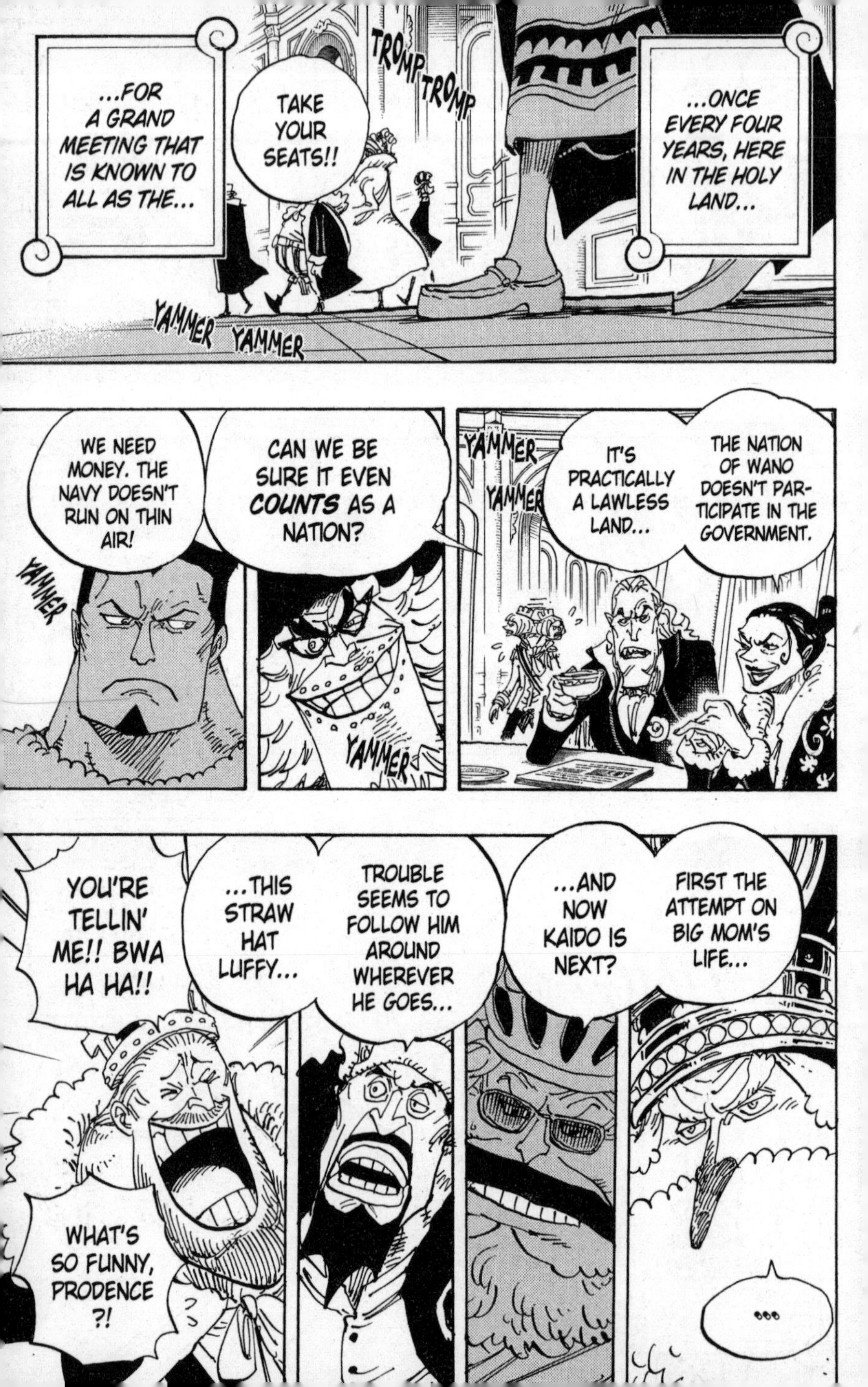
...ONCE EVERY FOUR YEARS, HERE IN THE HOLY LAND...
TROMP TROMP
TAKE YOUR SEATS!!
...FOR A GRAND MEETING THAT IS KNOWN TO ALL AS THE...
YAMMER YAMMER
THE NATION OF WANO DOESN'T PARTICIPATE IN THE GOVERNMENT.
IT'S PRACTICALLY A LAWLESS LAND...
YAMMER
YAMMER
CAN WE BE SURE IT EVEN *COUNTS* AS A NATION?
YAMMER
WE NEED MONEY. THE NAVY DOESN'T RUN ON THIN AIR!
YAMMER
FIRST THE ATTEMPT ON BIG MOM'S LIFE...
...
...AND NOW KAIDO IS NEXT?
TROUBLE SEEMS TO FOLLOW HIM AROUND WHEREVER HE GOES...
...THIS STRAW HAT LUFFY...
YOU'RE TELLIN' ME!! BWA HA HA!!
WHAT'S SO FUNNY, PRODENCE?!

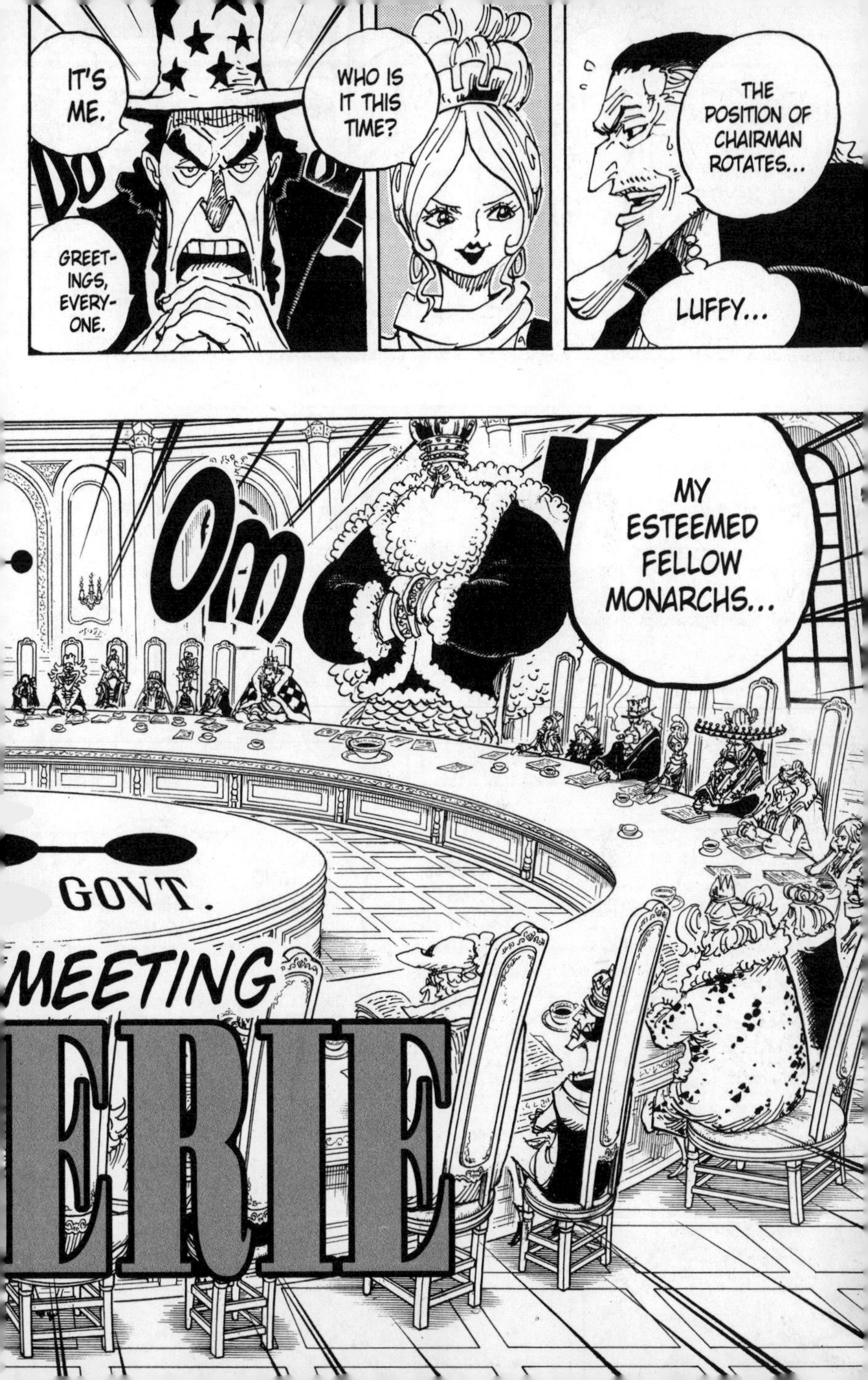
THE POSITION OF CHAIRMAN ROTATES...
LUFFY...
WHO IS IT THIS TIME?
IT'S ME.
GREETINGS, EVERYONE.
MY ESTEEMED FELLOW MONARCHS...
GOVT.
MEETING
ERIE

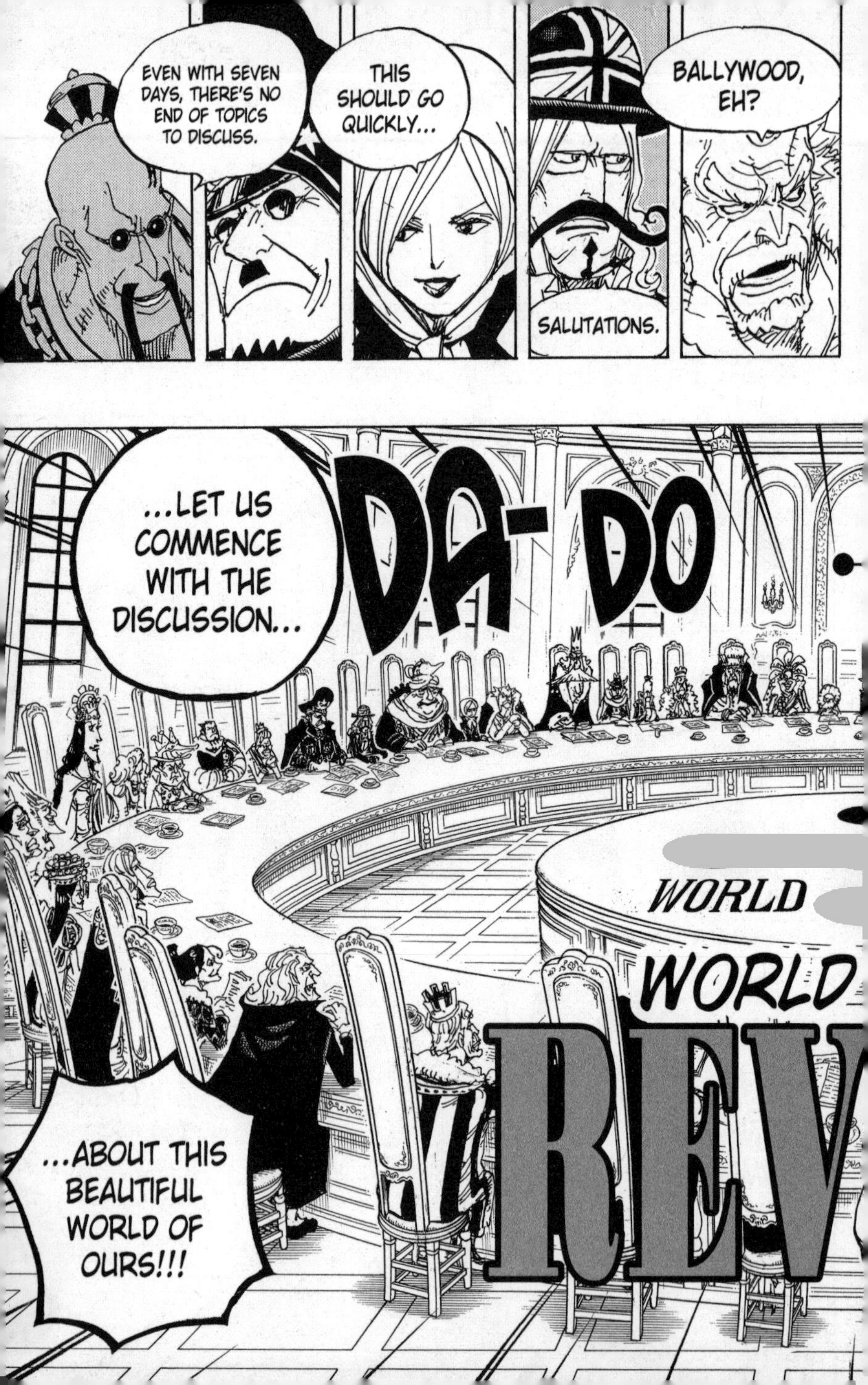
BALLYWOOD, EH?
SALUTATIONS.
THIS SHOULD GO QUICKLY...
EVEN WITH SEVEN DAYS, THERE'S NO END OF TOPICS TO DISCUSS.
DA-DO
...LET US COMMENCE WITH THE DISCUSSION...
WORLD
WORLD
REV
...ABOUT THIS BEAUTIFUL WORLD OF OURS!!!

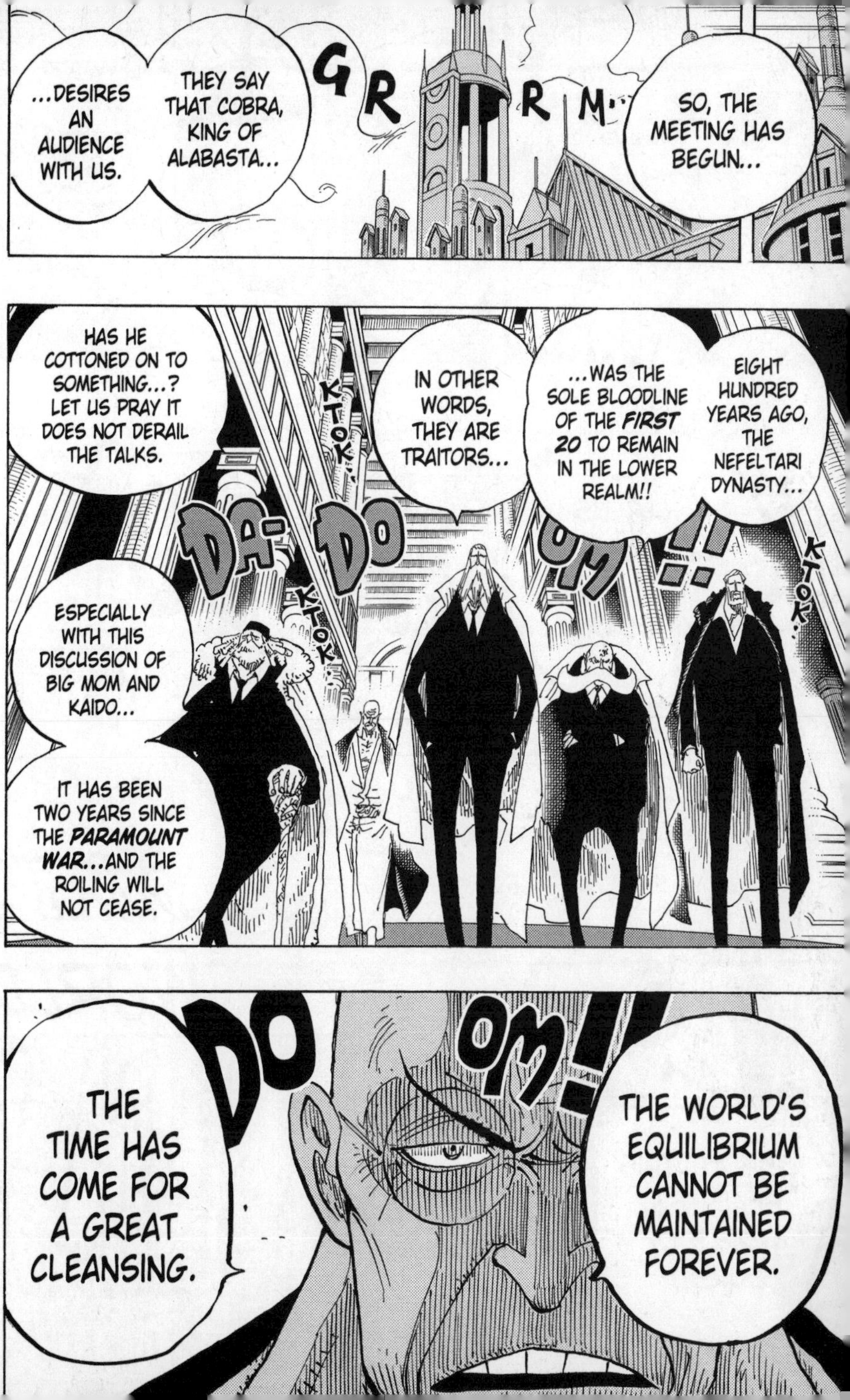
SO, THE MEETING HAS BEGUN...
GR R M
THEY SAY THAT COBRA, KING OF ALABASTA...
...DESIRES AN AUDIENCE WITH US.
EIGHT HUNDRED YEARS AGO, THE NEFELTARI DYNASTY...
KTOK
...WAS THE SOLE BLOODLINE OF THE *FIRST 20* TO REMAIN IN THE LOWER REALM!!
IN OTHER WORDS, THEY ARE TRAITORS...
DA-DO OM!!
KTOK
KTOK
HAS HE COTTONED ON TO SOMETHING...? LET US PRAY IT DOES NOT DERAIL THE TALKS.
ESPECIALLY WITH THIS DISCUSSION OF BIG MOM AND KAIDO...
IT HAS BEEN TWO YEARS SINCE THE *PARAMOUNT WAR*...AND THE ROILING WILL NOT CEASE.
THE WORLD'S EQUILIBRIUM CANNOT BE MAINTAINED FOREVER.
DO OM!!
THE TIME HAS COME FOR A GREAT CLEANSING.

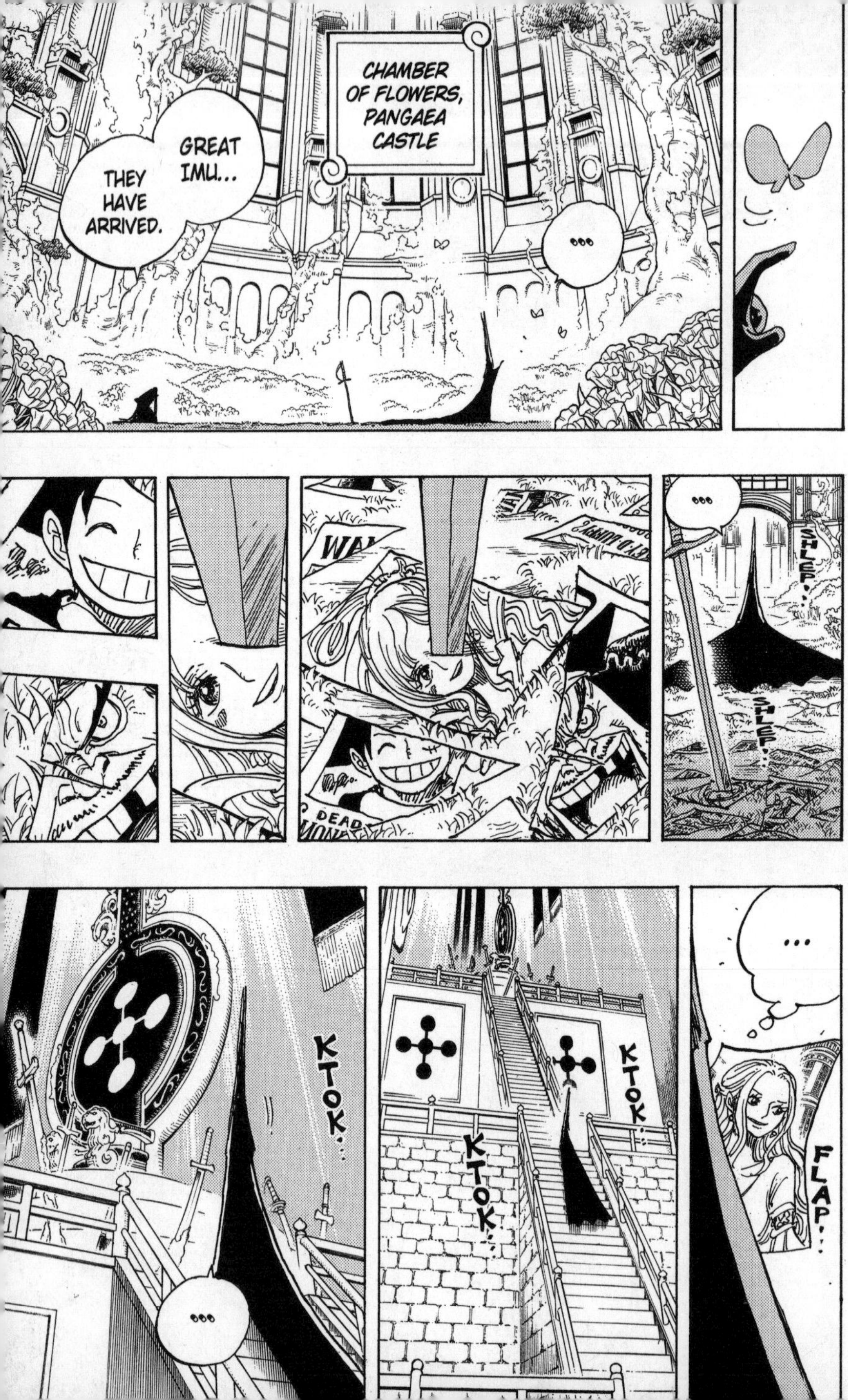
CHAMBER OF FLOWERS, PANGAEA CASTLE
GREAT IMU...
THEY HAVE ARRIVED.
...
...
SHLEP...
SHLEP...
WA
DEAD
...
FLAP...
KTOK...
KTOK...
KTOK...
...

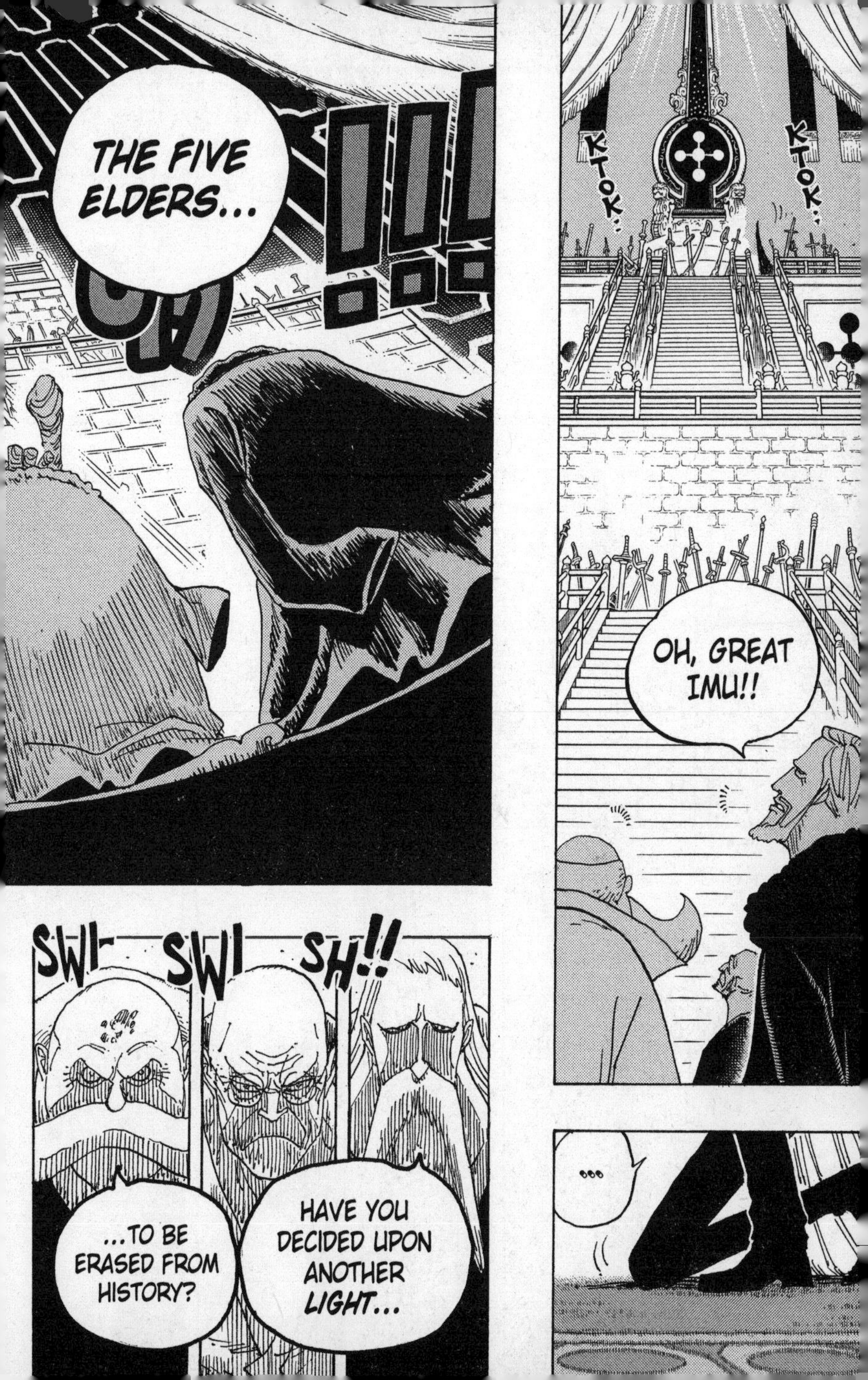
KTOK..
KTOK..
OH, GREAT IMU!!
THE FIVE ELDERS...
...
SWI- SWI- SH!!
HAVE YOU DECIDED UPON ANOTHER LIGHT...
...TO BE ERASED FROM HISTORY?

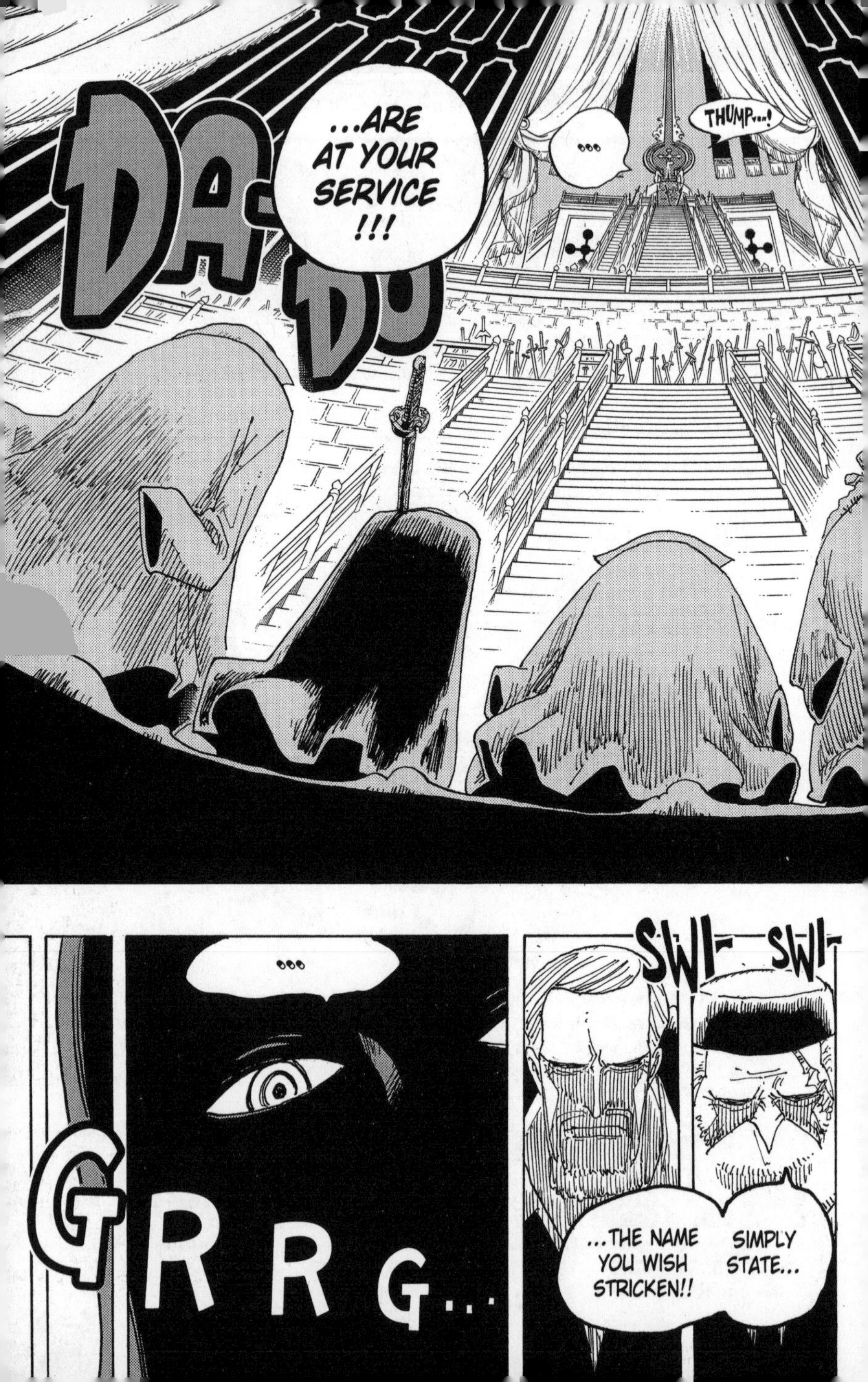
THUMP...!
...
...ARE AT YOUR SERVICE !!!
DA-DO
SWI- SWI-
SIMPLY STATE...
...THE NAME YOU WISH STRICKEN!!
...
GRRG...

SBS Question Corner

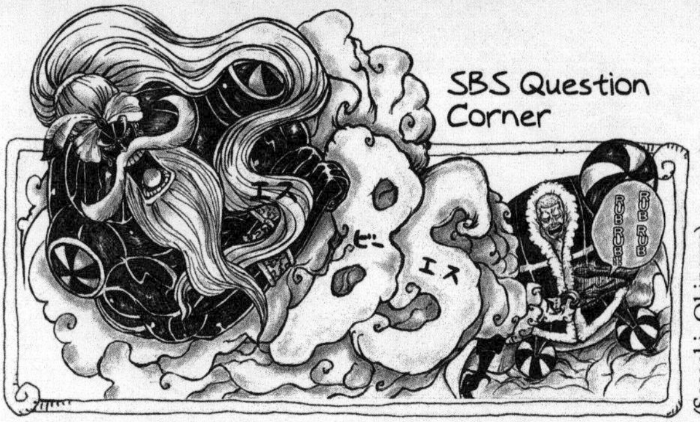
RUB RUB
RUB RUB

(Sasaaki, Okinawa)

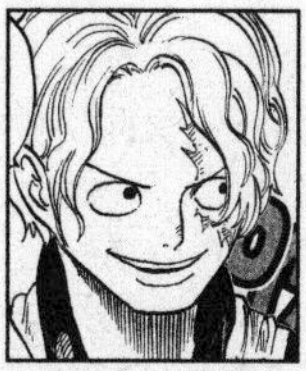

Q: Odacchi! Since we've seen Luffy and Ace at ages 40 and 60, please do Sabo next.
--Oda Freak's Older Brother

A: Okay, I'll draw it, but just to be clear, even I don't know the future of the series.

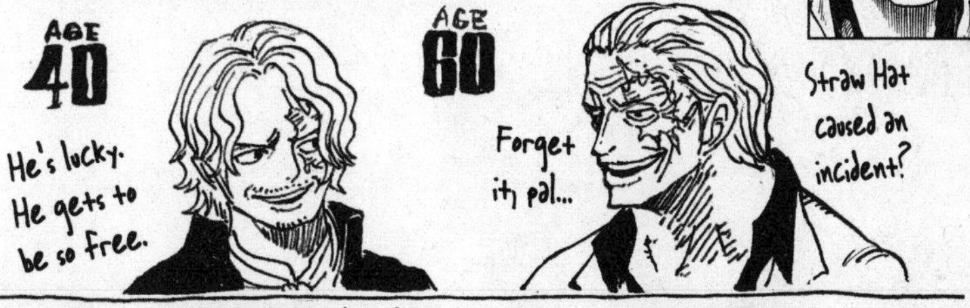
Straw Hat caused an incident?
Forget it pal...
AGE 60
AGE 40
He's lucky. He gets to be so free.

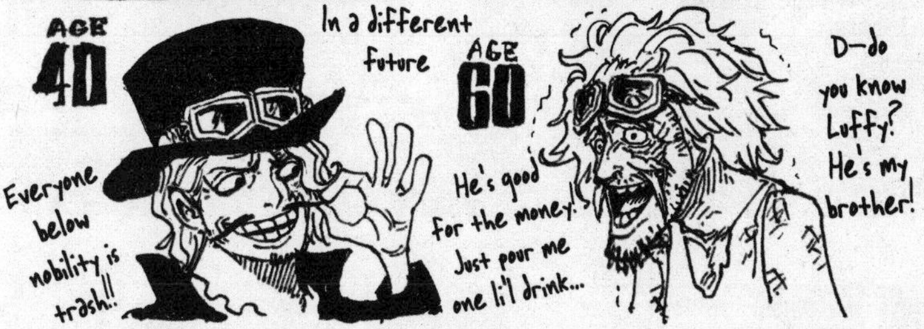
D-do you know Luffy? He's my brother!
He's good for the money. Just pour me one li'l drink...
AGE 60
In a different future
AGE 40
Everyone below nobility is trash!!

A: Also, I received some questions from Maccha-man, Atsugon, and Momota about various members of the Big Mom Pirates, like "What are their names?" and "How old are they?" So I'll answer them all in one go! These are mostly from chapters 848, 854, and 864.

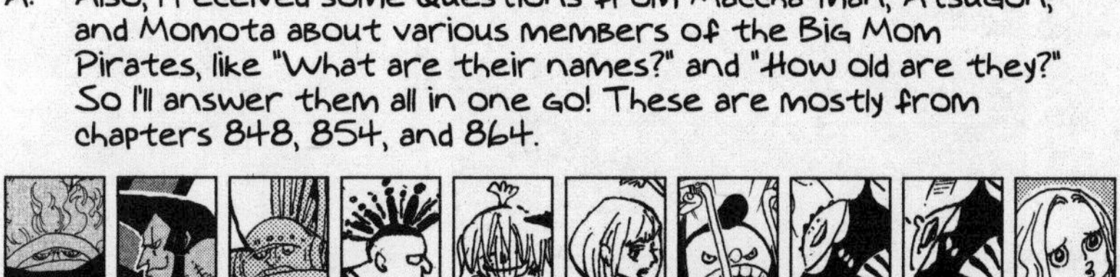

Bassquarte 13th Son (42)	Noisette 15th Son (41)	Saintmarc 22nd Son (34)	Dacquoise 24th Son (32)	Fructose 28th Son (28)	Myukuru 25th Daughter (25)	Anglais 42nd Son (14)	Dolce 45th Son (9)	Dragee 46th Son (9)	Anana 39th Daughter (8)

Chapter 909:
SEPPUKU

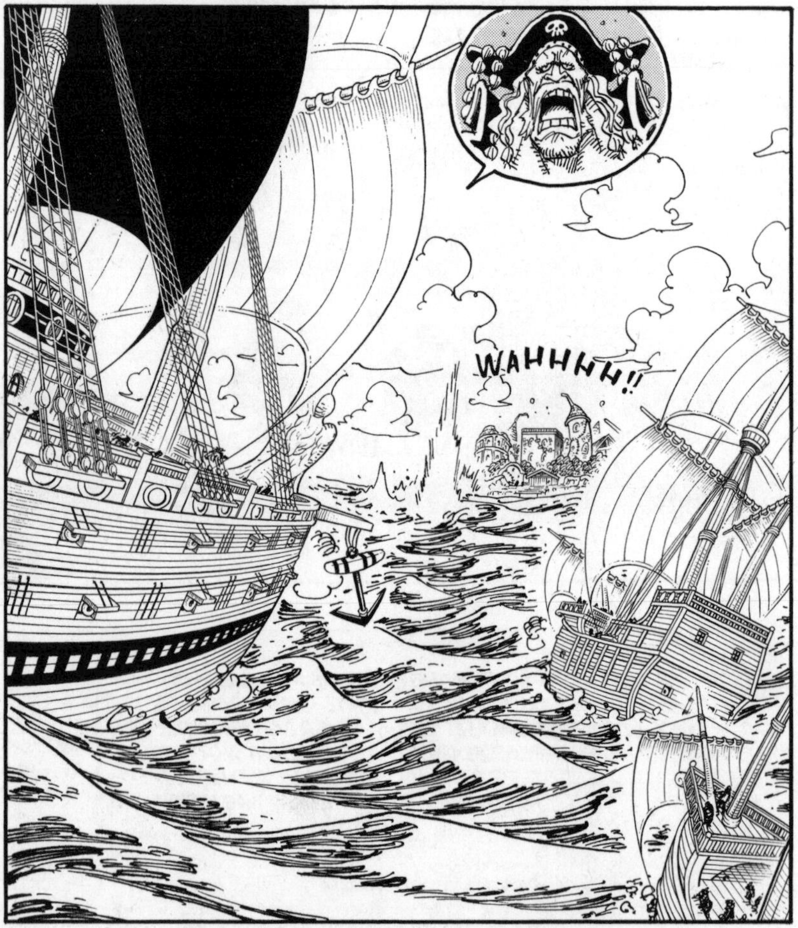
WAHHHHH!!

THE SAGA OF THE SELF-PROCLAIMED STRAW HAT FLEET, VOL. 39, ORLUMBUS: "4:00 P.M.: FIRST PIRATING CAMPAIGN! LAUNCH ATTACK!!"

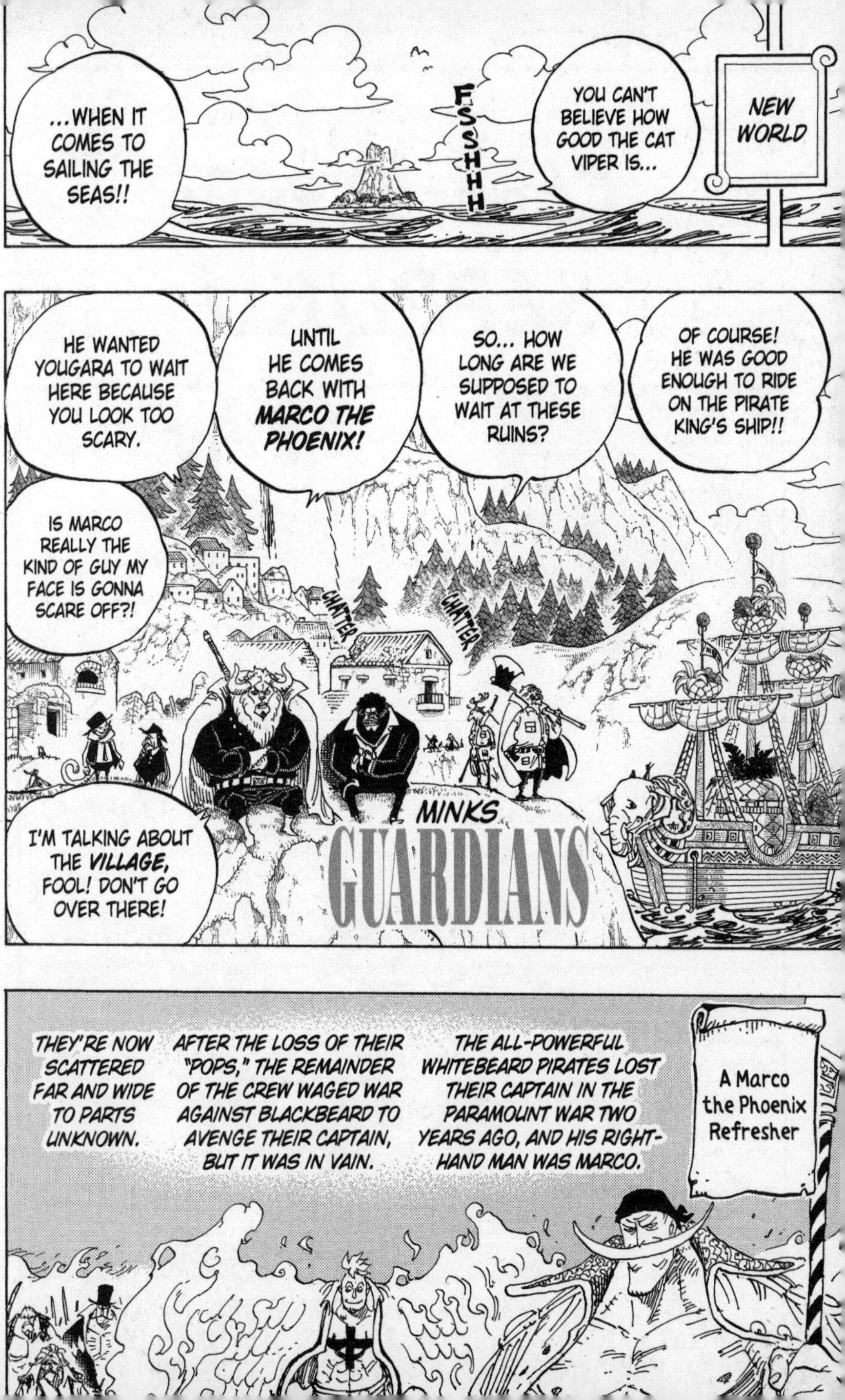
NEW WORLD
YOU CAN'T BELIEVE HOW GOOD THE CAT VIPER IS...
FSSHHH
...WHEN IT COMES TO SAILING THE SEAS!!
OF COURSE! HE WAS GOOD ENOUGH TO RIDE ON THE PIRATE KING'S SHIP!!
SO... HOW LONG ARE WE SUPPOSED TO WAIT AT THESE RUINS?
UNTIL HE COMES BACK WITH MARCO THE PHOENIX!
HE WANTED YOUGARA TO WAIT HERE BECAUSE YOU LOOK TOO SCARY.
IS MARCO REALLY THE KIND OF GUY MY FACE IS GONNA SCARE OFF?!
CHATTER
CHATTER
MINKS
GUARDIANS
I'M TALKING ABOUT THE VILLAGE, FOOL! DON'T GO OVER THERE!
A Marco the Phoenix Refresher
THE ALL-POWERFUL WHITEBEARD PIRATES LOST THEIR CAPTAIN IN THE PARAMOUNT WAR TWO YEARS AGO, AND HIS RIGHT-HAND MAN WAS MARCO.
AFTER THE LOSS OF THEIR "POPS," THE REMAINDER OF THE CREW WAGED WAR AGAINST BLACKBEARD TO AVENGE THEIR CAPTAIN, BUT IT WAS IN VAIN.
THEY'RE NOW SCATTERED FAR AND WIDE TO PARTS UNKNOWN.

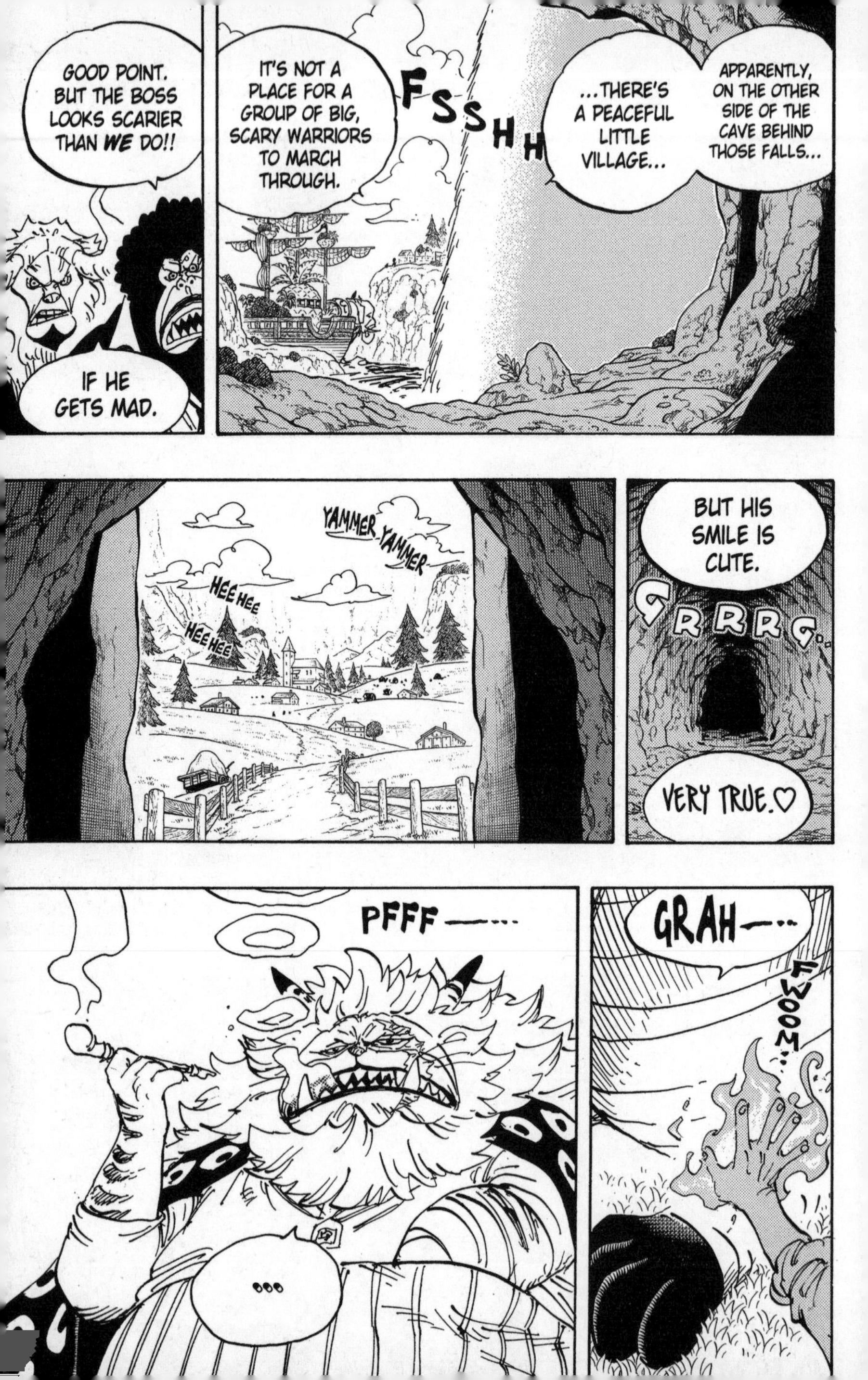
APPARENTLY, ON THE OTHER SIDE OF THE CAVE BEHIND THOSE FALLS...
...THERE'S A PEACEFUL LITTLE VILLAGE...
FSSHH
IT'S NOT A PLACE FOR A GROUP OF BIG, SCARY WARRIORS TO MARCH THROUGH.
GOOD POINT. BUT THE BOSS LOOKS SCARIER THAN WE DO!!
IF HE GETS MAD.
BUT HIS SMILE IS CUTE.
GRRRG..
VERY TRUE.♡
YAMMER YAMMER
HEEHEE
HEEHEE
GRAH—...
FWOOM
PFFF—...
...

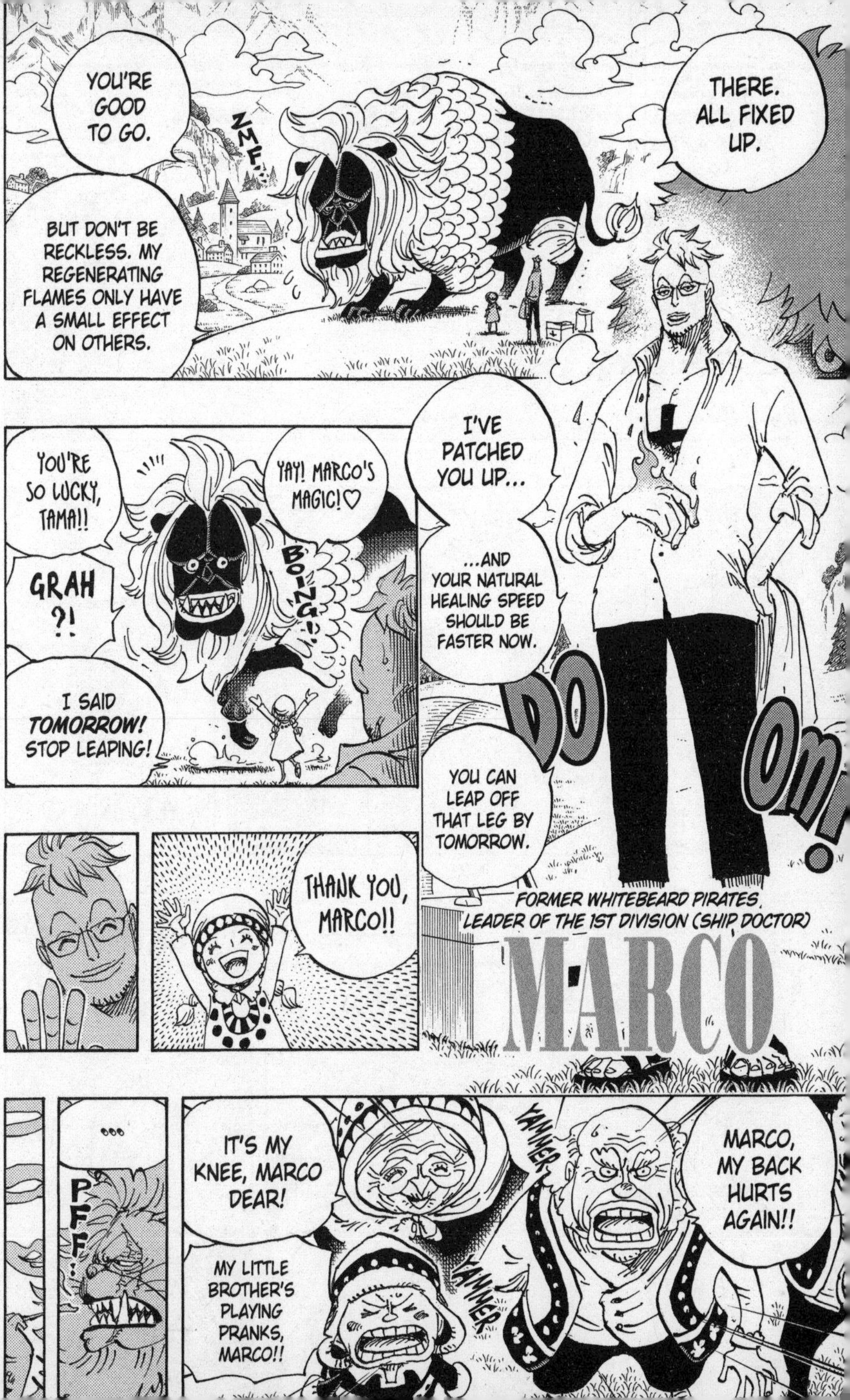
THERE. ALL FIXED UP.
YOU'RE GOOD TO GO.
ZMF
BUT DON'T BE RECKLESS. MY REGENERATING FLAMES ONLY HAVE A SMALL EFFECT ON OTHERS.
I'VE PATCHED YOU UP...
...AND YOUR NATURAL HEALING SPEED SHOULD BE FASTER NOW.
YOU CAN LEAP OFF THAT LEG BY TOMORROW.
DOOM!
FORMER WHITEBEARD PIRATES, LEADER OF THE 1ST DIVISION (SHIP DOCTOR)
MARCO
YAY! MARCO'S MAGIC!♡
BOING!!
YOU'RE SO LUCKY, TAMA!!
GRAH ?!
I SAID *TOMORROW!* STOP LEAPING!
THANK YOU, MARCO!!
MARCO, MY BACK HURTS AGAIN!!
YAMMER
IT'S MY KNEE, MARCO DEAR!
YAMMER
MY LITTLE BROTHER'S PLAYING PRANKS, MARCO!!
...
PFF

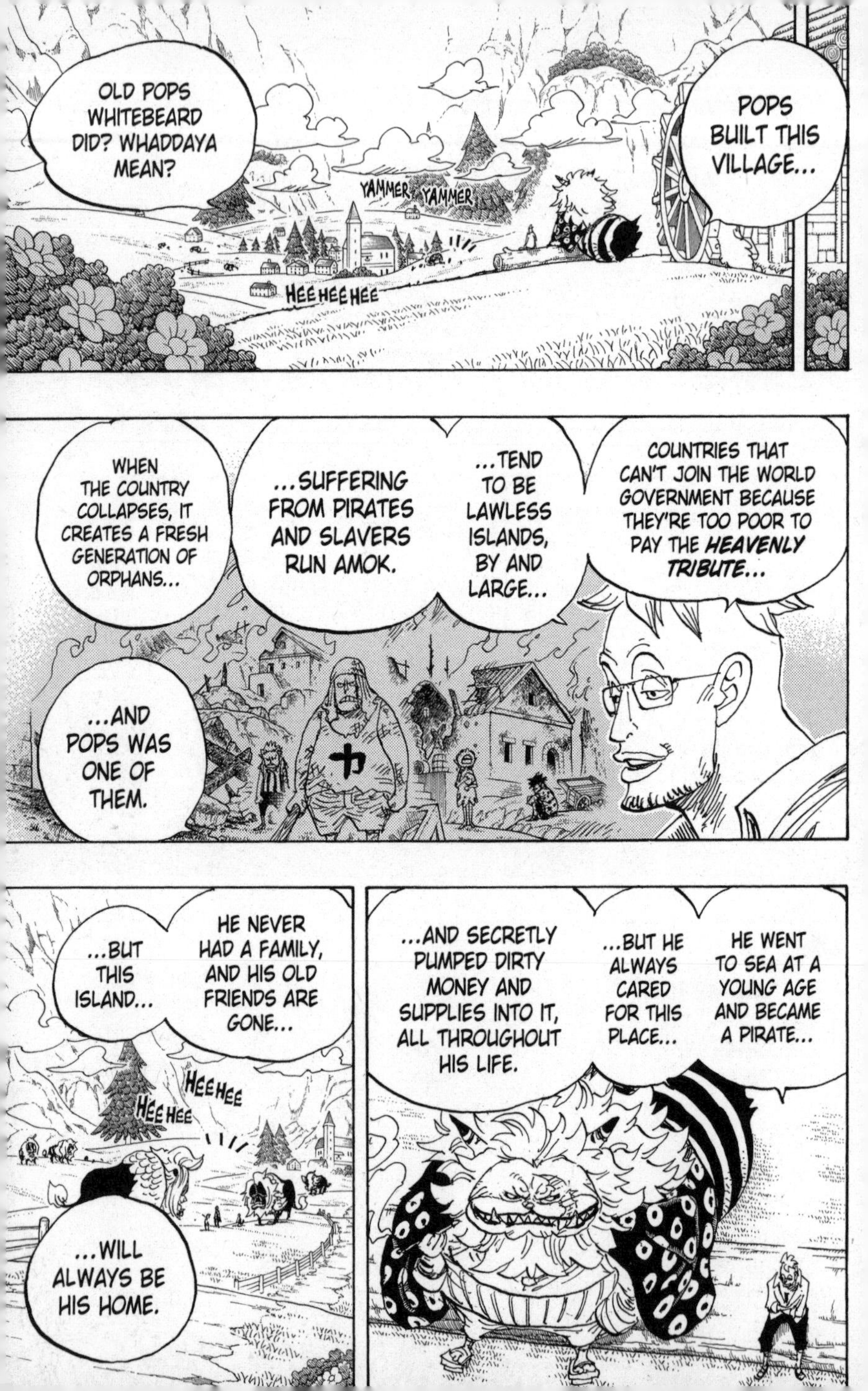
POPS BUILT THIS VILLAGE...
OLD POPS WHITEBEARD DID? WHADDAYA MEAN?
YAMMER YAMMER
HEE HEE HEE
COUNTRIES THAT CAN'T JOIN THE WORLD GOVERNMENT BECAUSE THEY'RE TOO POOR TO PAY THE *HEAVENLY TRIBUTE*...
...TEND TO BE LAWLESS ISLANDS, BY AND LARGE...
...SUFFERING FROM PIRATES AND SLAVERS RUN AMOK.
WHEN THE COUNTRY COLLAPSES, IT CREATES A FRESH GENERATION OF ORPHANS...
...AND POPS WAS ONE OF THEM.
HE WENT TO SEA AT A YOUNG AGE AND BECAME A PIRATE...
...BUT HE ALWAYS CARED FOR THIS PLACE...
...AND SECRETLY PUMPED DIRTY MONEY AND SUPPLIES INTO IT, ALL THROUGHOUT HIS LIFE.
HE NEVER HAD A FAMILY, AND HIS OLD FRIENDS ARE GONE...
...BUT THIS ISLAND...
HEE HEE
HEE HEE
...WILL ALWAYS BE HIS HOME.

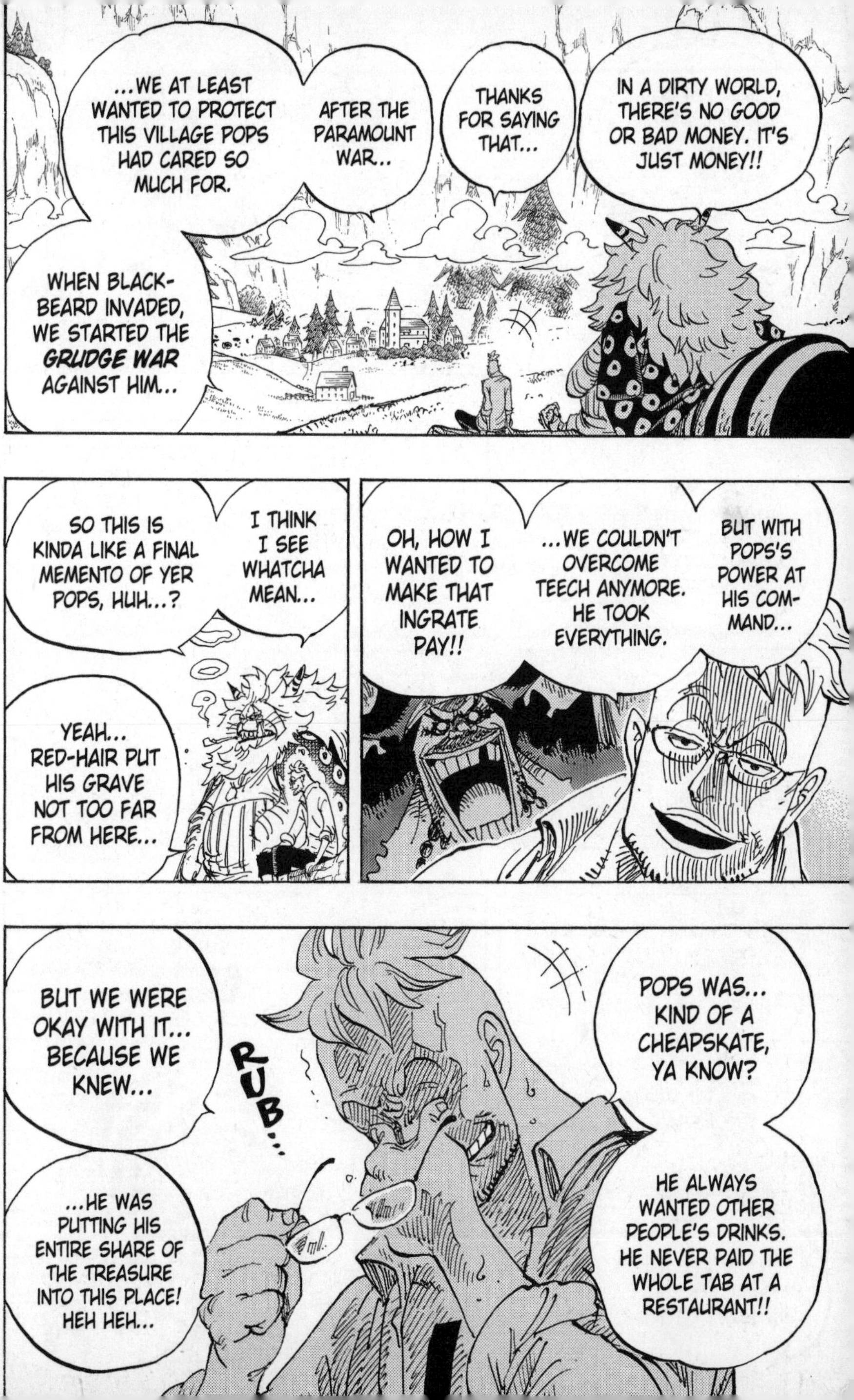
IN A DIRTY WORLD, THERE'S NO GOOD OR BAD MONEY. IT'S JUST MONEY!!
THANKS FOR SAYING THAT...
AFTER THE PARAMOUNT WAR...
...WE AT LEAST WANTED TO PROTECT THIS VILLAGE POPS HAD CARED SO MUCH FOR.
WHEN BLACK-BEARD INVADED, WE STARTED THE ***GRUDGE WAR*** AGAINST HIM...
BUT WITH POPS'S POWER AT HIS COM-MAND...
...WE COULDN'T OVERCOME TEECH ANYMORE. HE TOOK EVERYTHING.
OH, HOW I WANTED TO MAKE THAT INGRATE PAY!!
I THINK I SEE WHATCHA MEAN...
SO THIS IS KINDA LIKE A FINAL MEMENTO OF YER POPS, HUH...?
YEAH... RED-HAIR PUT HIS GRAVE NOT TOO FAR FROM HERE...
POPS WAS... KIND OF A CHEAPSKATE, YA KNOW?
BUT WE WERE OKAY WITH IT... BECAUSE WE KNEW...
RUB...
HE ALWAYS WANTED OTHER PEOPLE'S DRINKS. HE NEVER PAID THE WHOLE TAB AT A RESTAURANT!!
...HE WAS PUTTING HIS ENTIRE SHARE OF THE TREASURE INTO THIS PLACE! HEH HEH...

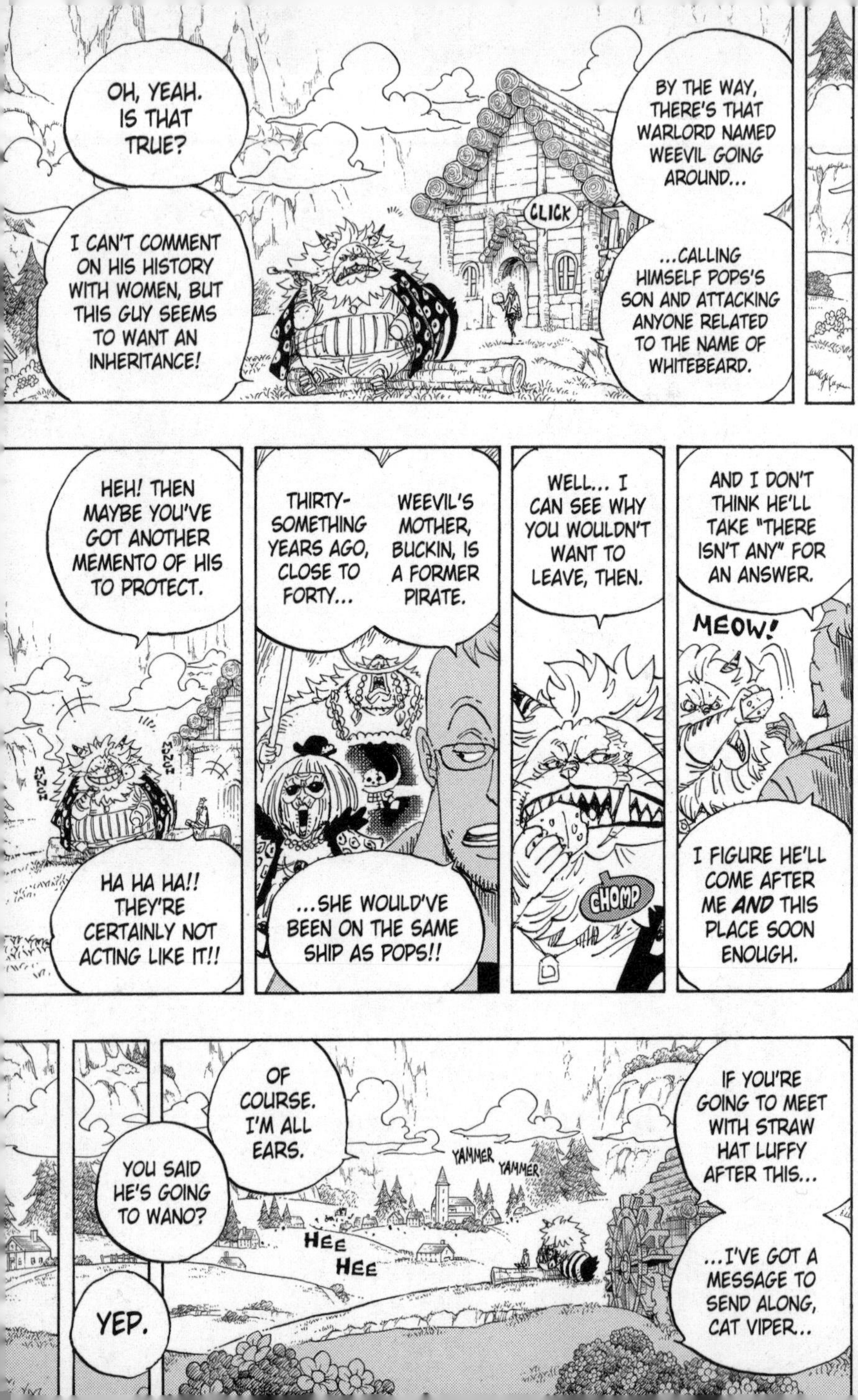

BY THE WAY, THERE'S THAT WARLORD NAMED WEEVIL GOING AROUND...
...CALLING HIMSELF POPS'S SON AND ATTACKING ANYONE RELATED TO THE NAME OF WHITEBEARD.
CLICK
OH, YEAH. IS THAT TRUE?
I CAN'T COMMENT ON HIS HISTORY WITH WOMEN, BUT THIS GUY SEEMS TO WANT AN INHERITANCE!
AND I DON'T THINK HE'LL TAKE "THERE ISN'T ANY" FOR AN ANSWER.
MEOW!
I FIGURE HE'LL COME AFTER ME *AND* THIS PLACE SOON ENOUGH.
WELL... I CAN SEE WHY YOU WOULDN'T WANT TO LEAVE, THEN.
CHOMP
WEEVIL'S MOTHER, BUCKIN, IS A FORMER PIRATE.
THIRTY-SOMETHING YEARS AGO, CLOSE TO FORTY...
...SHE WOULD'VE BEEN ON THE SAME SHIP AS POPS!!
HEH! THEN MAYBE YOU'VE GOT ANOTHER MEMENTO OF HIS TO PROTECT.
MUNCH
MUNCH
HA HA HA!! THEY'RE CERTAINLY NOT ACTING LIKE IT!!
IF YOU'RE GOING TO MEET WITH STRAW HAT LUFFY AFTER THIS...
...I'VE GOT A MESSAGE TO SEND ALONG, CAT VIPER...
YAMMER
YAMMER
HEE
HEE
OF COURSE. I'M ALL EARS.
YOU SAID HE'S GOING TO WANO?
YEP.

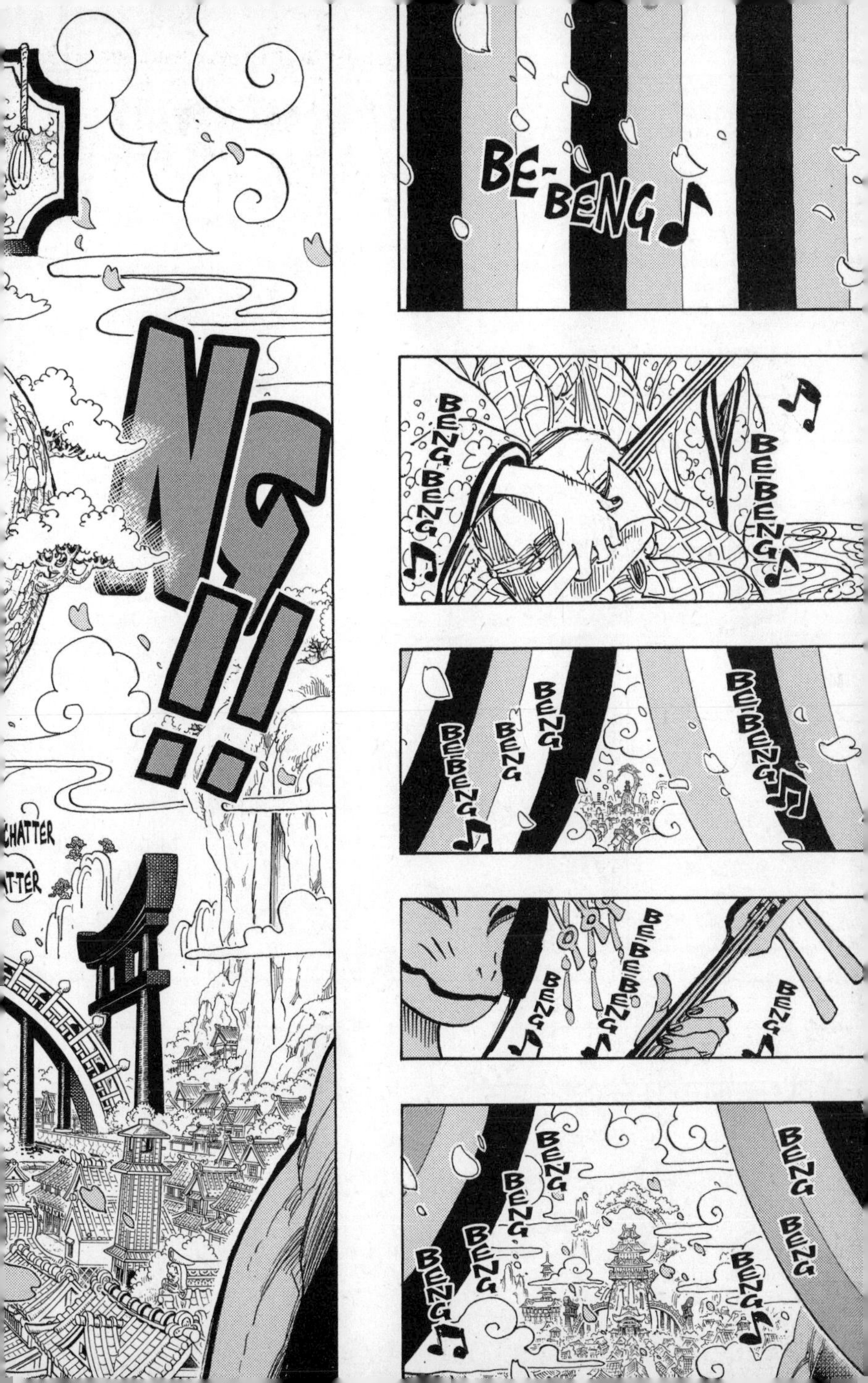
BE-BENG
BE-BENG
BENG BENG
BE-BENG
BENG BENG
BE-BENG
BENG
BE-BE-BE-BENG
BENG
BENG BENG
BENG
BENG BENG BENG BENG
N!!
CHATTER

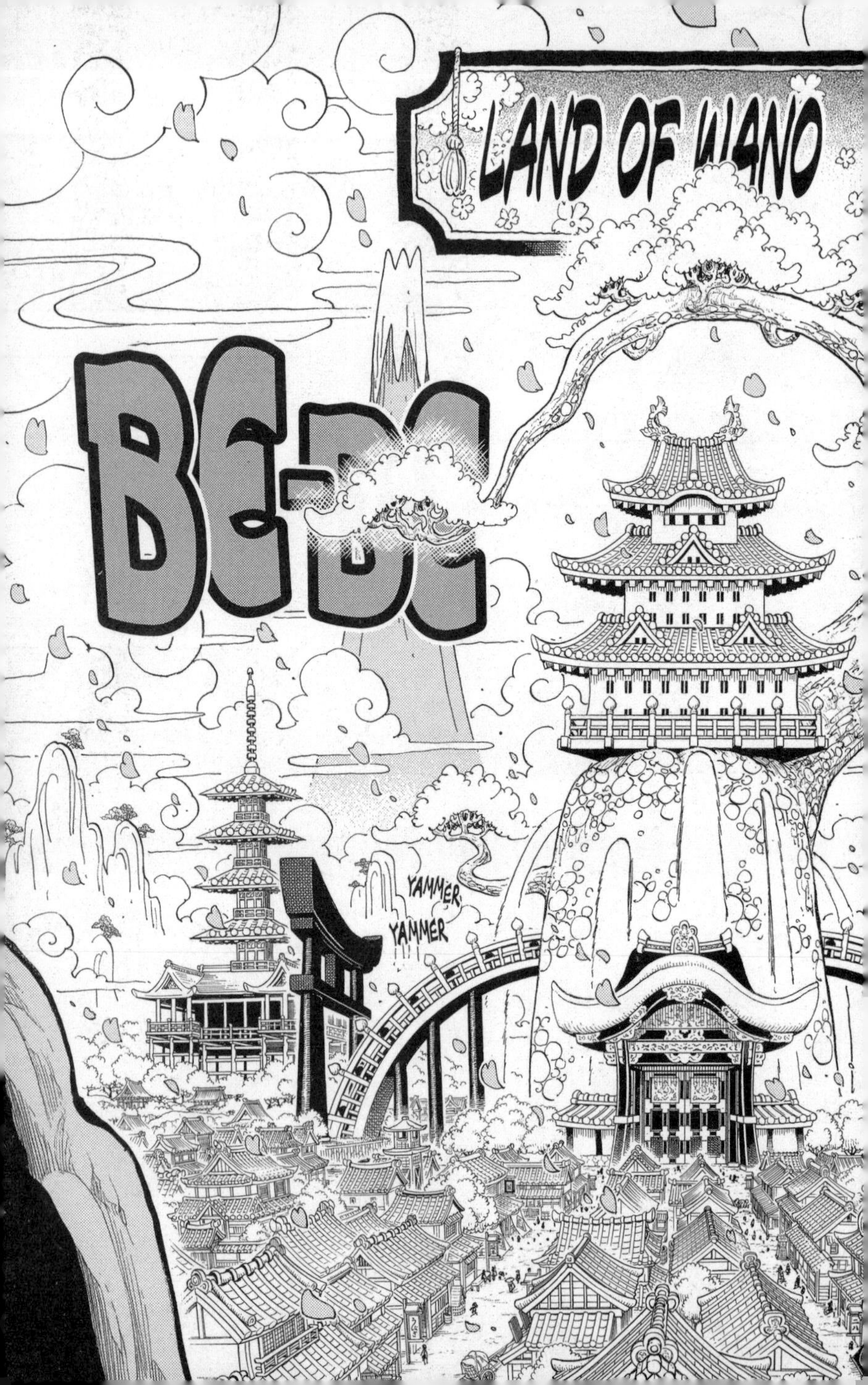
LAND OF WANO
BC-BC
YAMMER
YAMMER

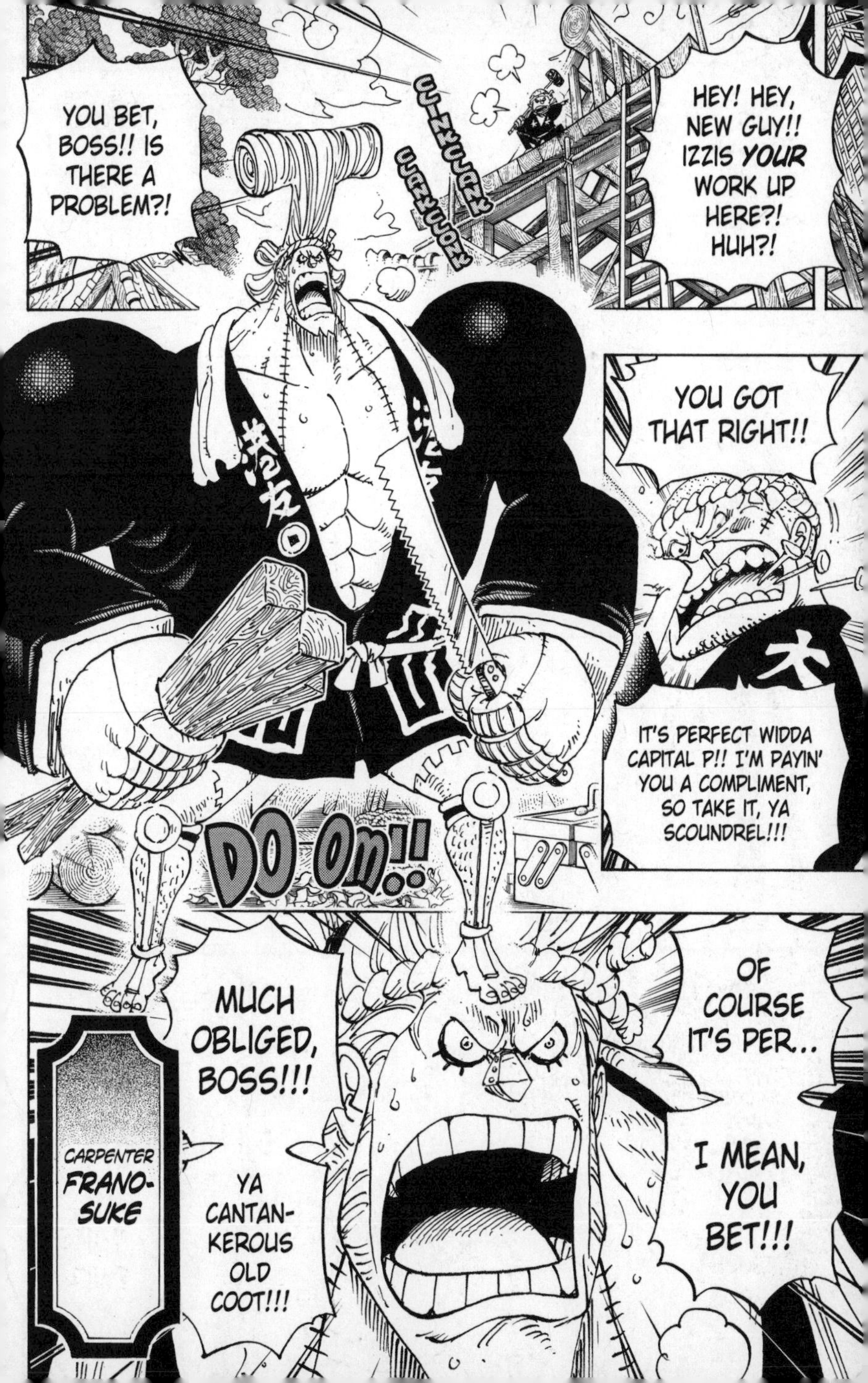

HEY! HEY, NEW GUY!! IZZIS *YOUR* WORK UP HERE?! HUH?!
CLINKCLANK
CLANKCLONK
YOU BET, BOSS!! IS THERE A PROBLEM?!
YOU GOT THAT RIGHT!!
IT'S PERFECT WIDDA CAPITAL P!! I'M PAYIN' YOU A COMPLIMENT, SO TAKE IT, YA SCOUNDREL!!!
DO-OM!!
OF COURSE IT'S PER...
I MEAN, YOU BET!!!
MUCH OBLIGED, BOSS!!!
YA CANTANKEROUS OLD COOT!!!
CARPENTER *FRANOSUKE*

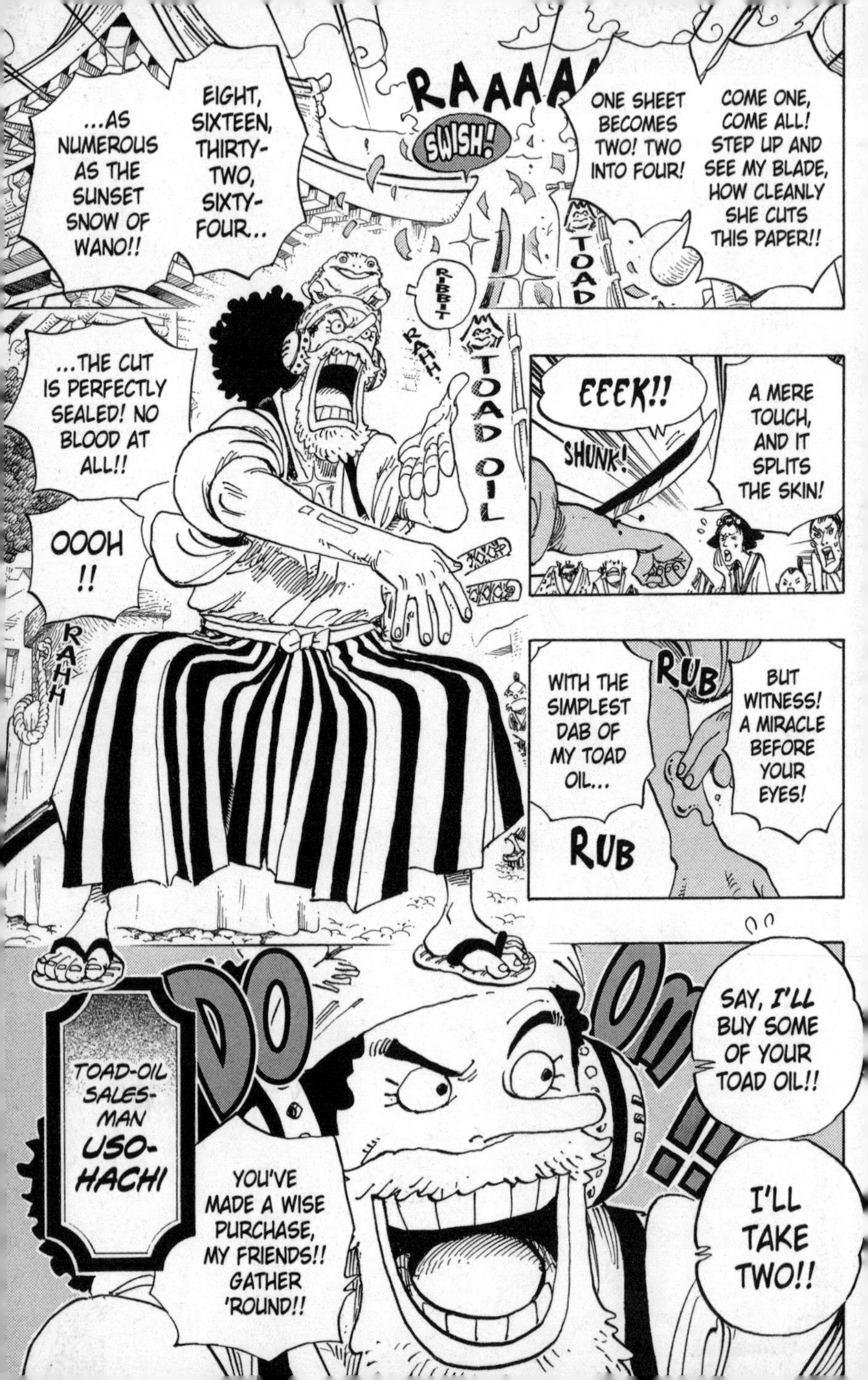
COME ONE, COME ALL! STEP UP AND SEE MY BLADE, HOW CLEANLY SHE CUTS THIS PAPER!!
ONE SHEET BECOMES TWO! TWO INTO FOUR!
RAAAA
SWISH!
TOAD
EIGHT, SIXTEEN, THIRTY-TWO, SIXTY-FOUR...
...AS NUMEROUS AS THE SUNSET SNOW OF WANO!!
A MERE TOUCH, AND IT SPLITS THE SKIN!
EEEK!!
SHUNK!
BUT WITNESS! A MIRACLE BEFORE YOUR EYES!
RUB
WITH THE SIMPLEST DAB OF MY TOAD OIL...
RUB
RIBBIT
RAHH
TOAD OIL
...THE CUT IS PERFECTLY SEALED! NO BLOOD AT ALL!!
OOOH !!
RAHH
SAY, I'LL BUY SOME OF YOUR TOAD OIL!!
I'LL TAKE TWO!!
DOOM
YOU'VE MADE A WISE PURCHASE, MY FRIENDS!! GATHER 'ROUND!!
TOAD-OIL SALESMAN USO-HACHI

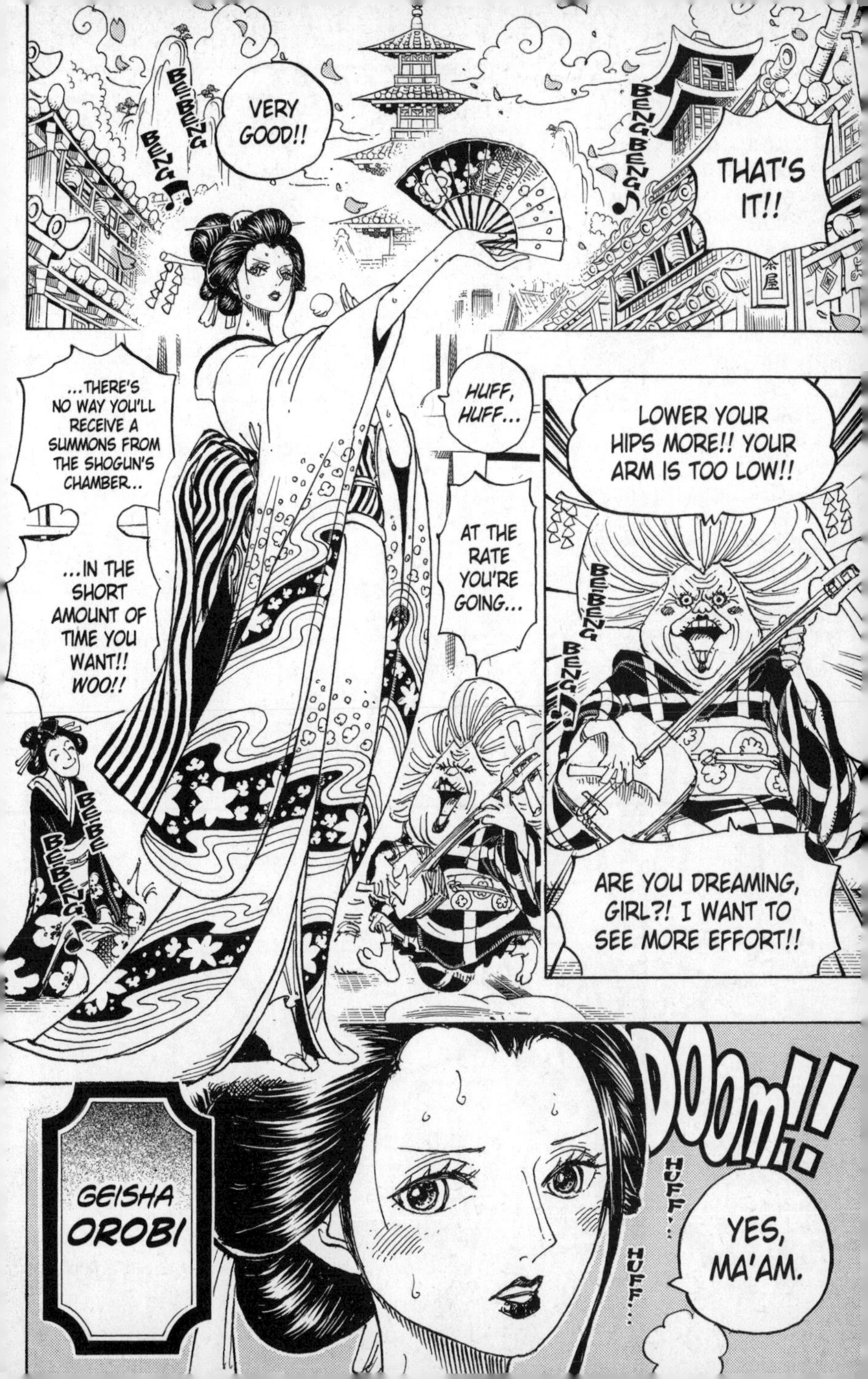
BENG BENG♪
THAT'S IT!!
VERY GOOD!!
BEBENG BENG♪
LOWER YOUR HIPS MORE!! YOUR ARM IS TOO LOW!!
BEBENG BENG♪
ARE YOU DREAMING, GIRL?! I WANT TO SEE MORE EFFORT!!
HUFF, HUFF...
AT THE RATE YOU'RE GOING...
...THERE'S NO WAY YOU'LL RECEIVE A SUMMONS FROM THE SHOGUN'S CHAMBER...
...IN THE SHORT AMOUNT OF TIME YOU WANT!! WOO!!
BEBE BEBENG
DOOM!!
HUFF... HUFF...
YES, MA'AM.
GEISHA OROBI

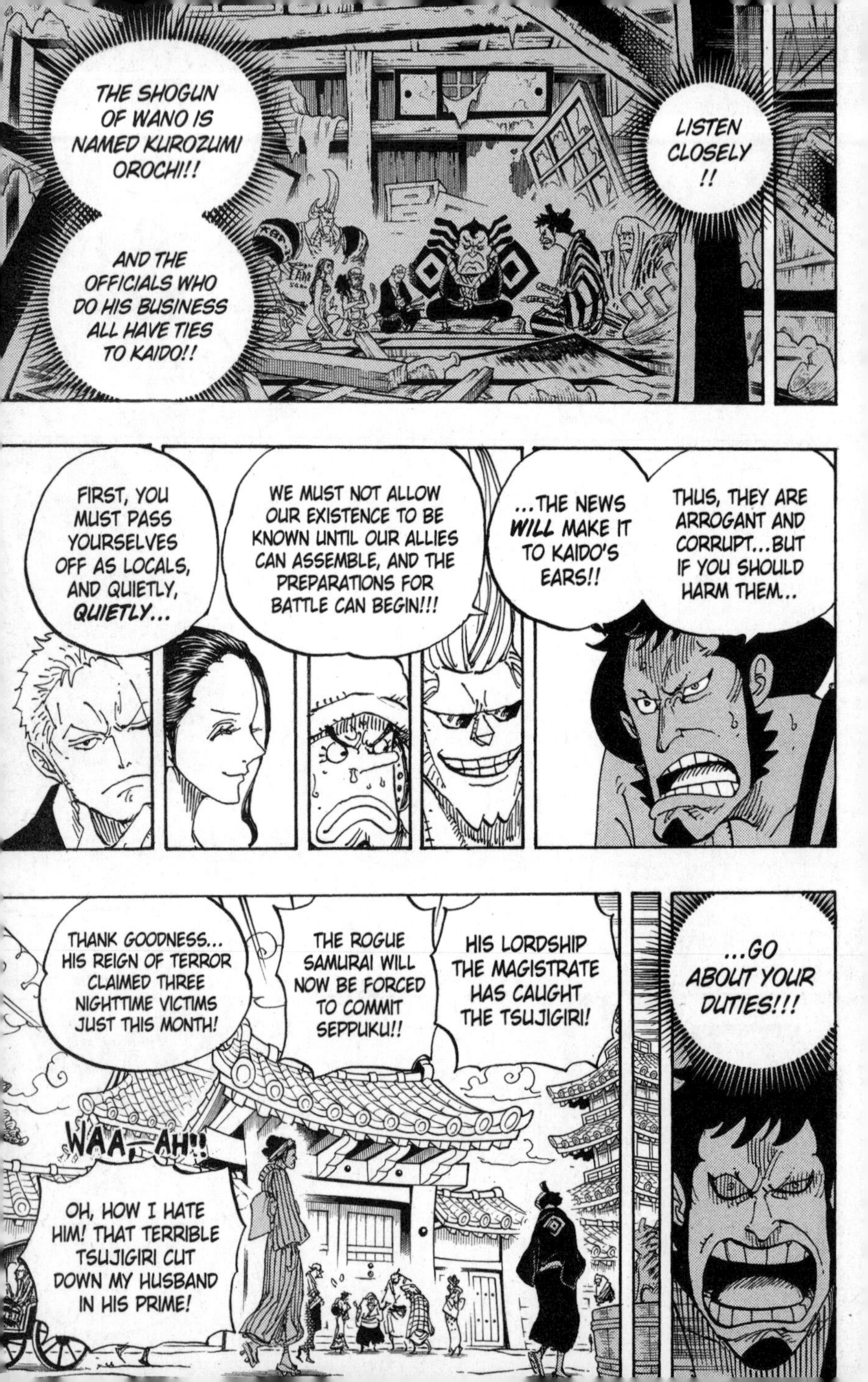
LISTEN CLOSELY!!
THE SHOGUN OF WANO IS NAMED KUROZUMI OROCHI!!
AND THE OFFICIALS WHO DO HIS BUSINESS ALL HAVE TIES TO KAIDO!!
THUS, THEY ARE ARROGANT AND CORRUPT...BUT IF YOU SHOULD HARM THEM...
...THE NEWS WILL MAKE IT TO KAIDO'S EARS!!
WE MUST NOT ALLOW OUR EXISTENCE TO BE KNOWN UNTIL OUR ALLIES CAN ASSEMBLE, AND THE PREPARATIONS FOR BATTLE CAN BEGIN!!!
FIRST, YOU MUST PASS YOURSELVES OFF AS LOCALS, AND QUIETLY, QUIETLY...
...GO ABOUT YOUR DUTIES!!!
HIS LORDSHIP THE MAGISTRATE HAS CAUGHT THE TSUJIGIRI!
THE ROGUE SAMURAI WILL NOW BE FORCED TO COMMIT SEPPUKU!!
THANK GOODNESS... HIS REIGN OF TERROR CLAIMED THREE NIGHTTIME VICTIMS JUST THIS MONTH!
WAA-AH!!
OH, HOW I HATE HIM! THAT TERRIBLE TSUJIGIRI CUT DOWN MY HUSBAND IN HIS PRIME!

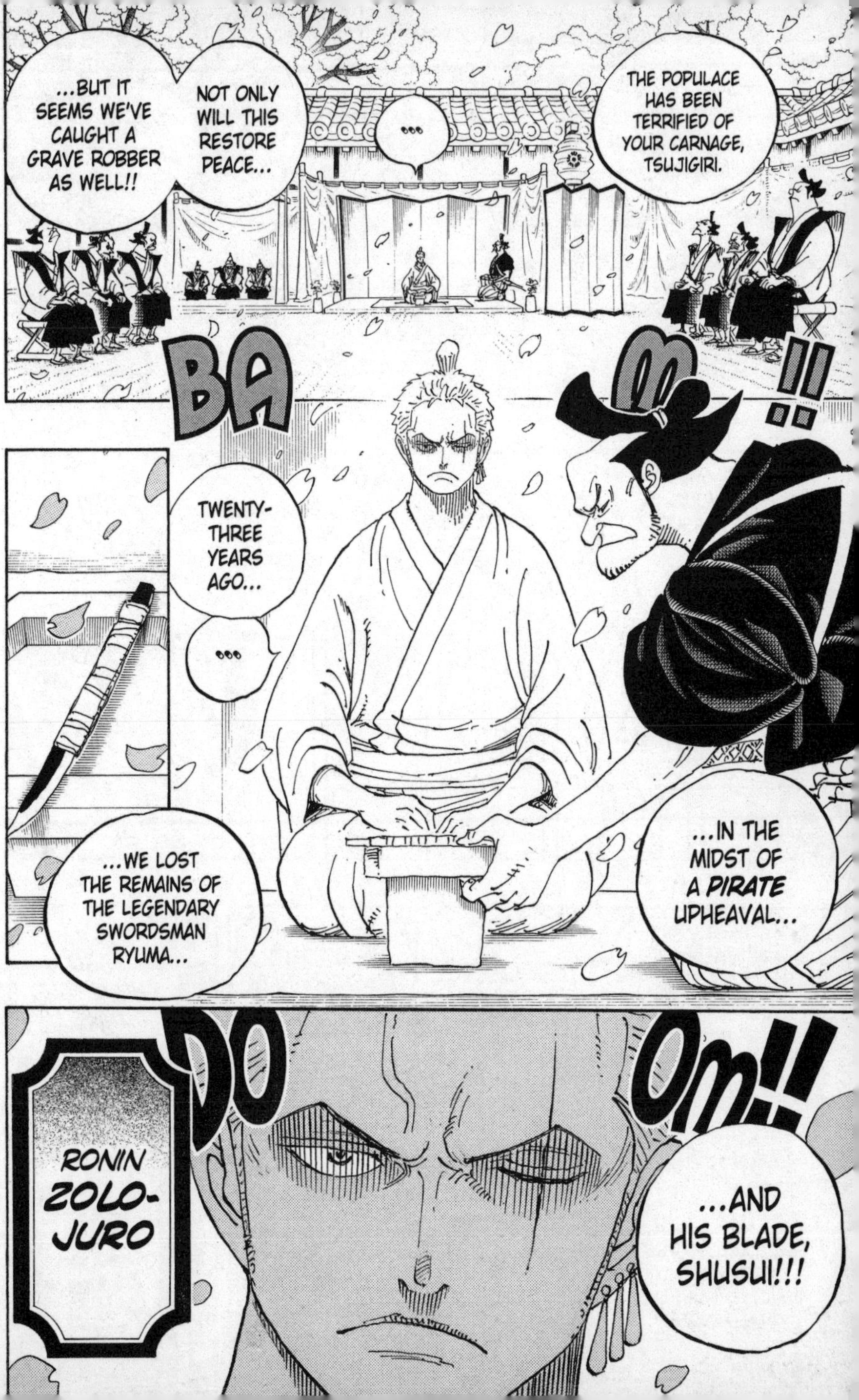
THE POPULACE HAS BEEN TERRIFIED OF YOUR CARNAGE, TSUJIGIRI.
...
NOT ONLY WILL THIS RESTORE PEACE...
...BUT IT SEEMS WE'VE CAUGHT A GRAVE ROBBER AS WELL!!
BAM!!
TWENTY-THREE YEARS AGO...
...
...IN THE MIDST OF A PIRATE UPHEAVAL...
...WE LOST THE REMAINS OF THE LEGENDARY SWORDSMAN RYUMA...
DOOM!!
...AND HIS BLADE, SHUSUI!!!
RONIN ZOLO-JURO

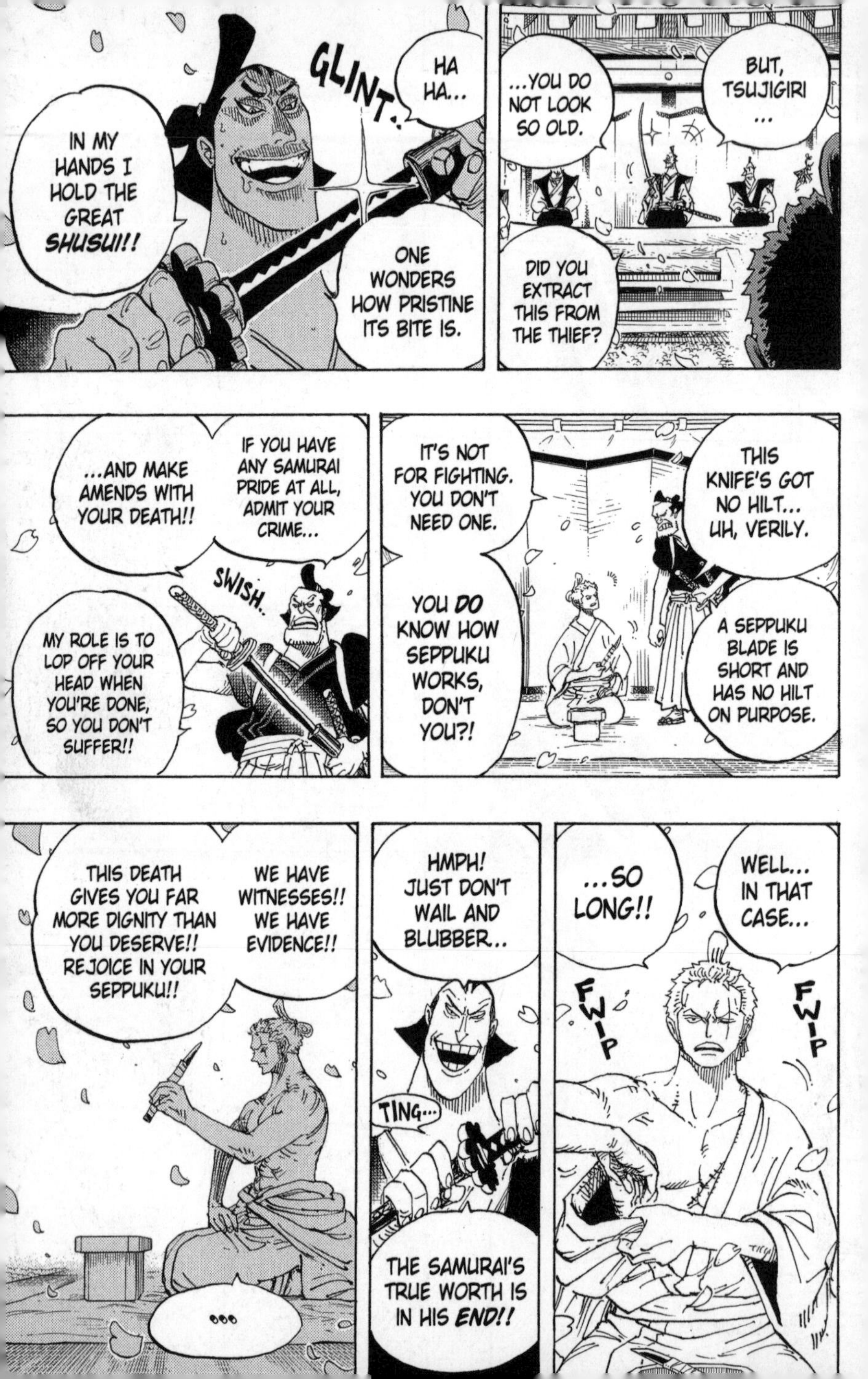
BUT, TSUJIGIRI ...
...YOU DO NOT LOOK SO OLD.
DID YOU EXTRACT THIS FROM THE THIEF?
HA HA...
GLINT
IN MY HANDS I HOLD THE GREAT *SHUSUI!!*
ONE WONDERS HOW PRISTINE ITS BITE IS.
THIS KNIFE'S GOT NO HILT... UH, VERILY.
IT'S NOT FOR FIGHTING. YOU DON'T NEED ONE.
A SEPPUKU BLADE IS SHORT AND HAS NO HILT ON PURPOSE.
YOU *DO* KNOW HOW SEPPUKU WORKS, DON'T YOU?!
IF YOU HAVE ANY SAMURAI PRIDE AT ALL, ADMIT YOUR CRIME...
...AND MAKE AMENDS WITH YOUR DEATH!!
SWISH
MY ROLE IS TO LOP OFF YOUR HEAD WHEN YOU'RE DONE, SO YOU DON'T SUFFER!!
WELL... IN THAT CASE...
...SO LONG!!
FWIP
FWIP
HMPH! JUST DON'T WAIL AND BLUBBER...
TING...
THE SAMURAI'S TRUE WORTH IS IN HIS *END!!*
WE HAVE WITNESSES!! WE HAVE EVIDENCE!!
THIS DEATH GIVES YOU FAR MORE DIGNITY THAN YOU DESERVE!! REJOICE IN YOUR SEPPUKU!!
...

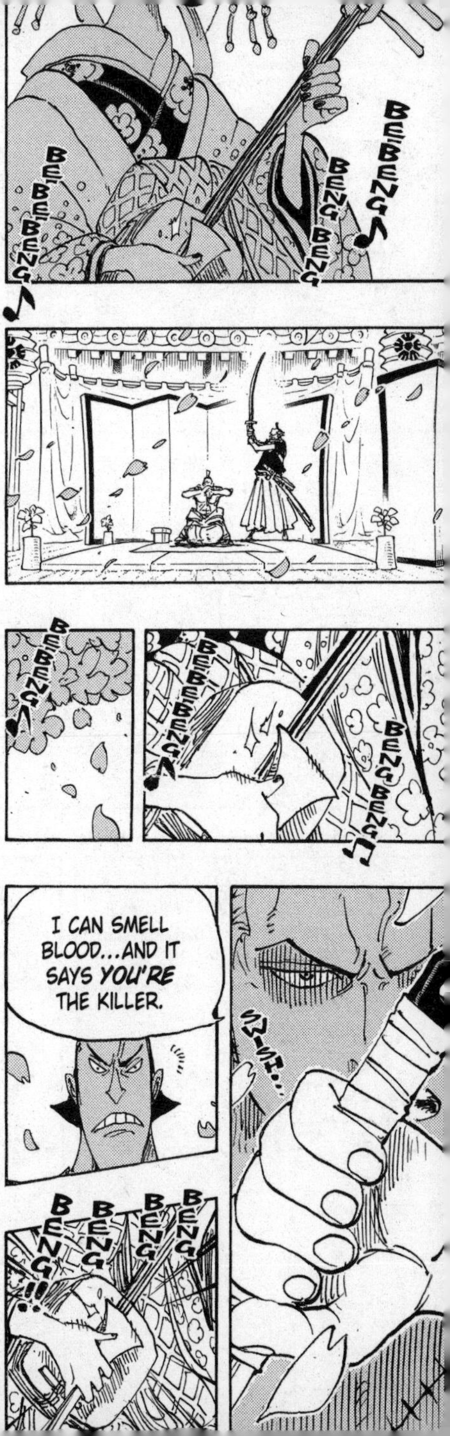
BEBENG♪
BENG BENG
BEBEBENG♪
BENG BENG♪
BEBEBENG♪
BEBENG♪
SWISH...
I CAN SMELL BLOOD...AND IT SAYS *YOU'RE* THE KILLER.
BENG BENG BENG BENG!!
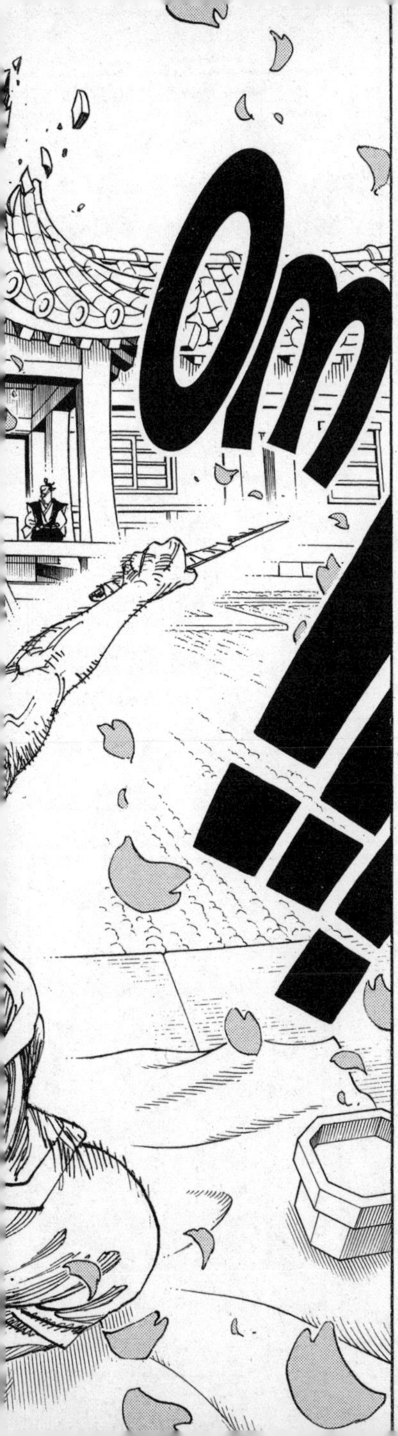
Om!!

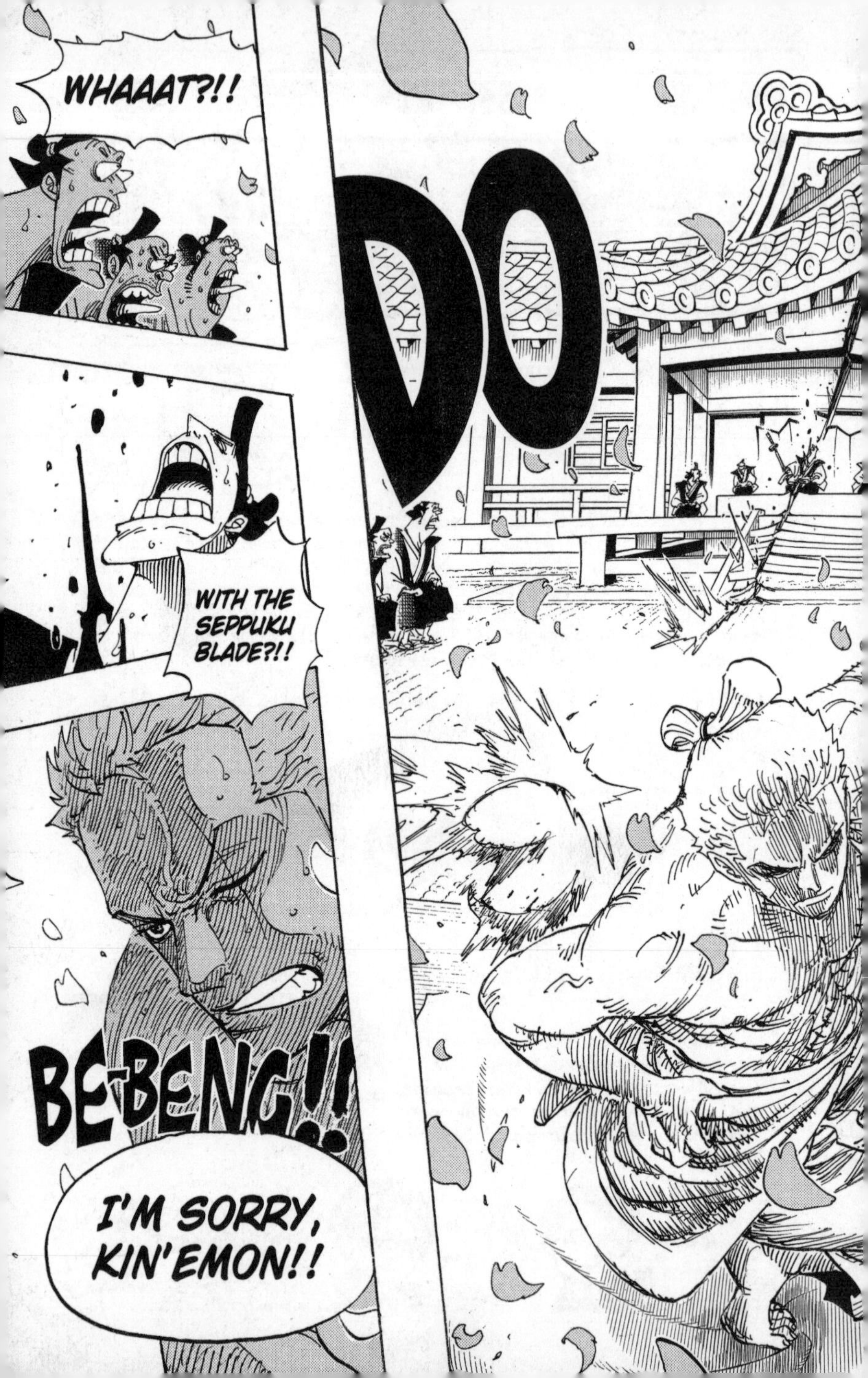
DO
WHAAAT?!!
WITH THE SEPPUKU BLADE?!!
BE-BENG!!
I'M SORRY, KIN'EMON!!

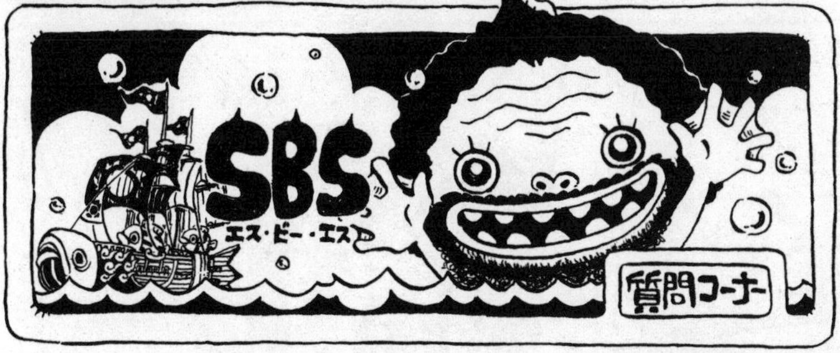
SBS
エス・ビー・エスD
質問コーナー

(I ♡ OP, Ishikawa)

Q: Hello, Mr. Oda! I have a question. Charlotte Montd'or and Charlotte Opera's Devil Fruit titles were never actually unveiled in the story, were they? Can you tell us what they are?

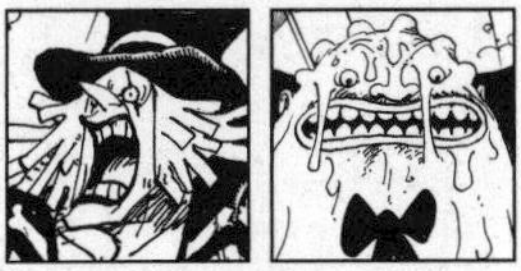

--Boil

A: Okay. Montd'or is the bookkeeper because he has the Book-Book Fruit. He can turn living things into living samples, use books to fly in the air, and pull people into the stories within books. It's a rich enough variety of powers that he could be the villain of his own story arc. Opera has the Cream-Cream Fruit. He's a very tricky enemy who controls the cream his body creates, and utilizes "sweetness" as a novel attack concept.

Q: Question for the SBS! What are the hobbies of Smoker, Tashigi, and Lady Hina?

--Itsuma

A: Interesting question.

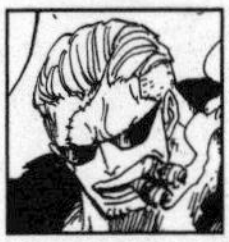

Pottery
Casinos

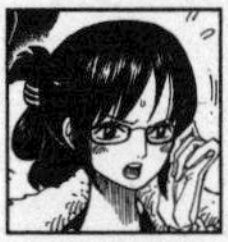

Reading books about swords
Paper-cutting art

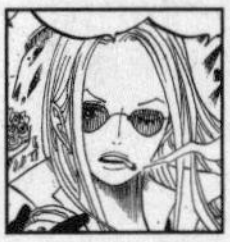

Horseback riding
Clubbing

Q: I love Crocodile, Mihawk and Doflamingo. Are they going to be bachelors forever, without having descendants? What would their children look like?

--Purple Panda

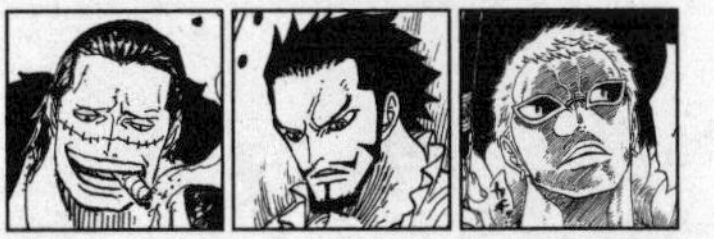

A: I wonder if any of them have been married. I don't know if they have kids or not, but here's how I imagine that going, for your entertainment. See you in next volume's SBS!

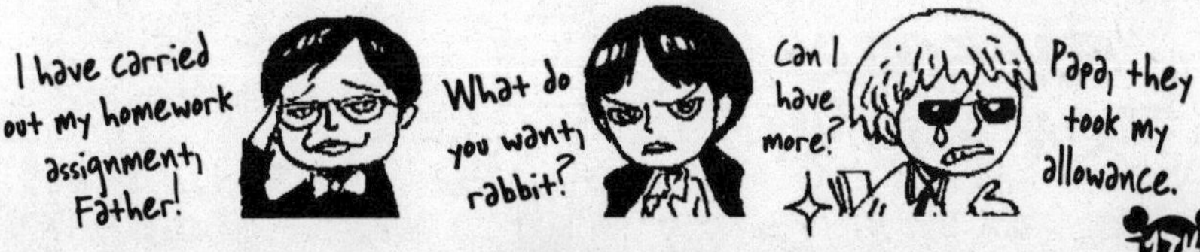
Papa, they took my allowance.
Can I have more?
What do you want, rabbit?
I have carried out my homework assignment, Father!

Chapter 910:
ONWARD TO WANO

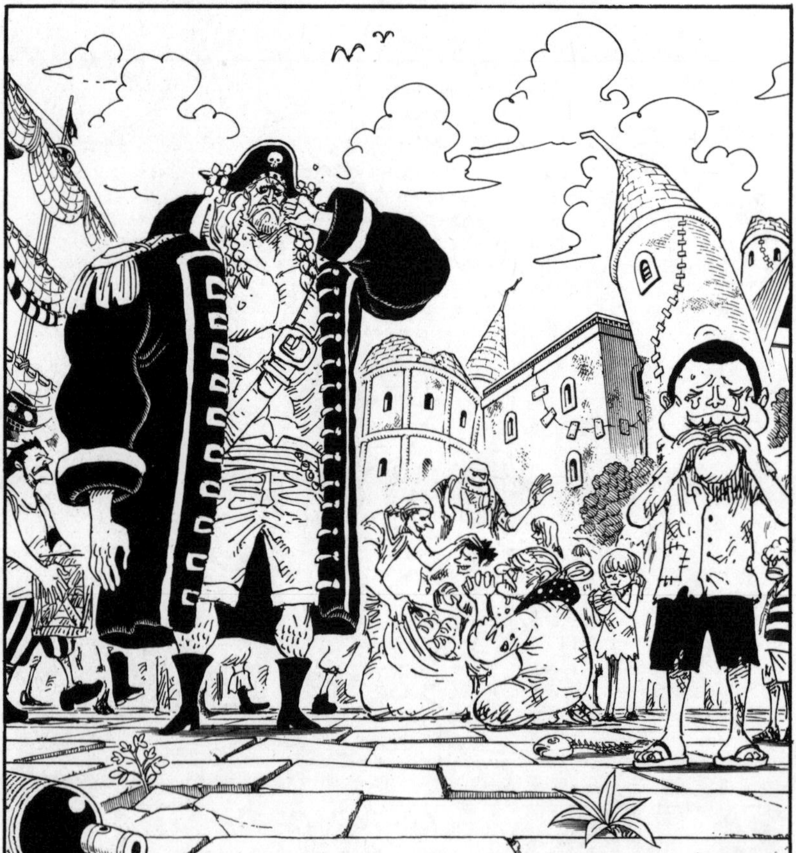

THE SAGA OF THE SELF-PROCLAIMED STRAW HAT FLEET, VOL. 40, ORLUMBUS: "4:30 P.M.: THEY WERE POORER THAN ANTICIPATED, NOW DISTRIBUTING SUPPLIES"

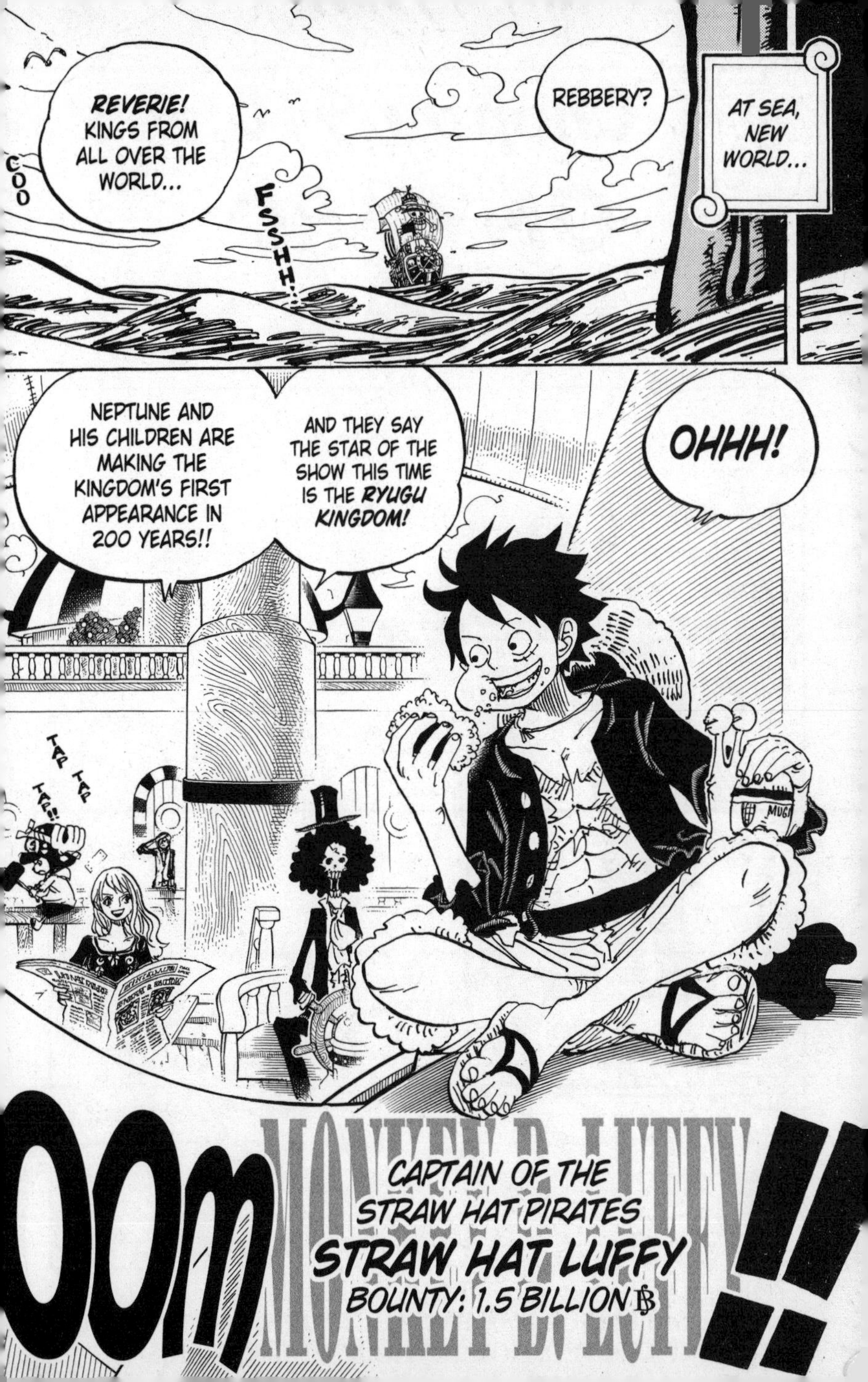
AT SEA, NEW WORLD...
REBBERY?
REVERIE! KINGS FROM ALL OVER THE WORLD...
FSSHH
COO
OHHH!
AND THEY SAY THE STAR OF THE SHOW THIS TIME IS THE RYUGU KINGDOM!
NEPTUNE AND HIS CHILDREN ARE MAKING THE KINGDOM'S FIRST APPEARANCE IN 200 YEARS!!
TAP TAP TAP!!
OOM
MONKEY D. LUFFY!!
CAPTAIN OF THE STRAW HAT PIRATES
STRAW HAT LUFFY
BOUNTY: 1.5 BILLION ฿

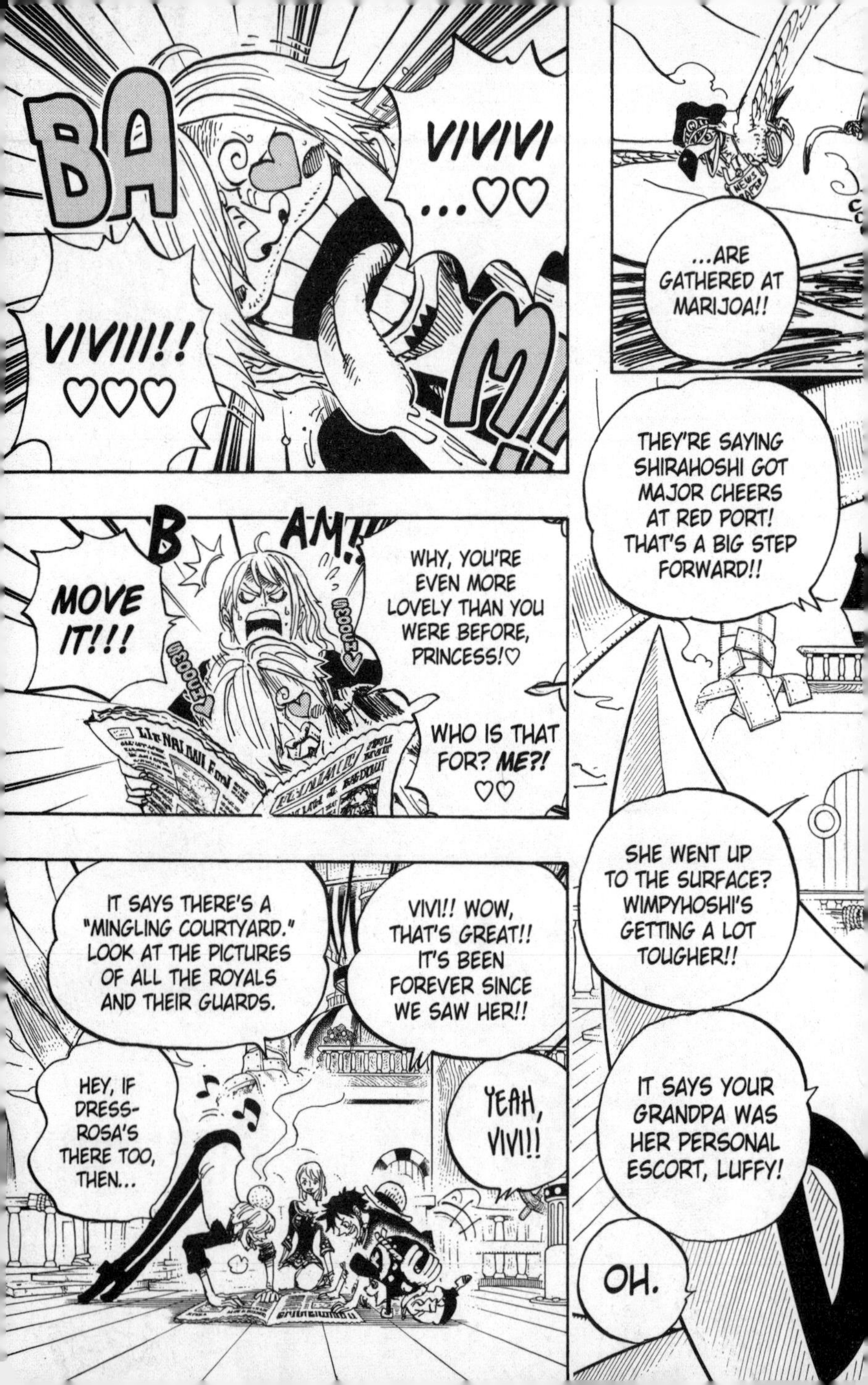
...ARE GATHERED AT MARIJOA!!
THEY'RE SAYING SHIRAHOSHI GOT MAJOR CHEERS AT RED PORT! THAT'S A BIG STEP FORWARD!!
SHE WENT UP TO THE SURFACE? WIMPYHOSHI'S GETTING A LOT TOUGHER!!
IT SAYS YOUR GRANDPA WAS HER PERSONAL ESCORT, LUFFY!
OH.
VIVIVI ...♡♡
BA
MI
VIVIII!! ♡♡♡
WHY, YOU'RE EVEN MORE LOVELY THAN YOU WERE BEFORE, PRINCESS!♡
AM!!
B
WHO IS THAT FOR? ME?! ♡♡
SMOOCH
MOVE IT!!!
SMOOCH
VIVI!! WOW, THAT'S GREAT!! IT'S BEEN FOREVER SINCE WE SAW HER!!
IT SAYS THERE'S A "MINGLING COURTYARD." LOOK AT THE PICTURES OF ALL THE ROYALS AND THEIR GUARDS.
YEAH, VIVI!!
HEY, IF DRESS-ROSA'S THERE TOO, THEN...

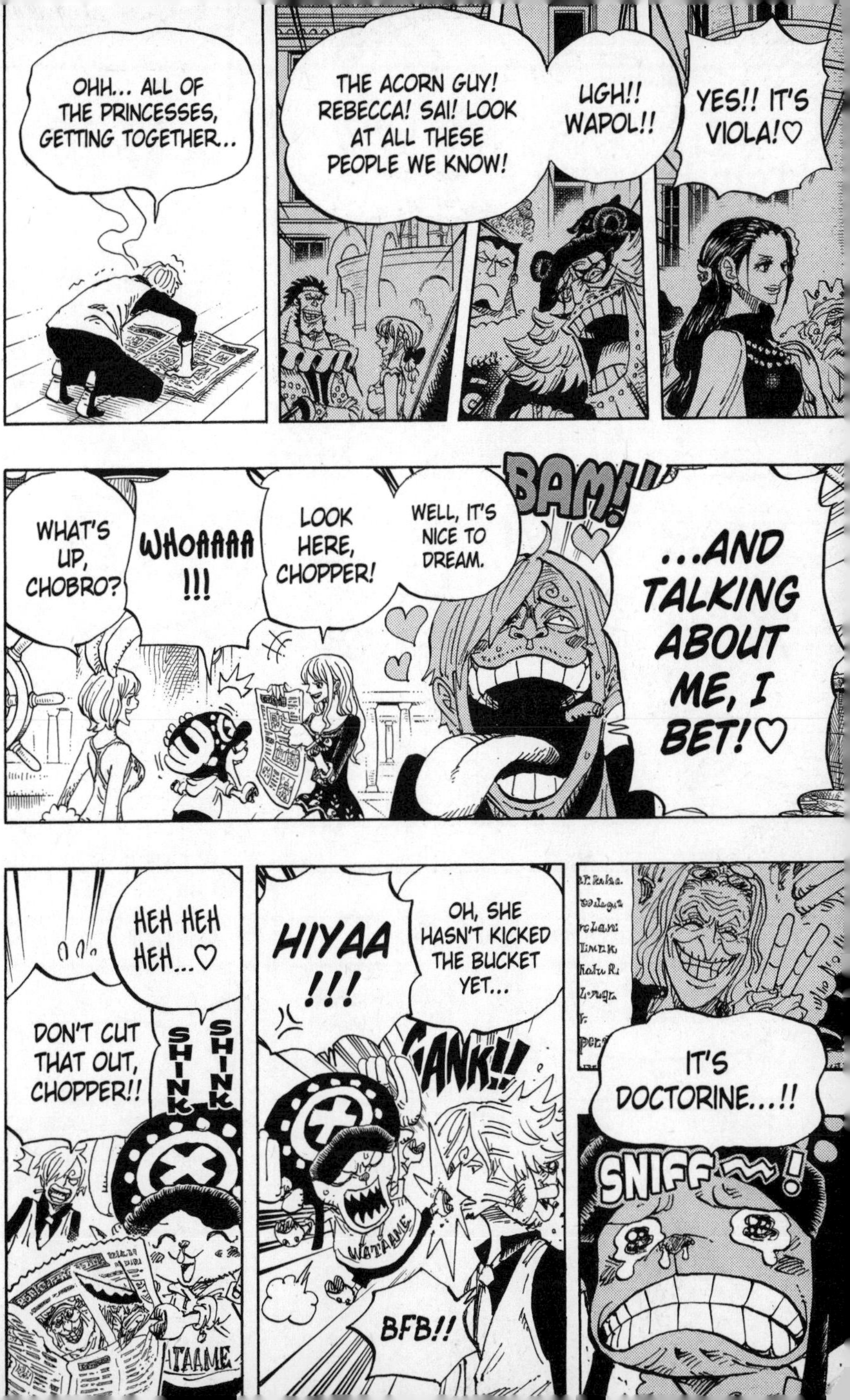
YES!! IT'S VIOLA!♡
UGH!! WAPOL!!
THE ACORN GUY! REBECCA! SAI! LOOK AT ALL THESE PEOPLE WE KNOW!
OHH... ALL OF THE PRINCESSES, GETTING TOGETHER...
BAM!!
...AND TALKING ABOUT ME, I BET!♡
WELL, IT'S NICE TO DREAM.
LOOK HERE, CHOPPER!
WHOAAAA!!!
WHAT'S UP, CHOBRO?
IT'S DOCTORINE...!!
SNIFF~!
OH, SHE HASN'T KICKED THE BUCKET YET...
HIYAA!!!
GANK!!
WATAAME
BFB!!
HEH HEH HEH...♡
SHINK
SHINK
DON'T CUT THAT OUT, CHOPPER!!

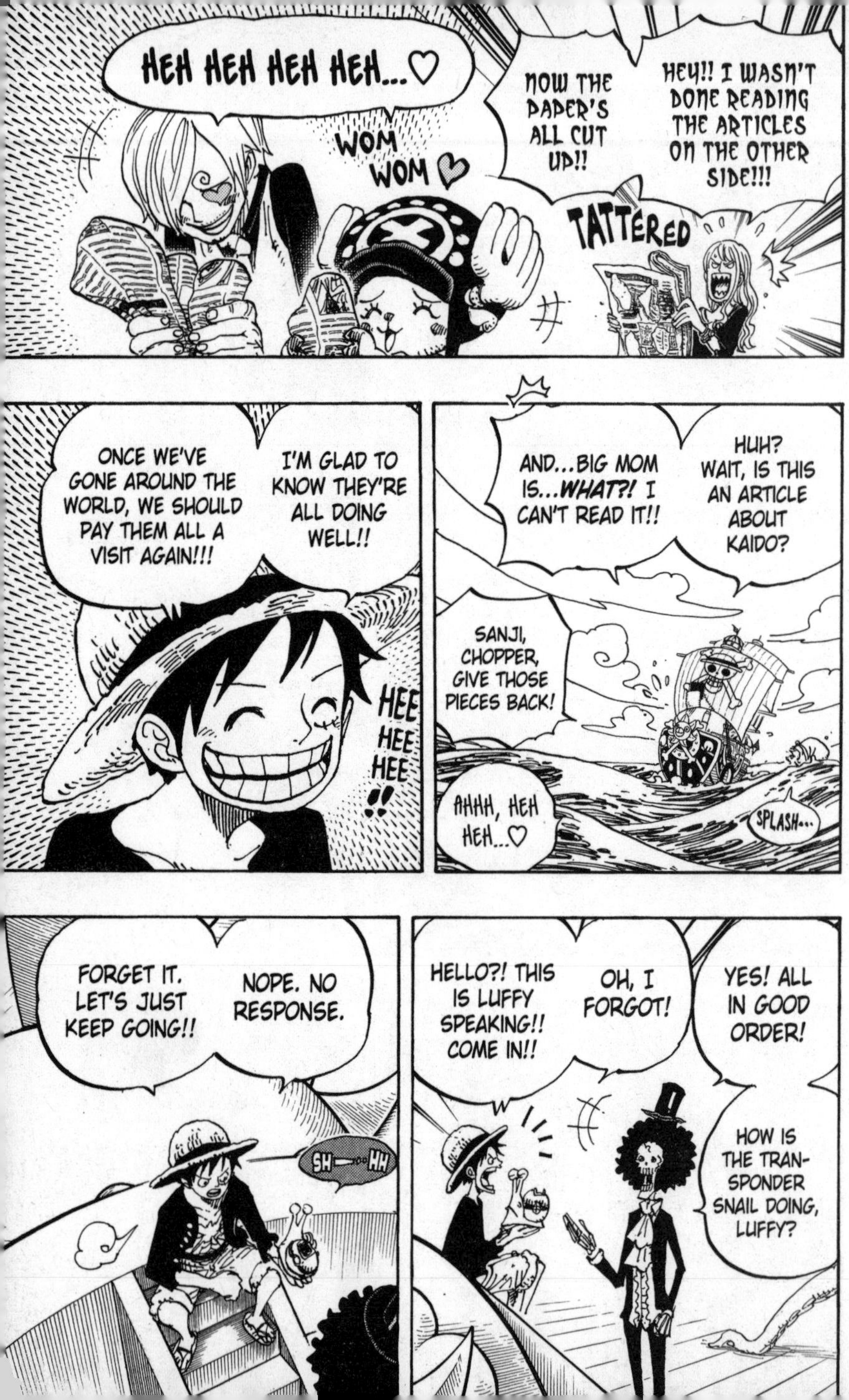
HEY!! I WASN'T DONE READING THE ARTICLES ON THE OTHER SIDE!!!
NOW THE PAPER'S ALL CUT UP!!
TATTERED
HEH HEH HEH HEH...♡
WOM WOM ♡
HUH? WAIT, IS THIS AN ARTICLE ABOUT KAIDO?
AND...BIG MOM IS...*WHAT?!* I CAN'T READ IT!!
SANJI, CHOPPER, GIVE THOSE PIECES BACK!
SPLASH...
AHHH, HEH HEH...♡
I'M GLAD TO KNOW THEY'RE ALL DOING WELL!!
ONCE WE'VE GONE AROUND THE WORLD, WE SHOULD PAY THEM ALL A VISIT AGAIN!!!
HEE HEE HEE!!
HOW IS THE TRAN-SPONDER SNAIL DOING, LUFFY?
YES! ALL IN GOOD ORDER!
OH, I FORGOT!
HELLO?! THIS IS LUFFY SPEAKING!! COME IN!!
NOPE. NO RESPONSE.
FORGET IT. LET'S JUST KEEP GOING!!
SH—HH

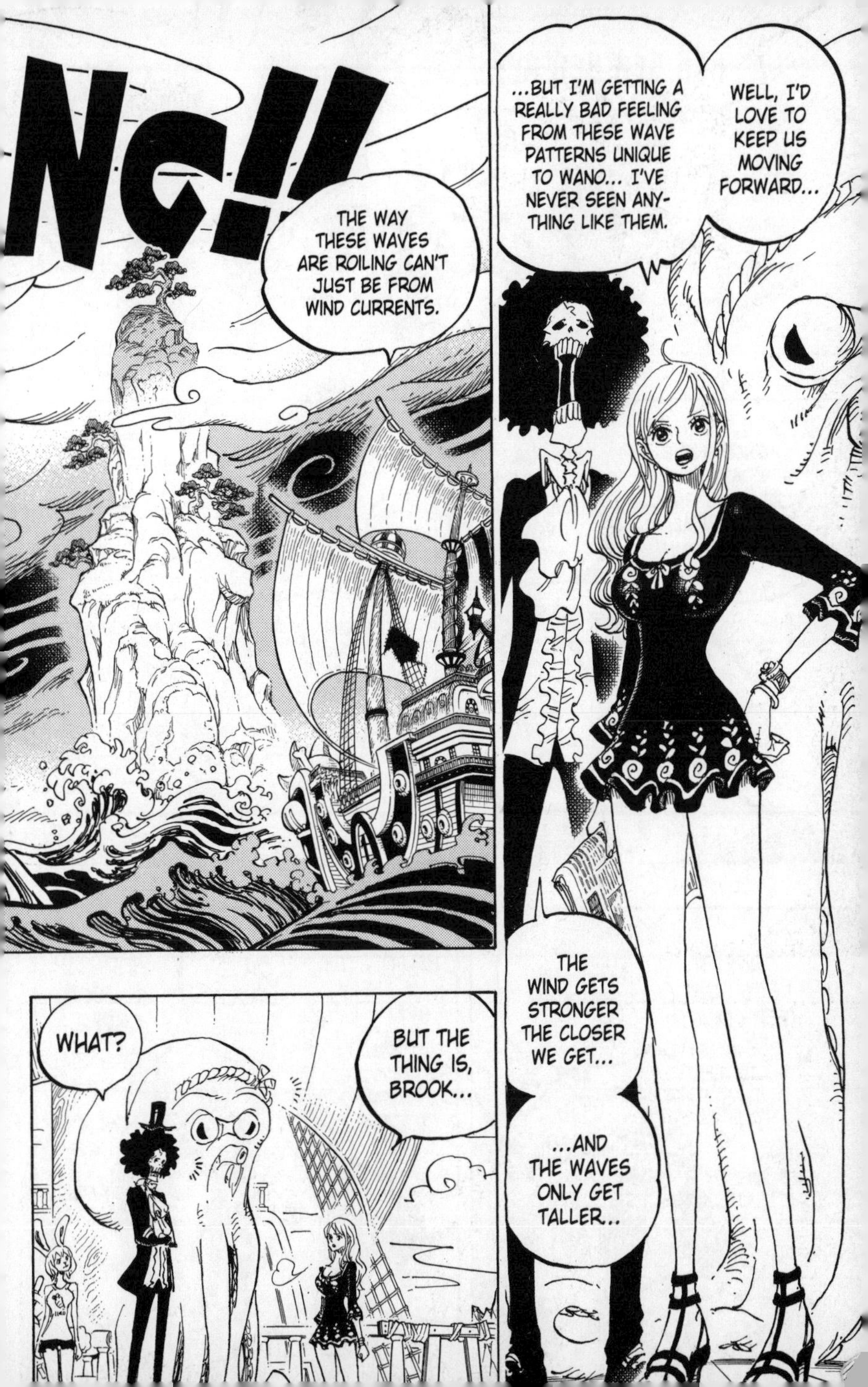
WELL, I'D LOVE TO KEEP US MOVING FORWARD...
...BUT I'M GETTING A REALLY BAD FEELING FROM THESE WAVE PATTERNS UNIQUE TO WANO... I'VE NEVER SEEN ANYTHING LIKE THEM.
THE WIND GETS STRONGER THE CLOSER WE GET...
...AND THE WAVES ONLY GET TALLER...
NG!!
THE WAY THESE WAVES ARE ROILING CAN'T JUST BE FROM WIND CURRENTS.
BUT THE THING IS, BROOK...
WHAT?

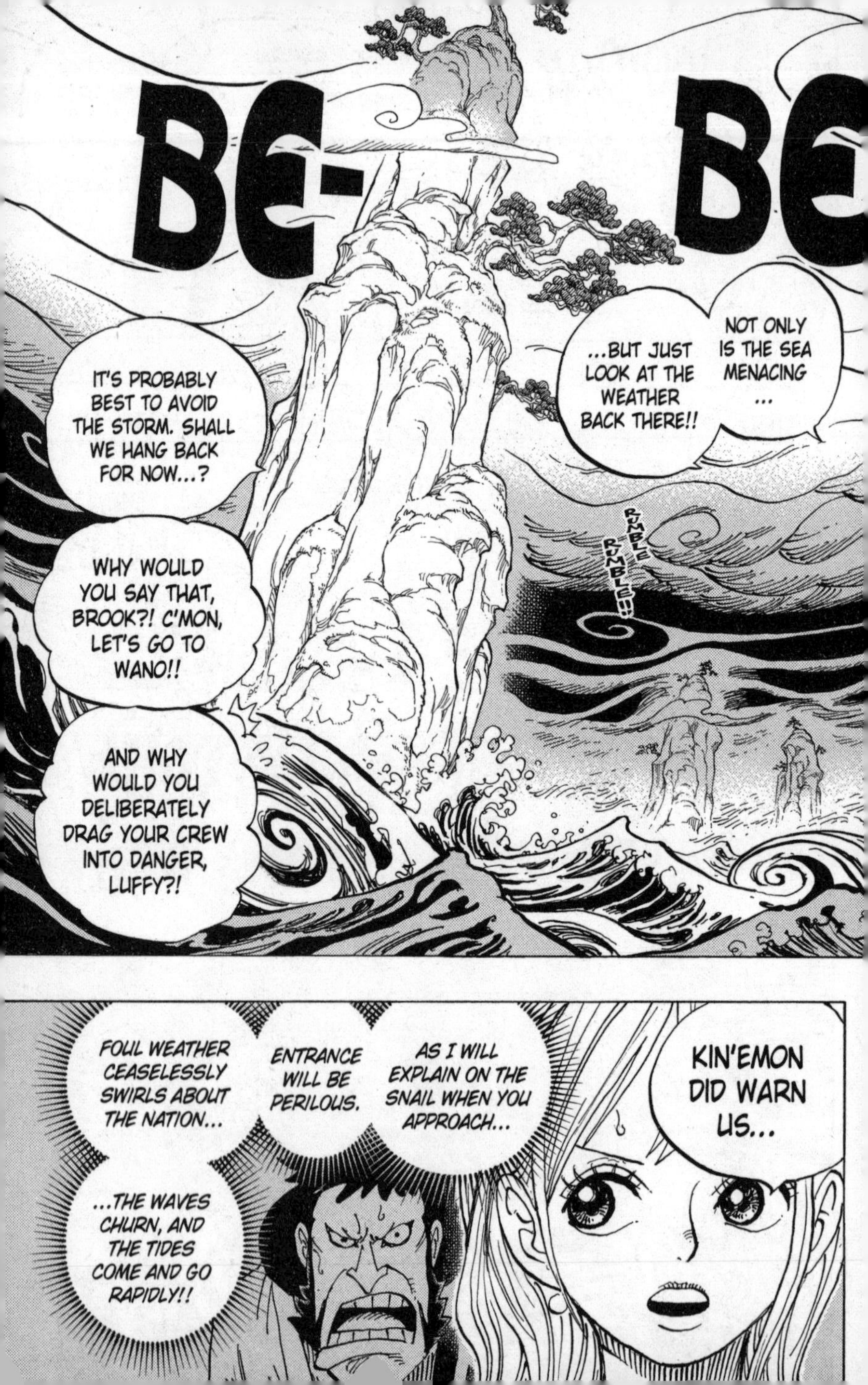
BE- BE
NOT ONLY IS THE SEA MENACING ...
...BUT JUST LOOK AT THE WEATHER BACK THERE!!
RUMBLE RUMBLE!!
IT'S PROBABLY BEST TO AVOID THE STORM. SHALL WE HANG BACK FOR NOW...?
WHY WOULD YOU SAY THAT, BROOK?! C'MON, LET'S GO TO WANO!!
AND WHY WOULD YOU DELIBERATELY DRAG YOUR CREW INTO DANGER, LUFFY?!
KIN'EMON DID WARN US...
AS I WILL EXPLAIN ON THE SNAIL WHEN YOU APPROACH...
ENTRANCE WILL BE PERILOUS.
FOUL WEATHER CEASELESSLY SWIRLS ABOUT THE NATION...
...THE WAVES CHURN, AND THE TIDES COME AND GO RAPIDLY!!

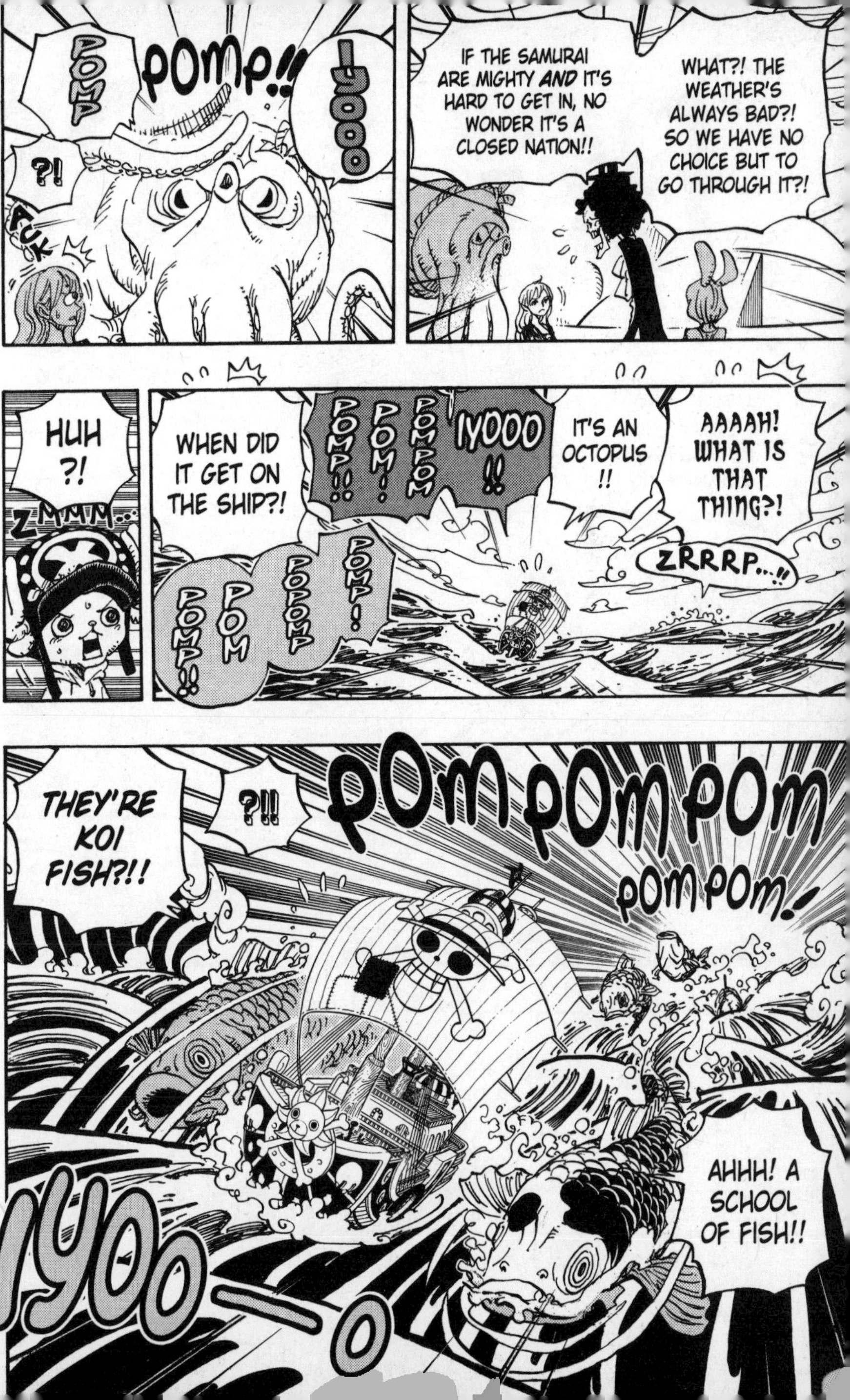
WHAT?! THE WEATHER'S ALWAYS BAD?! SO WE HAVE NO CHOICE BUT TO GO THROUGH IT?!
IF THE SAMURAI ARE MIGHTY AND IT'S HARD TO GET IN, NO WONDER IT'S A CLOSED NATION!!
IYOOO
POMP!!
POMP
?!
AUK
AAAAH! WHAT IS THAT THING?!
IT'S AN OCTOPUS !!
IYOOO !!
POMPOM POM! POMP!!
WHEN DID IT GET ON THE SHIP?!
ZRRRP...!!
POMP! POPOMP POM POMP!!
HUH ?!
ZMMM...
AHHH! A SCHOOL OF FISH!!
POM POM POM POM POM!
?!!
THEY'RE KOI FISH?!!
IYOO—O

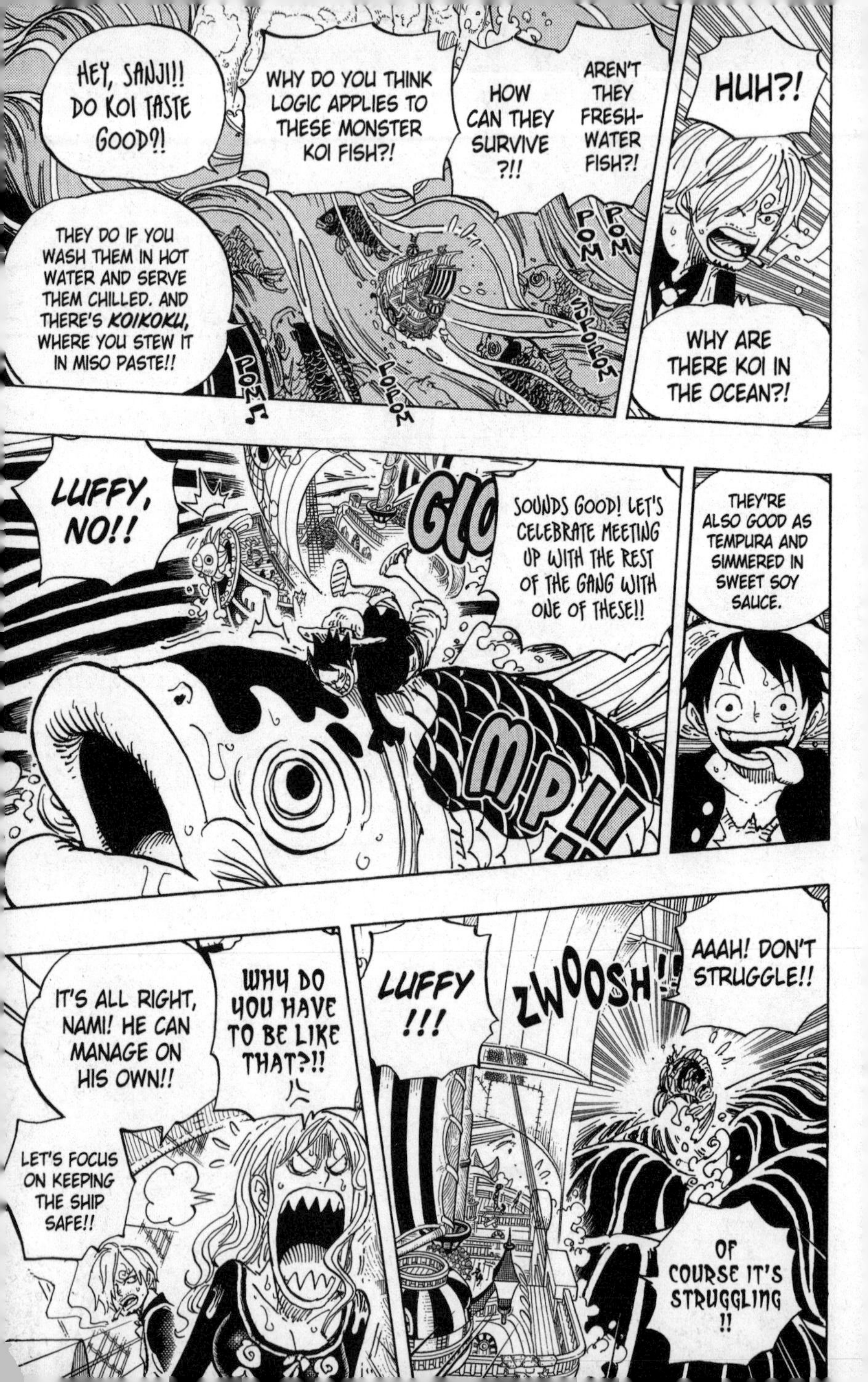
HUH?!
WHY ARE THERE KOI IN THE OCEAN?!
AREN'T THEY FRESH-WATER FISH?!
HOW CAN THEY SURVIVE?!!
WHY DO YOU THINK LOGIC APPLIES TO THESE MONSTER KOI FISH?!
POM POM
HEY, SANJI!! DO KOI TASTE GOOD?!
THEY DO IF YOU WASH THEM IN HOT WATER AND SERVE THEM CHILLED. AND THERE'S KOIKOKU, WHERE YOU STEW IT IN MISO PASTE!!
POM
THEY'RE ALSO GOOD AS TEMPURA AND SIMMERED IN SWEET SOY SAUCE.
SOUNDS GOOD! LET'S CELEBRATE MEETING UP WITH THE REST OF THE GANG WITH ONE OF THESE!!
GLO
MP!!
LUFFY, NO!!
AAAH! DON'T STRUGGLE!!
ZWOOSH!!
LUFFY!!!
OF COURSE IT'S STRUGGLING!!
WHY DO YOU HAVE TO BE LIKE THAT?!!
IT'S ALL RIGHT, NAMI! HE CAN MANAGE ON HIS OWN!!
LET'S FOCUS ON KEEPING THE SHIP SAFE!!

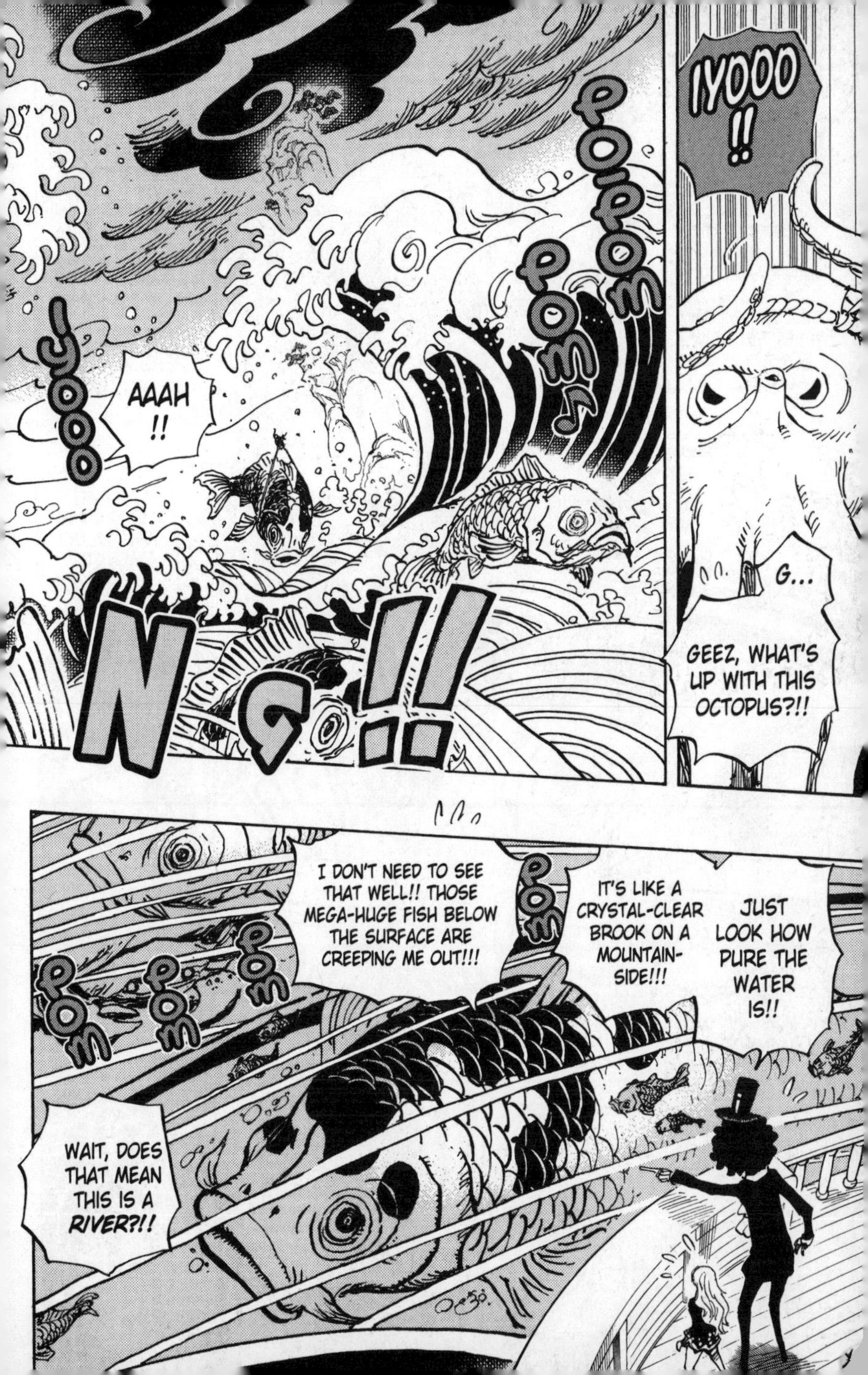
IYOOO!!
G...
GEEZ, WHAT'S UP WITH THIS OCTOPUS?!!
AAAH !!
NG!!
JUST LOOK HOW PURE THE WATER IS!!
IT'S LIKE A CRYSTAL-CLEAR BROOK ON A MOUNTAIN-SIDE!!!
I DON'T NEED TO SEE THAT WELL!! THOSE MEGA-HUGE FISH BELOW THE SURFACE ARE CREEPING ME OUT!!!
WAIT, DOES THAT MEAN THIS IS A RIVER?!!

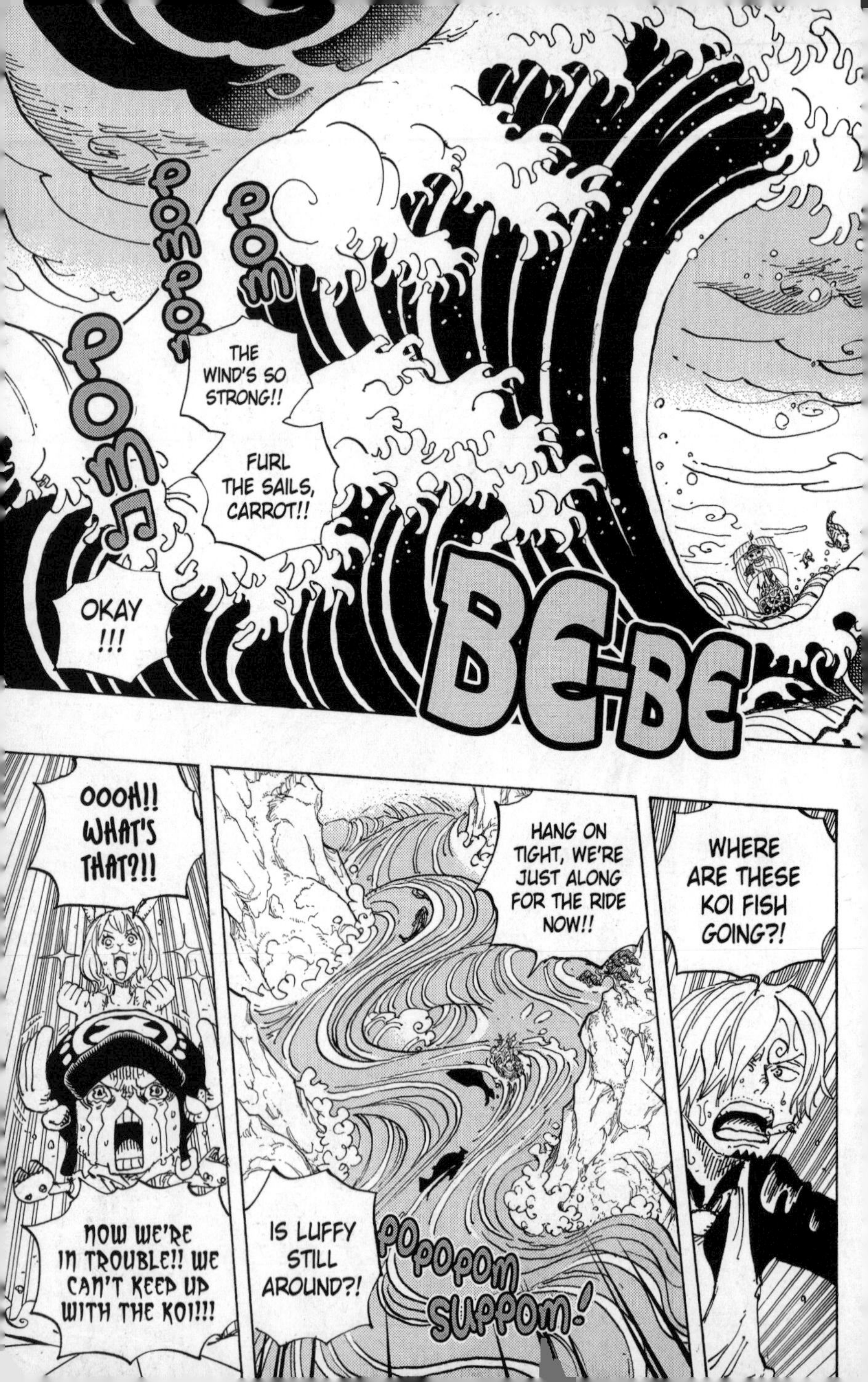
BE-BE
POM
POMPOM
THE WIND'S SO STRONG!!
FURL THE SAILS, CARROT!!
POM♫
OKAY!!!
WHERE ARE THESE KOI FISH GOING?!
HANG ON TIGHT, WE'RE JUST ALONG FOR THE RIDE NOW!!
POPOPOM SUPPOM!
IS LUFFY STILL AROUND?!
OOOH!! WHAT'S THAT?!!
NOW WE'RE IN TROUBLE!! WE CAN'T KEEP UP WITH THE KOI!!!

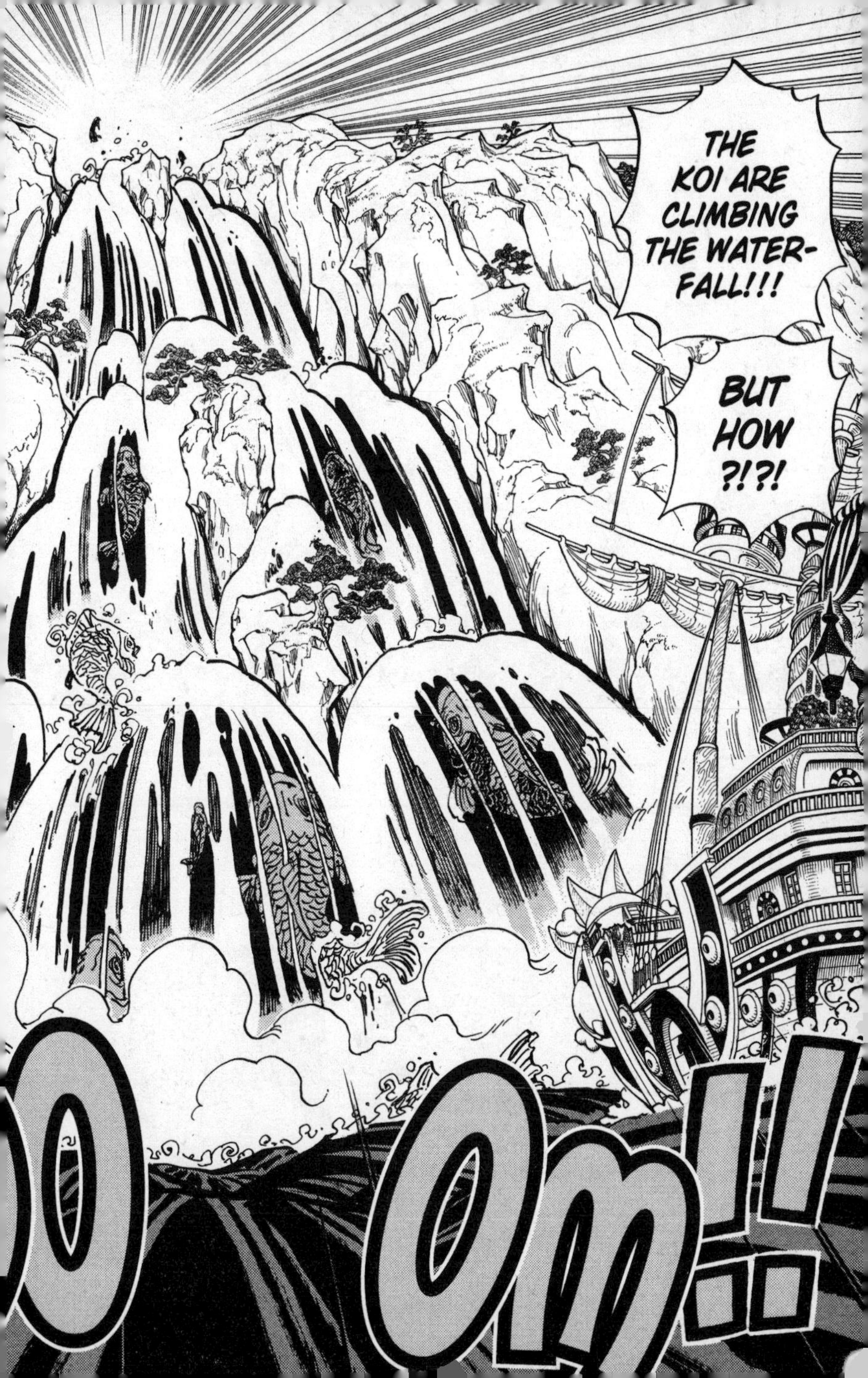
THE KOI ARE CLIMBING THE WATER-FALL!!!
BUT HOW ?!?!
OOM!!

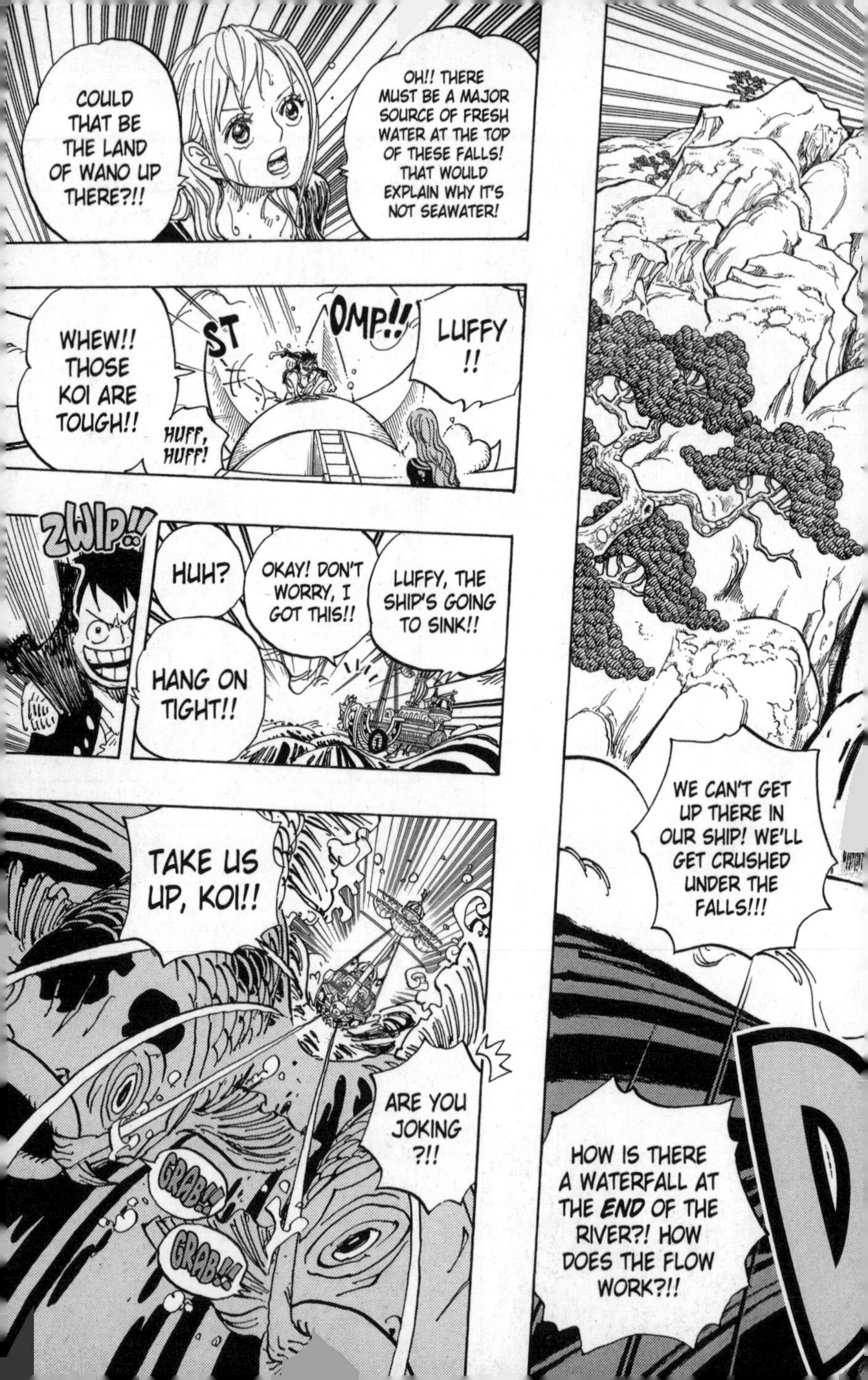
WE CAN'T GET UP THERE IN OUR SHIP! WE'LL GET CRUSHED UNDER THE FALLS!!!
HOW IS THERE A WATERFALL AT THE *END* OF THE RIVER?! HOW DOES THE FLOW WORK?!!
OH!! THERE MUST BE A MAJOR SOURCE OF FRESH WATER AT THE TOP OF THESE FALLS! THAT WOULD EXPLAIN WHY IT'S NOT SEAWATER!
COULD THAT BE THE LAND OF WANO UP THERE?!!
LUFFY!!
ST
OMP!!
WHEW!! THOSE KOI ARE TOUGH!!
HUFF, HUFF!
LUFFY, THE SHIP'S GOING TO SINK!!
OKAY! DON'T WORRY, I GOT THIS!!
HUH?
HANG ON TIGHT!!
ZWIP!!
TAKE US UP, KOI!!
ARE YOU JOKING?!!
GRAB!!
GRAB!!

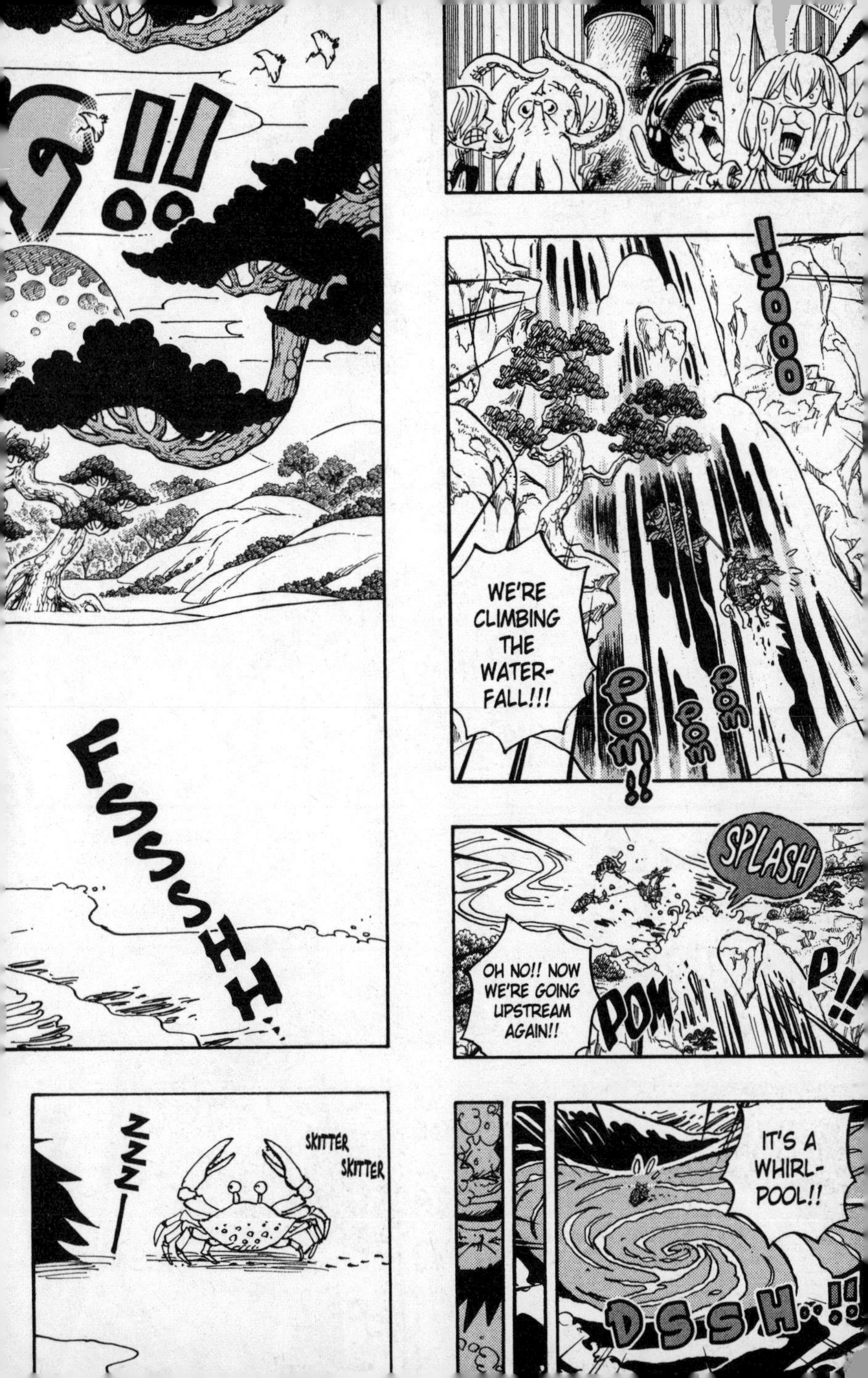
WE'RE CLIMBING THE WATER-FALL!!!
POM POM POM!!
SPLASH
OH NO!! NOW WE'RE GOING UPSTREAM AGAIN!!
POMP!!
IT'S A WHIRL-POOL!!
DSSH..!!
FSSSHH..
ZZZ—
SKITTER SKITTER

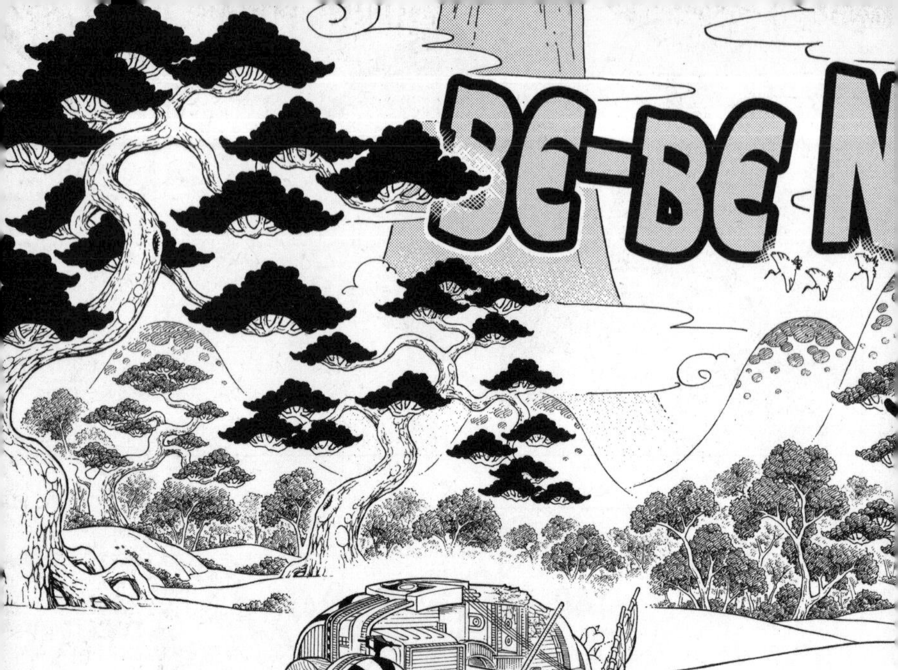
BE-BE N
ZZZ...
SPLISH...
SPLISH...
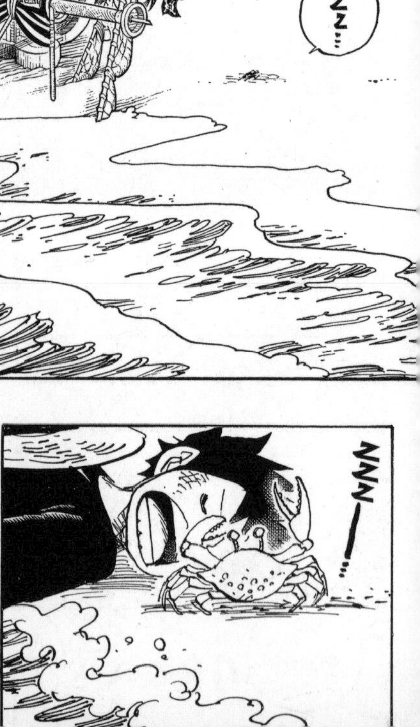
ZNN—...
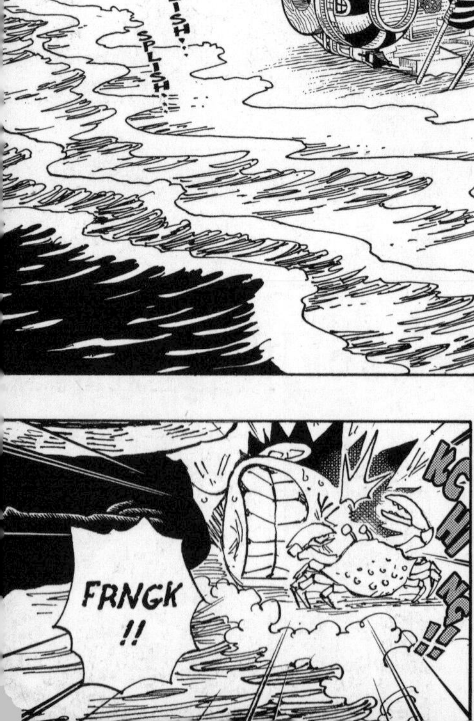
KCHING!!
FRNGK !!

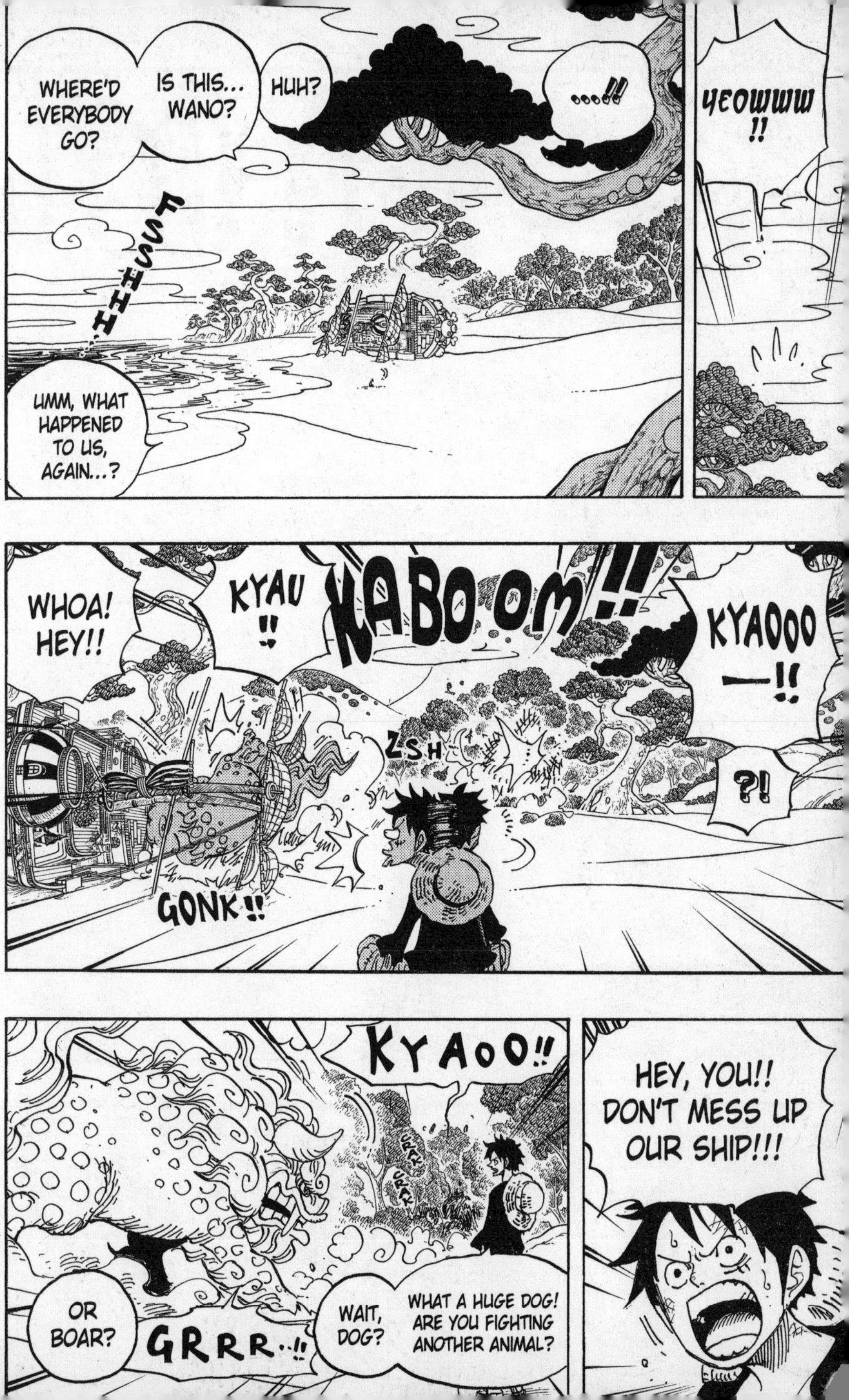
YEOWWW!!
....!!
HUH?
IS THIS... WANO?
WHERE'D EVERYBODY GO?
FSSHHHH
UMM, WHAT HAPPENED TO US, AGAIN...?
KYAOOO—!!
?!
KABOOM!!
KYAU!!
WHOA! HEY!!
ZSH
GONK!!
HEY, YOU!! DON'T MESS UP OUR SHIP!!!
KYAOO!!
CRAK
CRAK
WHAT A HUGE DOG! ARE YOU FIGHTING ANOTHER ANIMAL?
WAIT, DOG?
OR BOAR?
GRRR..!!

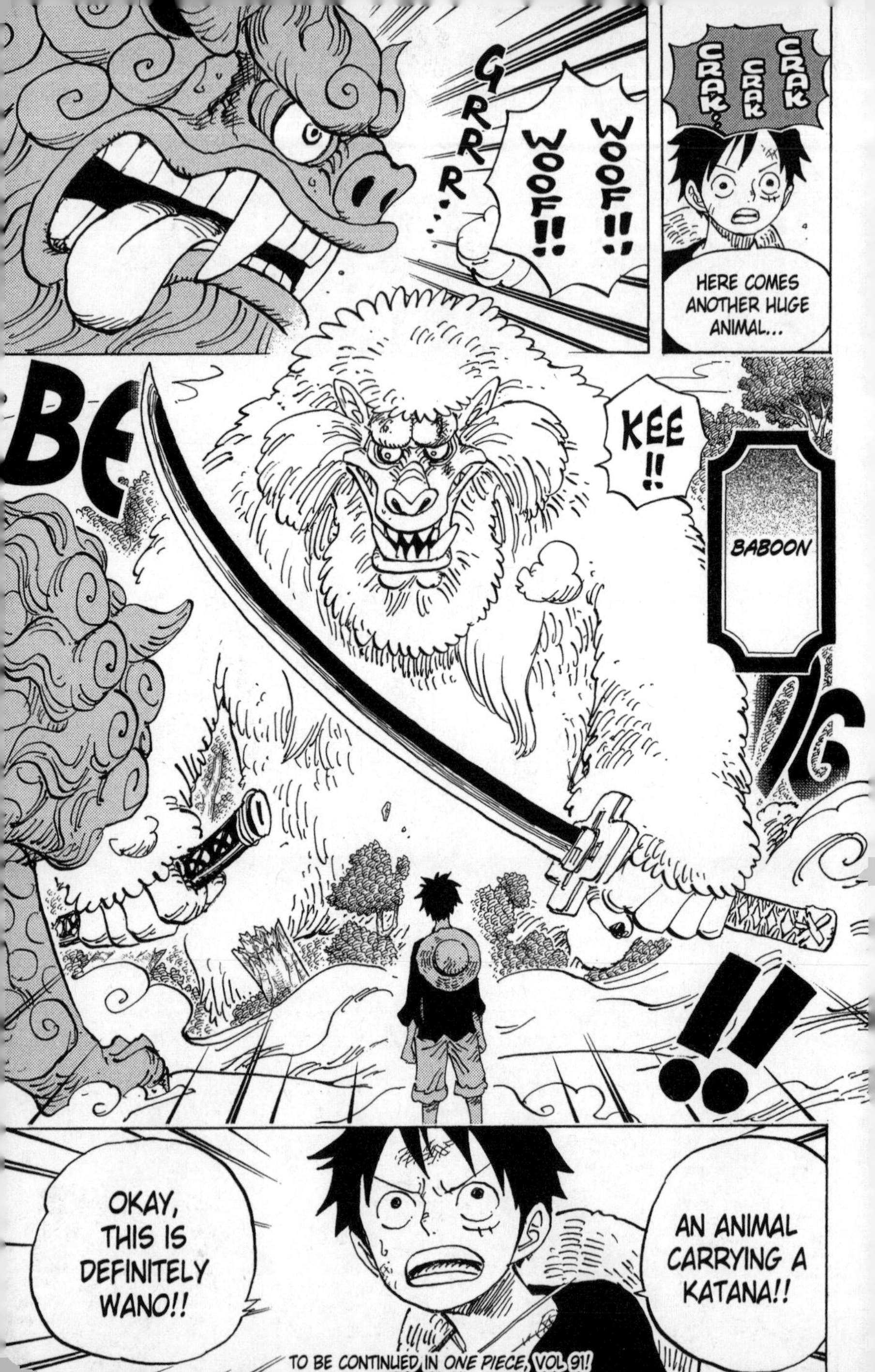
CRAK CRAK CRAK
HERE COMES ANOTHER HUGE ANIMAL...
WOOF!! WOOF!!
GRRR...
KEE!!
BABOON
BE
IG
!!
AN ANIMAL CARRYING A KATANA!!
OKAY, THIS IS DEFINITELY WANO!!

TO BE CONTINUED IN *ONE PIECE*, VOL 91!

COMING NEXT VOLUME:

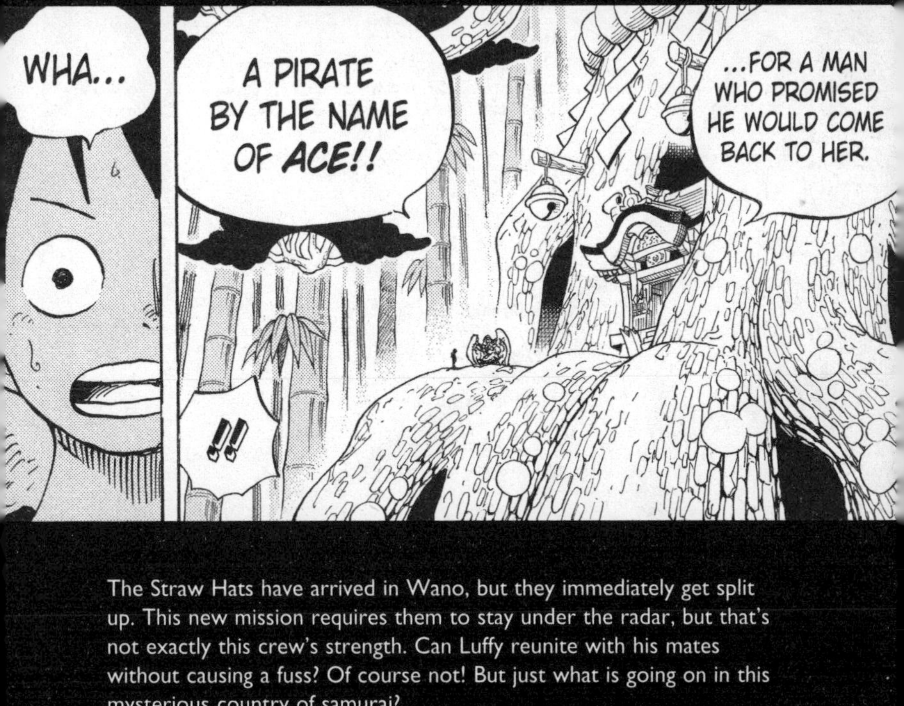
...FOR A MAN WHO PROMISED HE WOULD COME BACK TO HER.
A PIRATE BY THE NAME OF ACE!!
!!
WHA...

The Straw Hats have arrived in Wano, but they immediately get split up. This new mission requires them to stay under the radar, but that's not exactly this crew's strength. Can Luffy reunite with his mates without causing a fuss? Of course not! But just what is going on in this mysterious country of samurai?

ON SALE AUGUST 2019!

ONE PIECE VOL. 90
WANO PART 1

SHONEN JUMP Manga Edition

STORY AND ART BY EIICHIRO ODA

Translation/Stephen Paul
Touch-up Art & Lettering/Vanessa Satone
Design/Yukiko Whitley
Editor/Alexis Kirsch

Published by VIZ Media, LLC
P.O. Box 77010
San Francisco, CA 94107

10 9 8 7 6 5 4 3 2 1
First printing, May 2019

viz.com

shonenjump.com

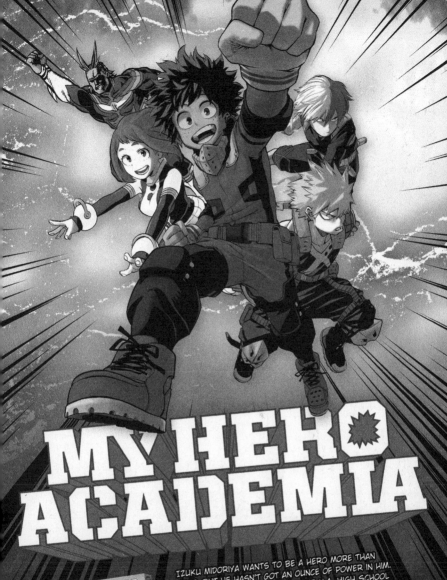

MY HERO ACADEMIA

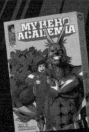

IZUKU MIDORIYA WANTS TO BE A HERO MORE THAN ANYTHING, BUT HE HASN'T GOT AN OUNCE OF POWER IN HIM. WITH NO CHANCE OF GETTING INTO THE U.A. HIGH SCHOOL FOR HEROES, HIS LIFE IS LOOKING LIKE A DEAD END. THEN AN ENCOUNTER WITH ALL MIGHT, THE GREATEST HERO OF ALL, GIVES HIM A CHANCE TO CHANGE HIS DESTINY...

SHONEN JUMP

VIZ media
www.viz.com

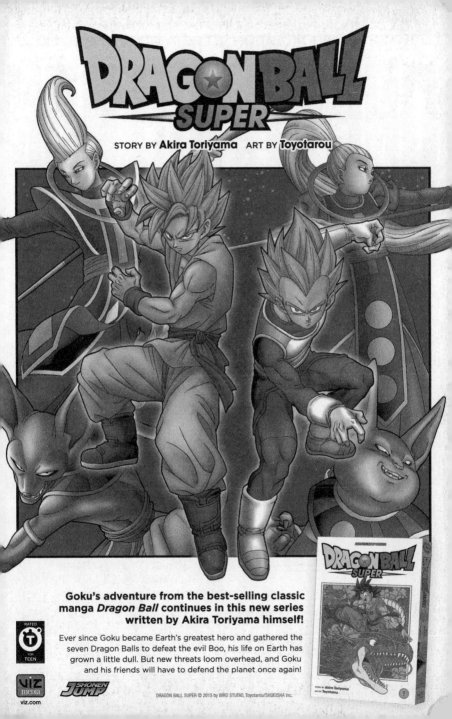

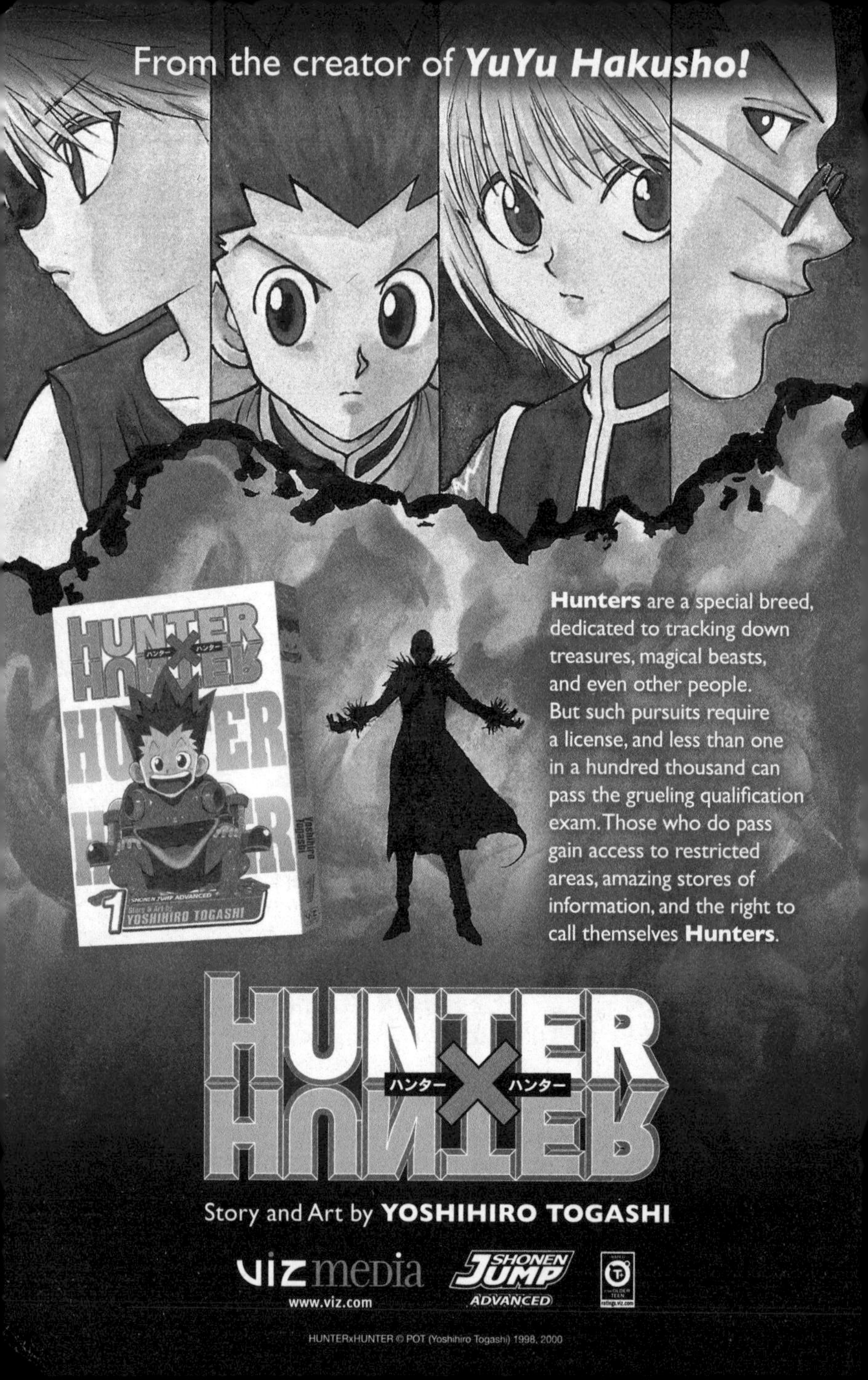
From the creator of YuYu Hakusho!
Hunters are a special breed, dedicated to tracking down treasures, magical beasts, and even other people. But such pursuits require a license, and less than one in a hundred thousand can pass the grueling qualification exam. Those who do pass gain access to restricted areas, amazing stores of information, and the right to call themselves Hunters.
HUNTER×HUNTER
ハンター ハンター
Story and Art by YOSHIHIRO TOGASHI
VIZ media
www.viz.com
SHONEN JUMP ADVANCED
HUNTERxHUNTER © POT (Yoshihiro Togashi) 1998, 2000

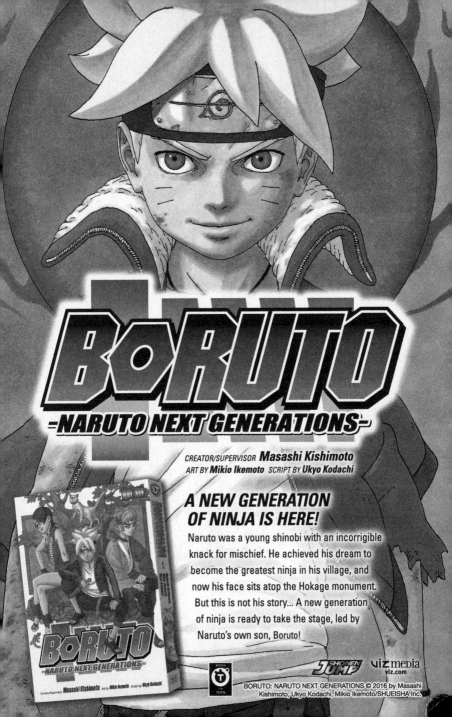

BORUTO
=NARUTO NEXT GENERATIONS=

CREATOR/SUPERVISOR **Masashi Kishimoto**
ART BY **Mikio Ikemoto** SCRIPT BY **Ukyo Kodachi**

A NEW GENERATION OF NINJA IS HERE!

Naruto was a young shinobi with an incorrigible knack for mischief. He achieved his dream to become the greatest ninja in his village, and now his face sits atop the Hokage monument. But this is not his story... A new generation of ninja is ready to take the stage, led by Naruto's own son, Boruto!

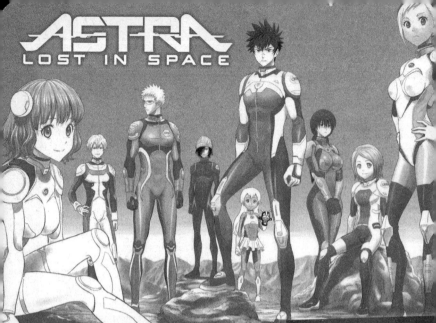

ASTRA
LOST IN SPACE

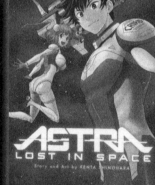

CAN EIGHT TEENAGERS FIND THEIR WAY HOME FROM 5,000 LIGHT-YEARS AWAY?

It's the year 2063, and interstellar space travel has become the norm. Eight students from Caird High School and one child set out on a routine planet camp excursion. While there, the students are mysteriously transported 5,000 light-years away to the middle of nowhere! Will they ever make it back home?!

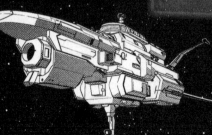

ASTRA
LOST IN SPACE
Story and Art by KENTA SHINOHARA

VIZ
viz.com

RATED
TEEN

You're Reading in the Wrong Direction!!

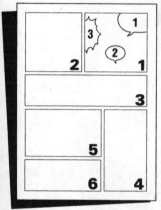

Whoops! Guess what? You're starting at the wrong end of the comic!

…It's true! In keeping with the original Japanese format, **One Piece** is meant to be read from right to left, starting in the upper-right corner.

Unlike English, which is read from left to right, Japanese is read from right to left, meaning that action, sound effects and word-balloon order are completely reversed…something which can make readers unfamiliar with Japanese feel pretty backwards themselves. For this reason, manga or Japanese comics published in the U.S. in English have sometimes been published "flopped"— that is, printed in exact reverse order, as though seen from the other side of a mirror.

By flopping pages, U.S. publishers can avoid confusing readers, but the compromise is not without its downside. For one thing, a character in a flopped manga series who once wore in the original Japanese version a T-shirt emblazoned with "M A Y" (as in "the merry month of") now wears one which reads "Y A M"! Additionally, many manga creators in Japan are themselves unhappy with the process, as some feel the mirror-imaging of their art skews their original intentions.

We are proud to bring you Eiichiro Oda's **One Piece** in the original unflopped format. For now, though, turn to the other side of the book and let the journey begin…!

—Editor

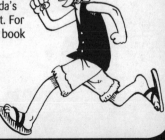